Noah is coming back.

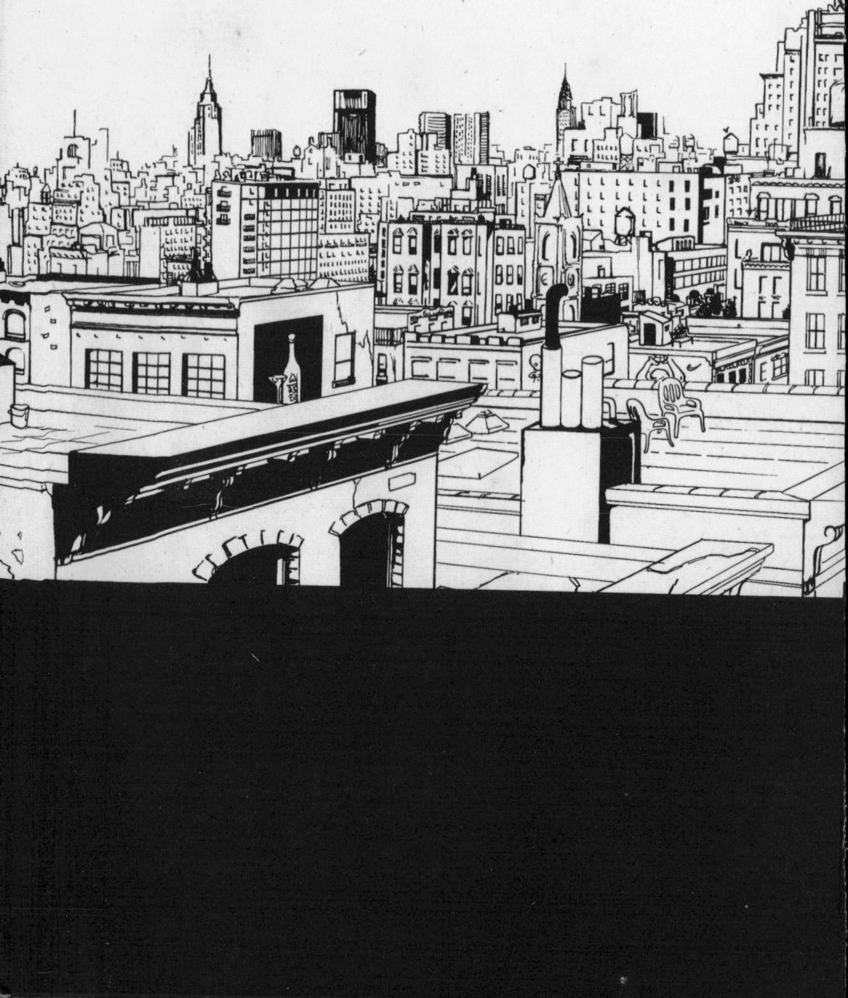

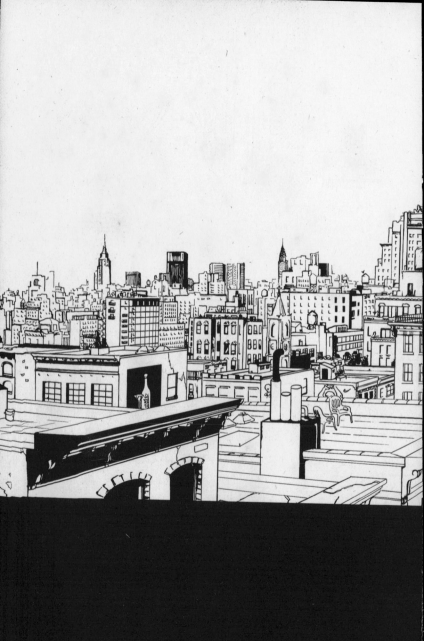

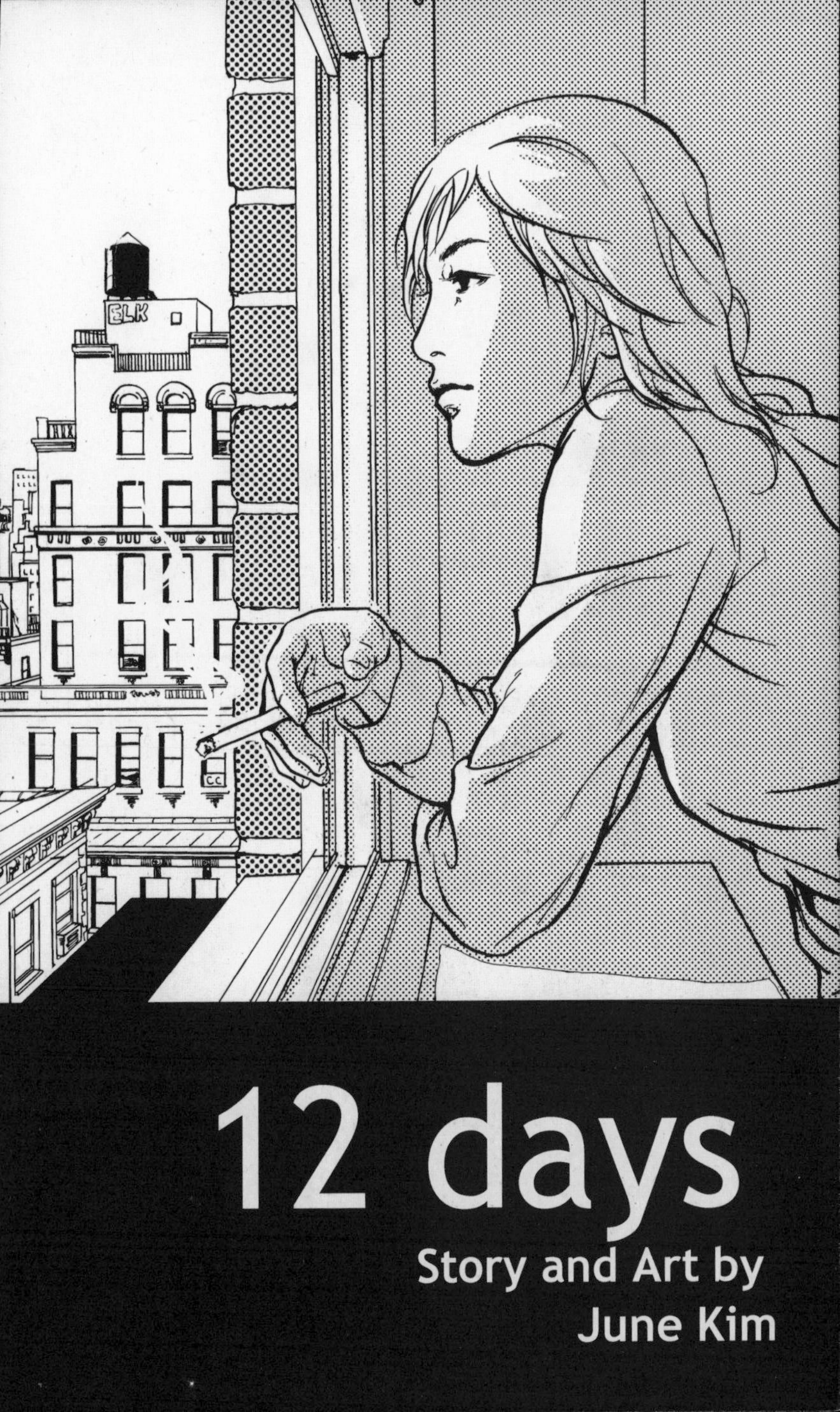
ELK

12 days

Story and Art by
June Kim

TABLE OF CONTENTS

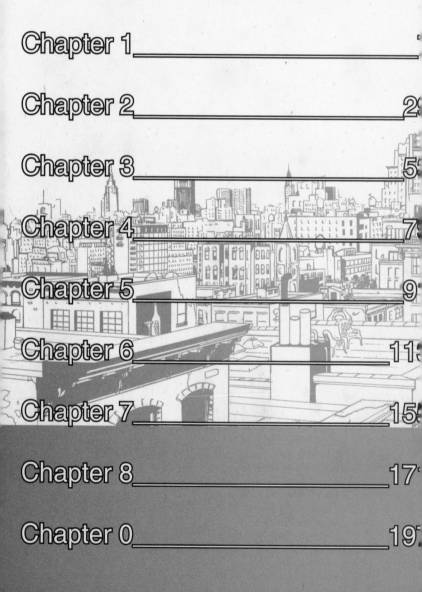

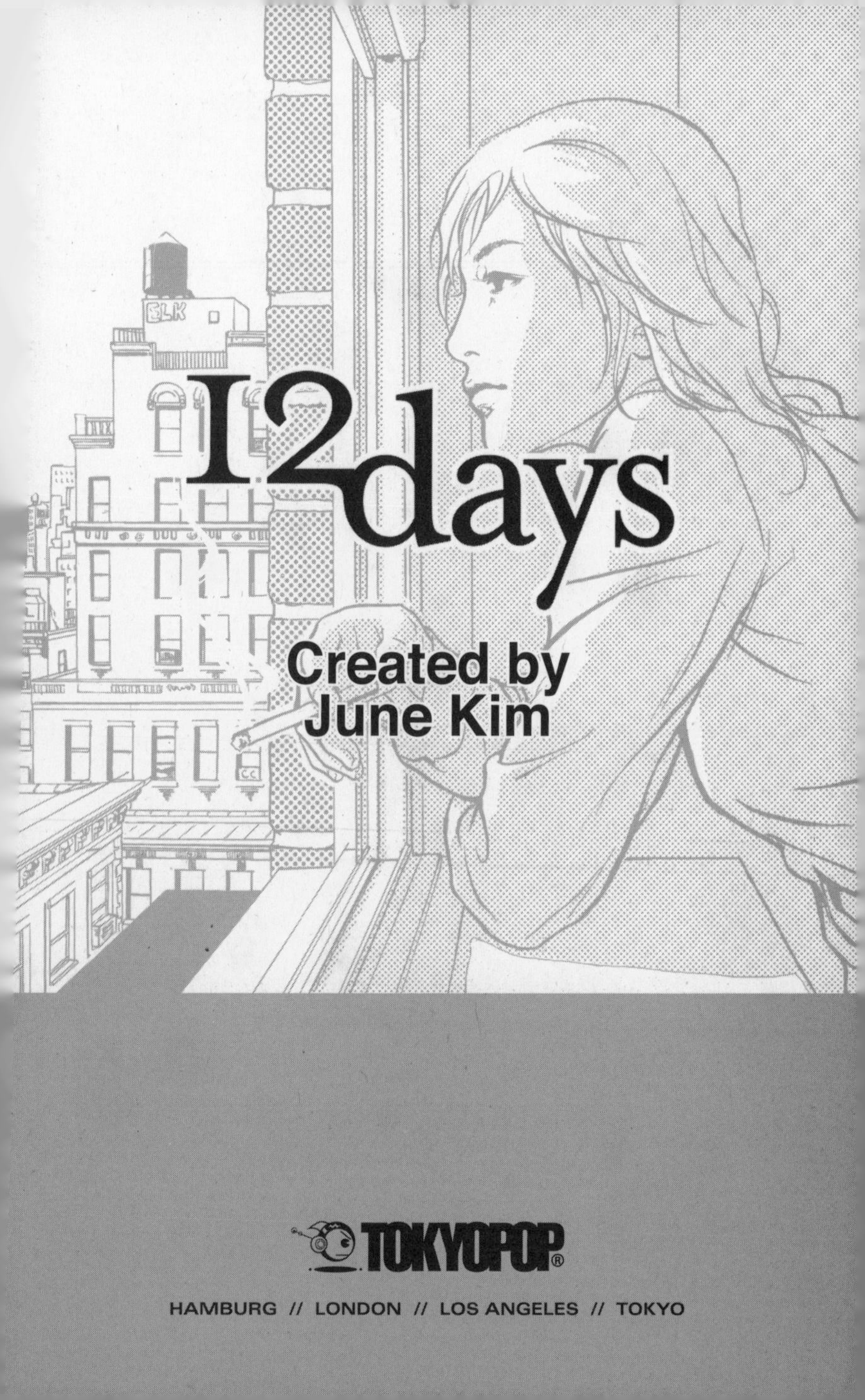

12 days

Created by June Kim

TOKYOPOP®

HAMBURG // LONDON // LOS ANGELES // TOKYO

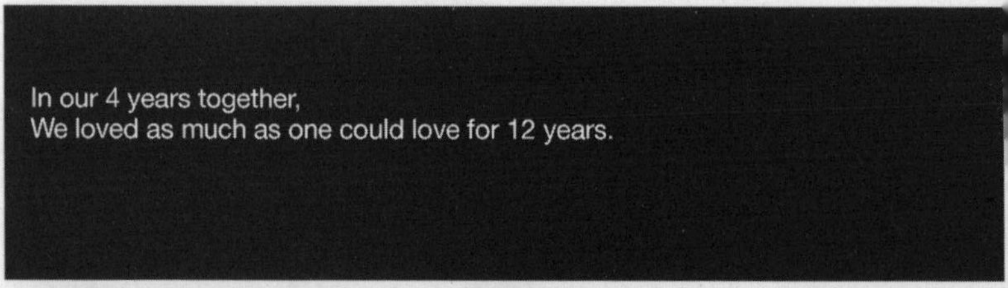
In our 4 years together,
We loved as much as one could love for 12 years.

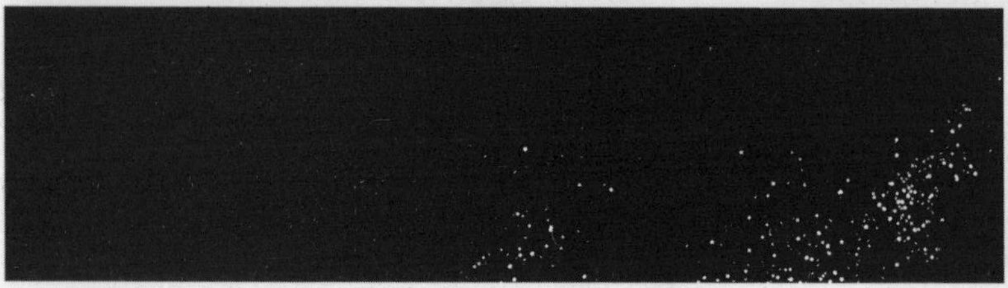

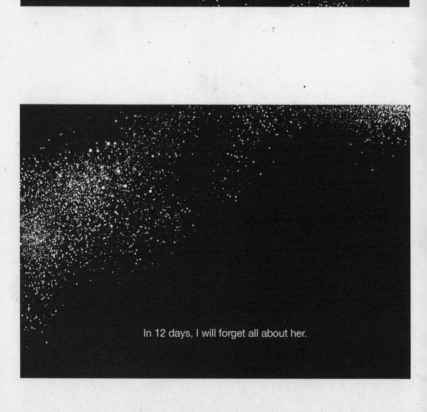

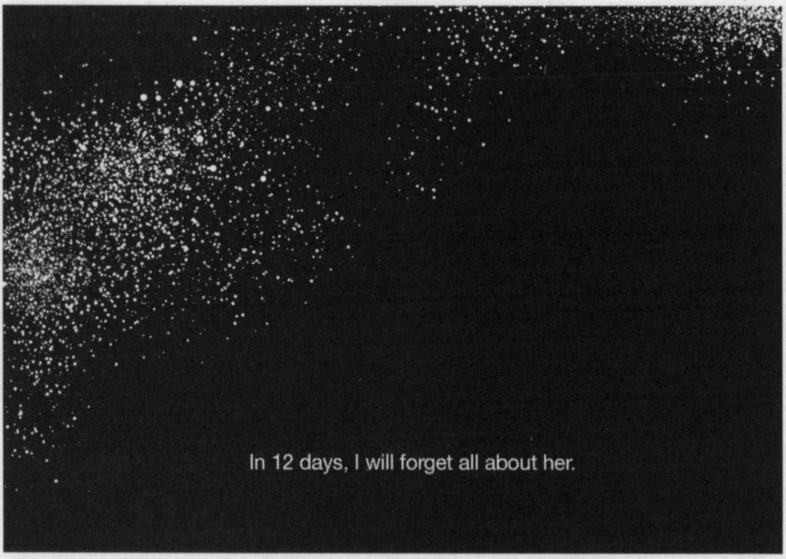
In 12 days, I will forget all about her.

12days

Chapter 1

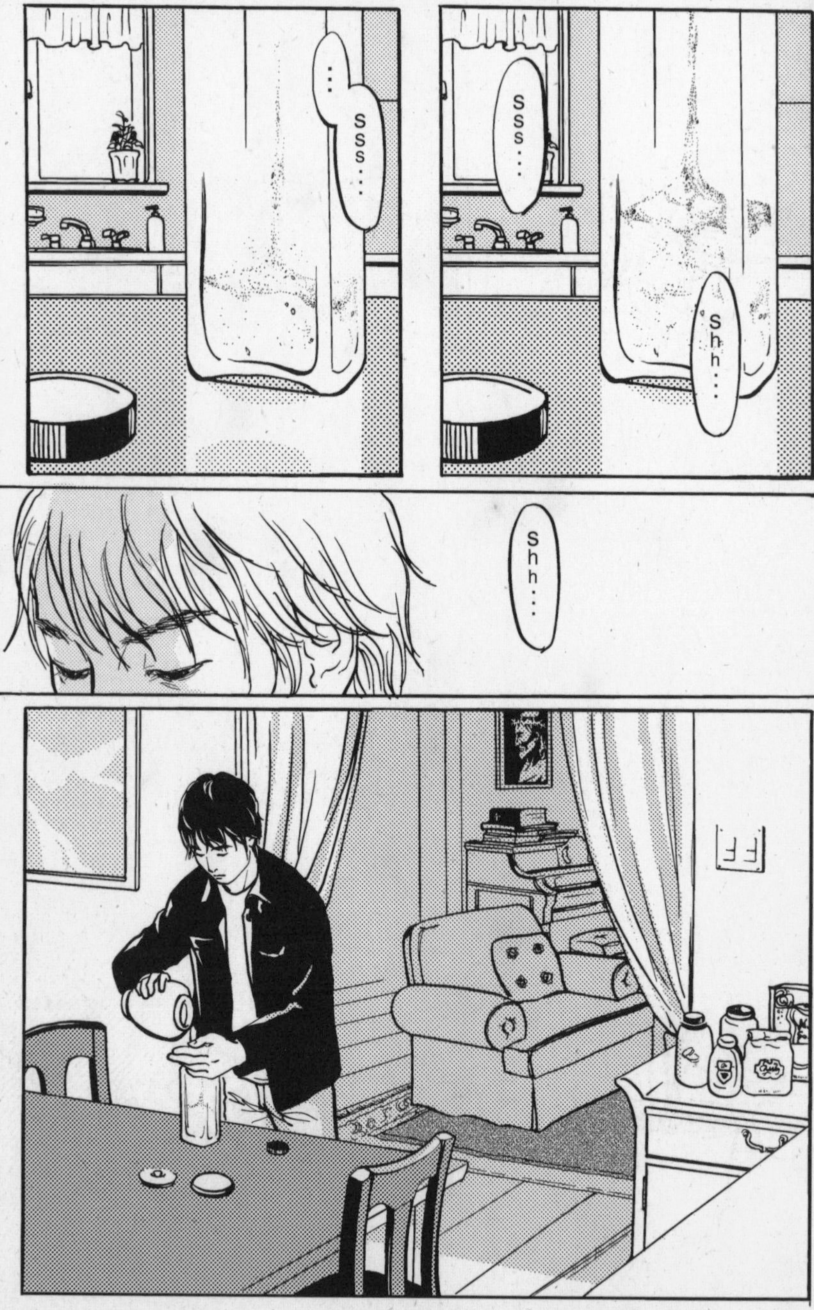
…
Sss….
Sss….
Shh….
Shh….

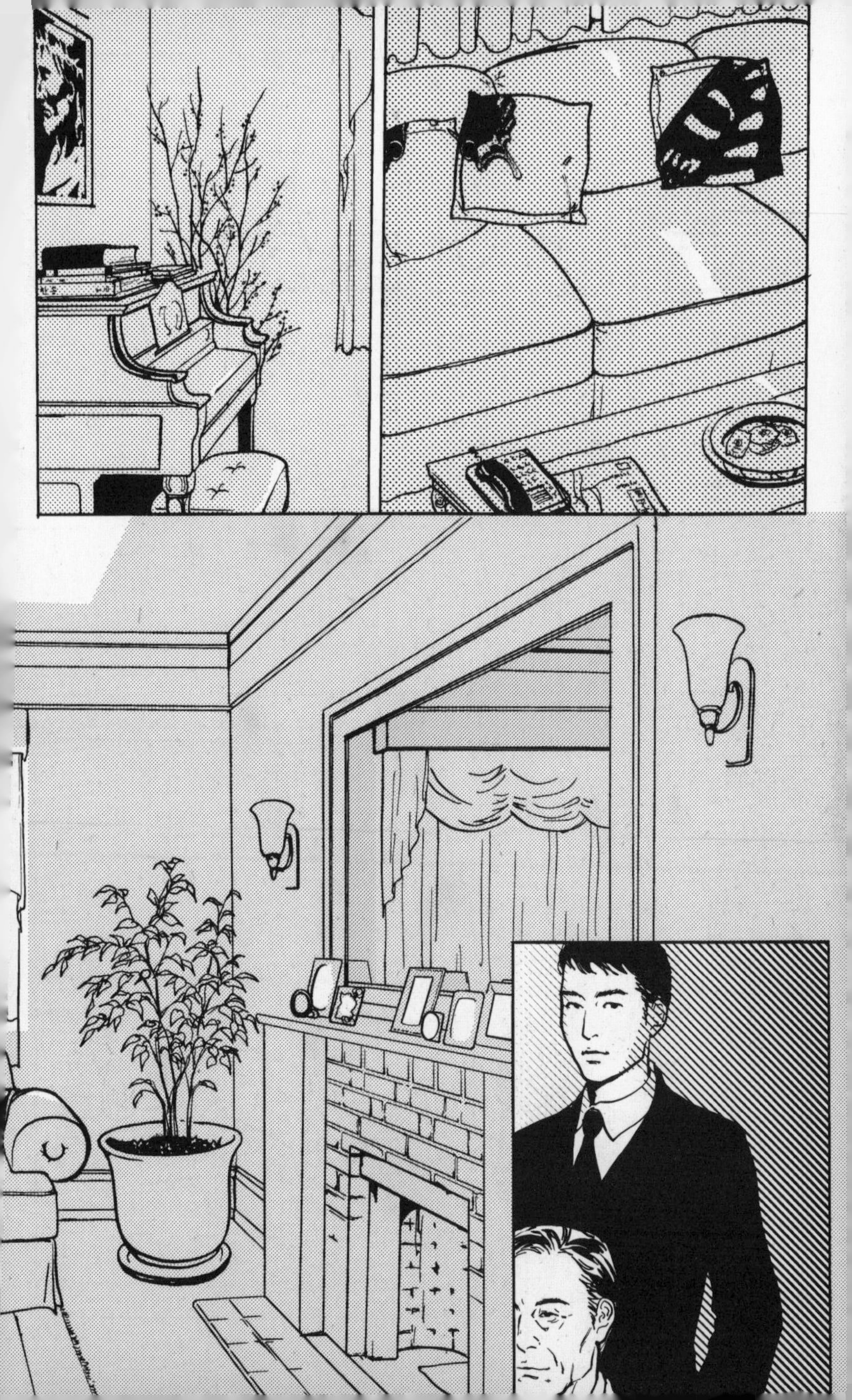

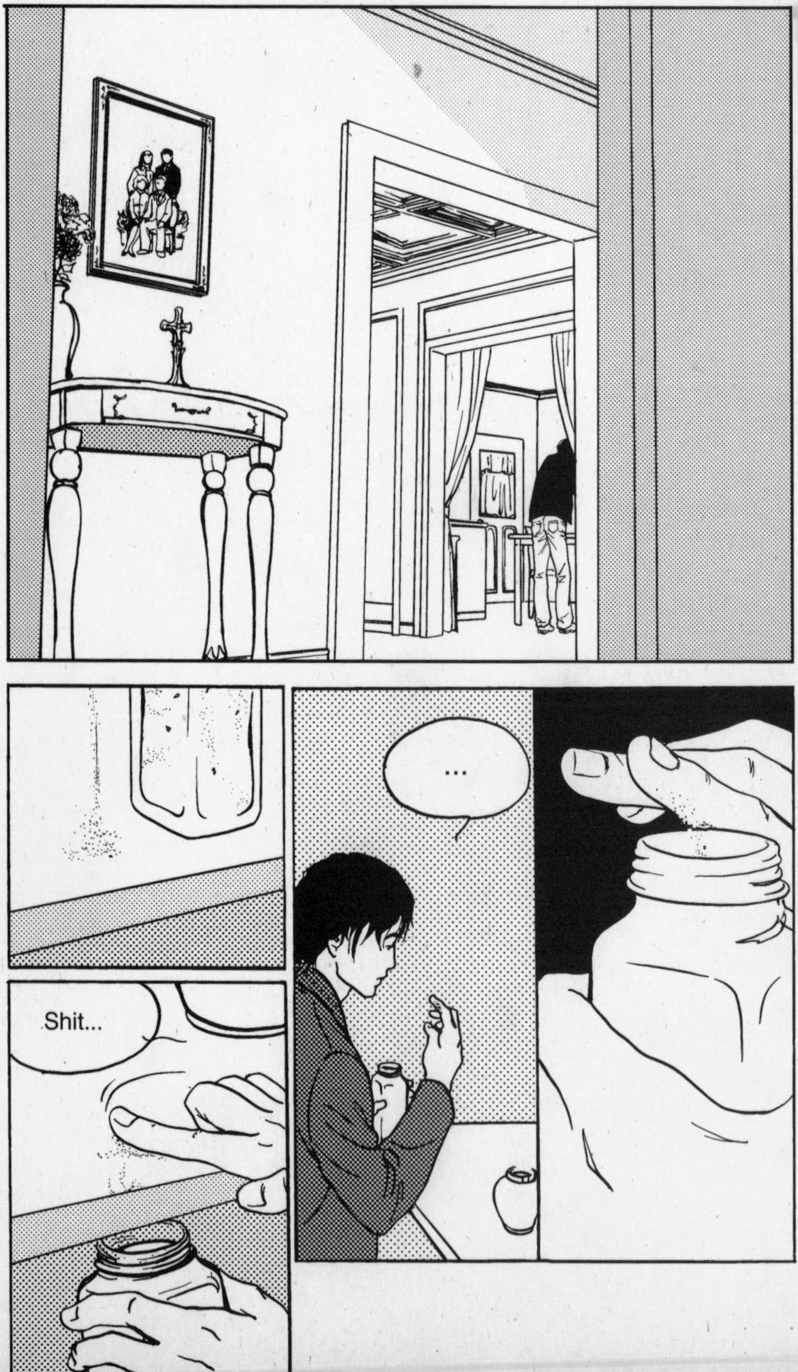
Shit...
...

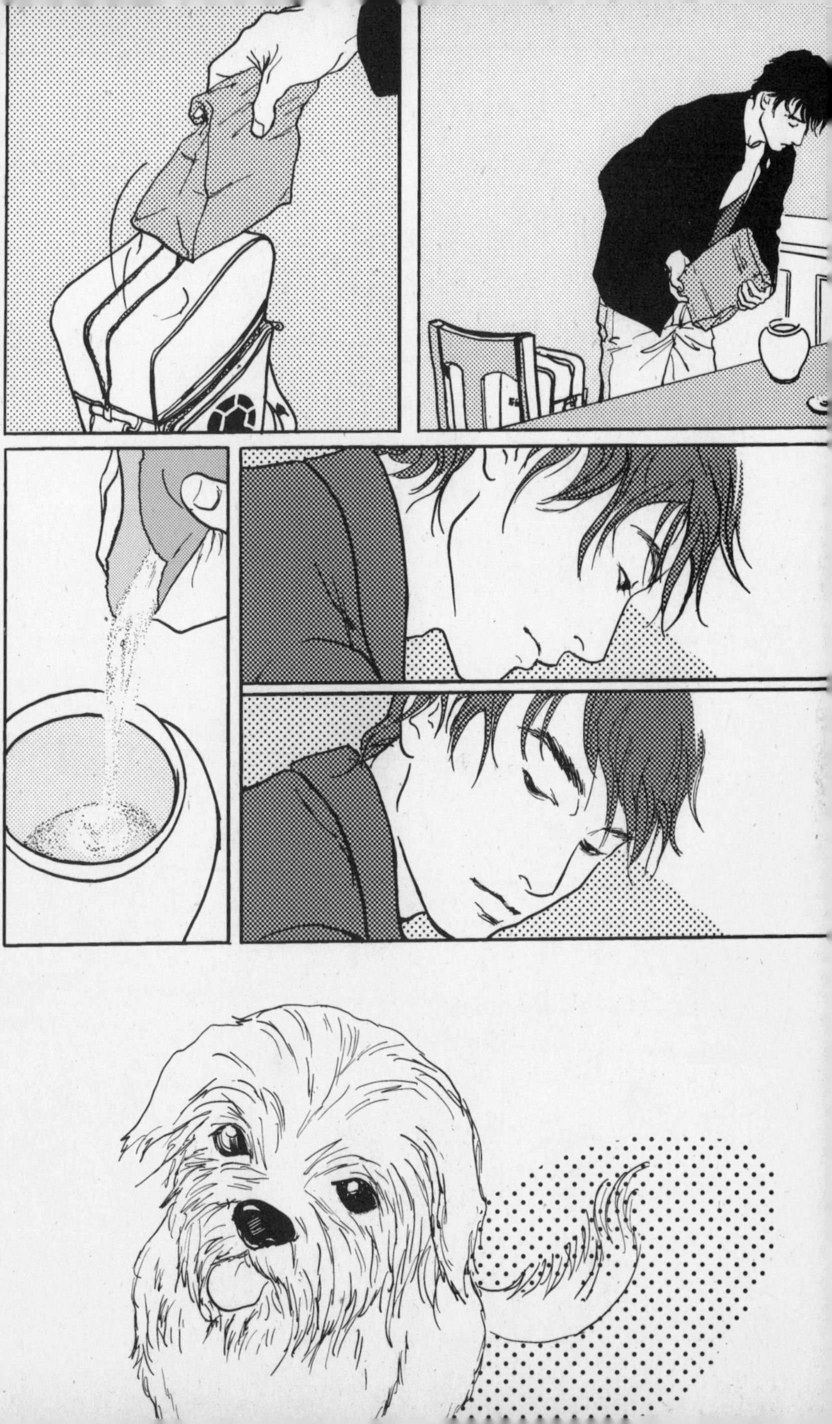

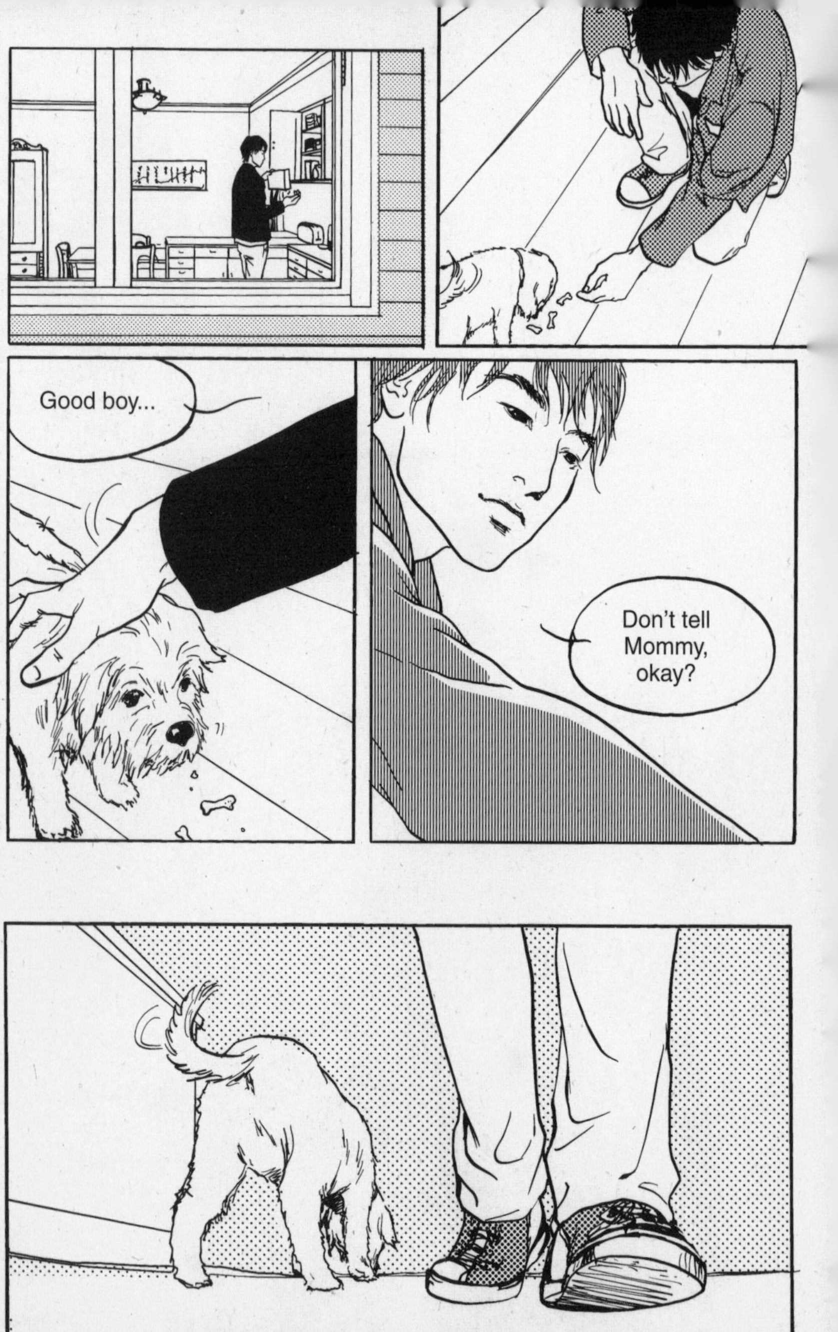
Good boy...
Don't tell Mommy, okay?

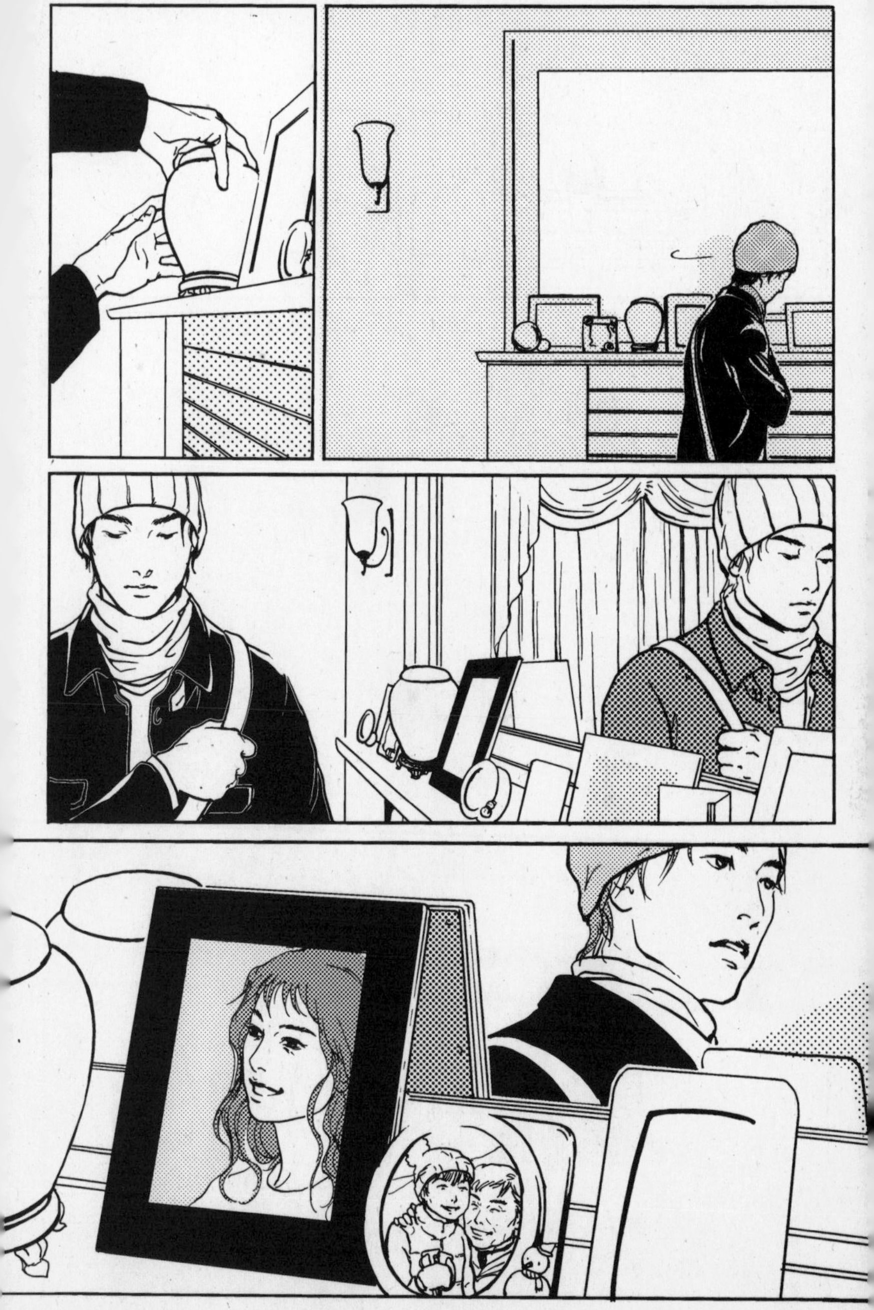

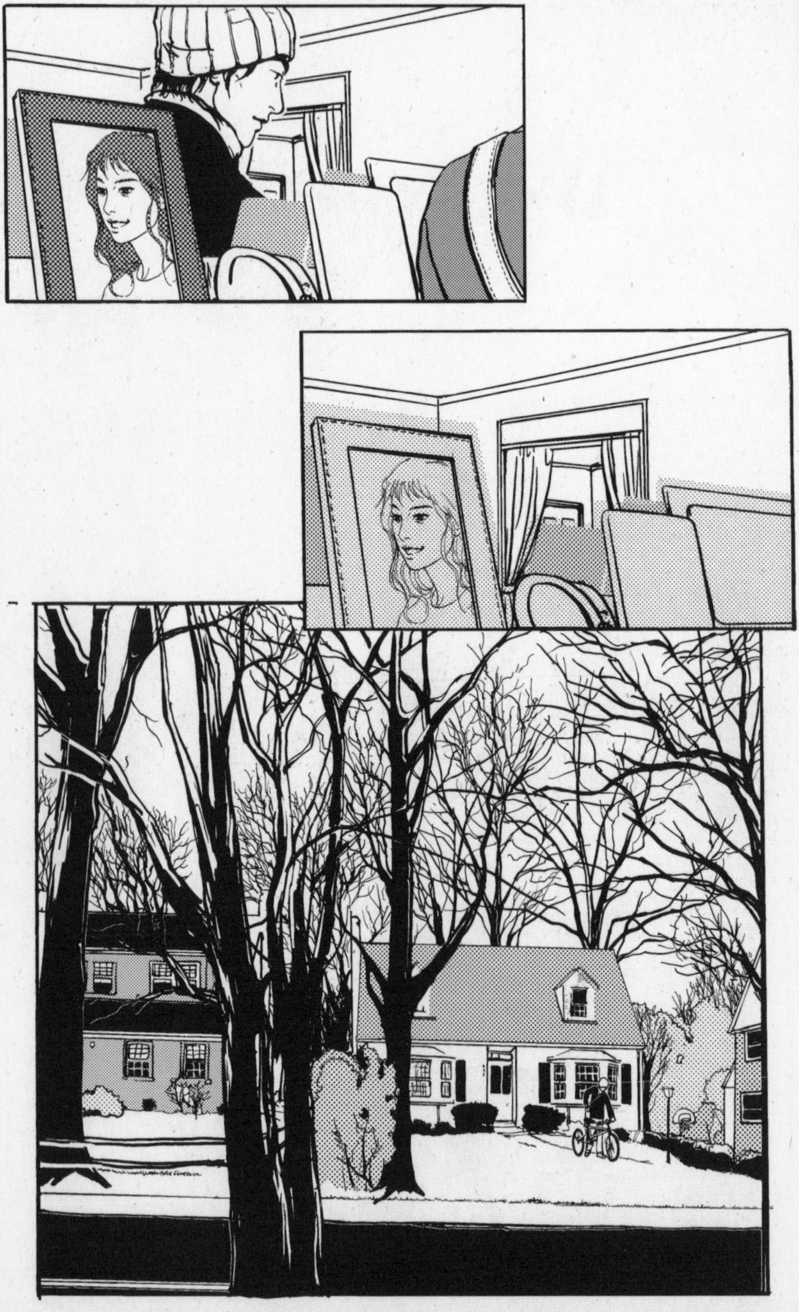

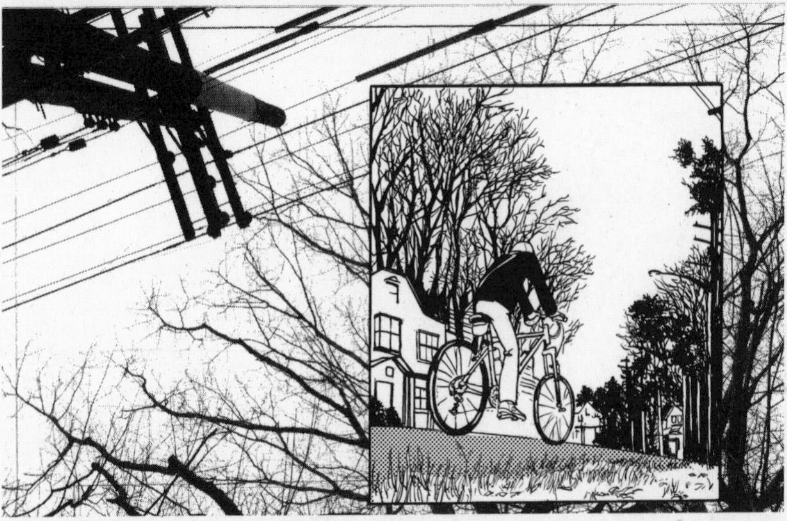

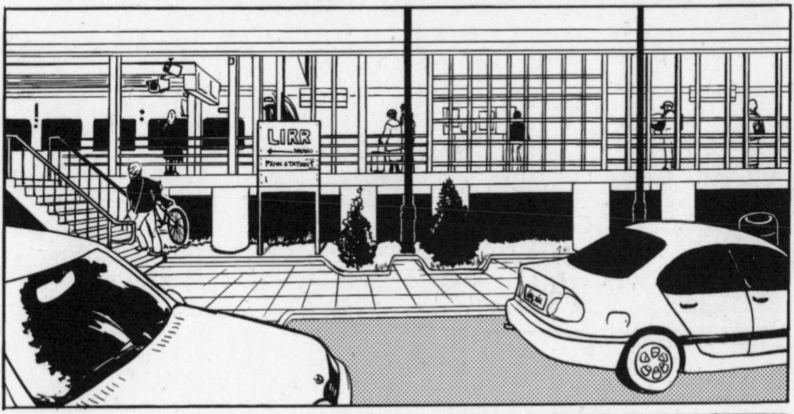
LIRR
PENN STATION

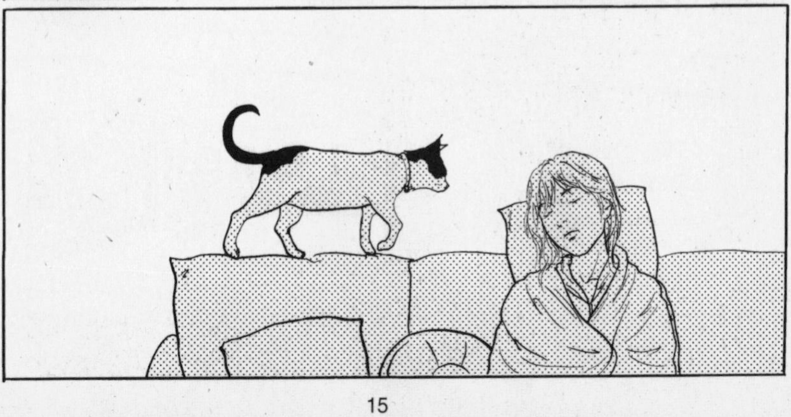

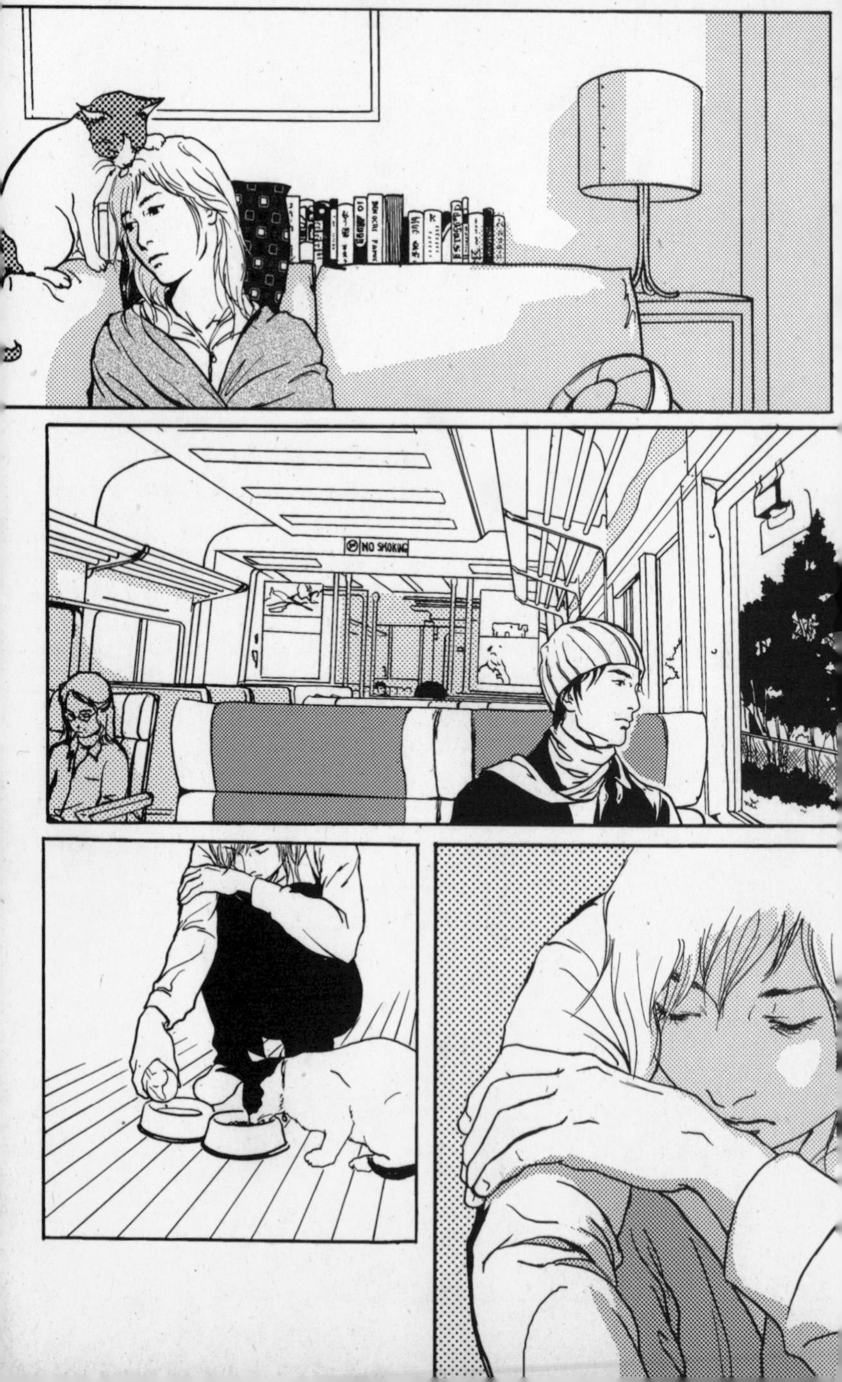
NO SMOKING

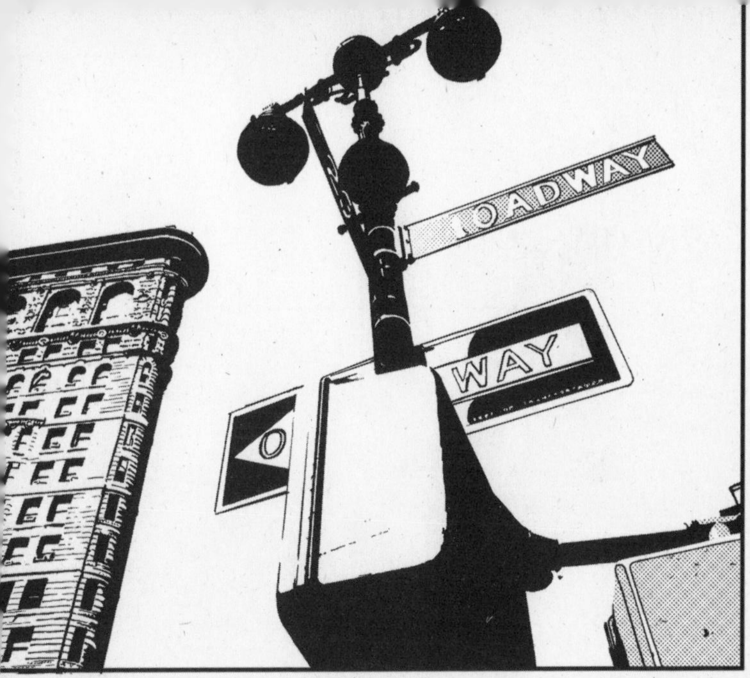
OADWAY
WAY
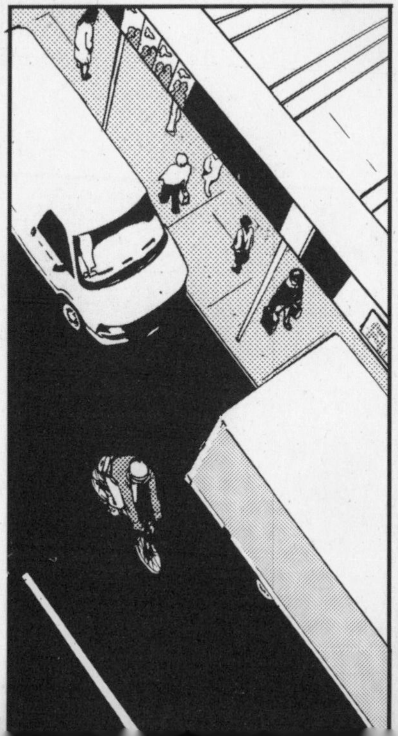
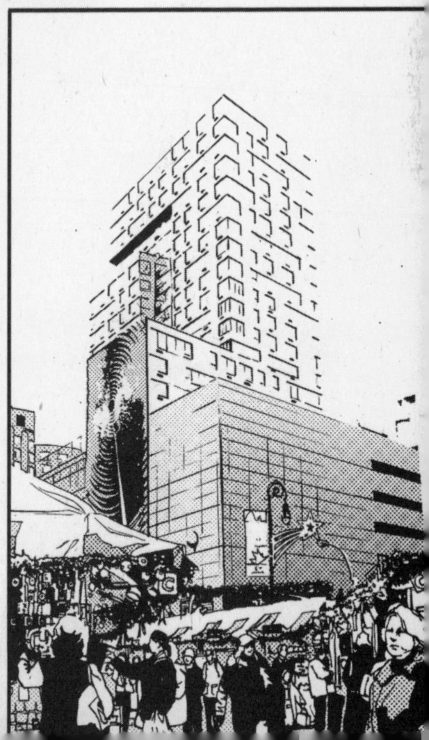

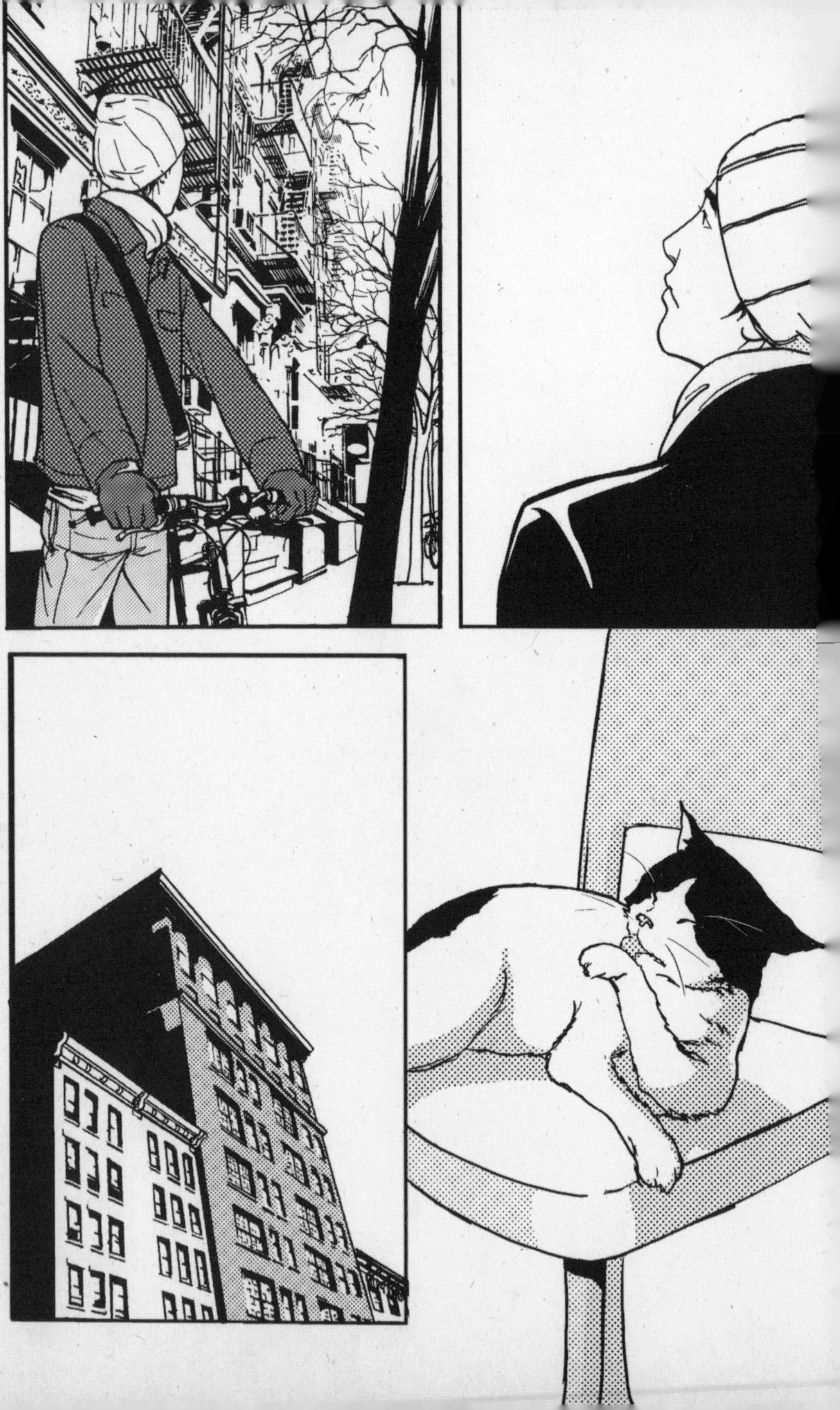

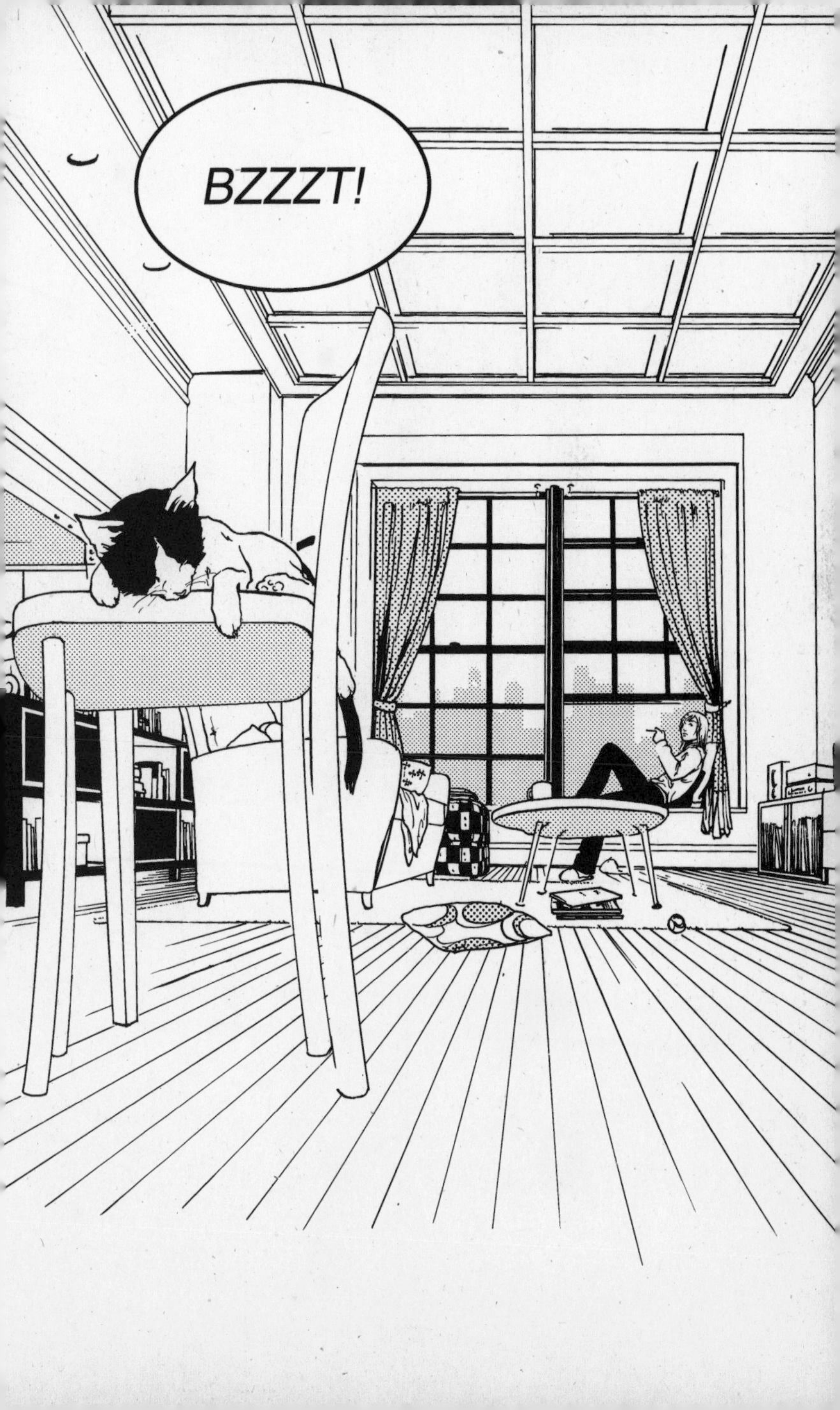
BZZZT!

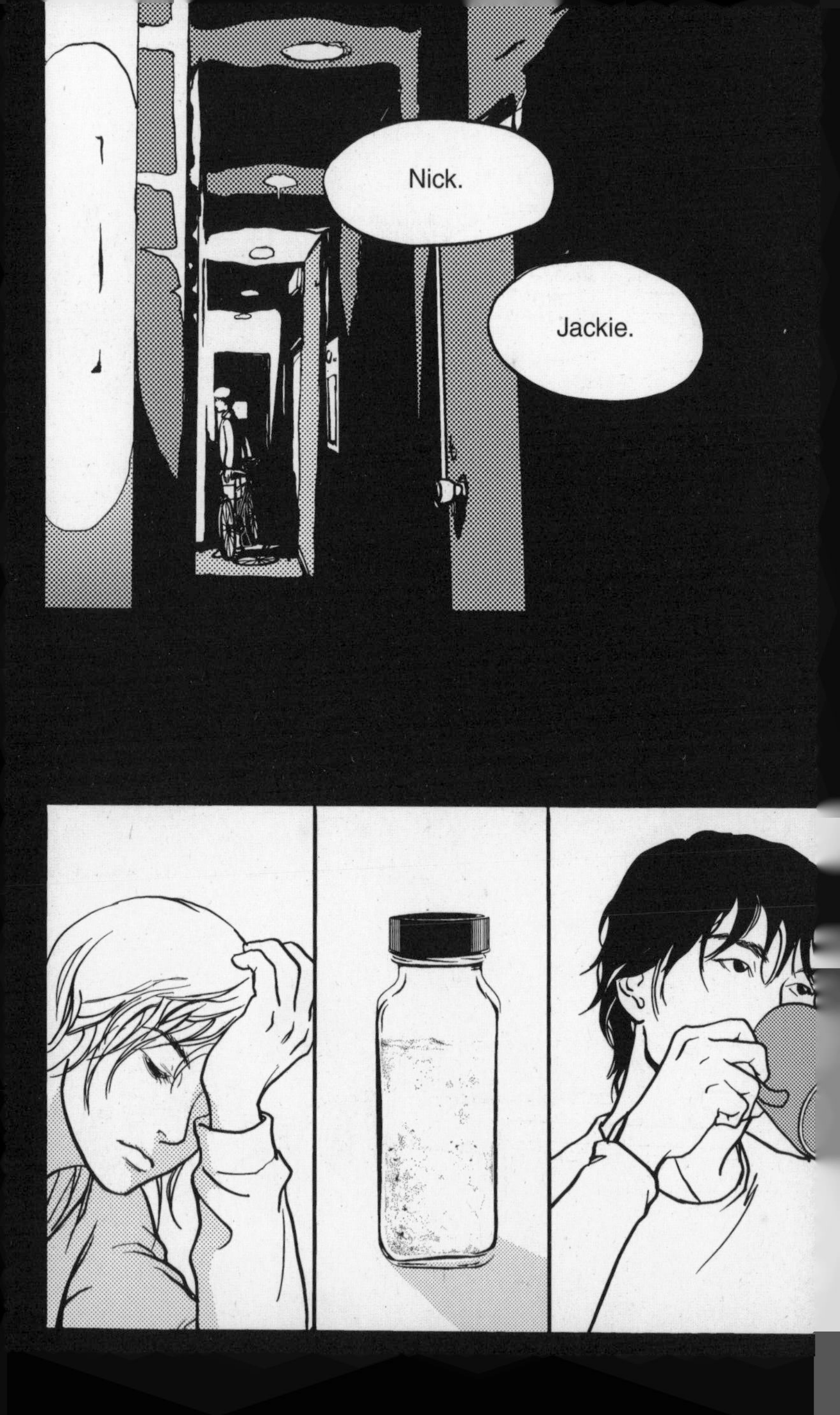
Nick.
Jackie.

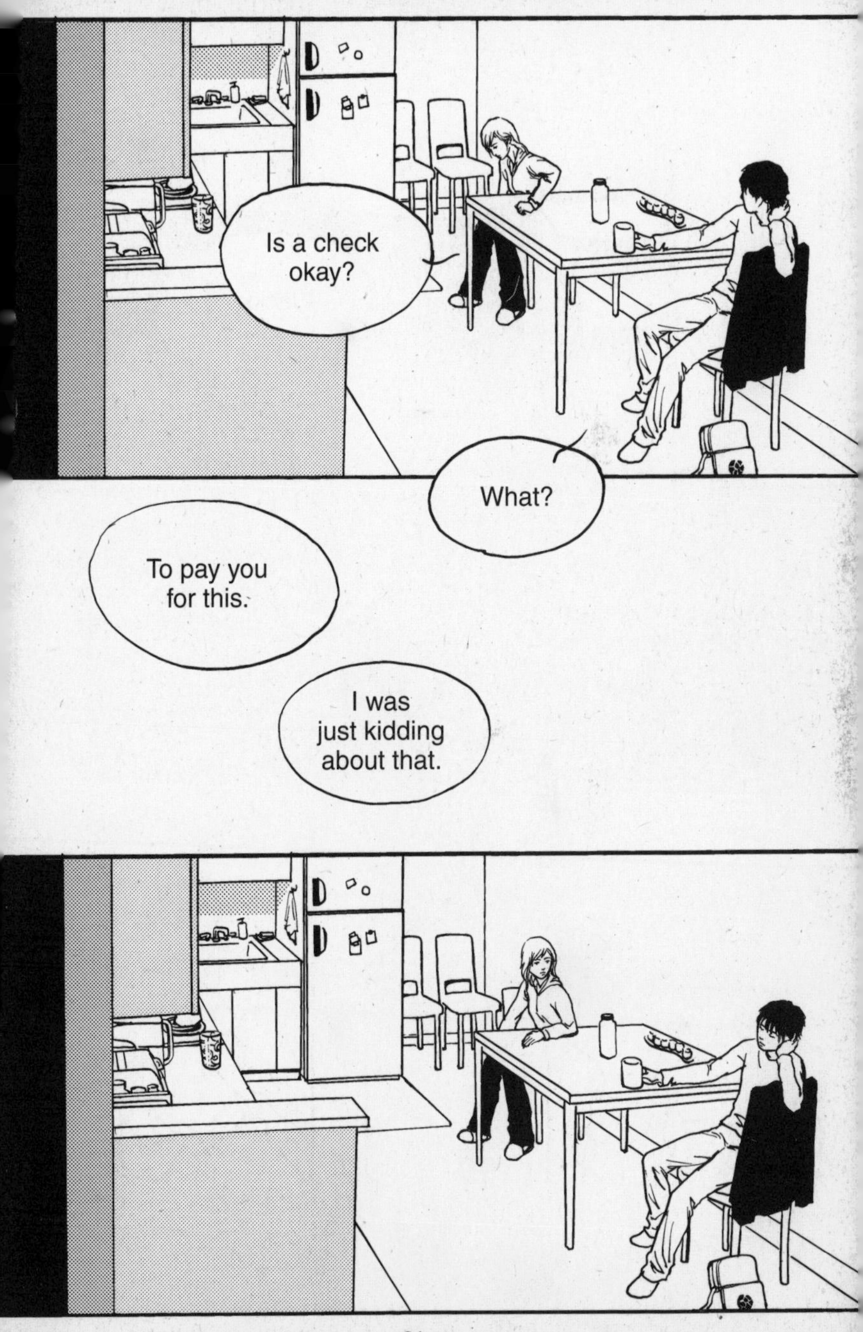
Is a check okay?
What?
To pay you for this.
I was just kidding about that.

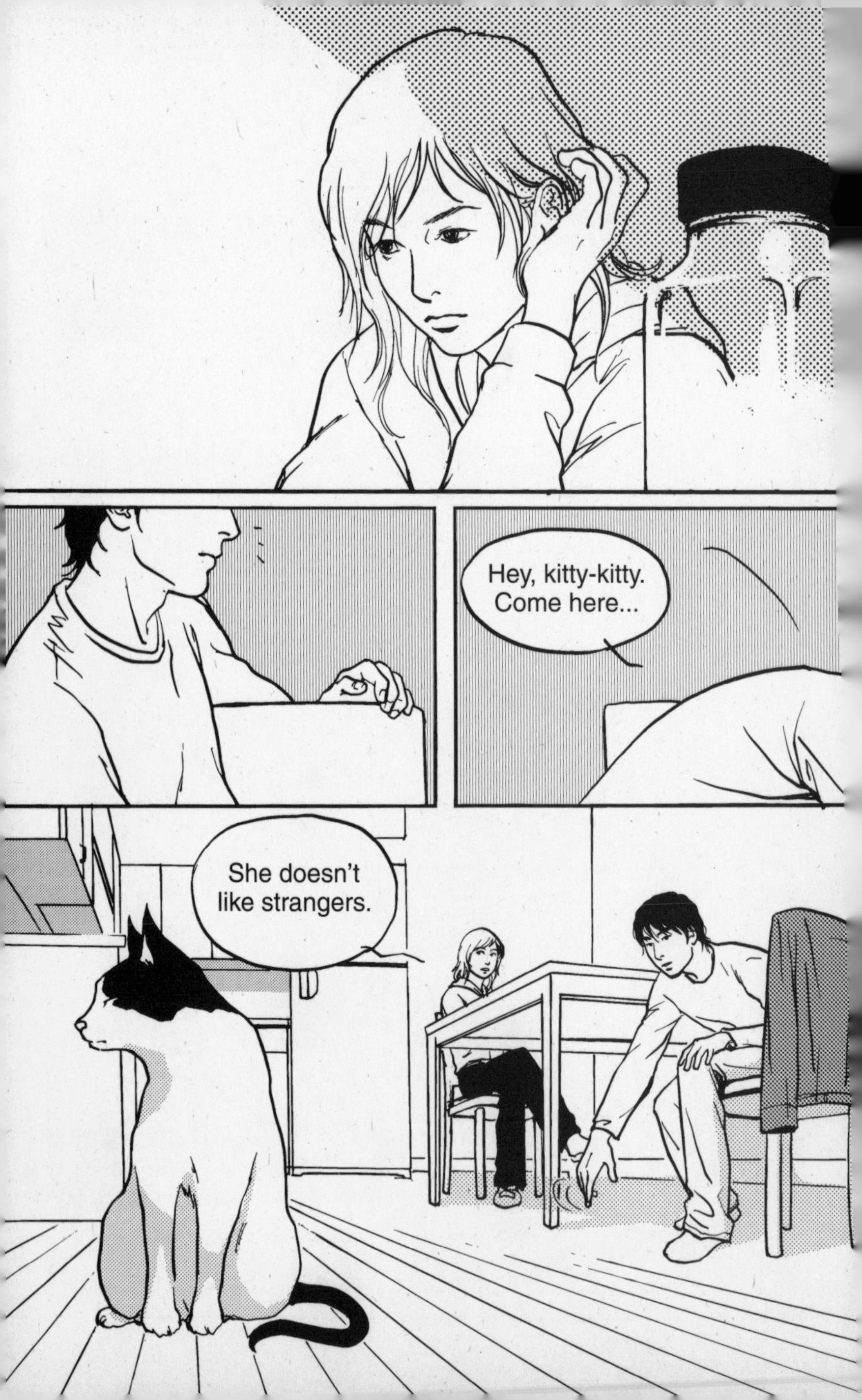
Hey, kitty-kitty. Come here...
She doesn't like strangers.

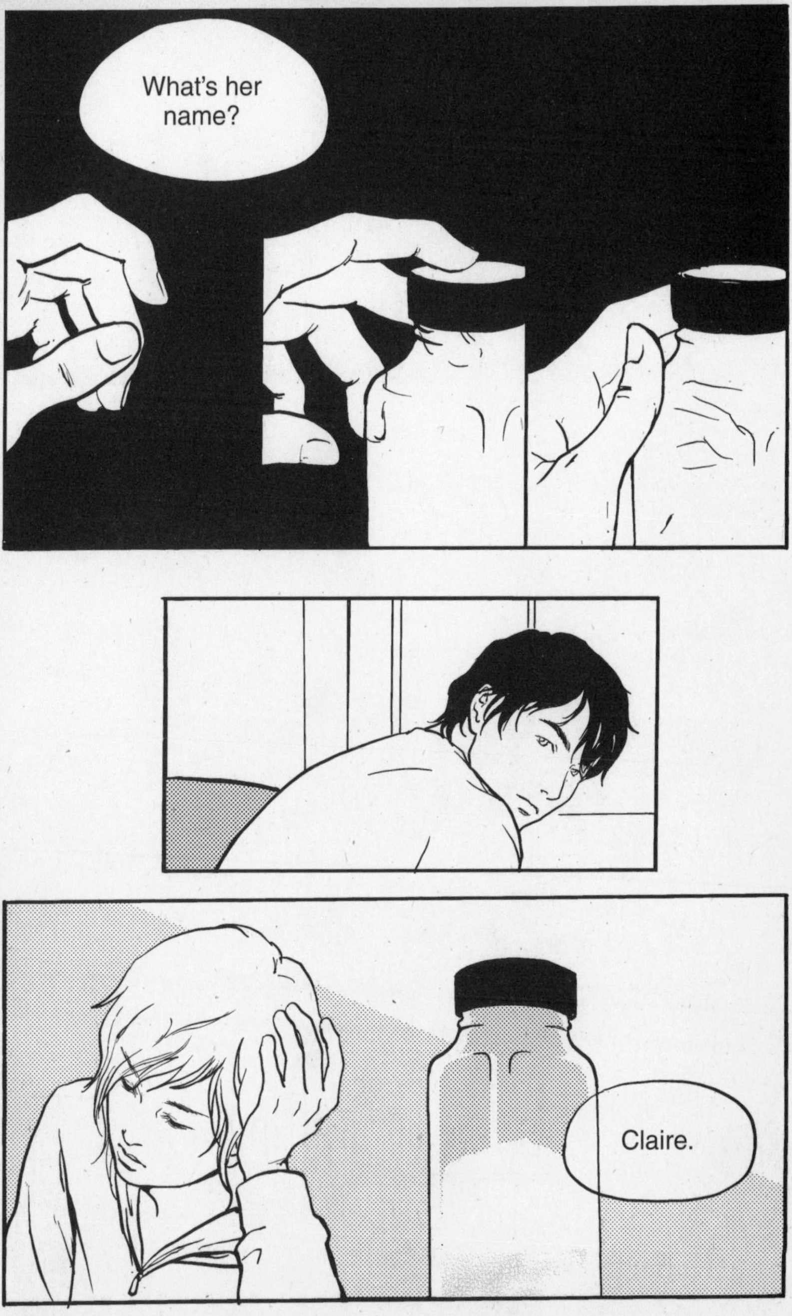
What's her name?
Claire.

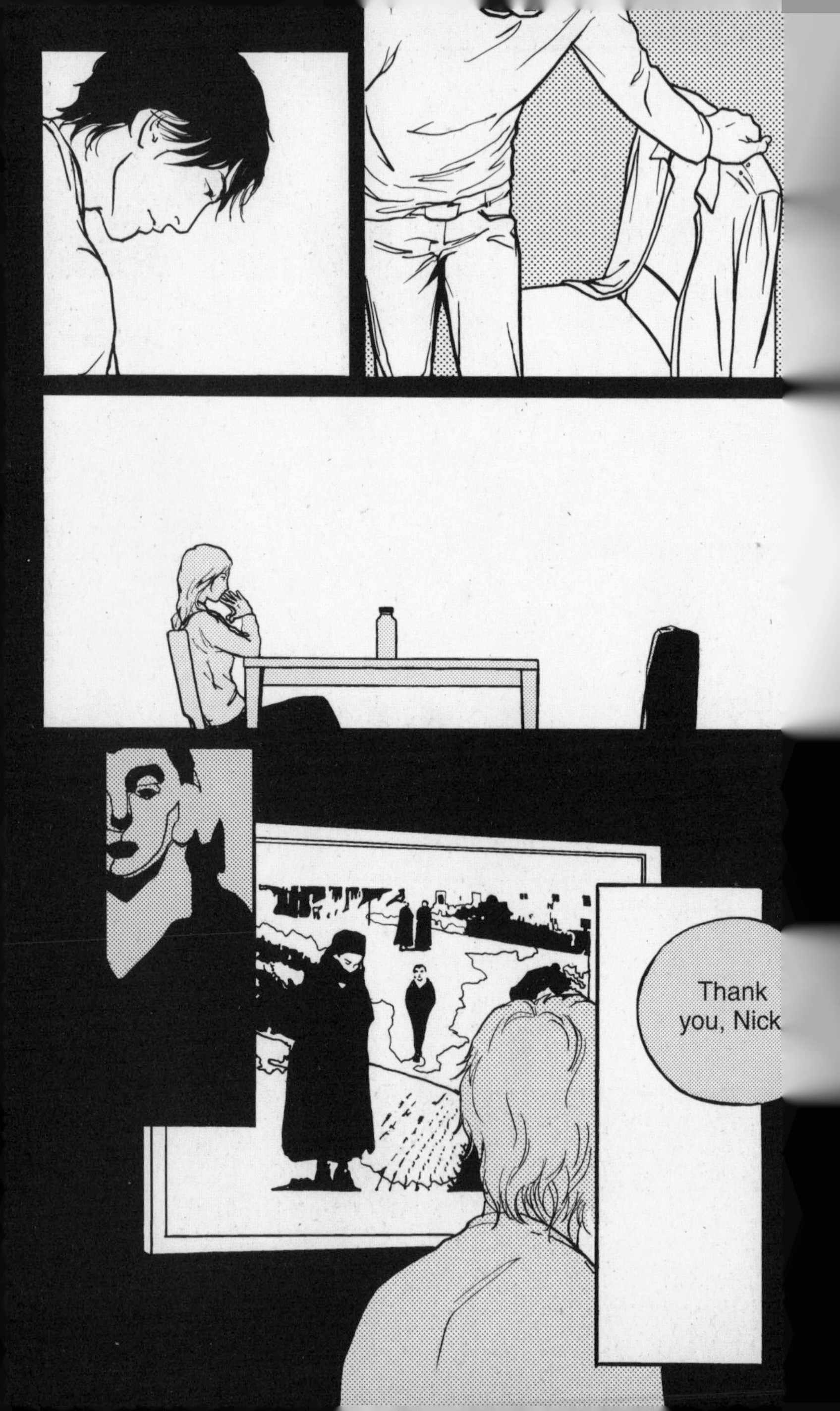
Thank you, Nick

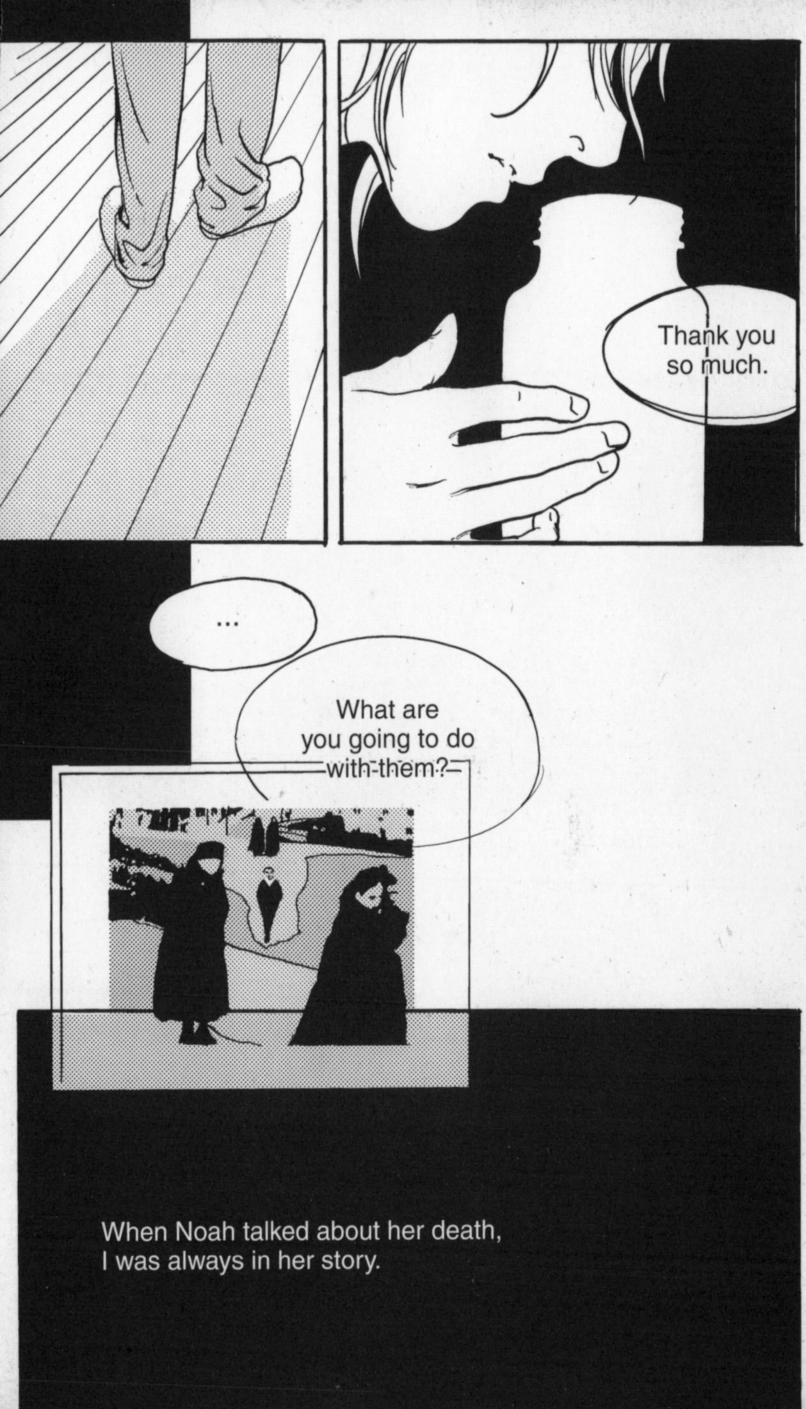
Thank you so much.
...
What are you going to do with them?
When Noah talked about her death, I was always in her story.

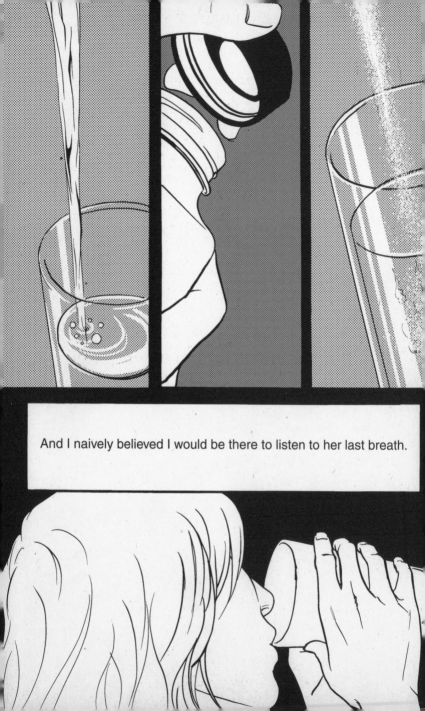

And I naively believed I would be there to listen to her last breath.

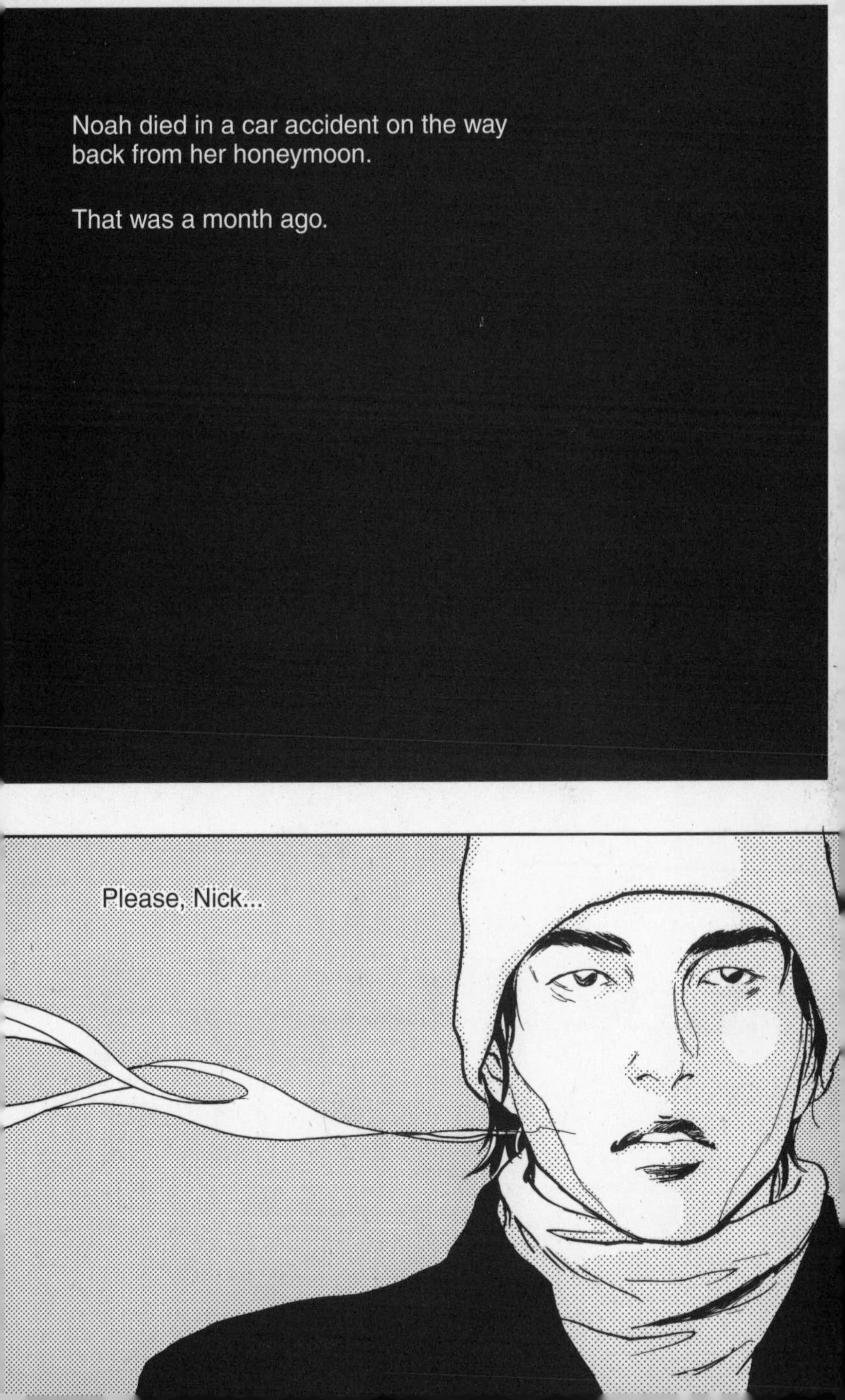
Noah died in a car accident on the way back from her honeymoon.
That was a month ago.
Please, Nick...

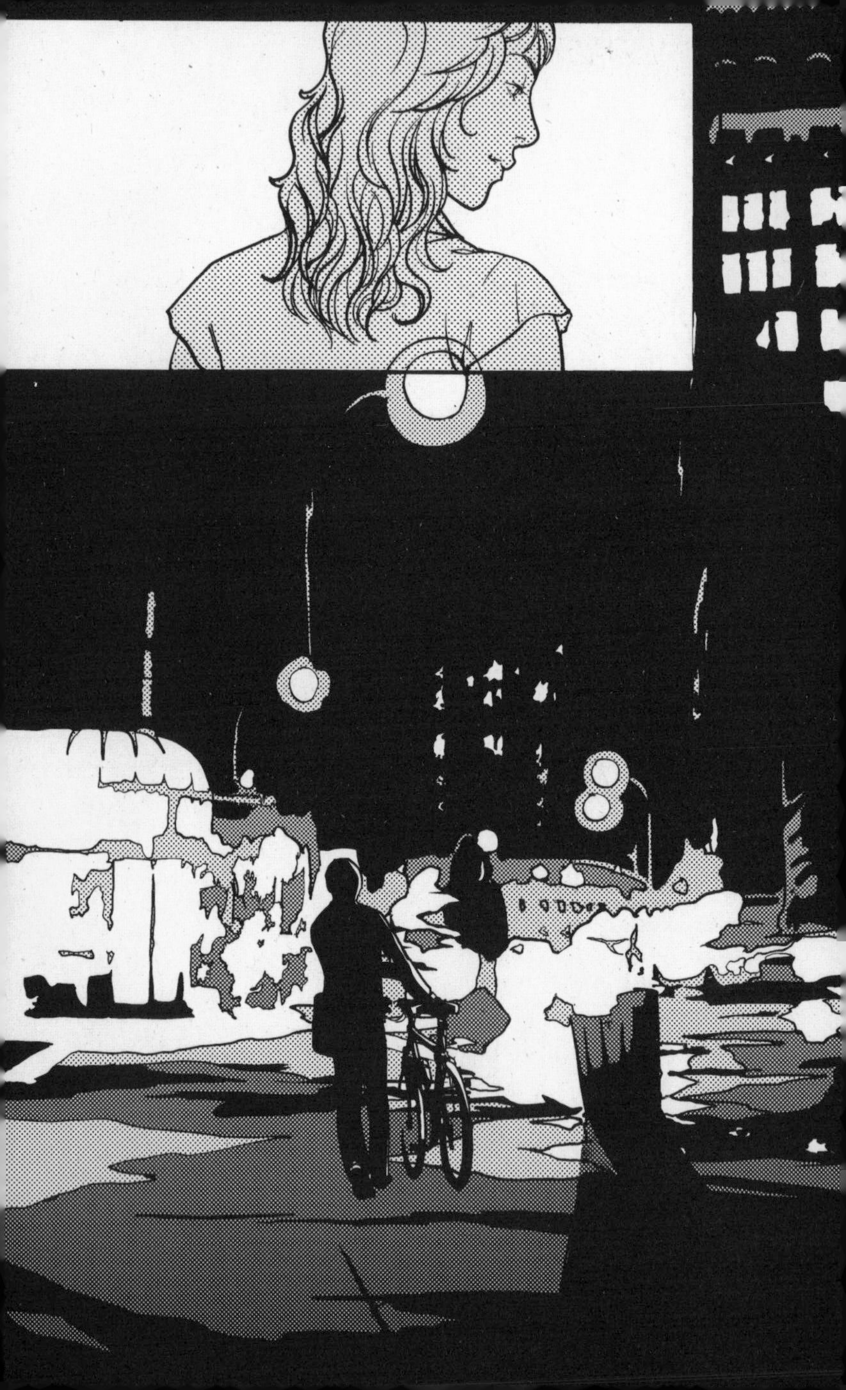

Chapter 2

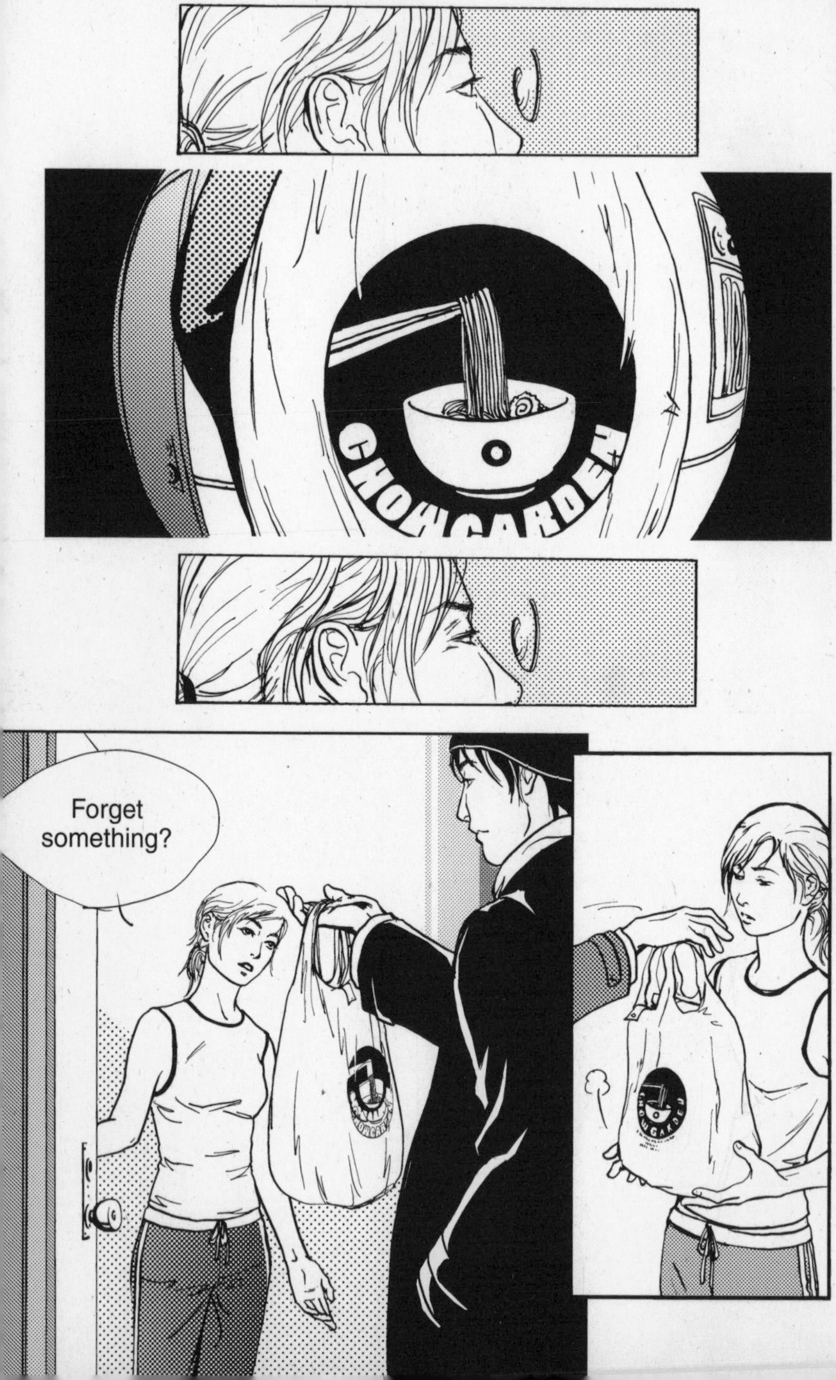
Forget something?

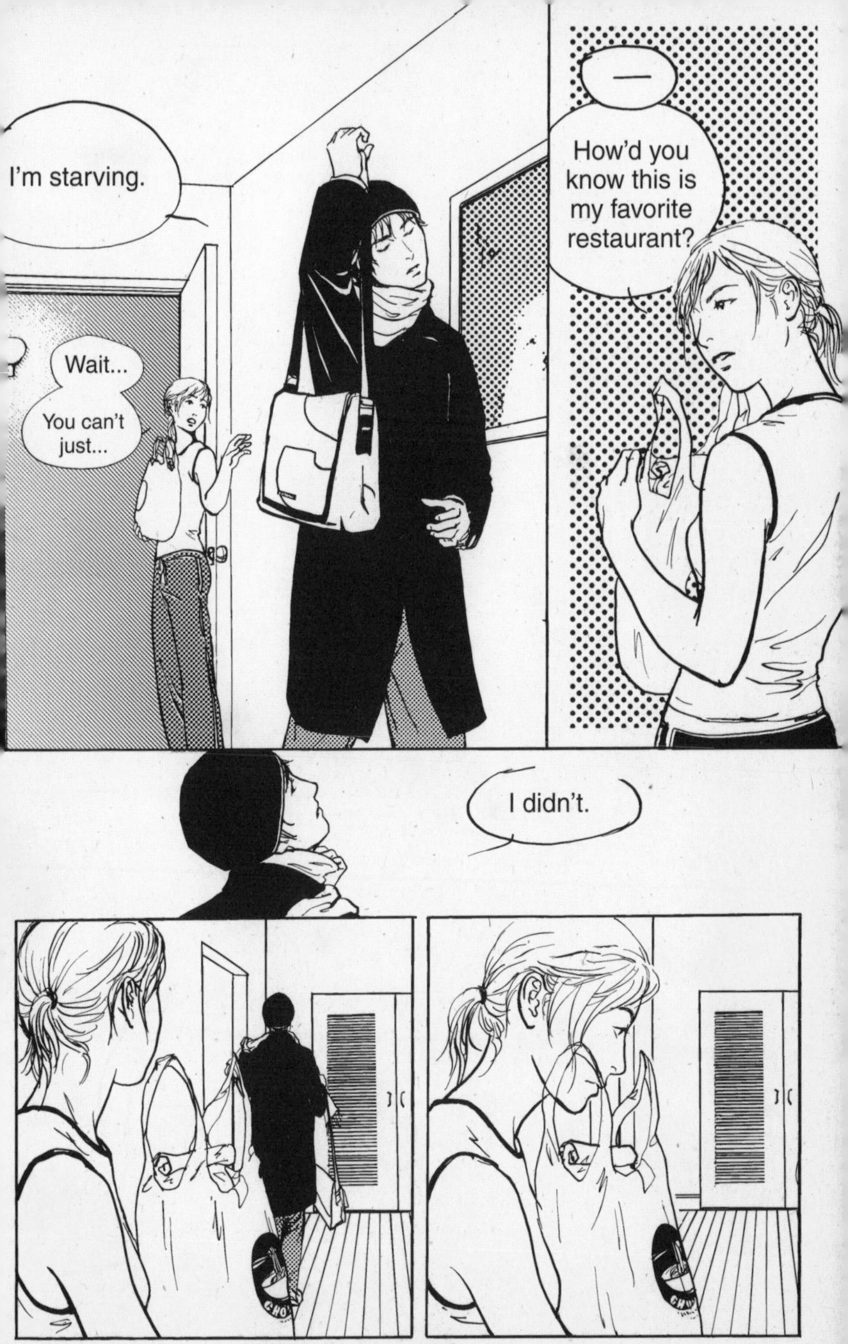
I'm starving.
Wait...
You can't just...
—
How'd you know this is my favorite restaurant?
I didn't.

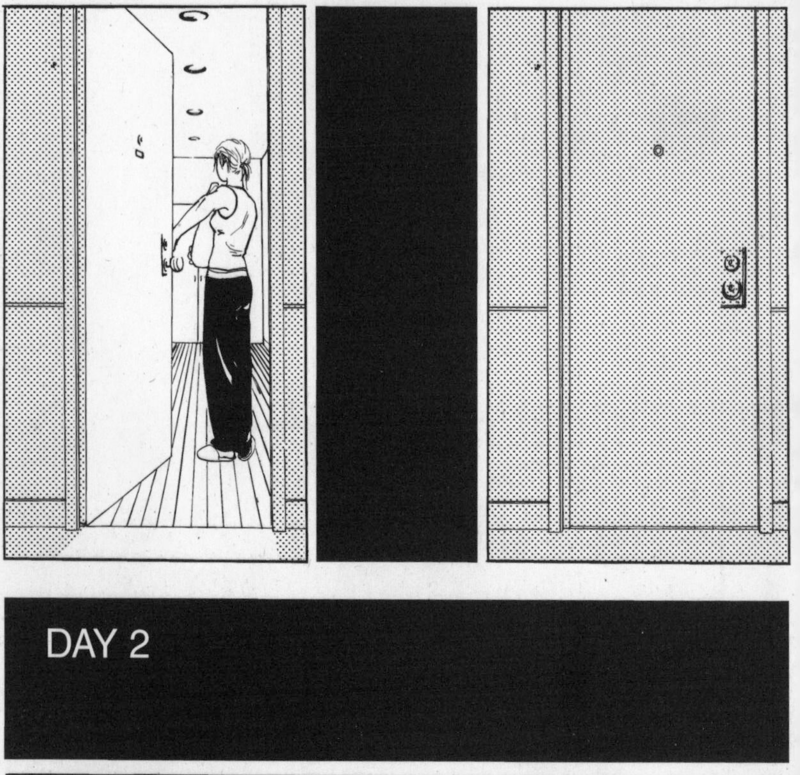

DAY 2

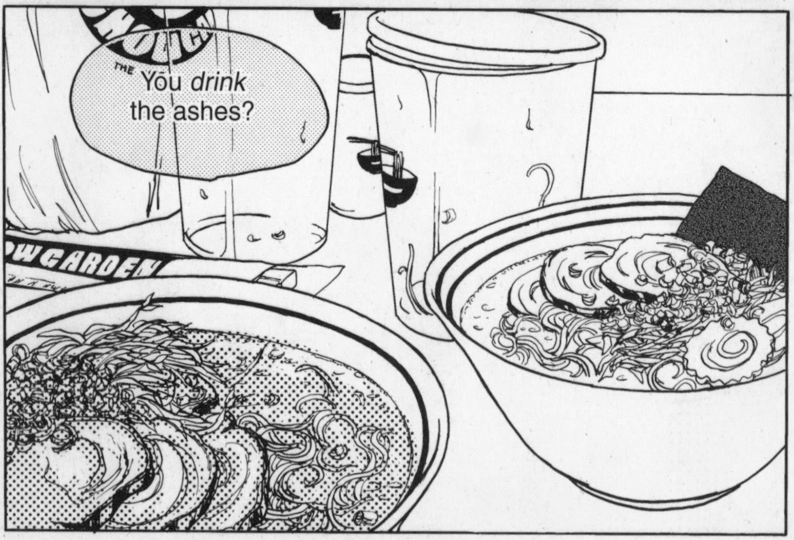
You *drink* the ashes?

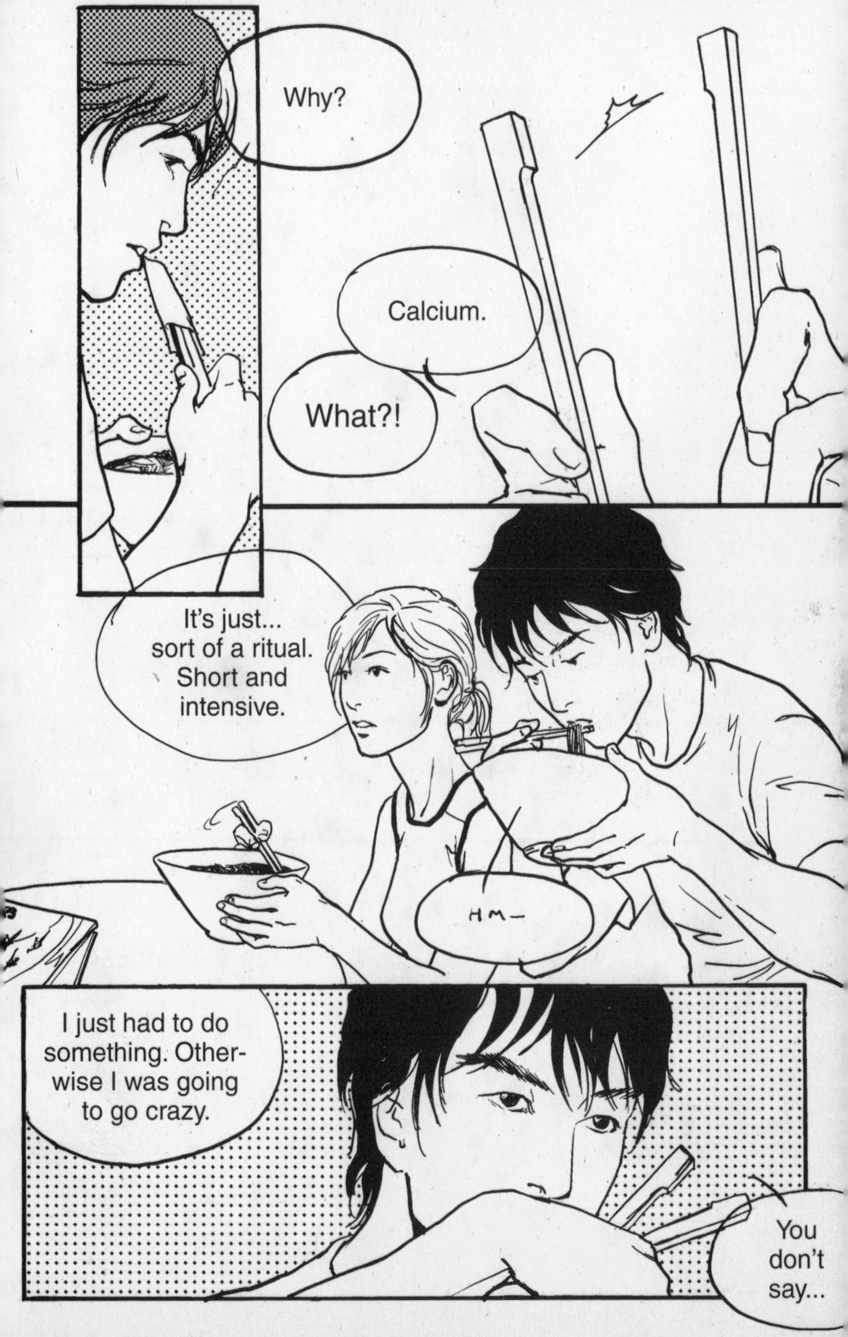
Why?
Calcium.
What?!
It's just... sort of a ritual. Short and intensive.
HM—
I just had to do something. Other-wise I was going to go crazy.
You don't say...

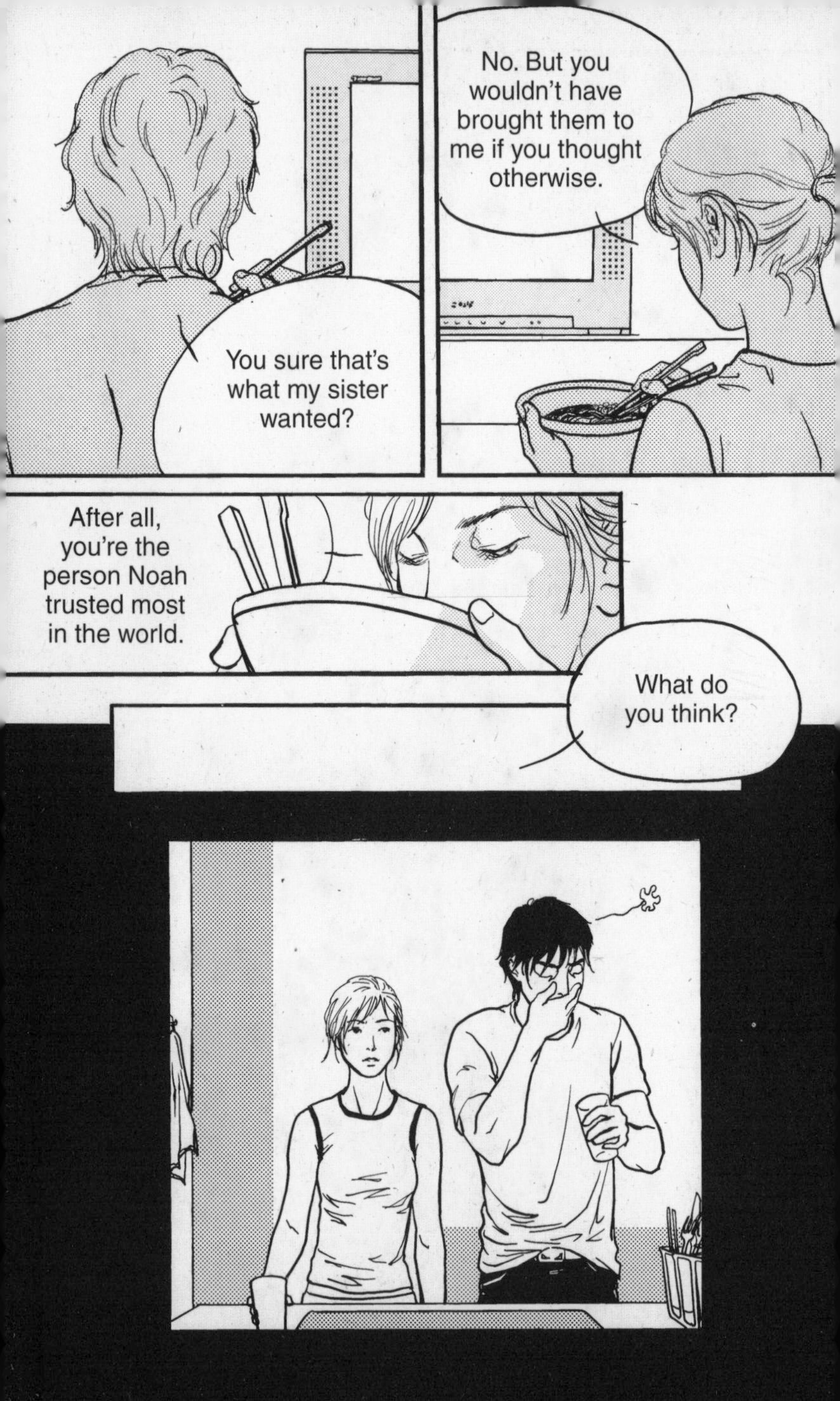
You sure that's what my sister wanted?
No. But you wouldn't have brought them to me if you thought otherwise.
After all, you're the person Noah trusted most in the world.
What do you think?

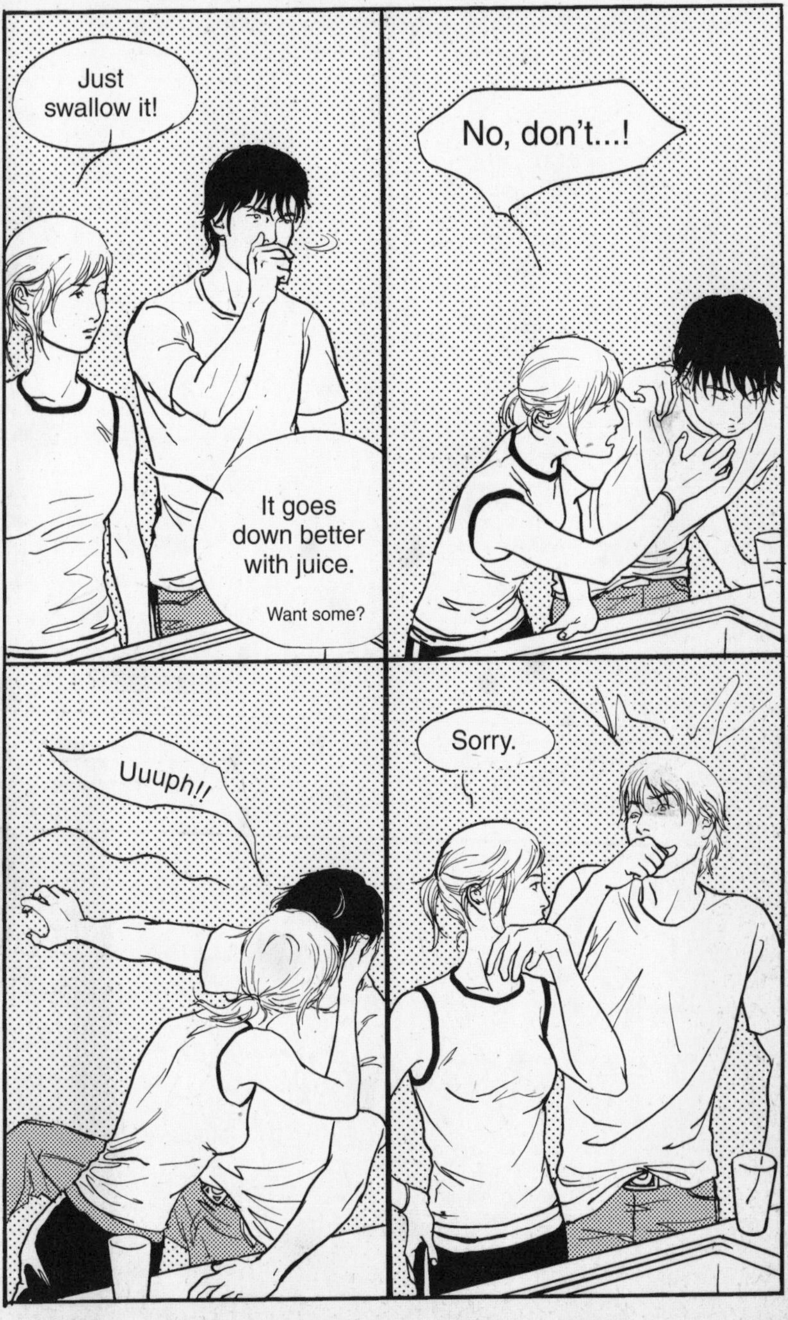
Just swallow it!
It goes down better with juice.
Want some?
No, don't...!
Uuuph!!
Sorry.

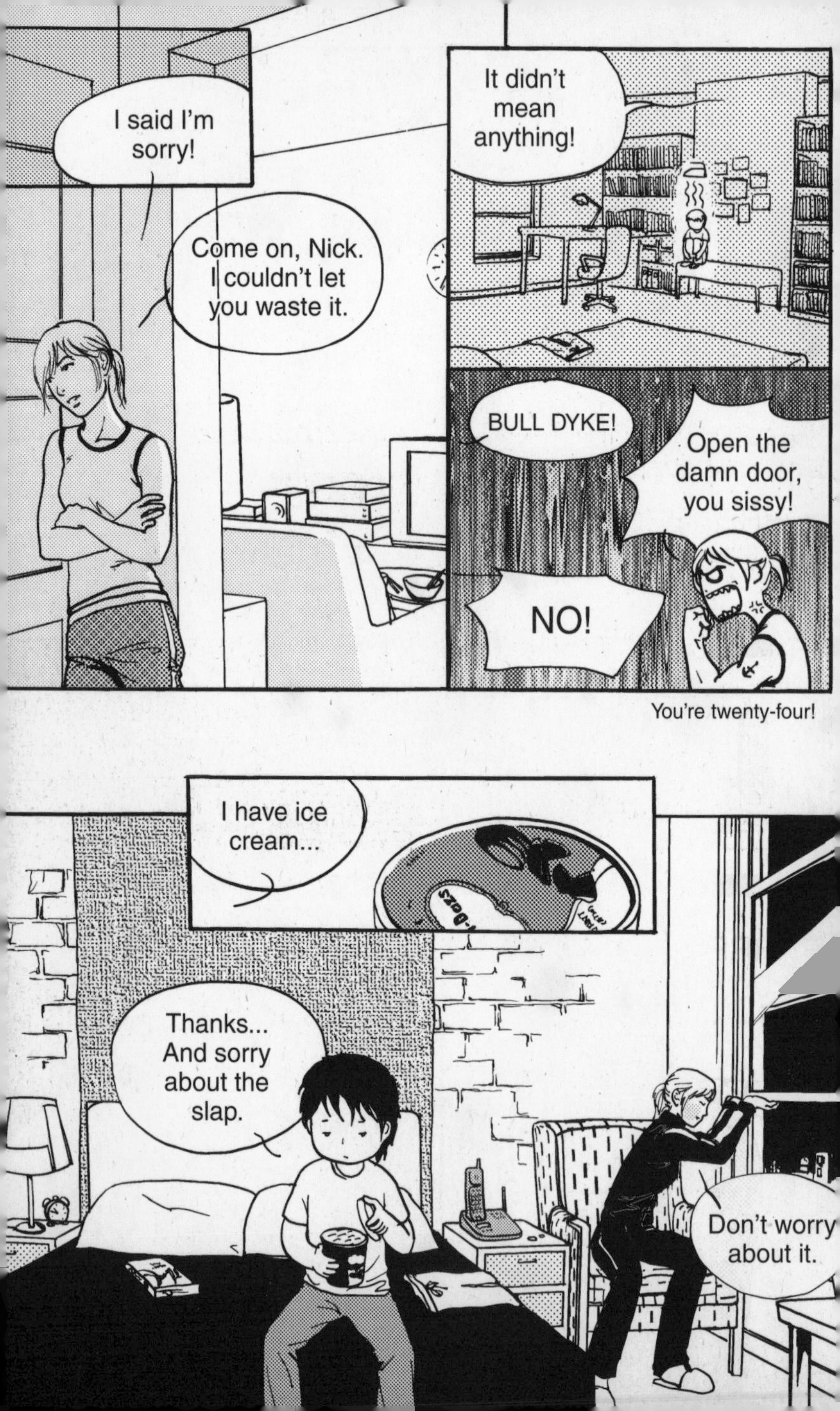
I said I'm sorry!
Come on, Nick. I couldn't let you waste it.
It didn't mean anything!
BULL DYKE!
Open the damn door, you sissy!
NO!
You're twenty-four!
I have ice cream...
Thanks... And sorry about the slap.
Don't worry about it.

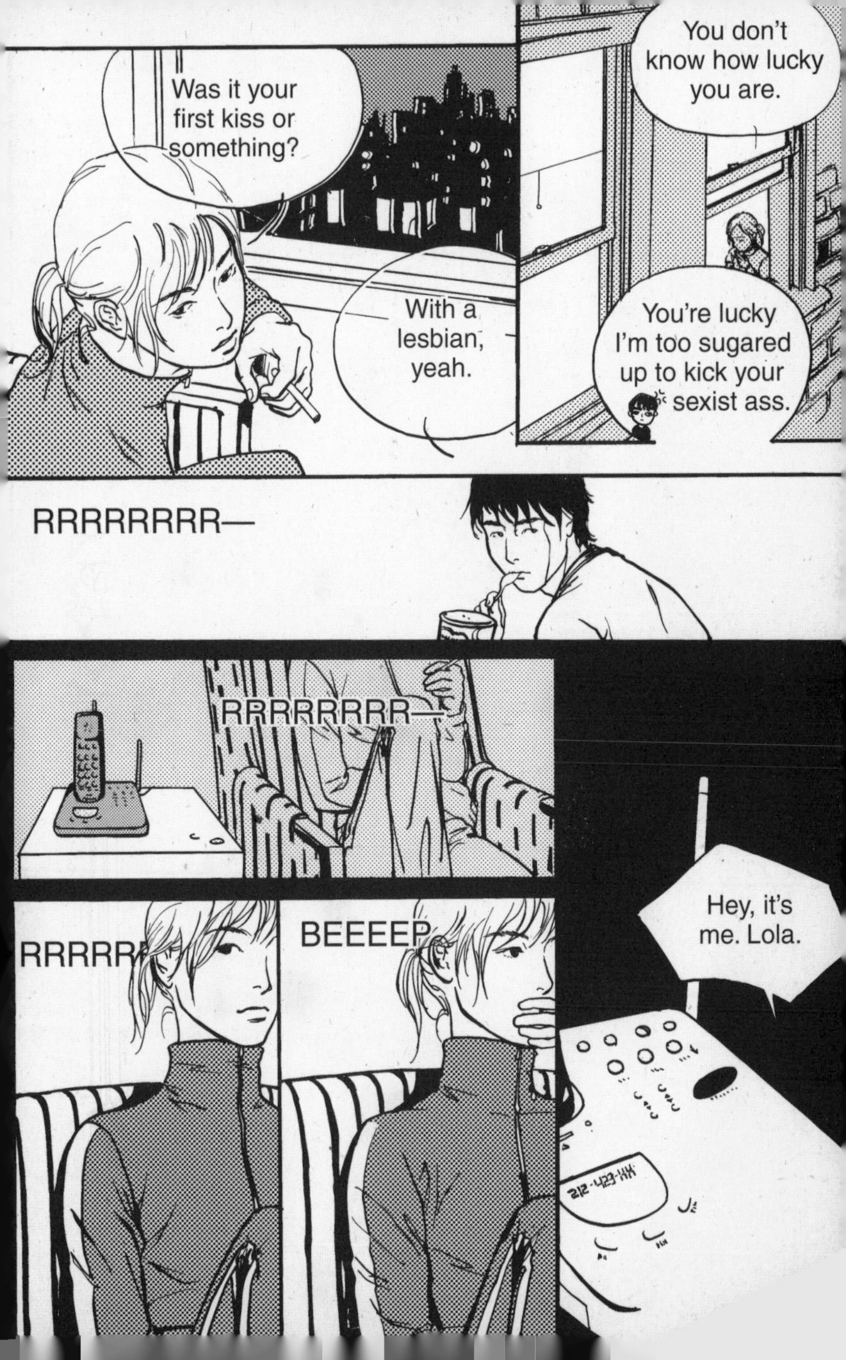
Was it your first kiss or something?
With a lesbian, yeah.
You don't know how lucky you are.
You're lucky I'm too sugared up to kick your sexist ass.
RRRRRRRR—
RRRRRRRRR—
RRRRR
BEEEEP
Hey, it's me. Lola.
212-423-

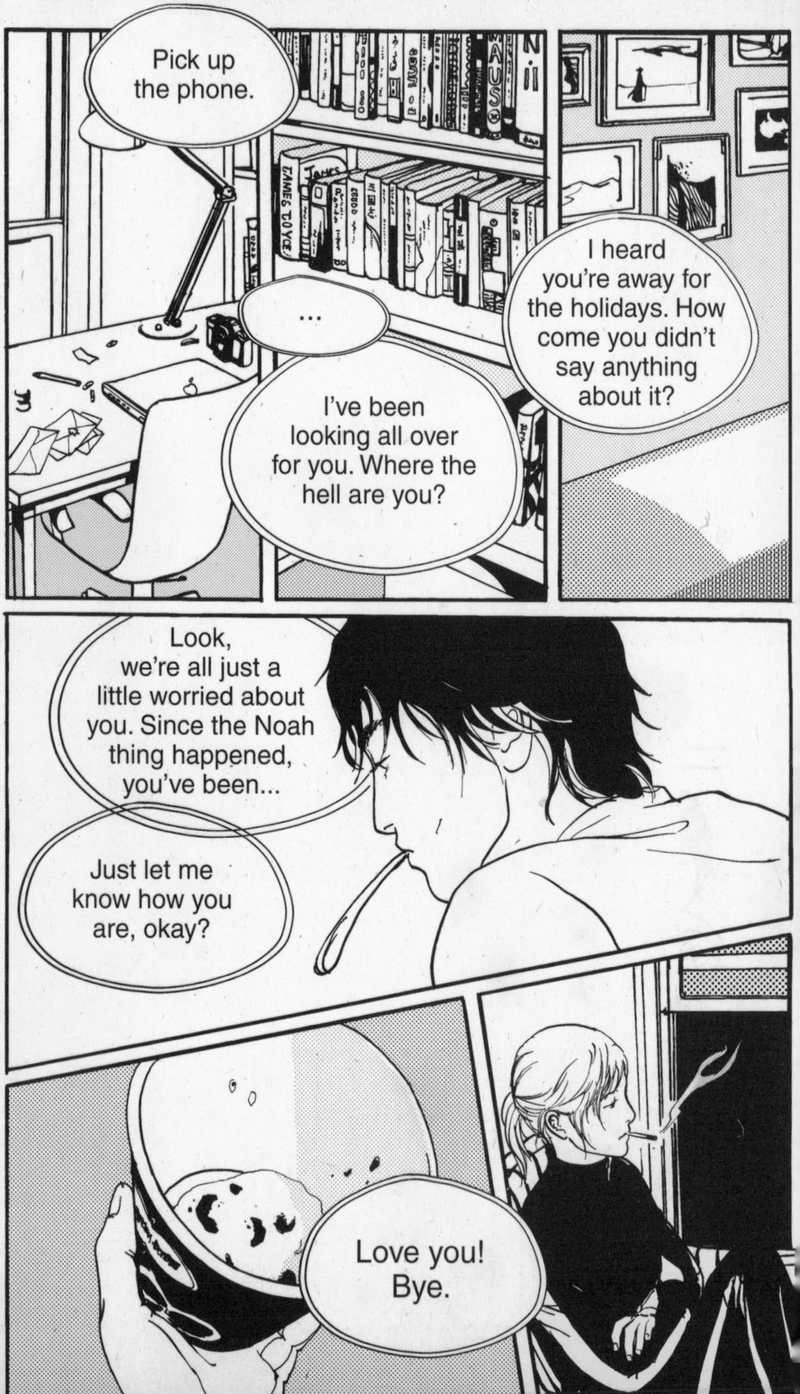
Pick up the phone.
...
I've been looking all over for you. Where the hell are you?
I heard you're away for the holidays. How come you didn't say anything about it?
Look, we're all just a little worried about you. Since the Noah thing happened, you've been...
Just let me know how you are, okay?
Love you! Bye.

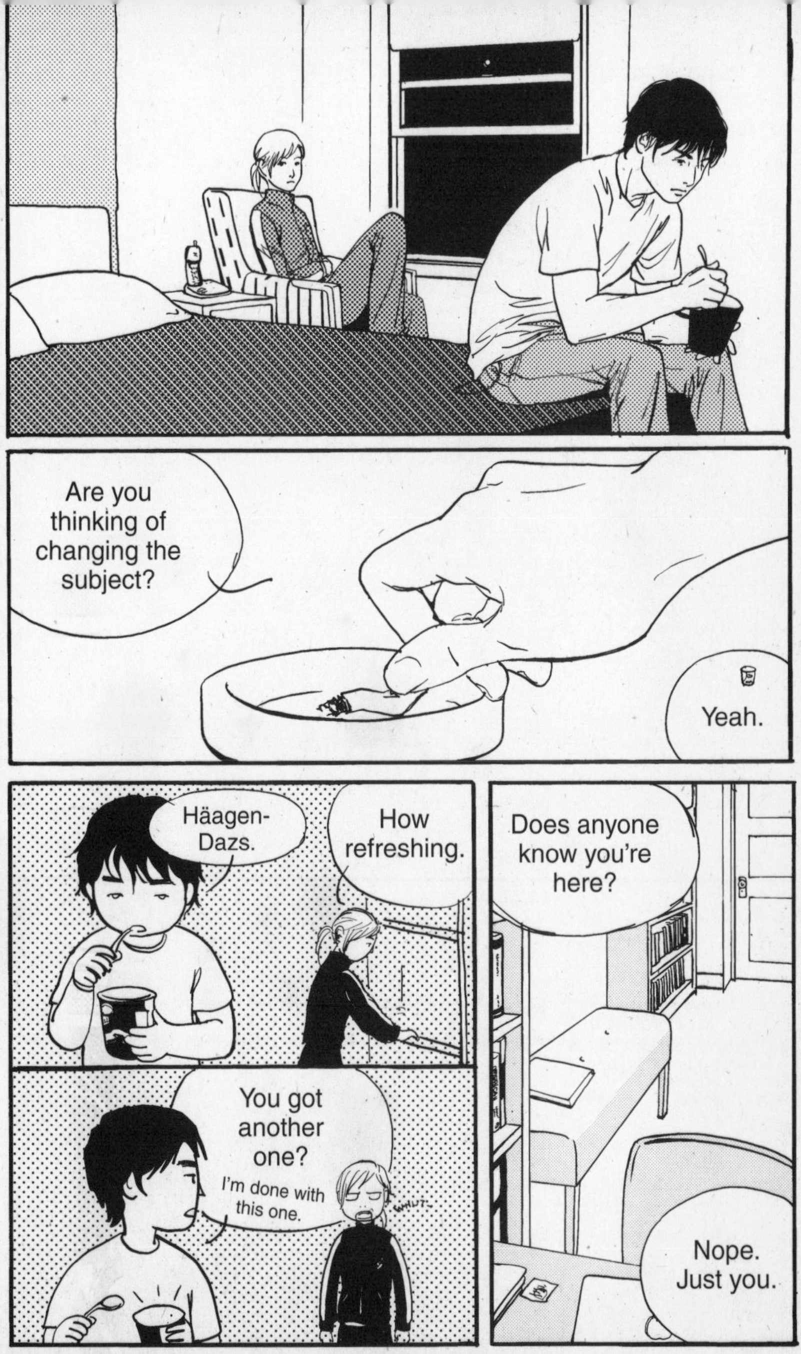
Are you thinking of changing the subject?
Yeah.
Häagen-Dazs.
How refreshing.
You got another one?
I'm done with this one.
Does anyone know you're here?
Nope. Just you.

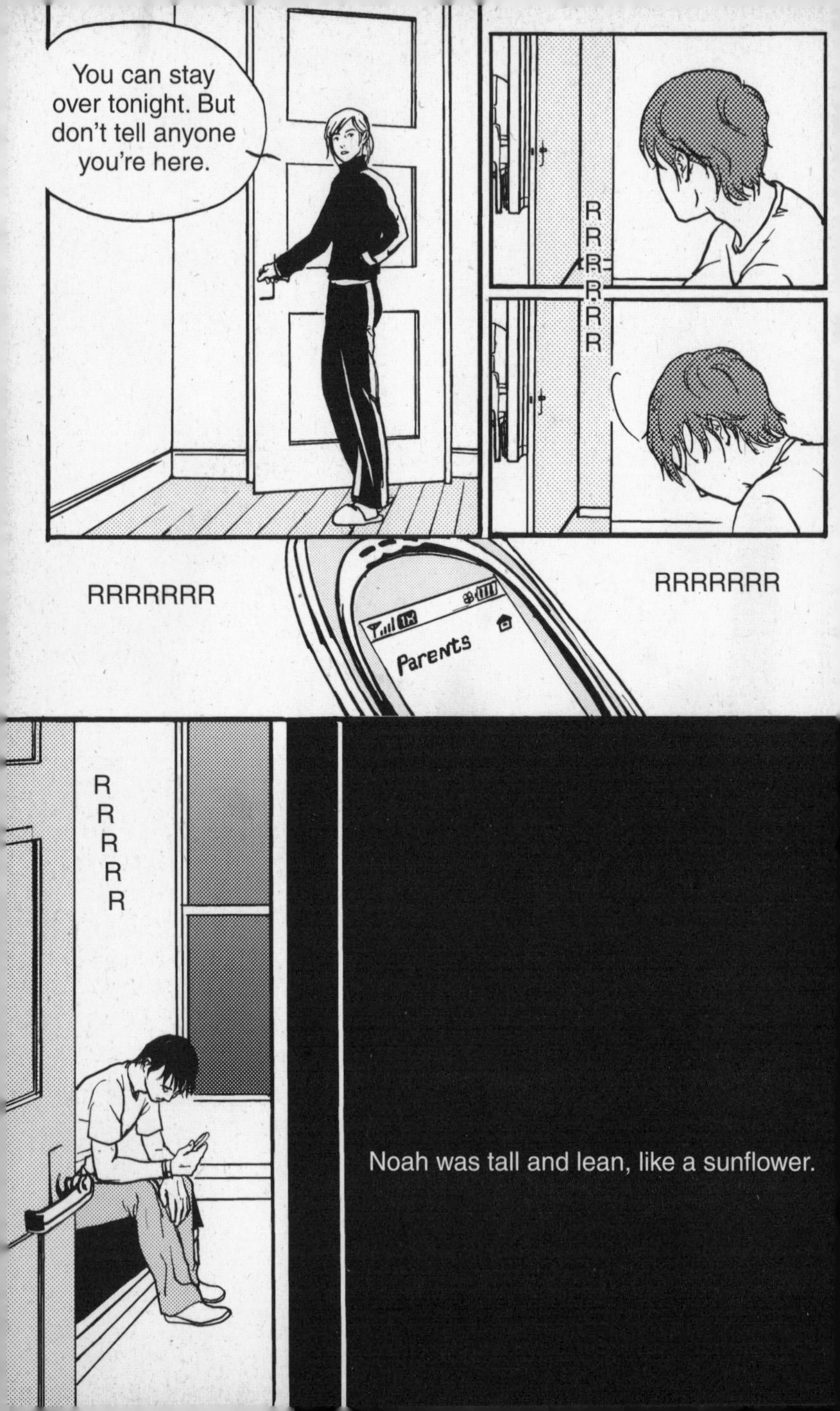
You can stay over tonight. But don't tell anyone you're here.
RRRRRRR
RRRRRRR
Parents
RRRRRRR
RRRRR
Noah was tall and lean, like a sunflower.

Her curly hair that stubbornly covered her face.
Her long limbs that coiled into my dreams.
Her warm neck and breast against my back.
Her pulse I couldn't tell from mine.

Is this really you?

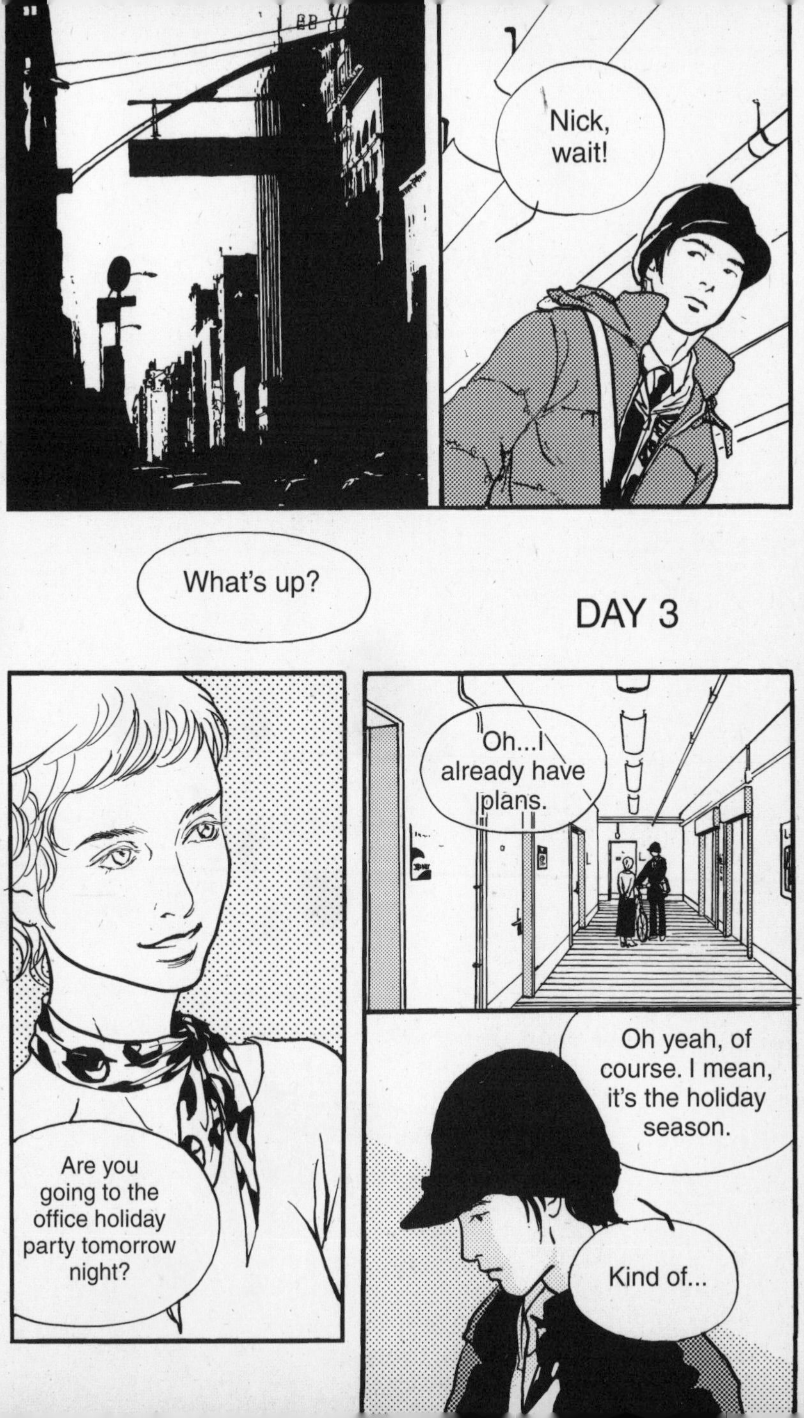

Nick, wait!
What's up?
DAY 3
Are you going to the office holiday party tomorrow night?
Oh...I already have plans.
Oh yeah, of course. I mean, it's the holiday season.
Kind of...

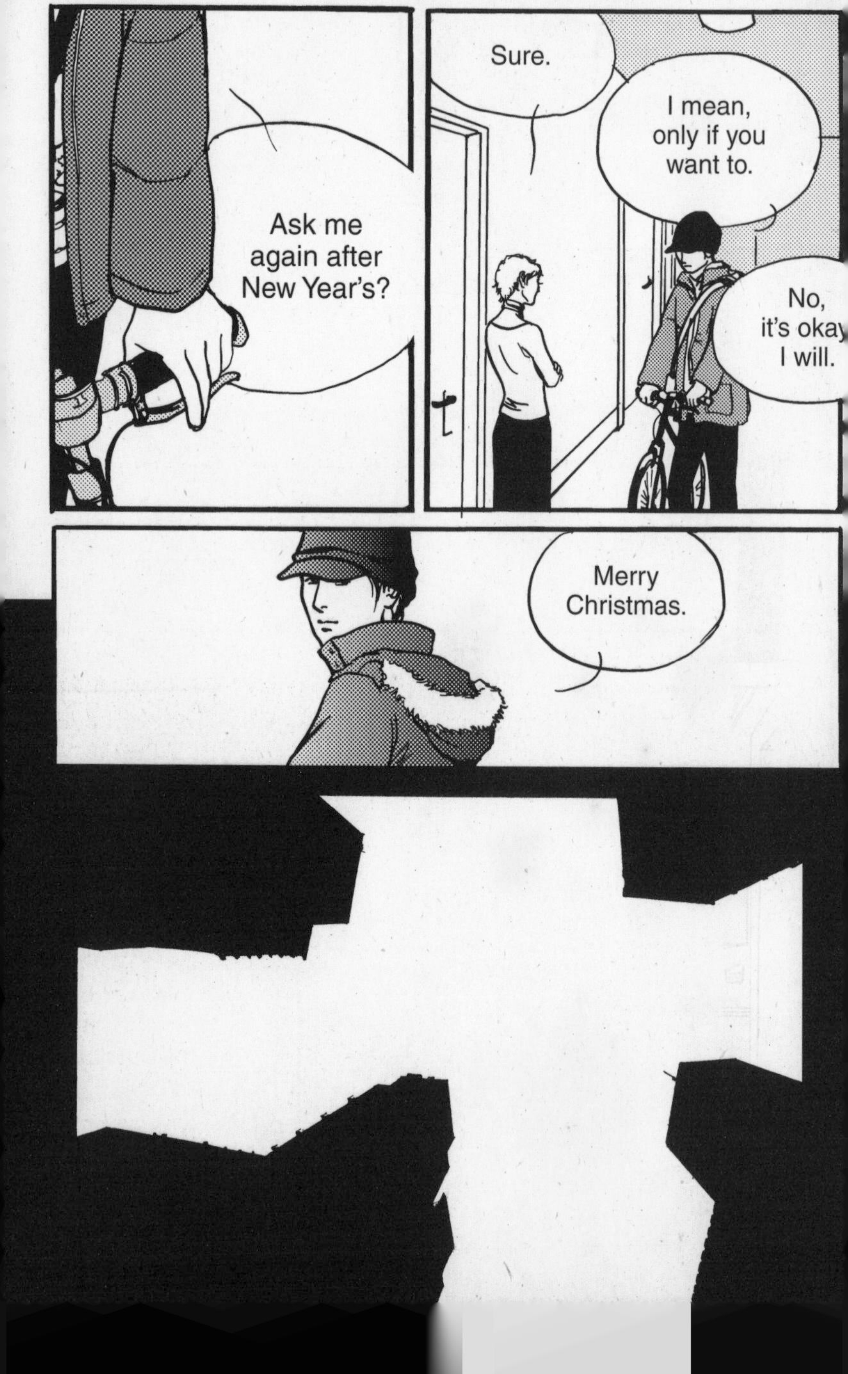
Ask me again after New Year's?
Sure.
I mean, only if you want to.
No, it's okay I will.
Merry Christmas.

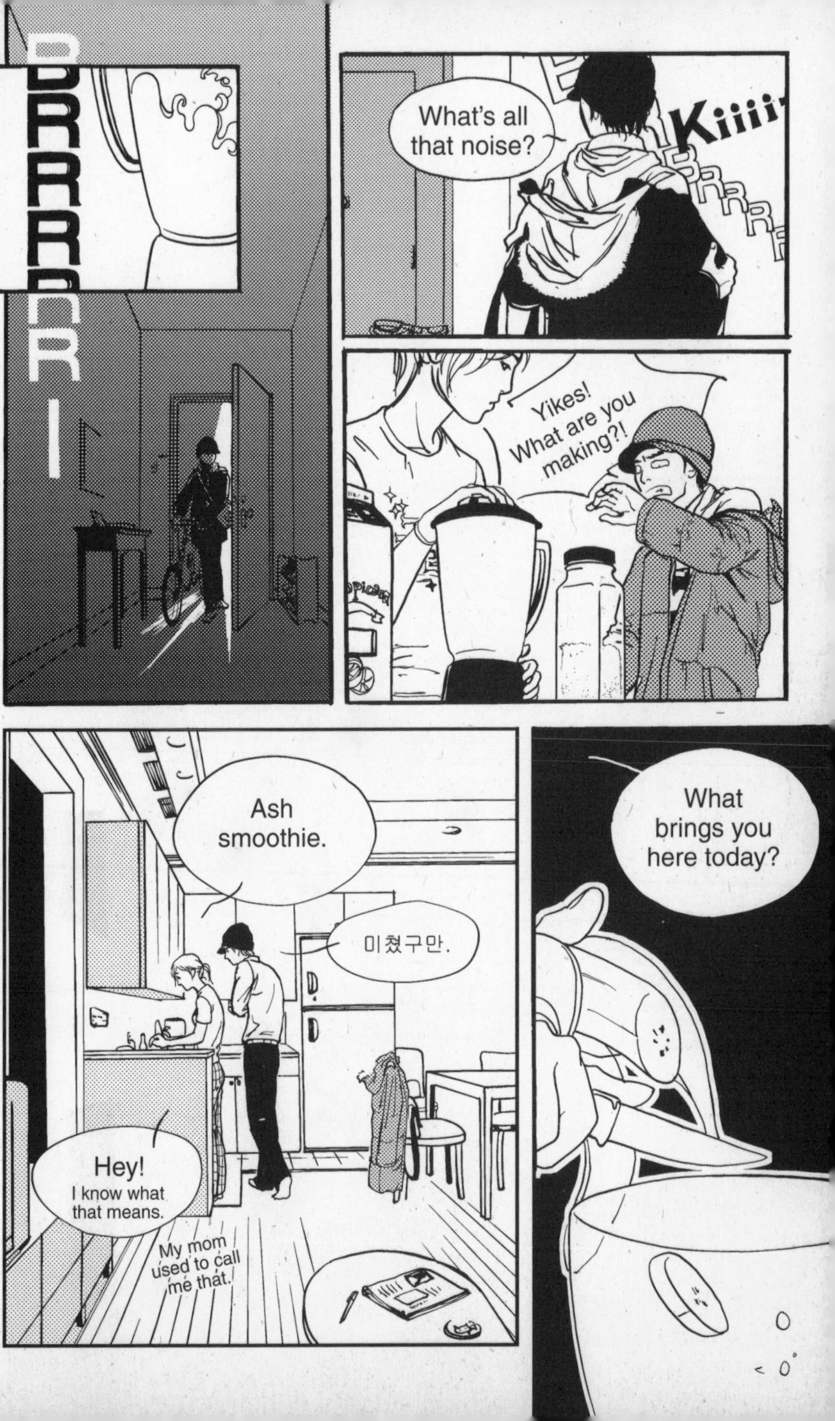
BRRRRRRI
What's all that noise?
Kiiii
BRRRRR
Yikes! What are you making?!
Ash smoothie.
미쳤구만.
Hey! I know what that means.
My mom used to call me that.
What brings you here today?

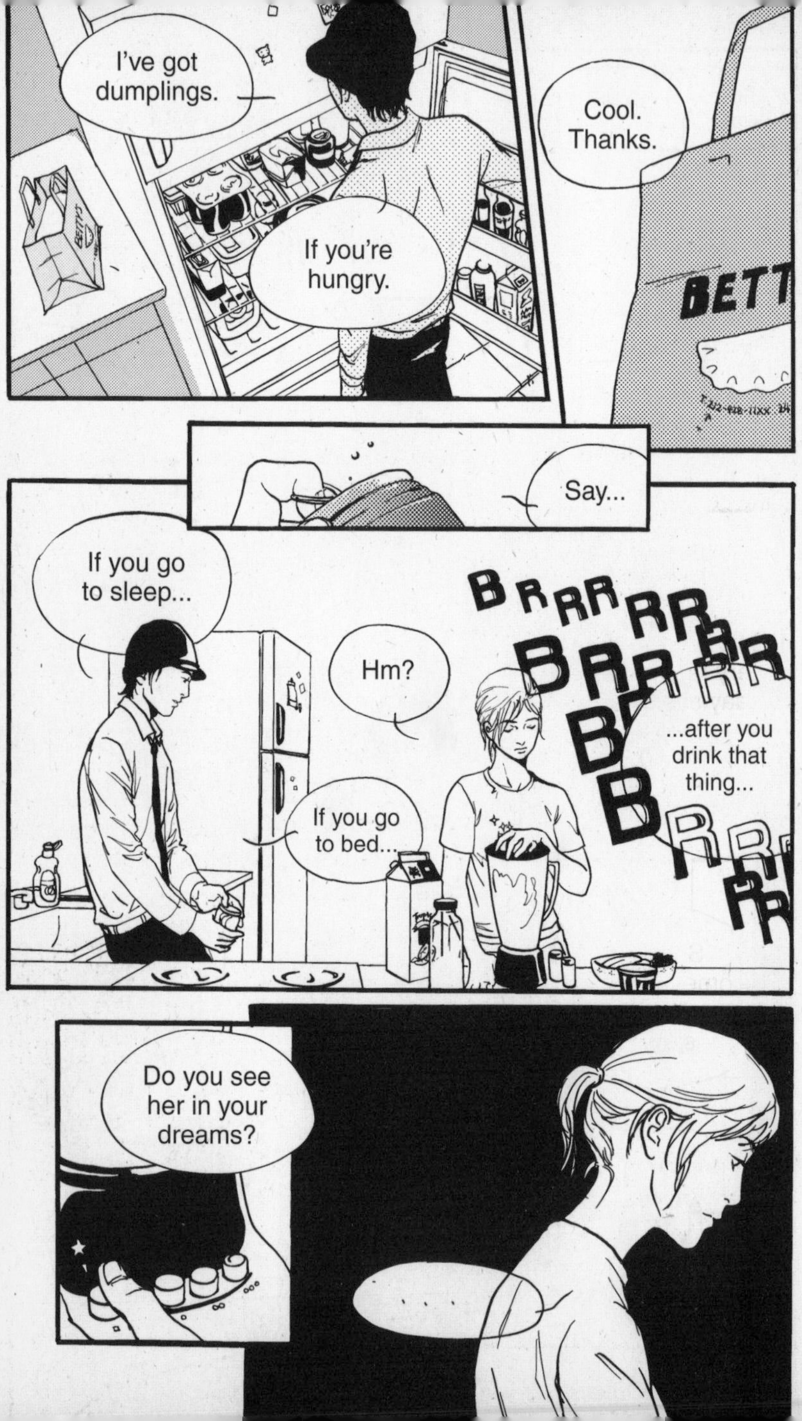
I've got dumplings.
If you're hungry.
Cool. Thanks.
Say...
If you go to sleep...
Hm?
BRRRRRR BRRRRR BRRRR
If you go to bed...
...after you drink that thing...
Do you see her in your dreams?
. . .

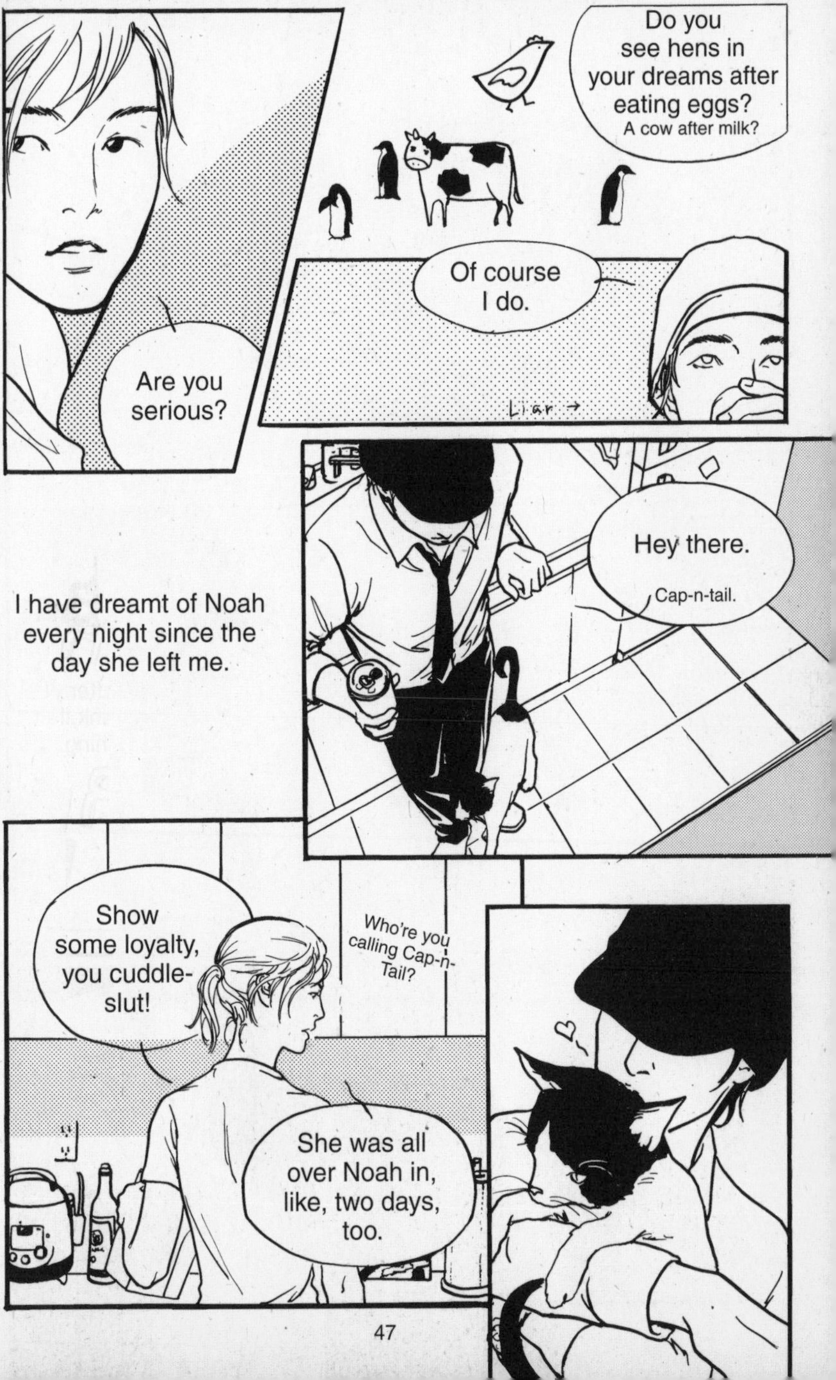
Are you serious?
Do you see hens in your dreams after eating eggs?
A cow after milk?
Of course I do.
Liar →
I have dreamt of Noah every night since the day she left me.
Hey there.
Cap-n-tail.
Show some loyalty, you cuddle-slut!
Who're you calling Cap-n-Tail?
She was all over Noah in, like, two days, too.

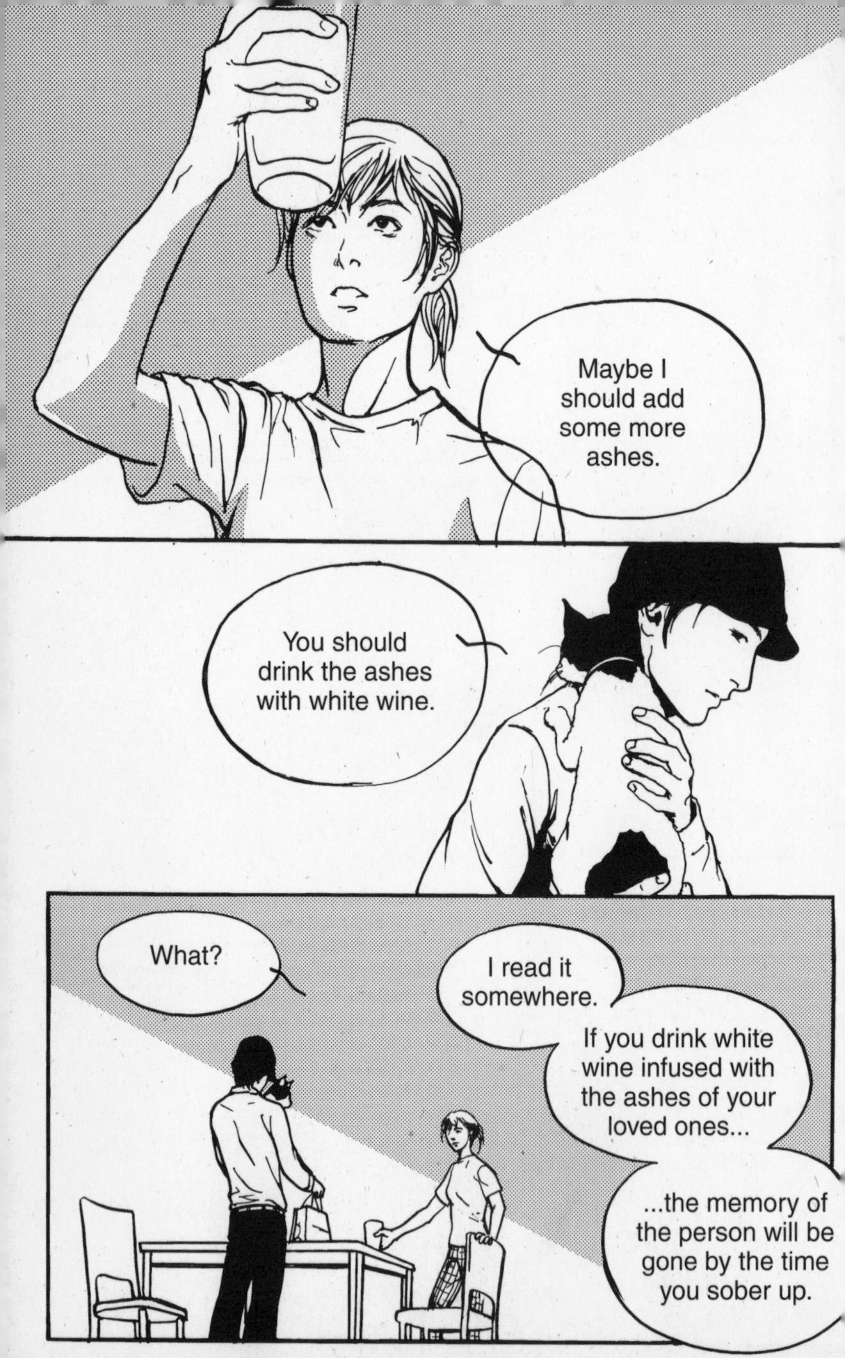
Maybe I should add some more ashes.
You should drink the ashes with white wine.
What?
I read it somewhere.
If you drink white wine infused with the ashes of your loved ones...
...the memory of the person will be gone by the time you sober up.

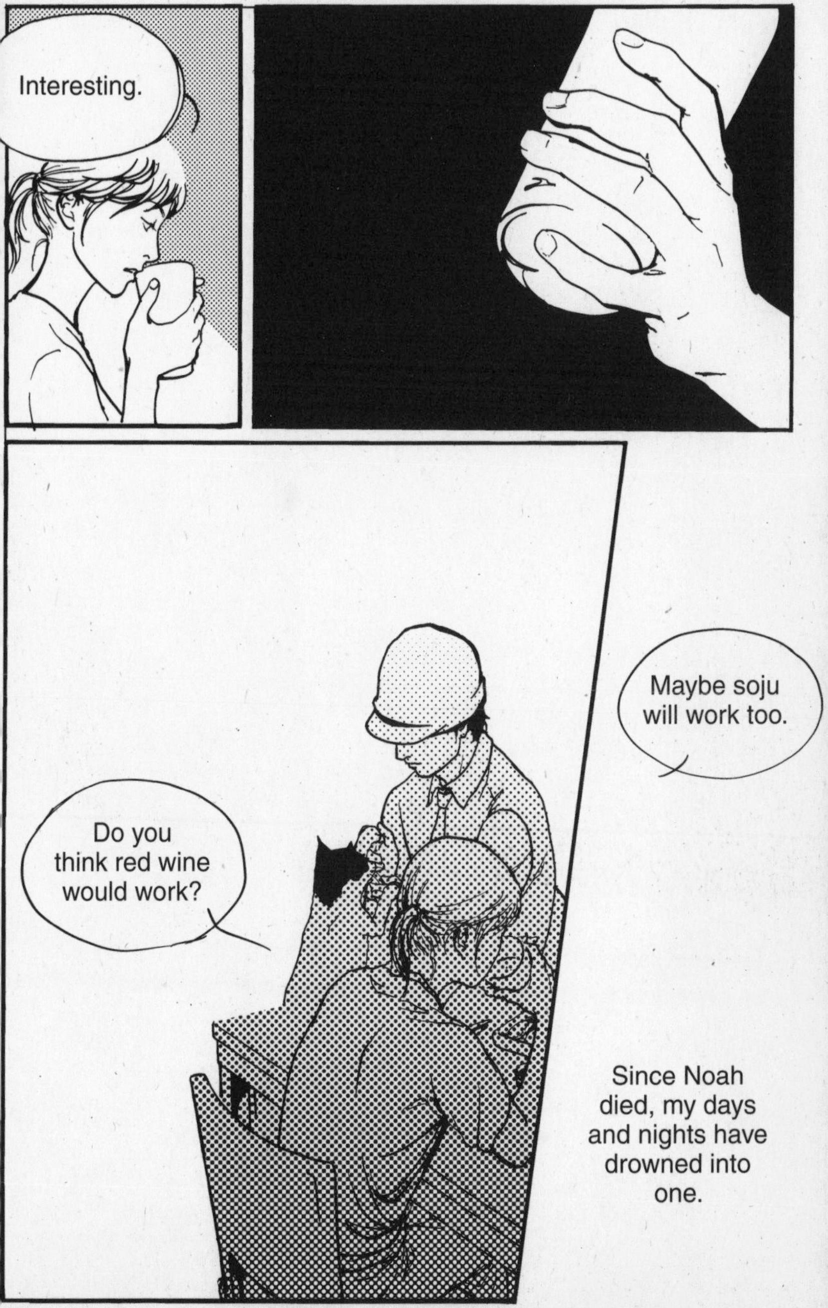
Interesting.
Do you think red wine would work?
Maybe soju will work too.
Since Noah died, my days and nights have drowned into one.

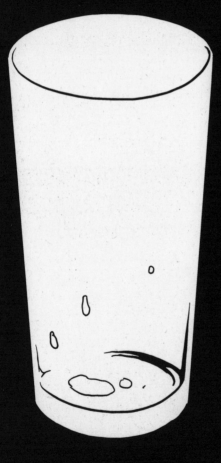

I just sit there clutching the
hem of my empty dreams
like a deranged woman
cherishing her treasure.

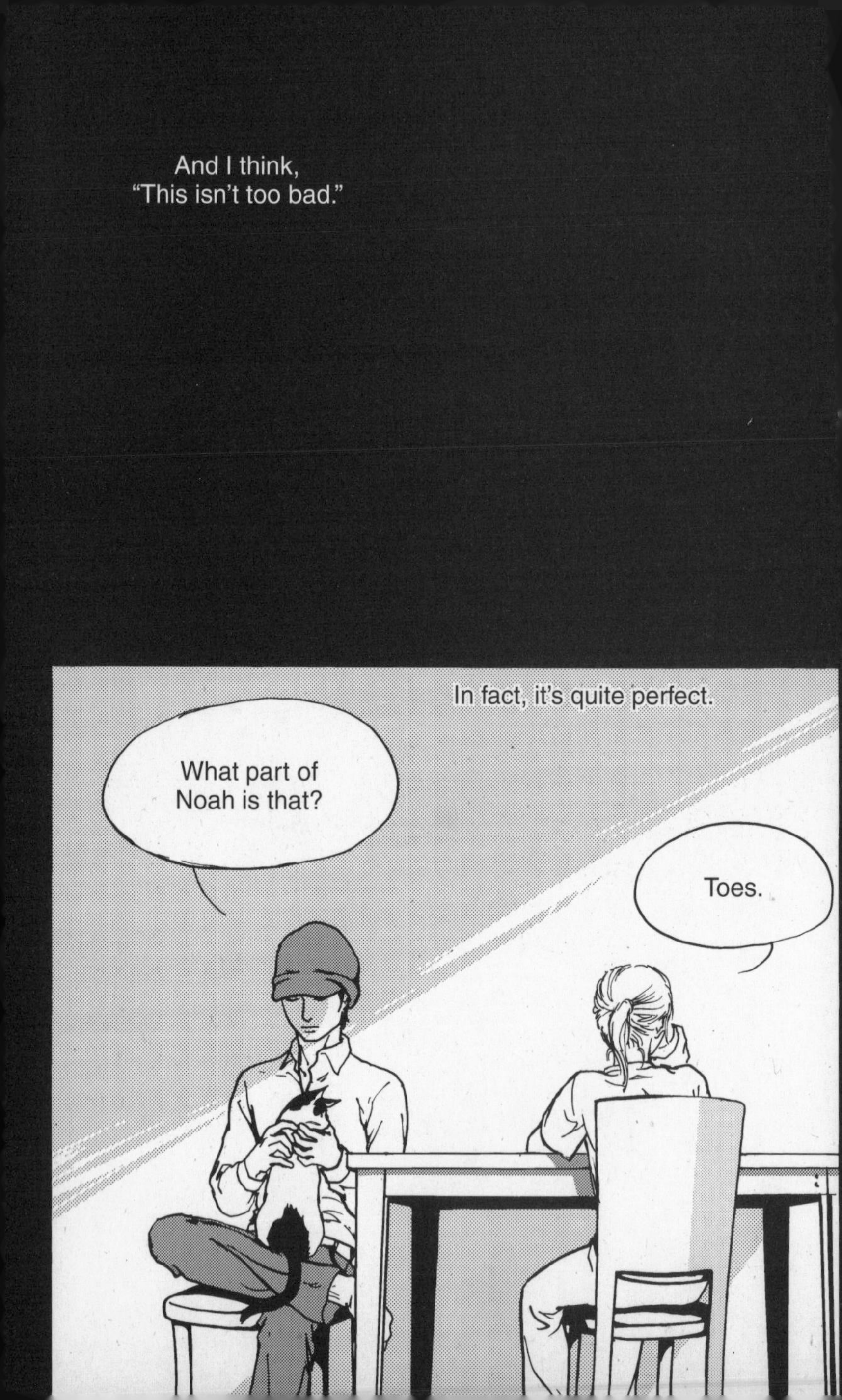
And I think,
"This isn't too bad."
In fact, it's quite perfect.
What part of Noah is that?
Toes.

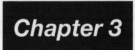

Chapter 3

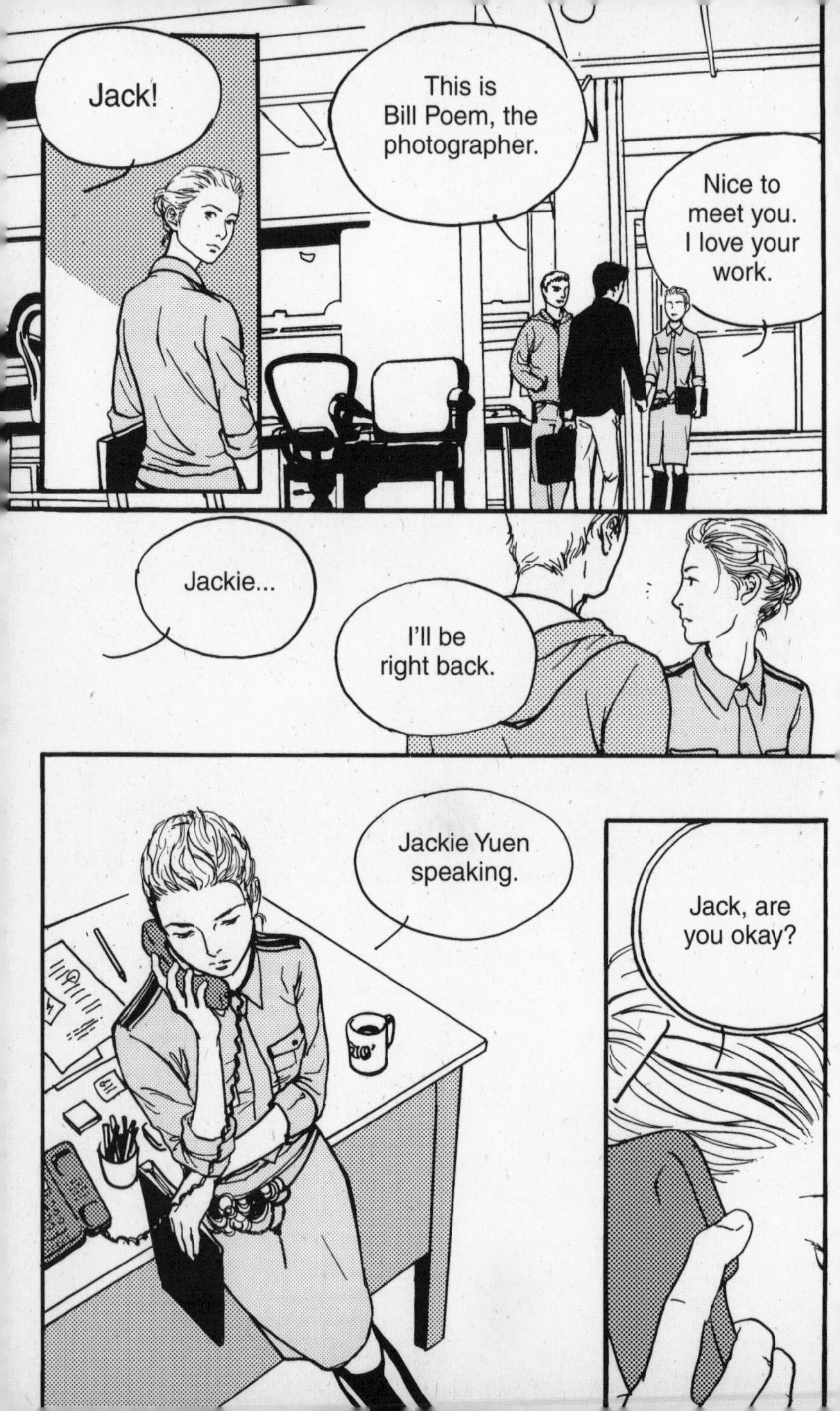
Jack!
This is Bill Poem, the photographer.
Nice to meet you. I love your work.
Jackie...
I'll be right back.
Jackie Yuen speaking.
Jack, are you okay?

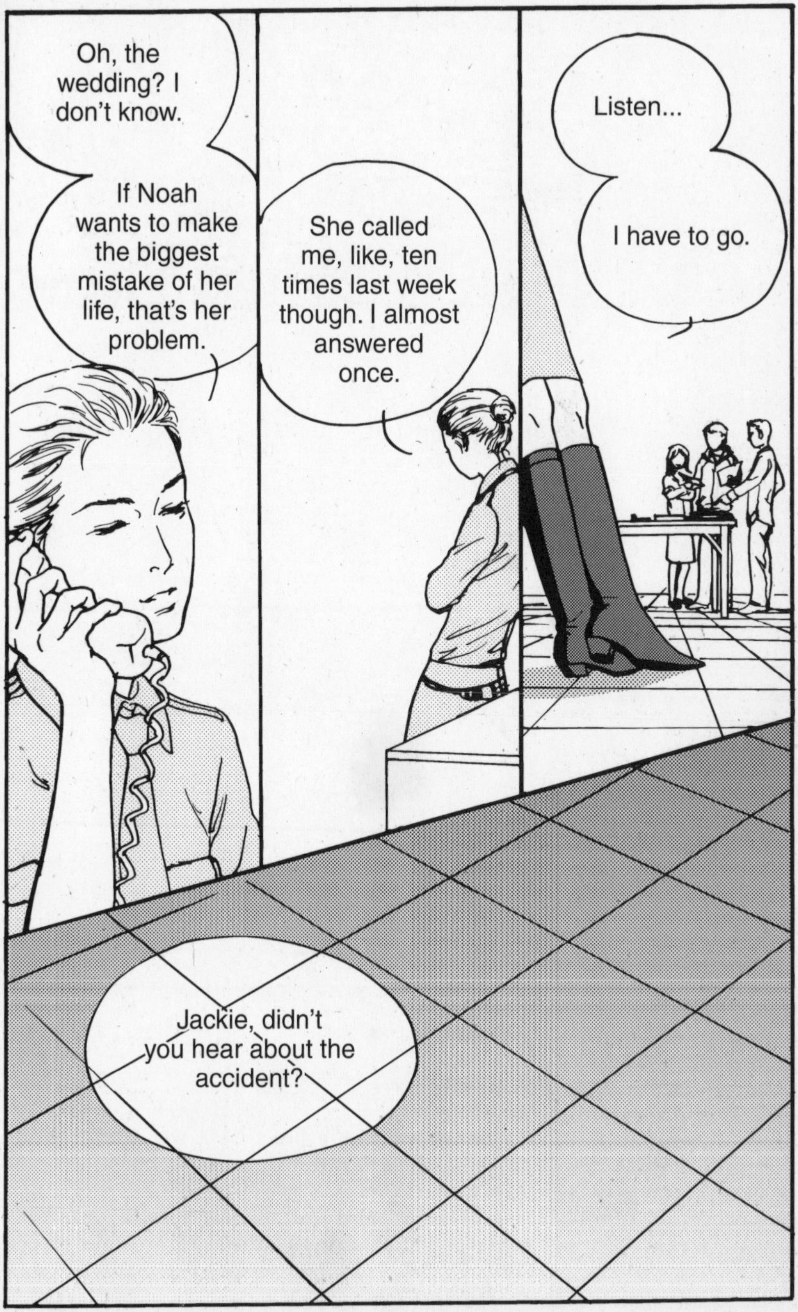
Oh, the wedding? I don't know.
If Noah wants to make the biggest mistake of her life, that's her problem.
She called me, like, ten times last week though. I almost answered once.
Listen...
I have to go.
Jackie, didn't you hear about the accident?

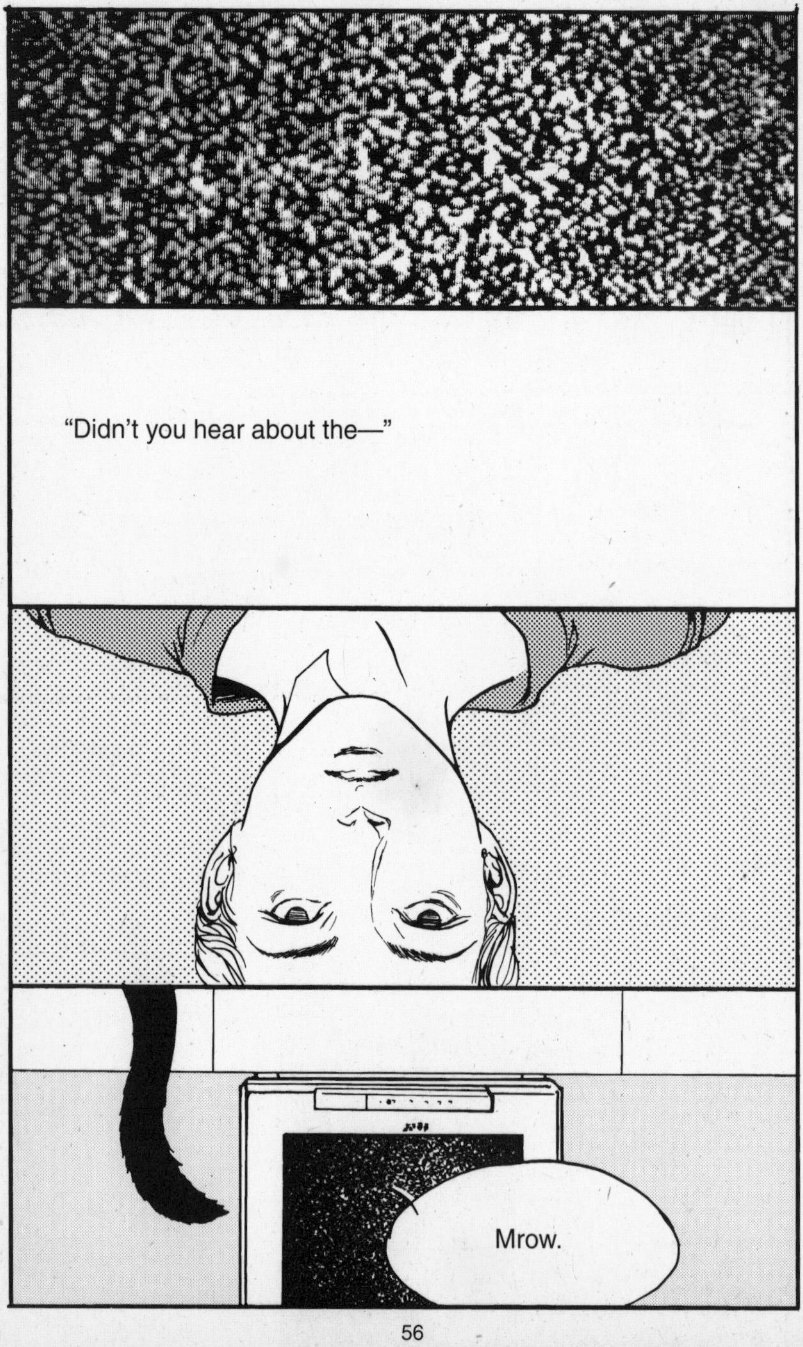
"Didn't you hear about the—"
Mrow.

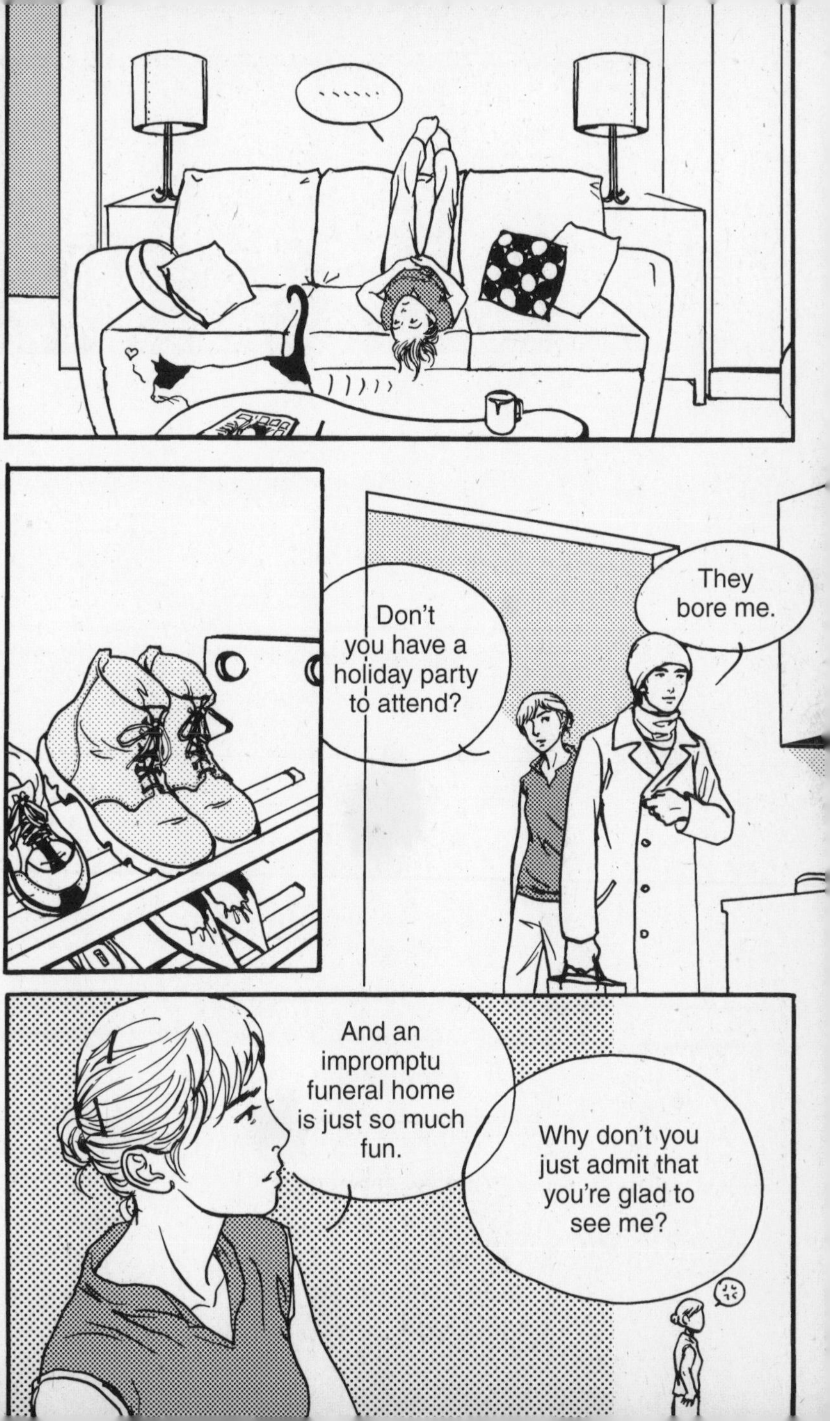
. . . . . .
Don't you have a holiday party to attend?
They bore me.
And an impromptu funeral home is just so much fun.
Why don't you just admit that you're glad to see me?

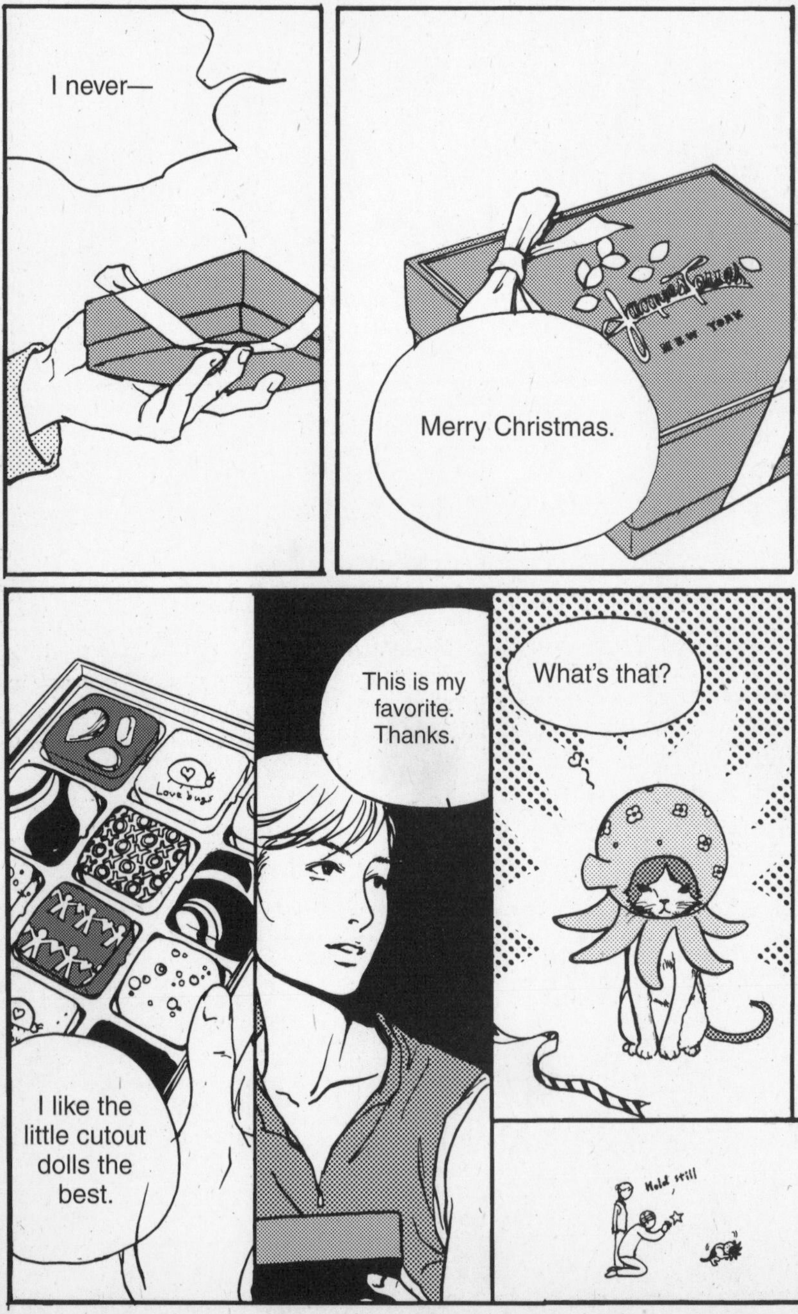
I never—
Merry Christmas.
NEW YORK
Love bugs
I like the little cutout dolls the best.
This is my favorite. Thanks.
What's that?
Hold still

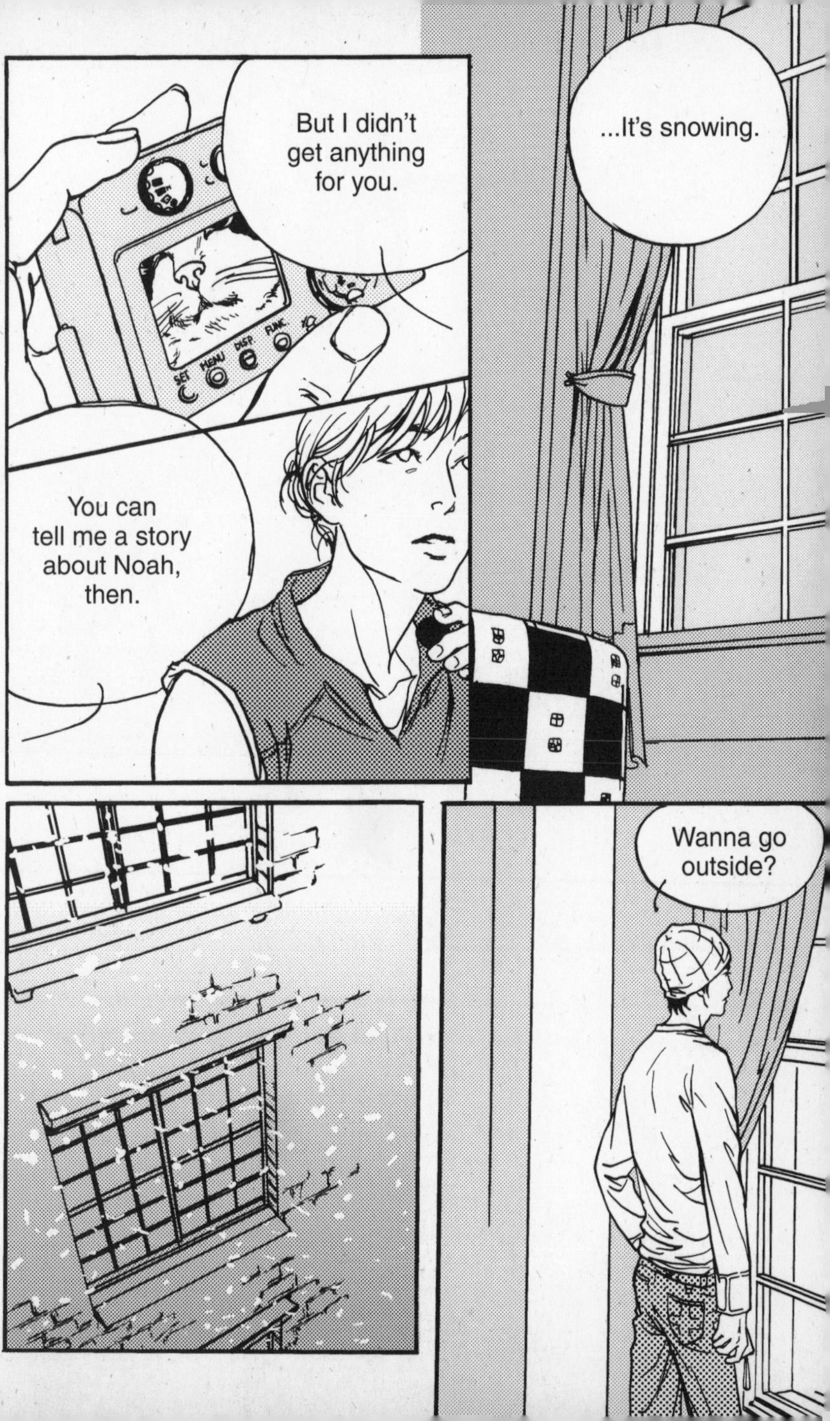
But I didn't get anything for you.
You can tell me a story about Noah, then.
...It's snowing.
Wanna go outside?

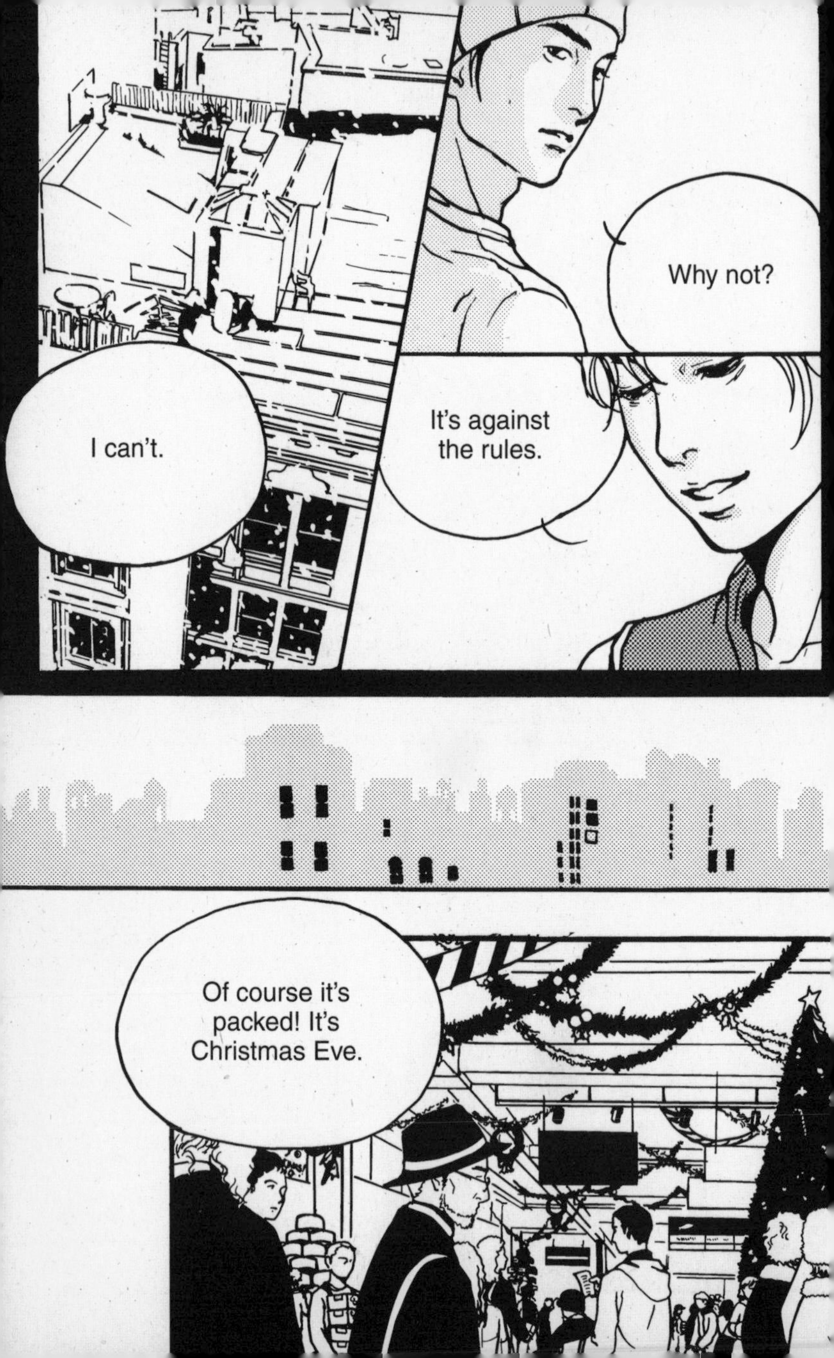
Why not?
I can't.
It's against the rules.
Of course it's packed! It's Christmas Eve.

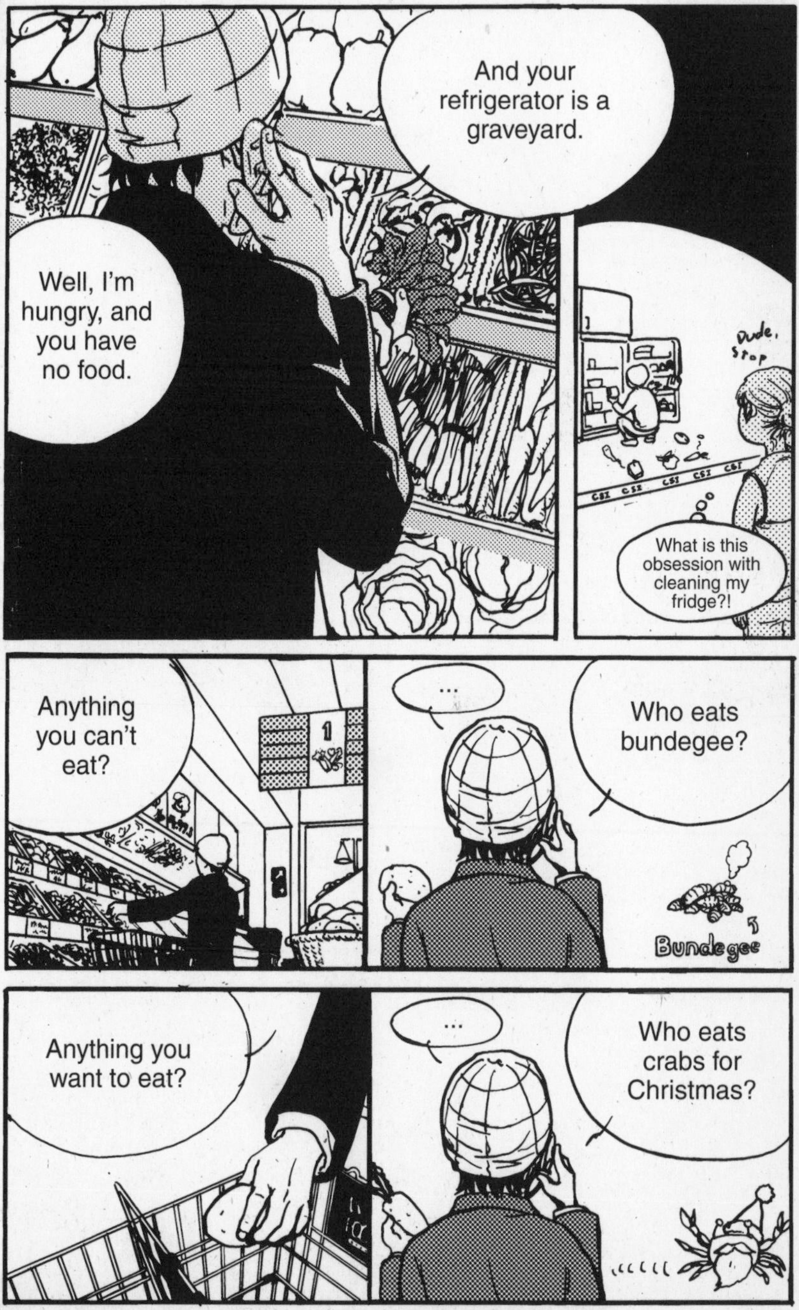
And your refrigerator is a graveyard.
Well, I'm hungry, and you have no food.
Dude, Stop
CSI CSI CSI CSI CSI
What is this obsession with cleaning my fridge?!
Anything you can't eat?
...
Who eats bundegee?
Bundegee
Anything you want to eat?
...
Who eats crabs for Christmas?

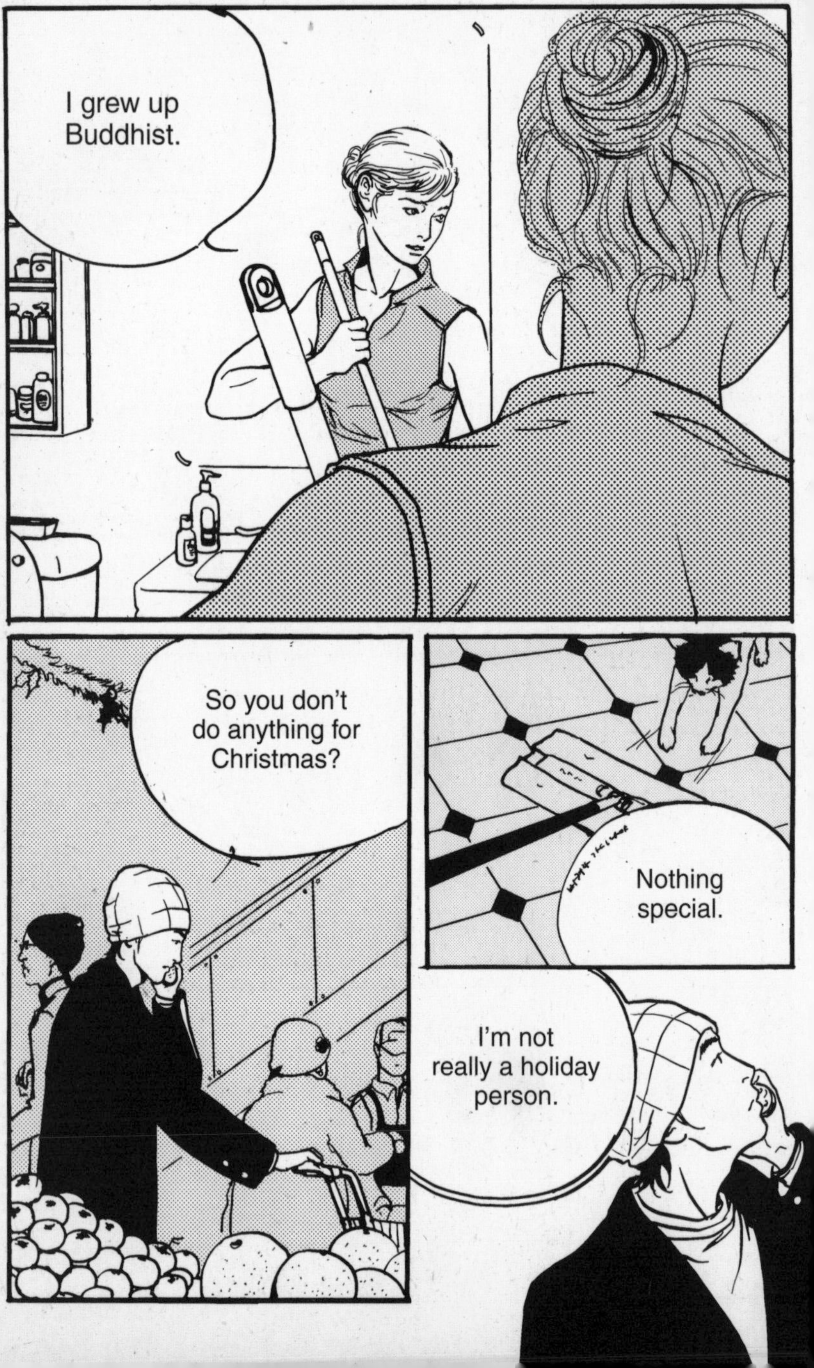
I grew up Buddhist.
So you don't do anything for Christmas?
Nothing special.
I'm not really a holiday person.

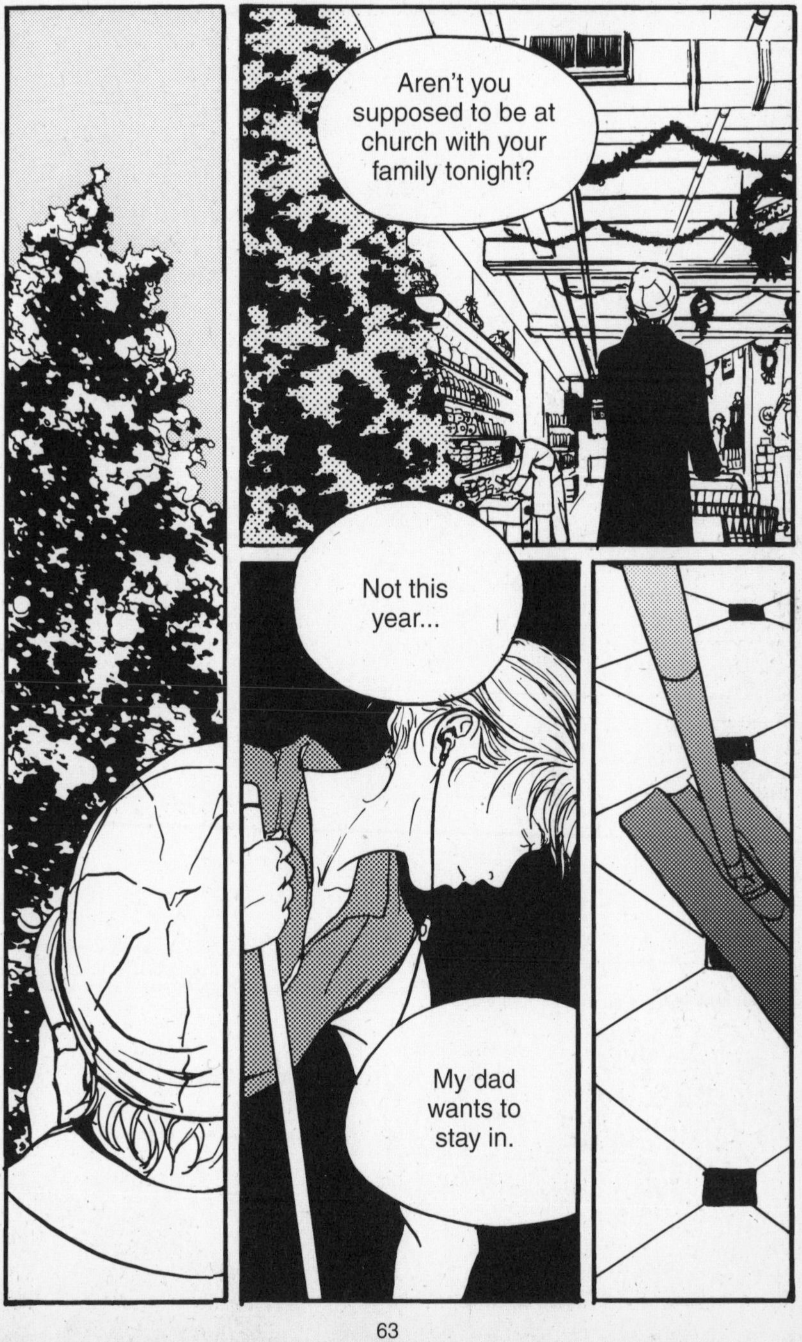
Aren't you supposed to be at church with your family tonight?
Not this year...
My dad wants to stay in.

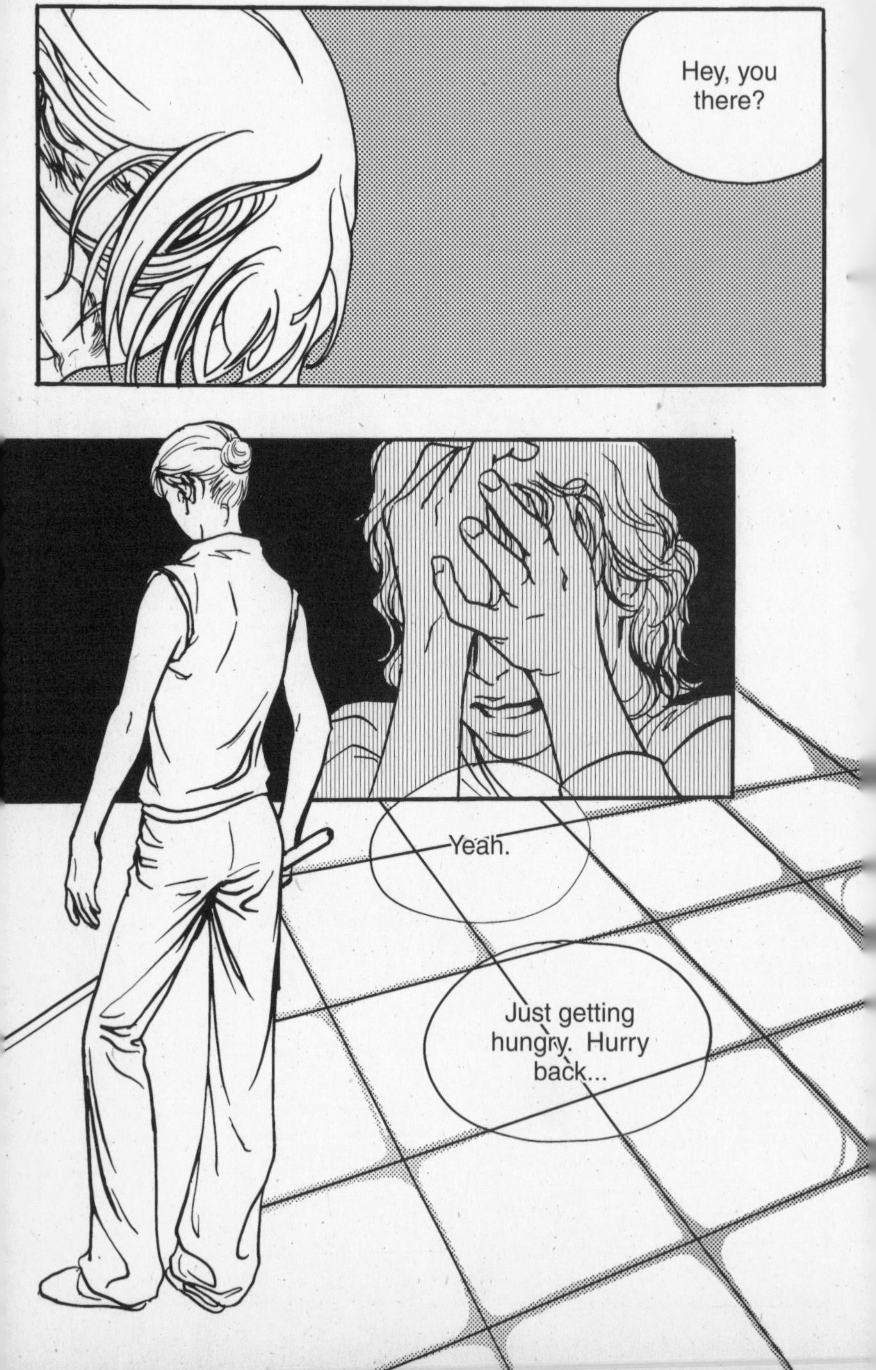
Hey, you there?
Yeah.
Just getting hungry. Hurry back...

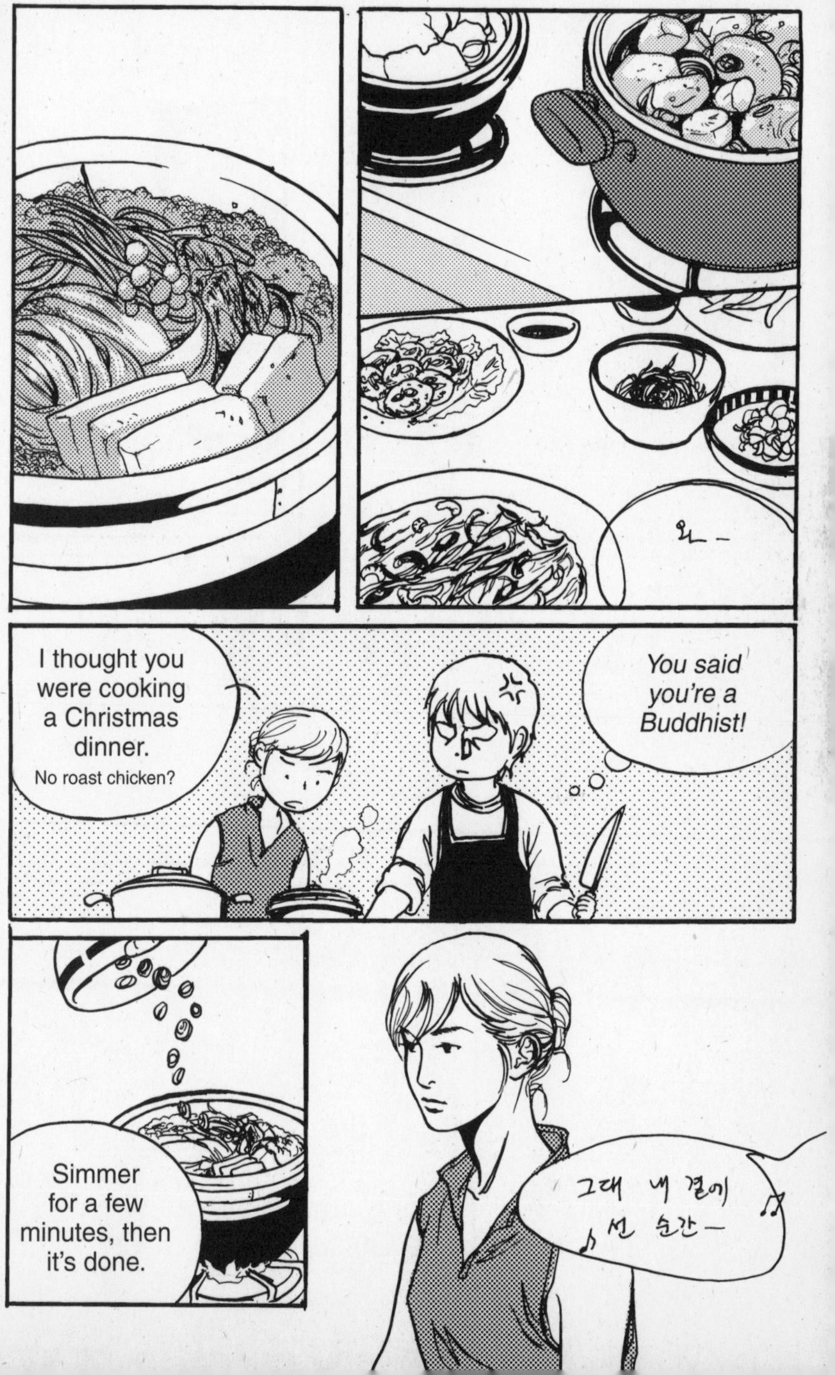

와—
I thought you were cooking a Christmas dinner. No roast chicken?
You said you're a Buddhist!
Simmer for a few minutes, then it's done.
그대 내 곁에 선 순간—

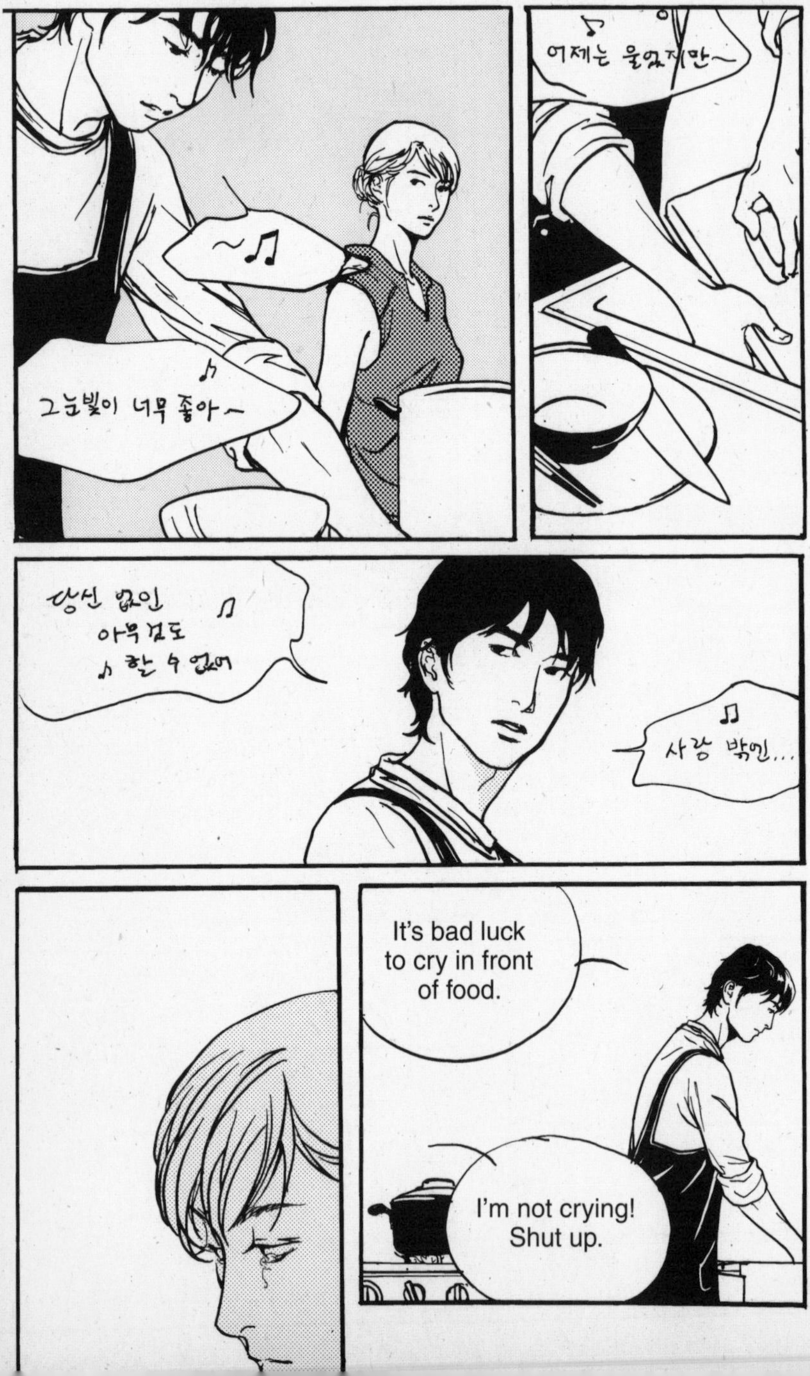
~♫
♪ 그눈빛이 너무 좋아~
♪ 어제는 울었지만~
당신 없인 ♫ 아무 것도 ♪ 할 수 없어
♫ 사랑 밖엔...
It's bad luck to cry in front of food.
I'm not crying! Shut up.

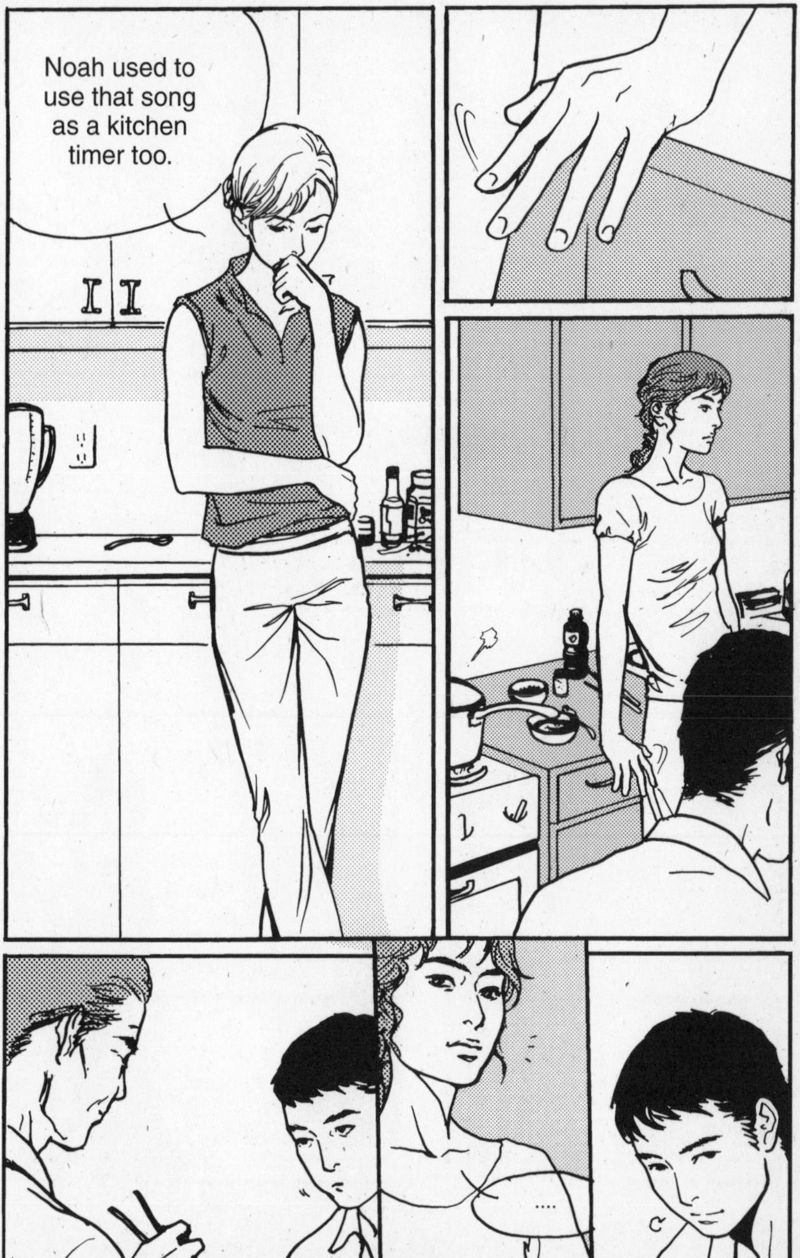
Noah used to use that song as a kitchen timer too.
....

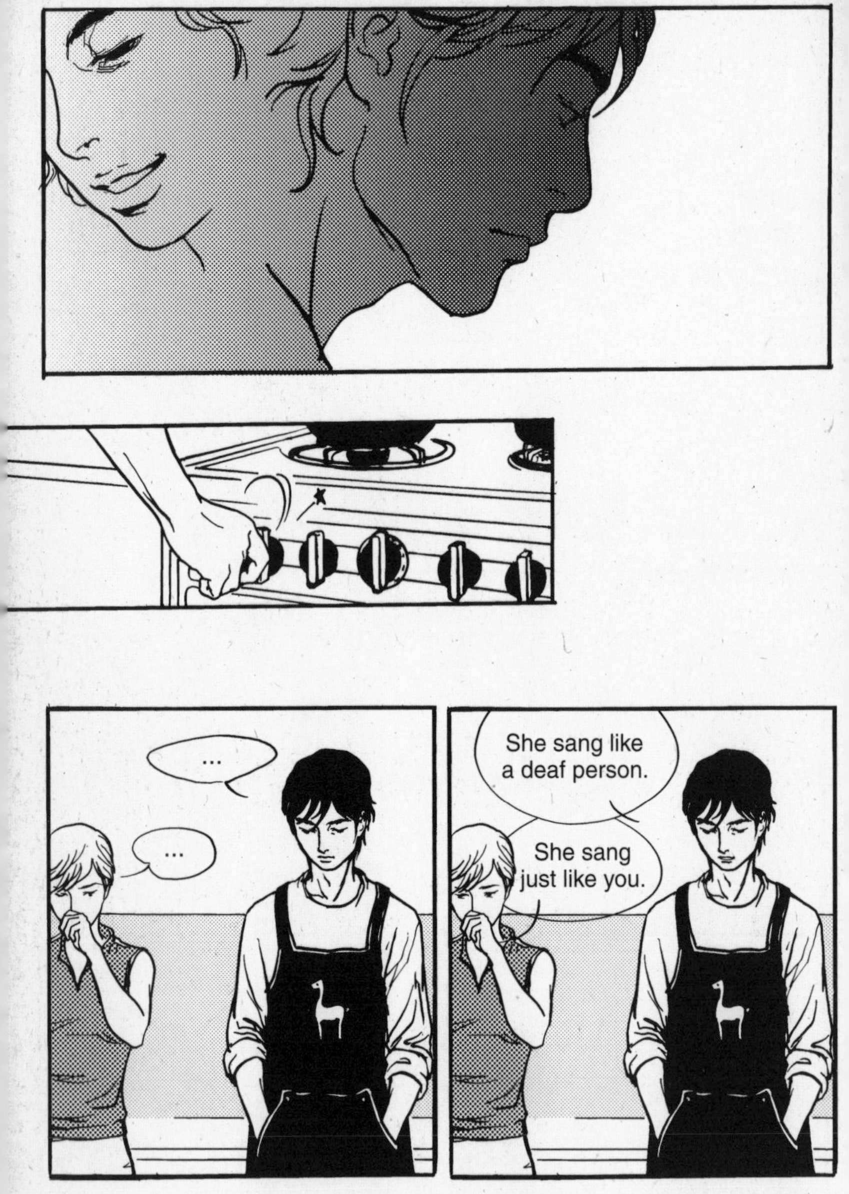
...
...
She sang like a deaf person.
She sang just like you.

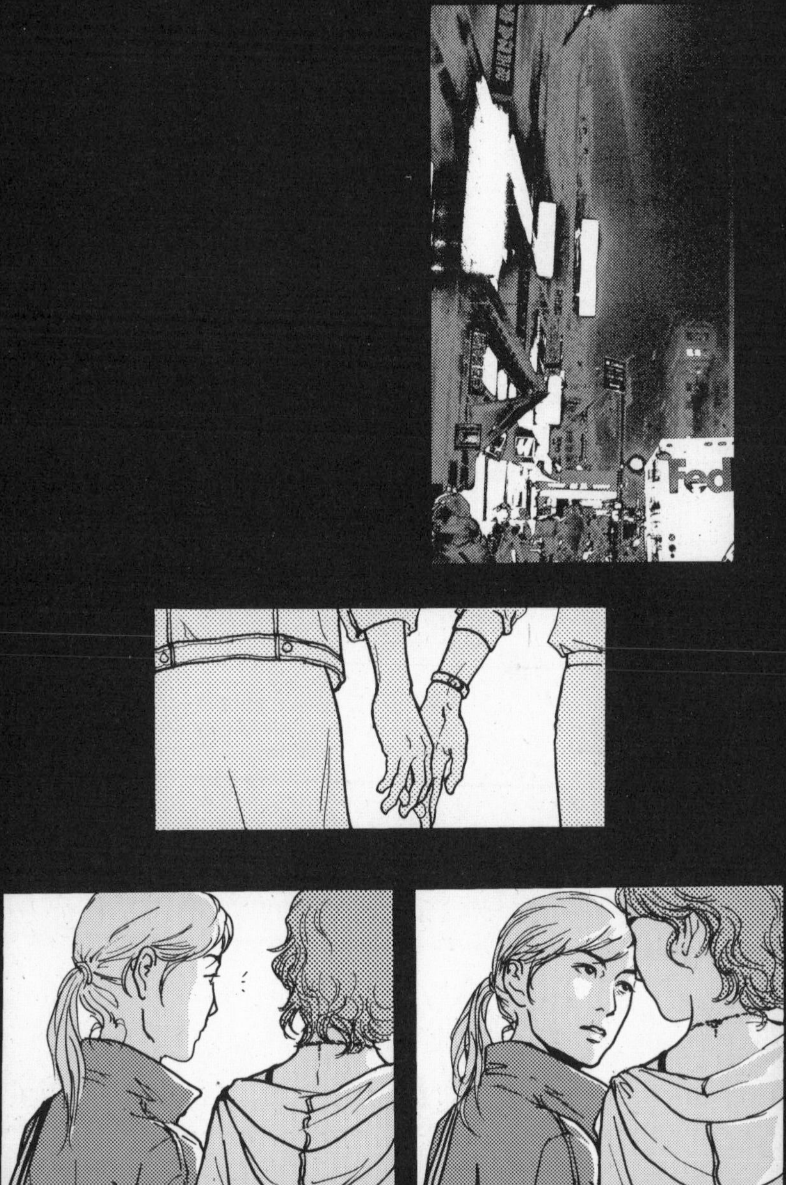

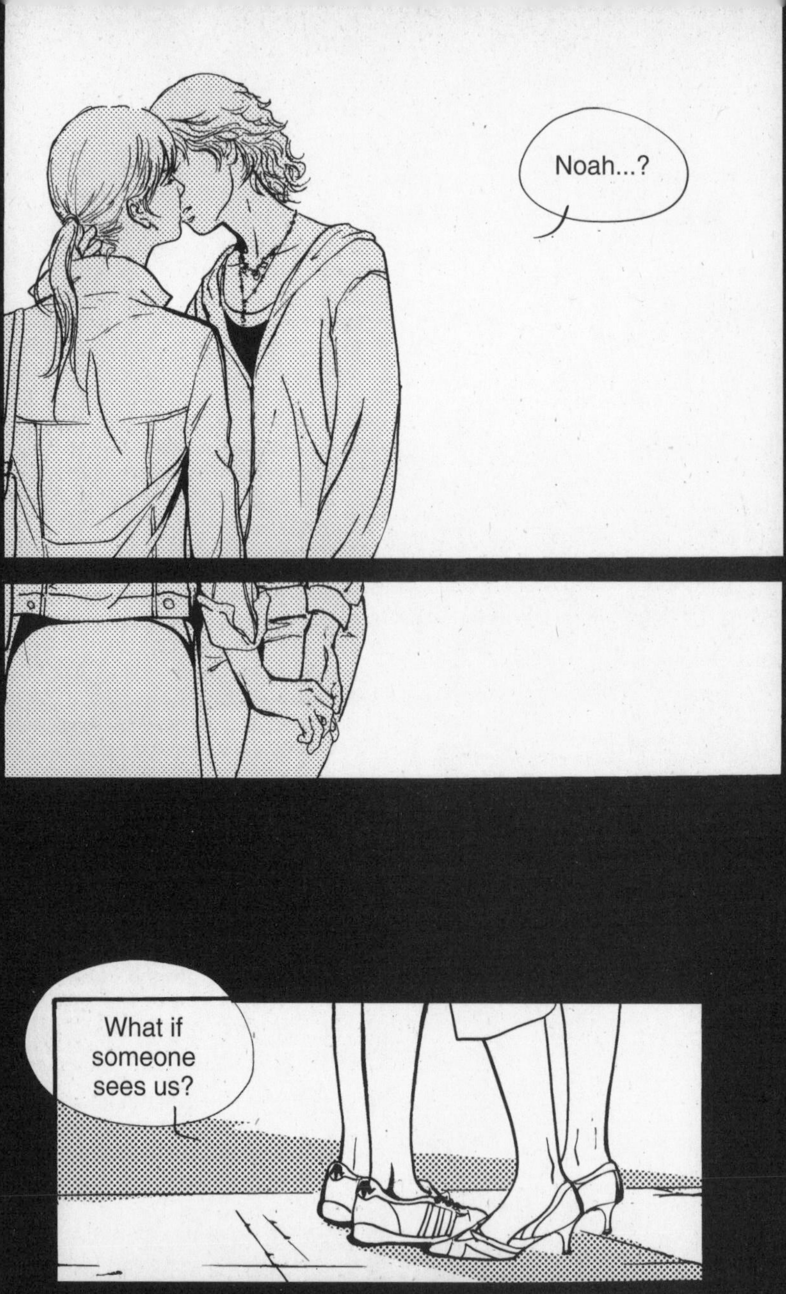
Noah...?
What if someone sees us?

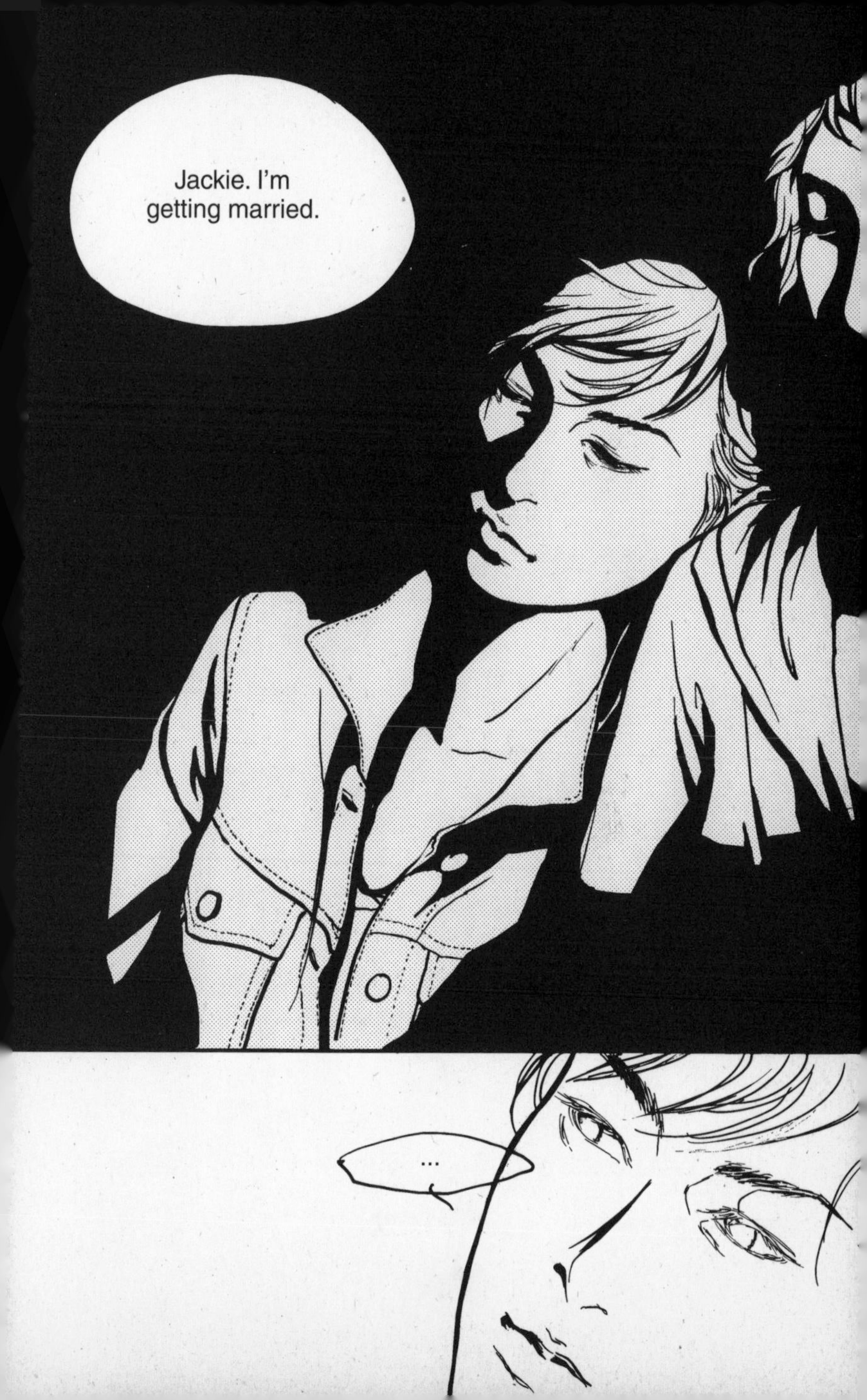
Jackie. I'm getting married.
...

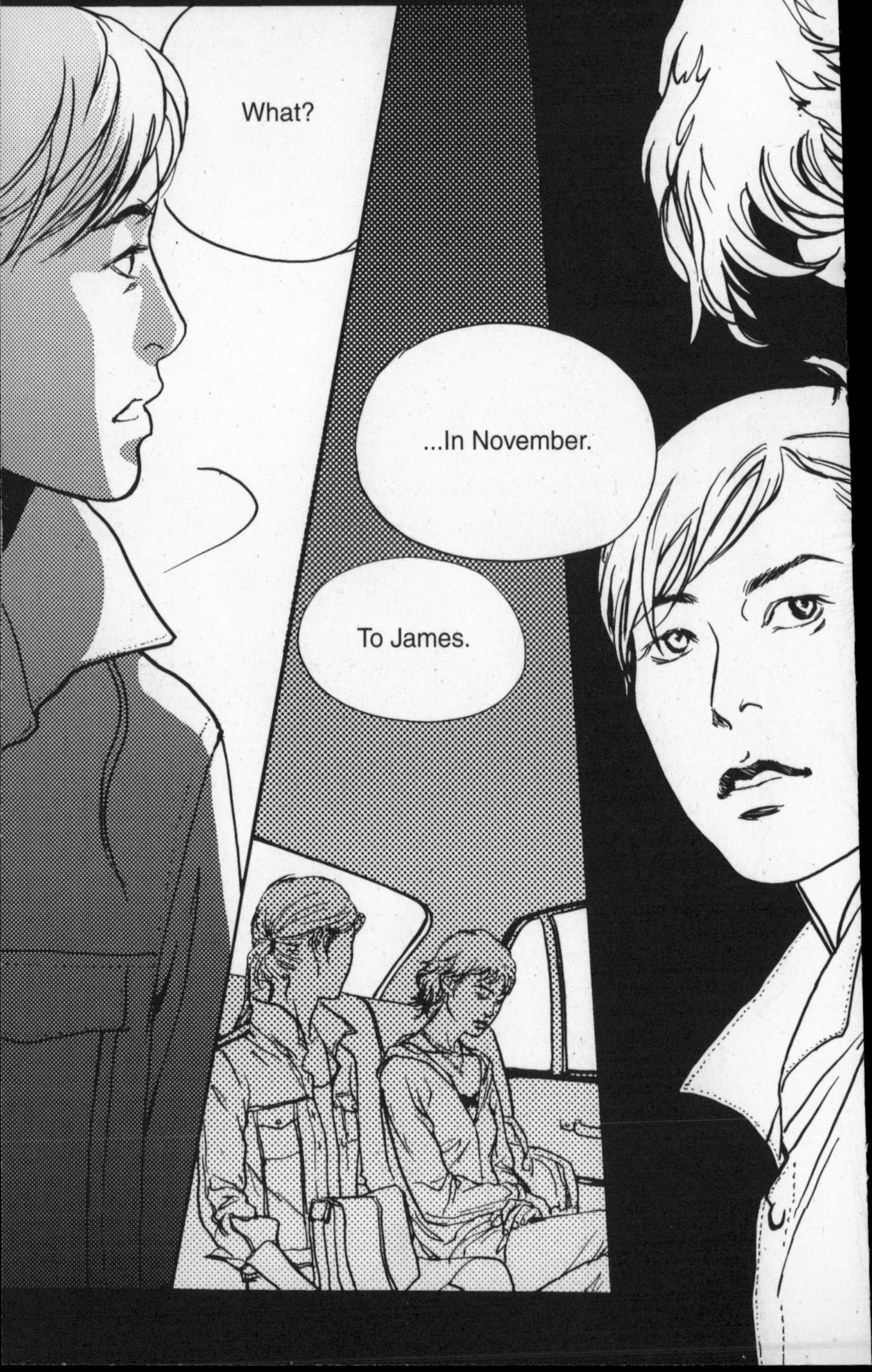
What?
...In November.
To James.

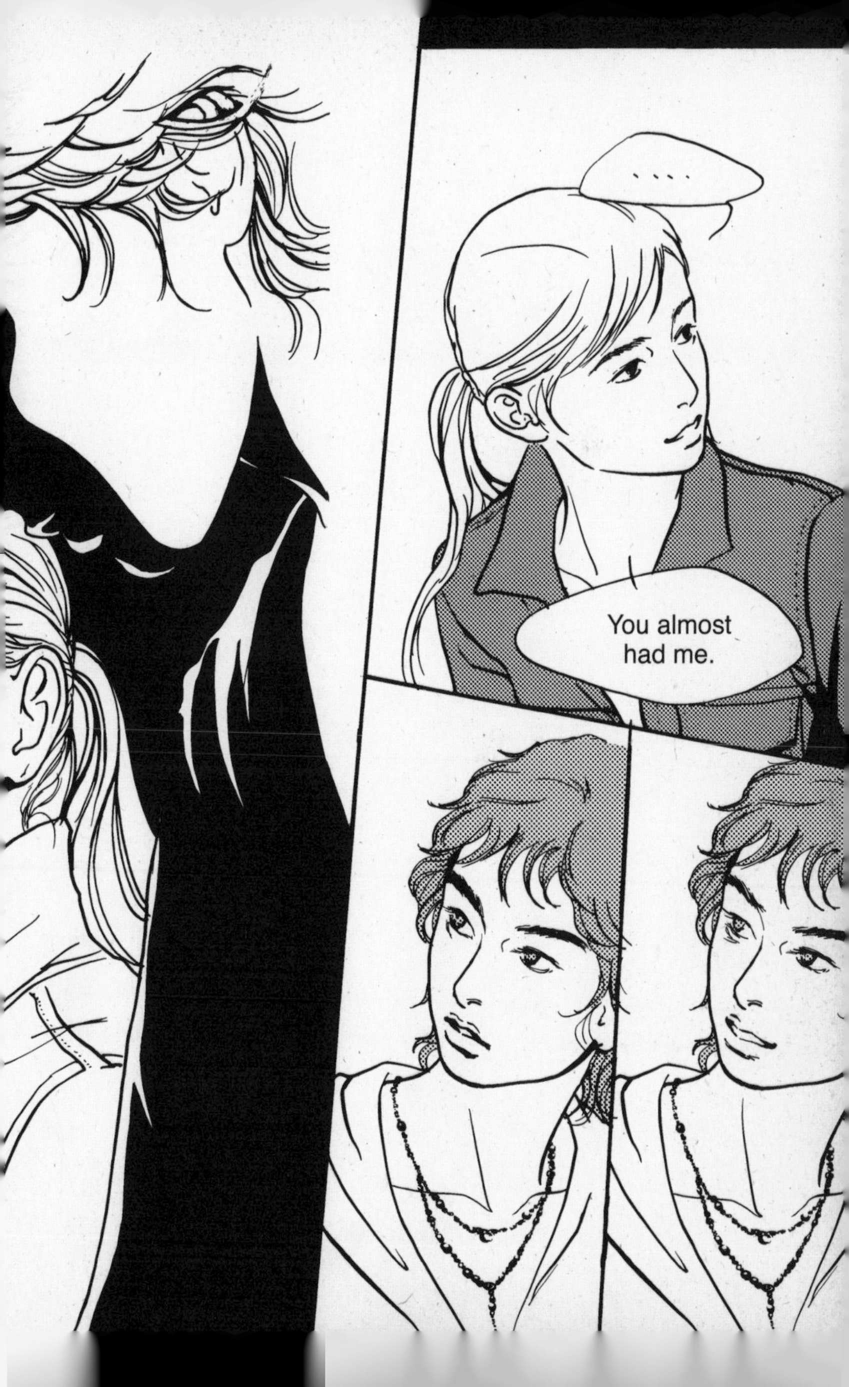
....
You almost had me.

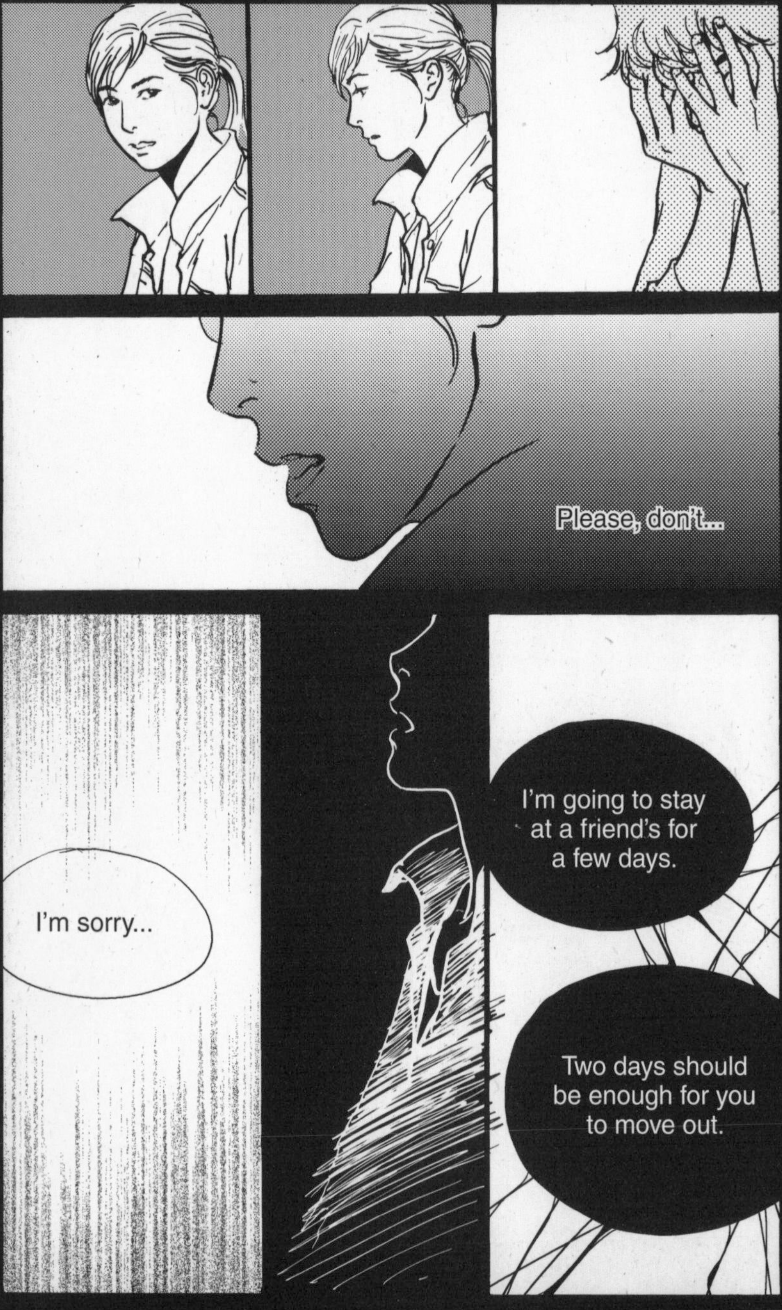
Please, don't...
I'm sorry...
I'm going to stay at a friend's for a few days.
Two days should be enough for you to move out.

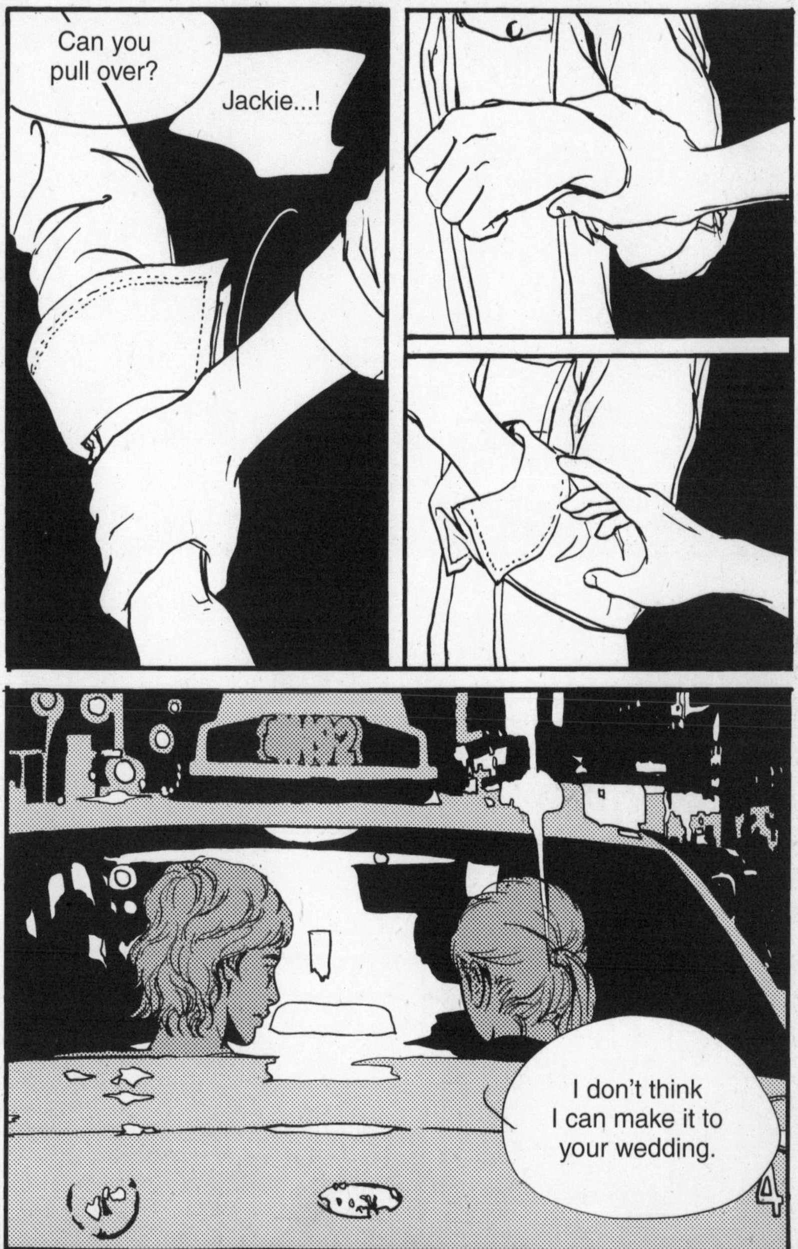
Can you pull over?
Jackie...!
I don't think I can make it to your wedding.

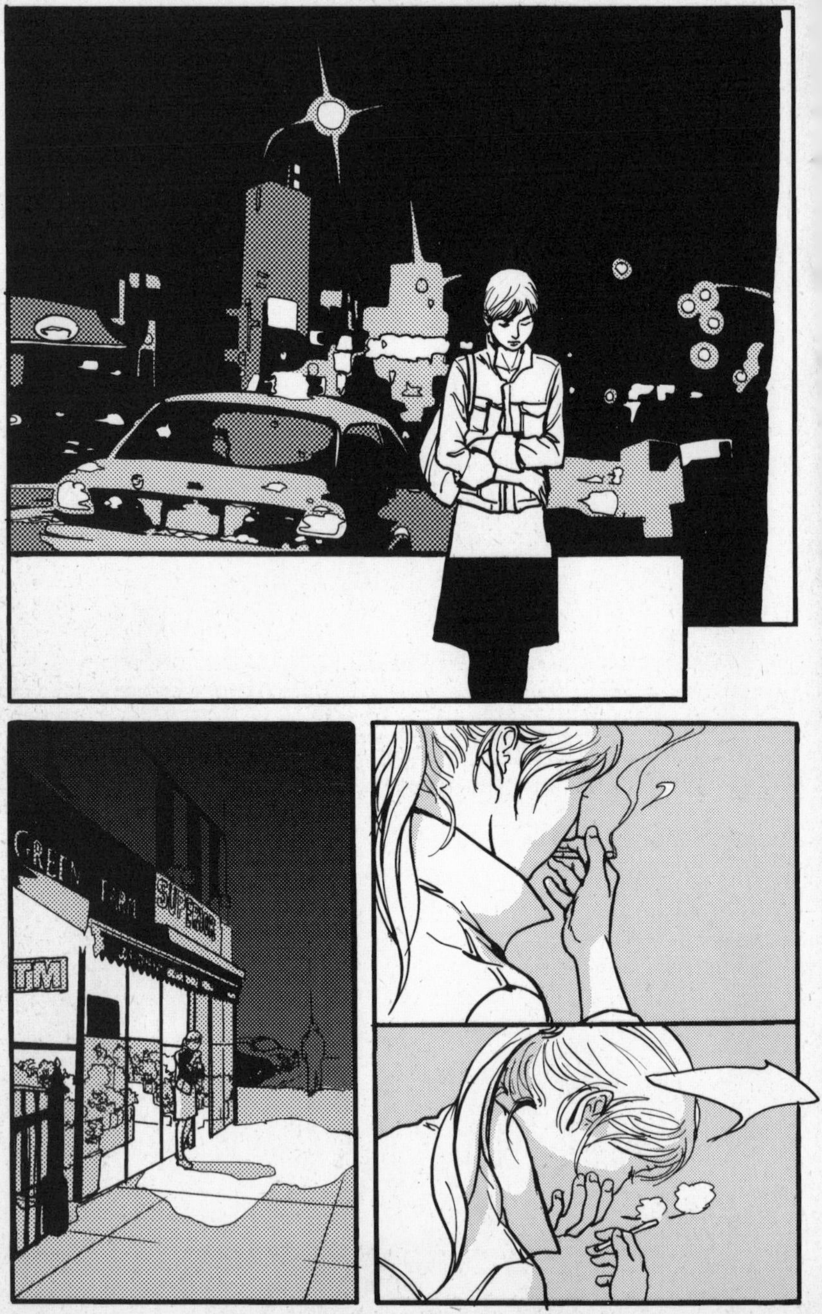

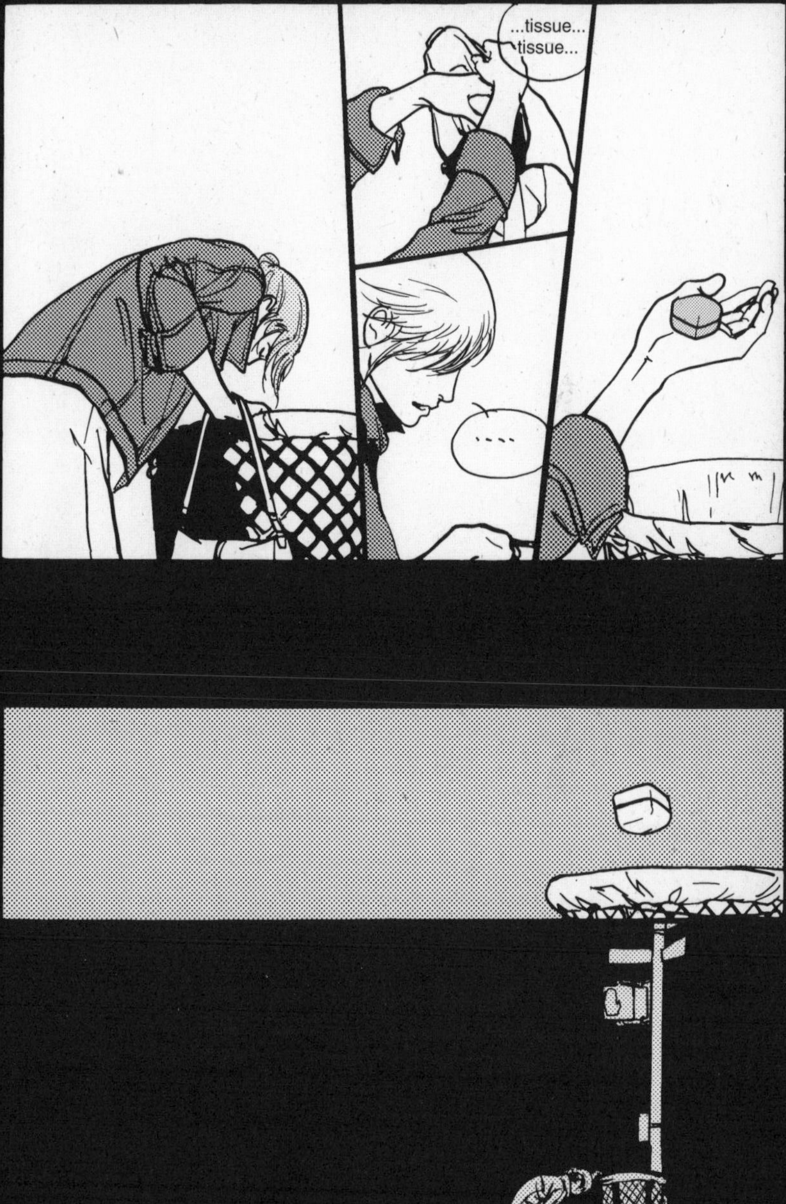
...tissue... tissue...
....

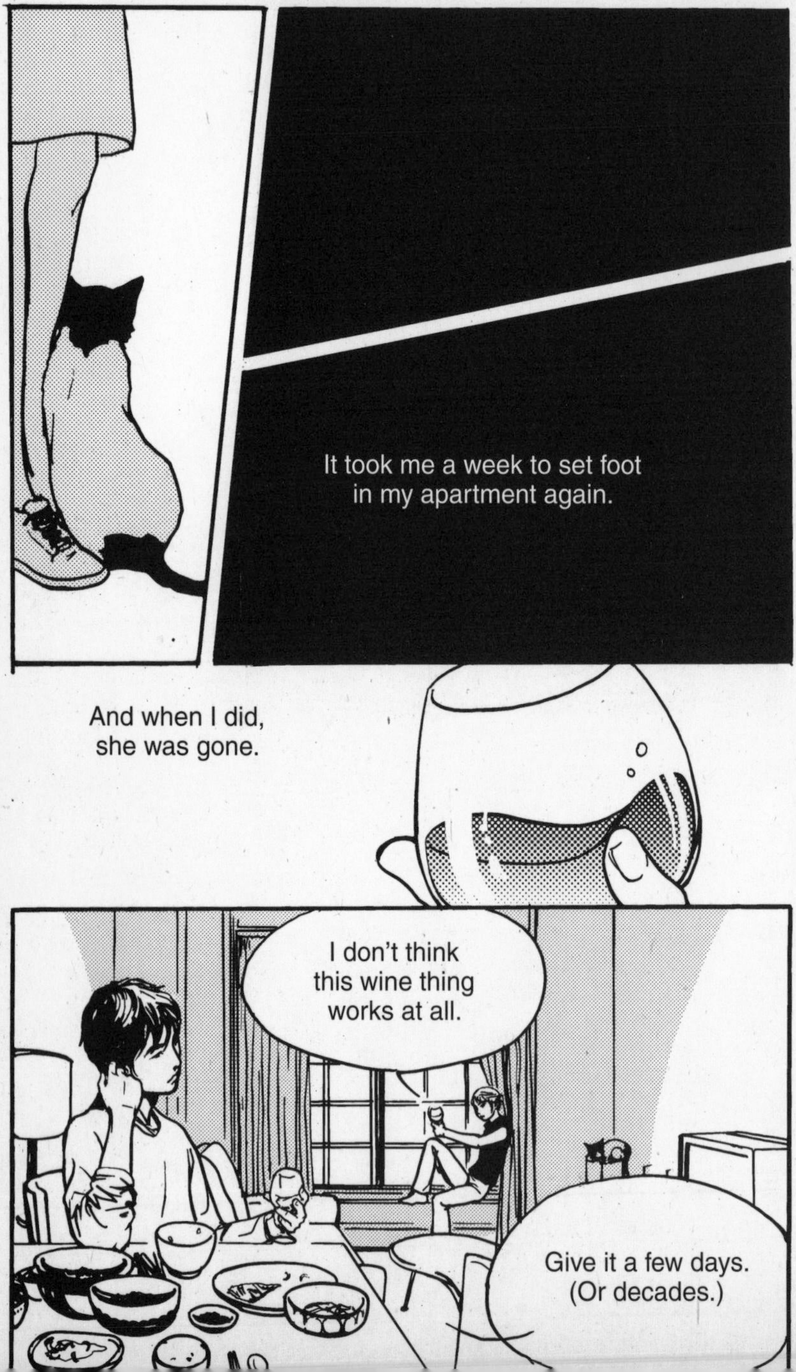
It took me a week to set foot in my apartment again.
And when I did, she was gone.
I don't think this wine thing works at all.
Give it a few days. (Or decades.)

Chapter 4

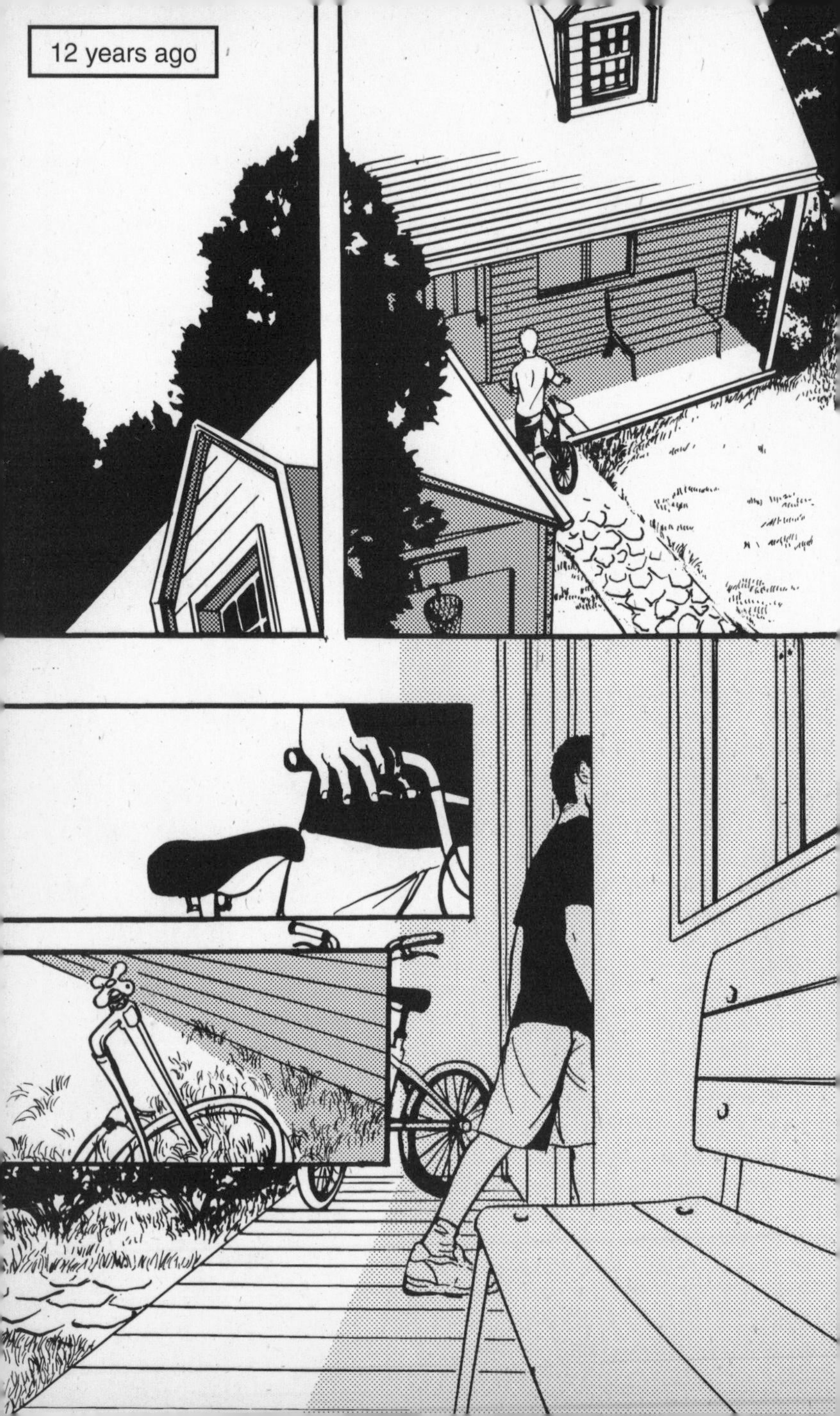

12 years ago

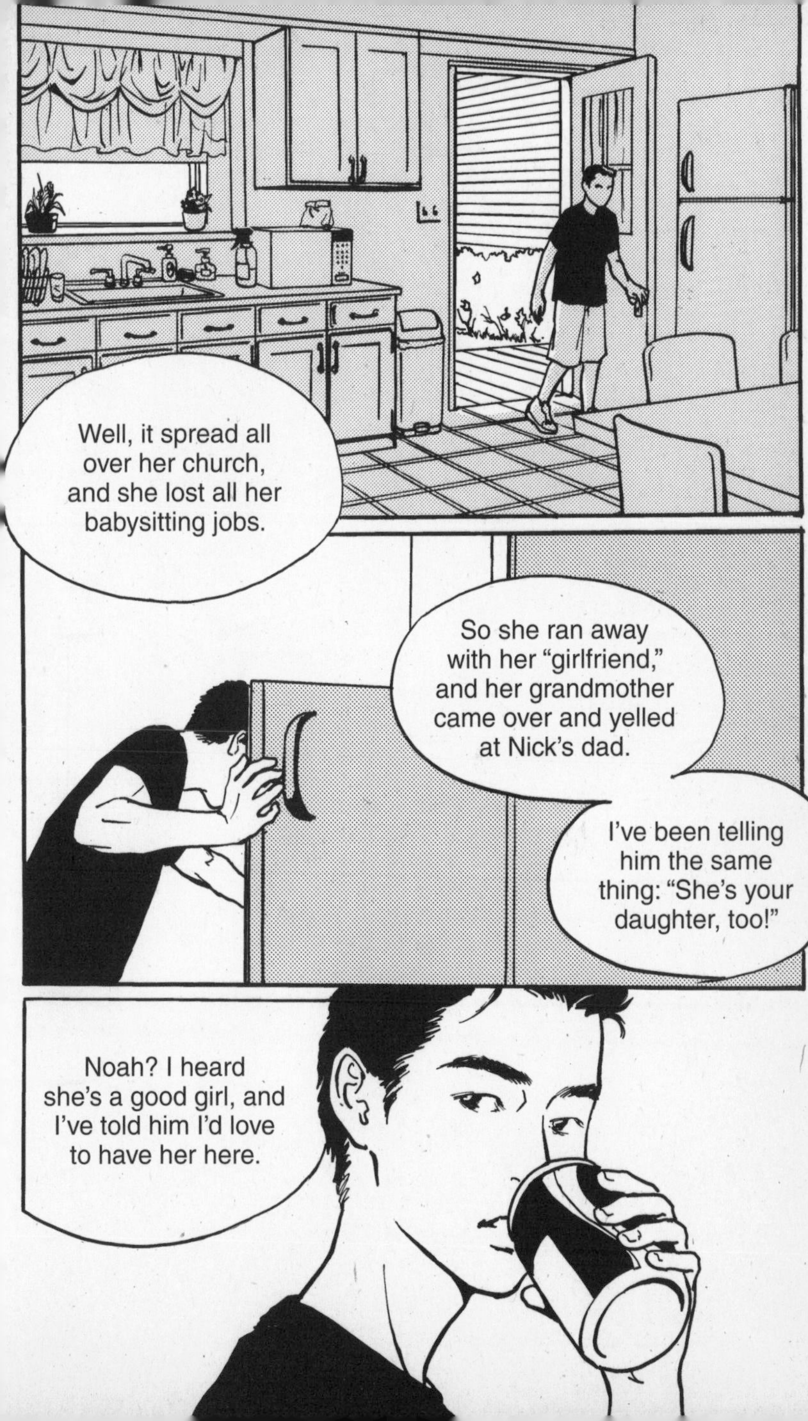
Well, it spread all over her church, and she lost all her babysitting jobs.
So she ran away with her "girlfriend," and her grandmother came over and yelled at Nick's dad.
I've been telling him the same thing: "She's your daughter, too!"
Noah? I heard she's a good girl, and I've told him I'd love to have her here.

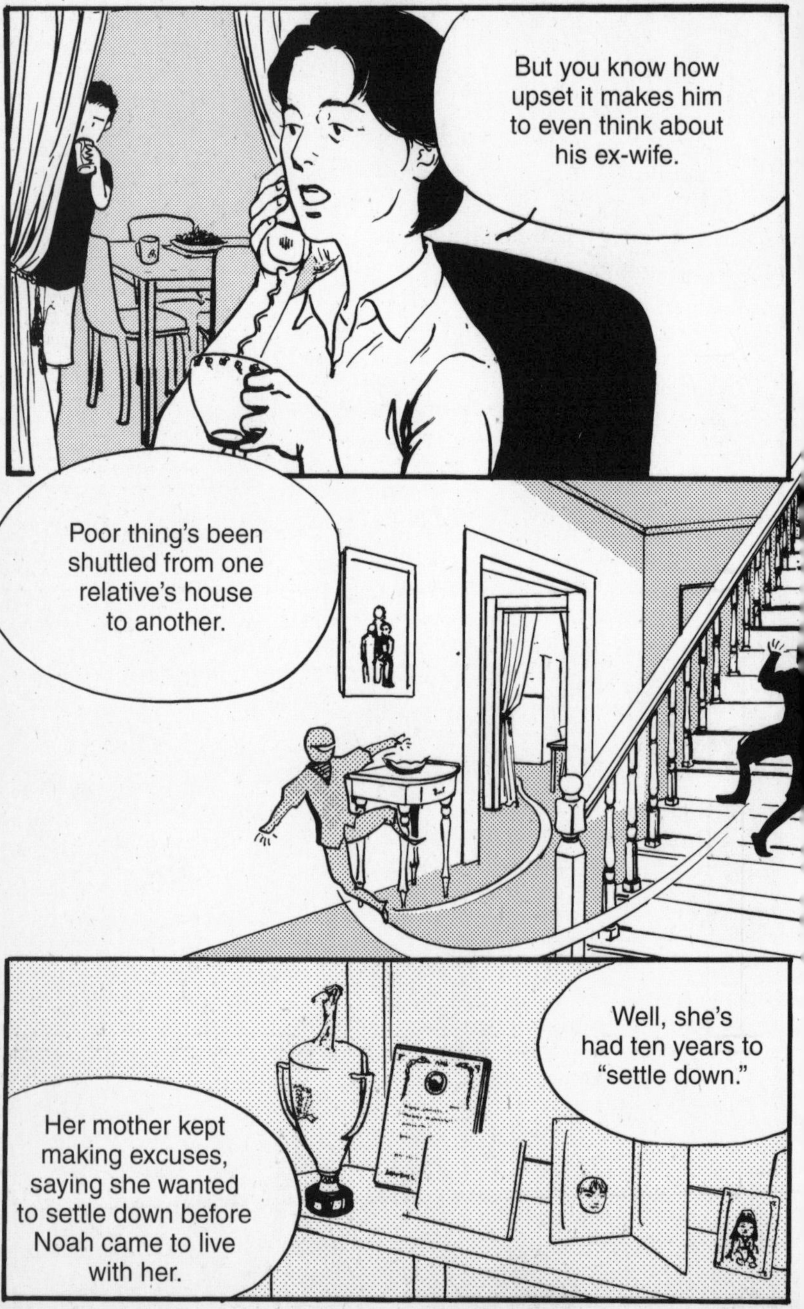
But you know how upset it makes him to even think about his ex-wife.
Poor thing's been shuttled from one relative's house to another.
Her mother kept making excuses, saying she wanted to settle down before Noah came to live with her.
Well, she's had ten years to "settle down."

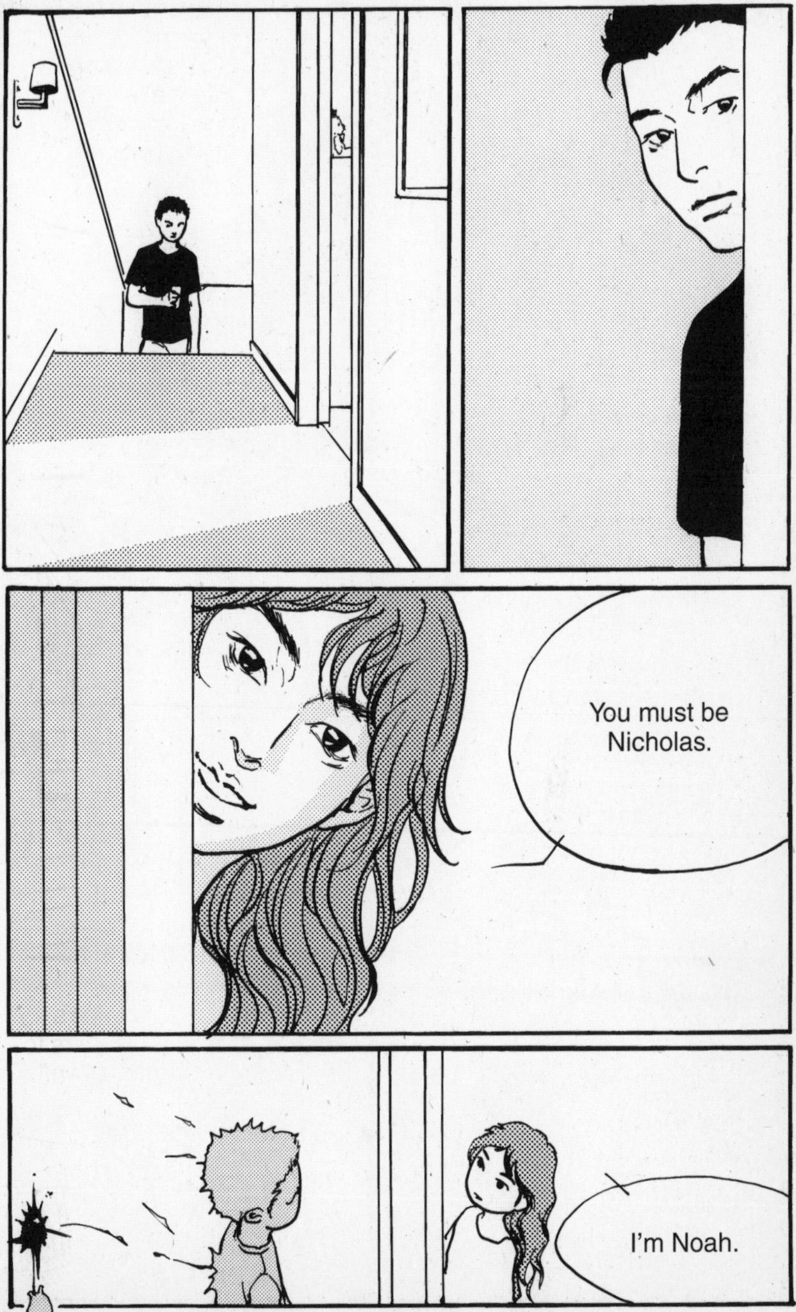
You must be Nicholas.
I'm Noah.

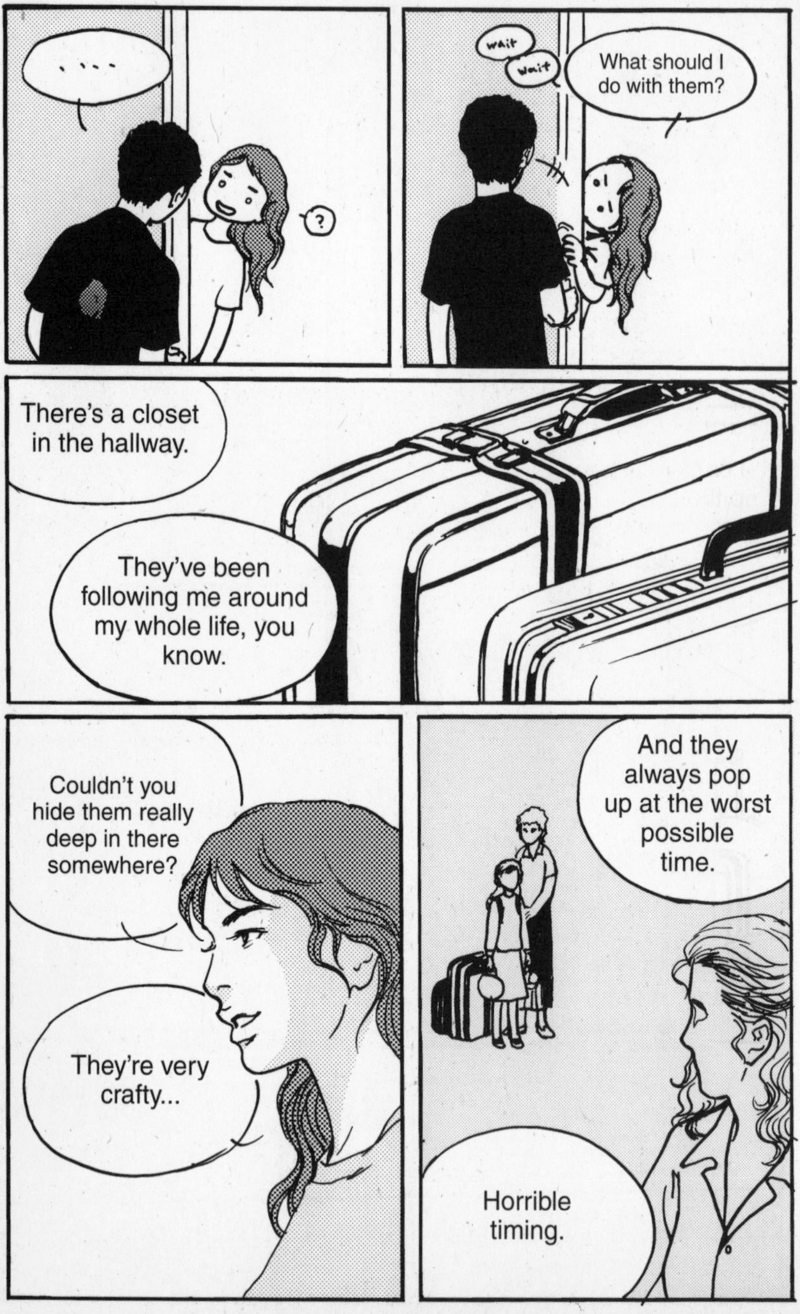
. . . .
wait
wait
What should I do with them?
There's a closet in the hallway.
They've been following me around my whole life, you know.
Couldn't you hide them really deep in there somewhere?
They're very crafty...
And they always pop up at the worst possible time.
Horrible timing.

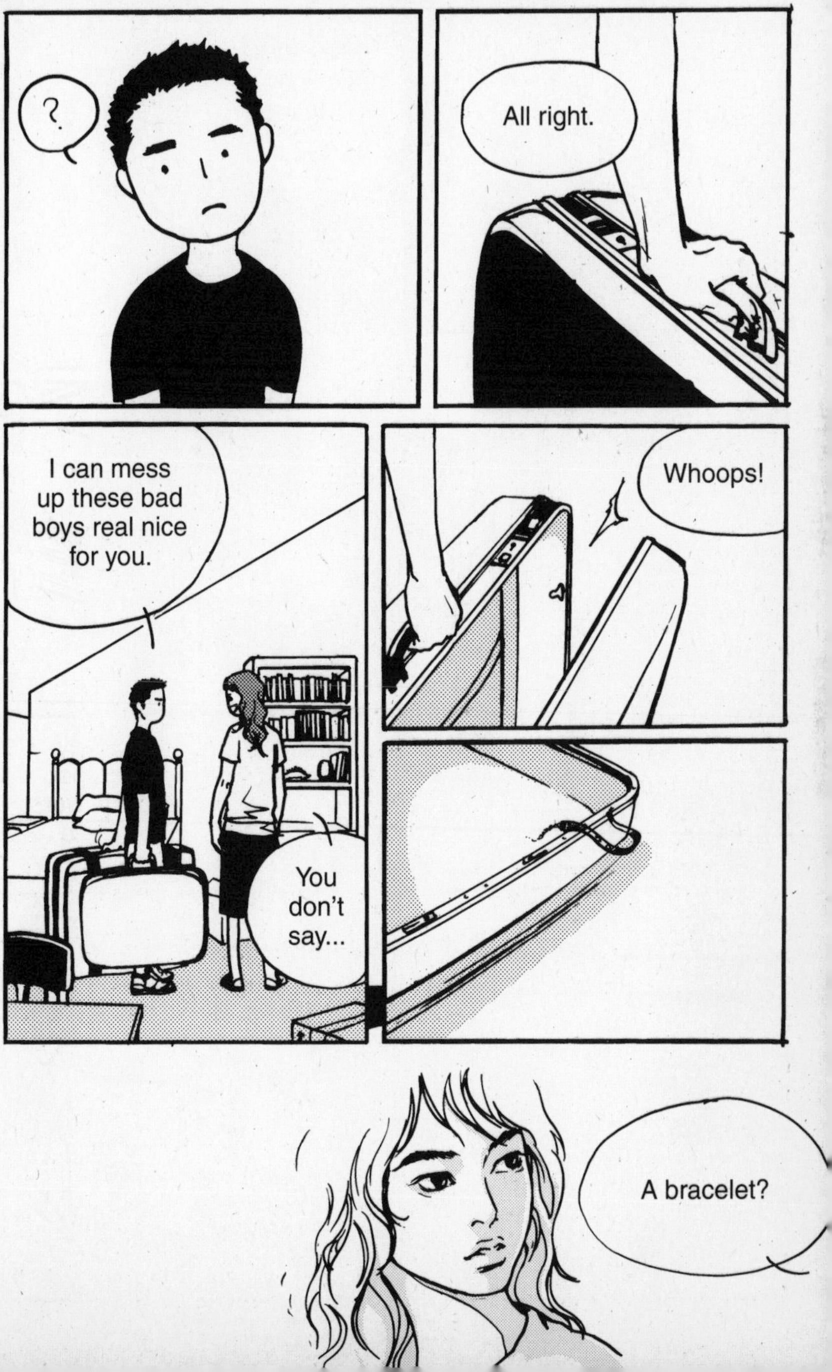
?
All right.
I can mess up these bad boys real nice for you.
You don't say...
Whoops!
A bracelet?

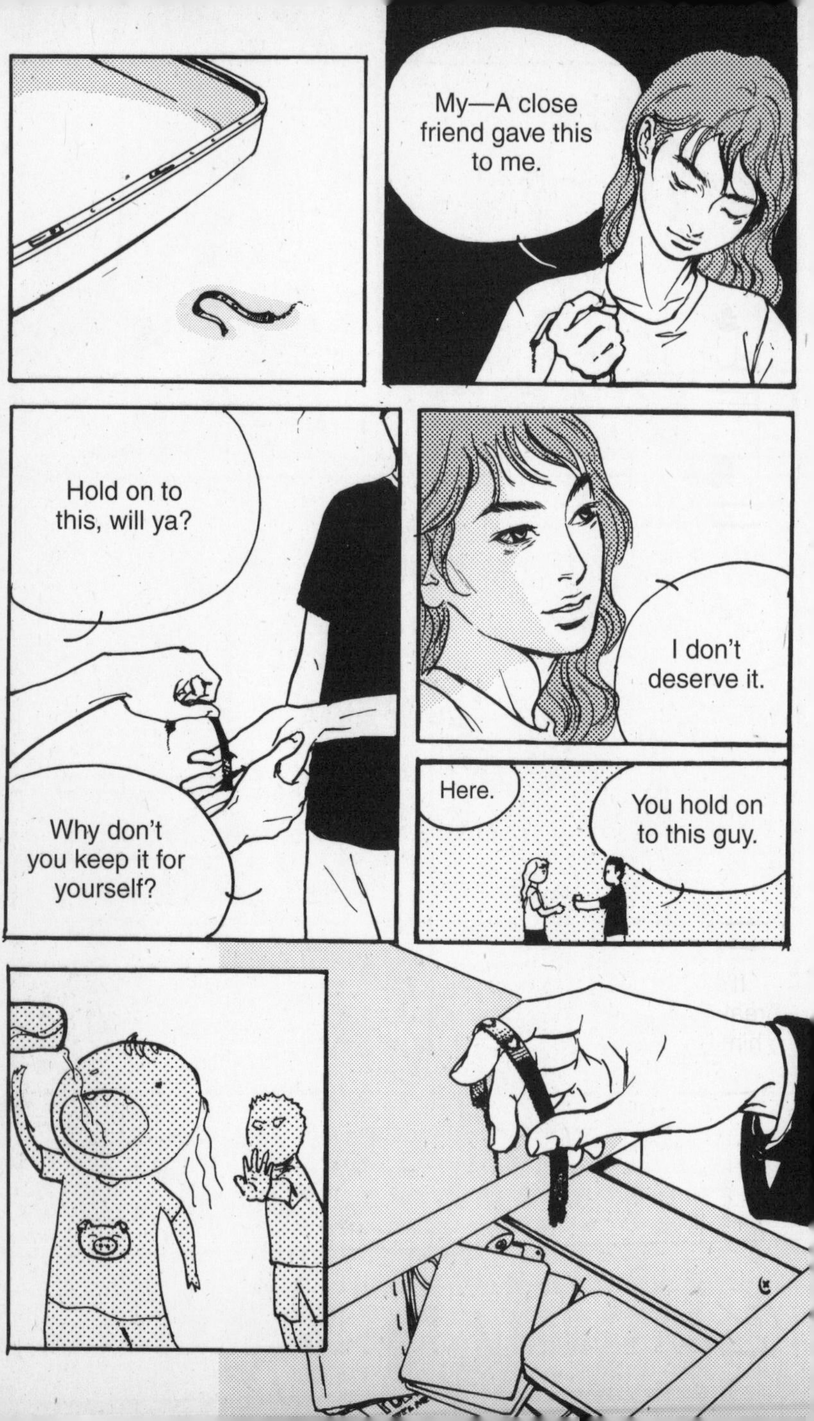
My—A close friend gave this to me.
Hold on to this, will ya?
Why don't you keep it for yourself?
I don't deserve it.
Here.
You hold on to this guy.

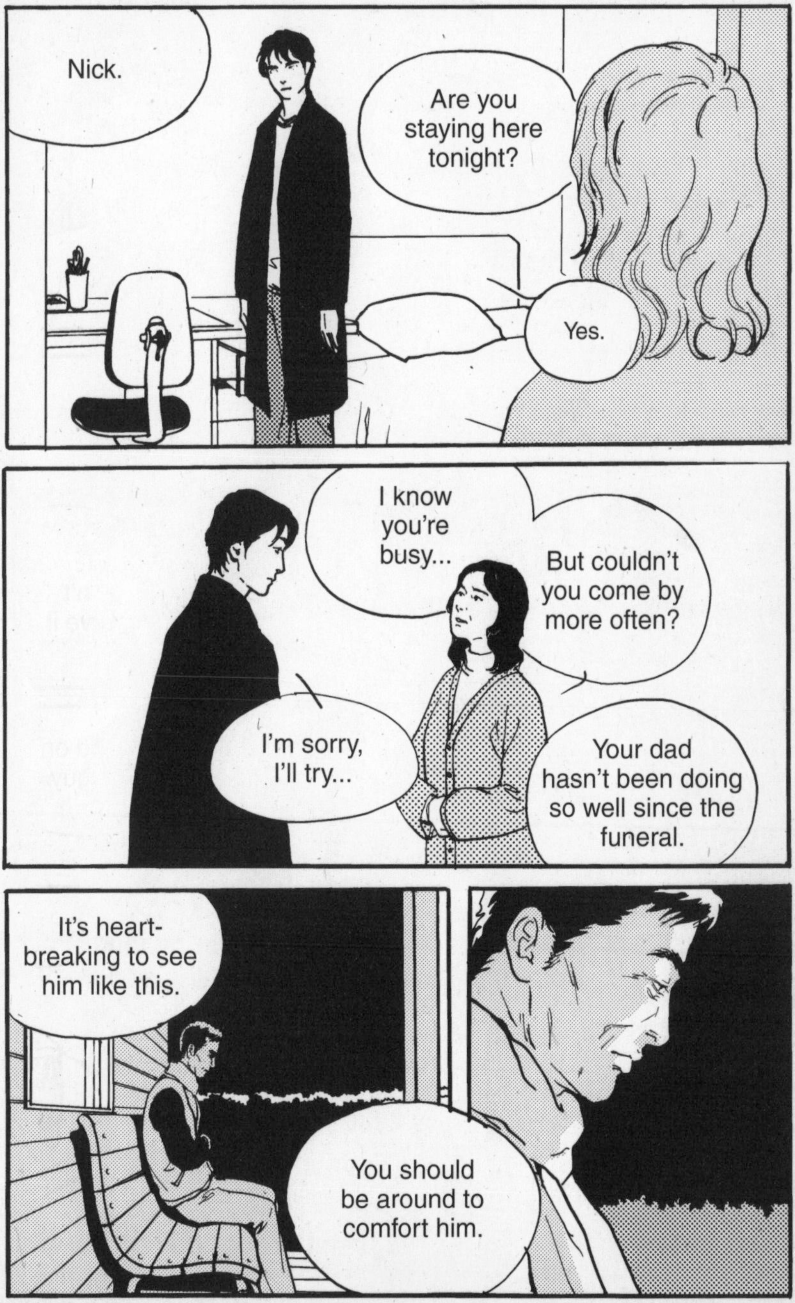
Nick.
Are you staying here tonight?
Yes.
I know you're busy...
But couldn't you come by more often?
I'm sorry, I'll try...
Your dad hasn't been doing so well since the funeral.
It's heart-breaking to see him like this.
You should be around to comfort him.

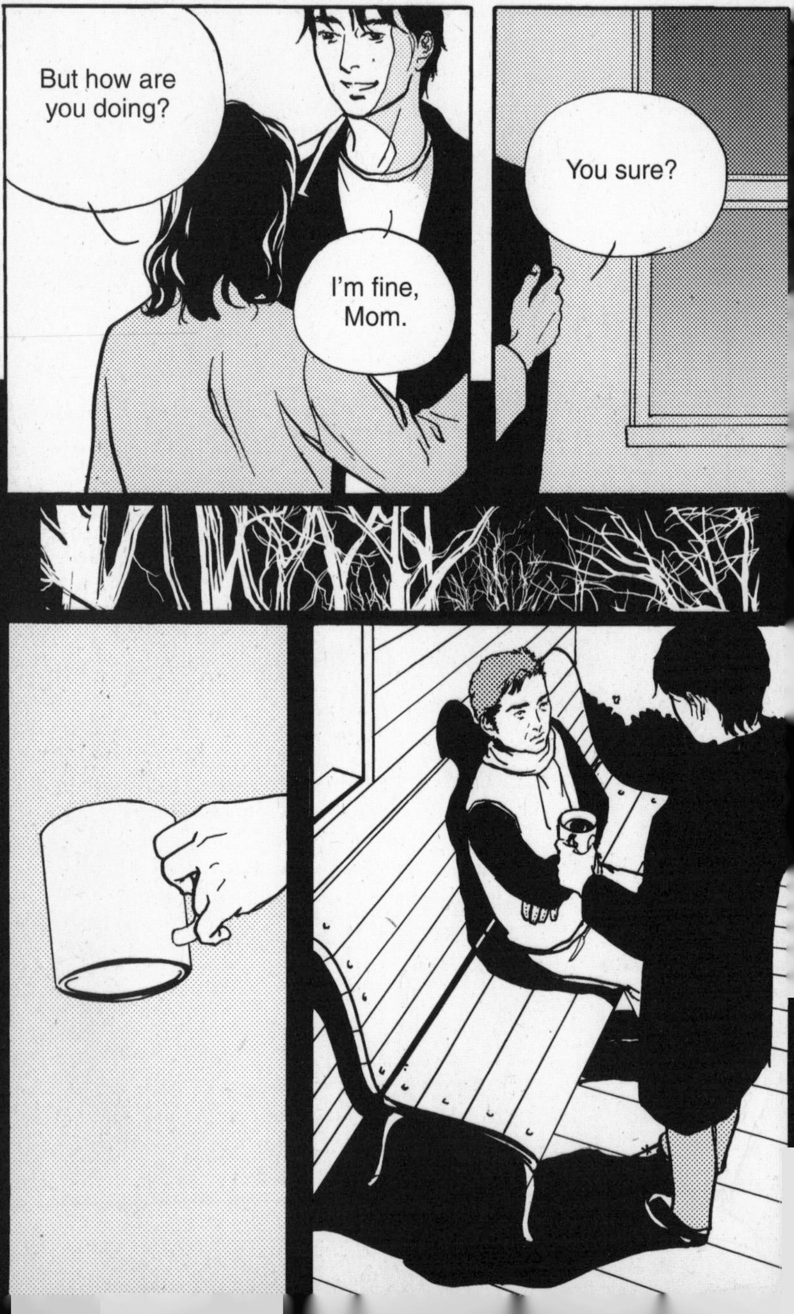
But how are you doing?
I'm fine, Mom.
You sure?

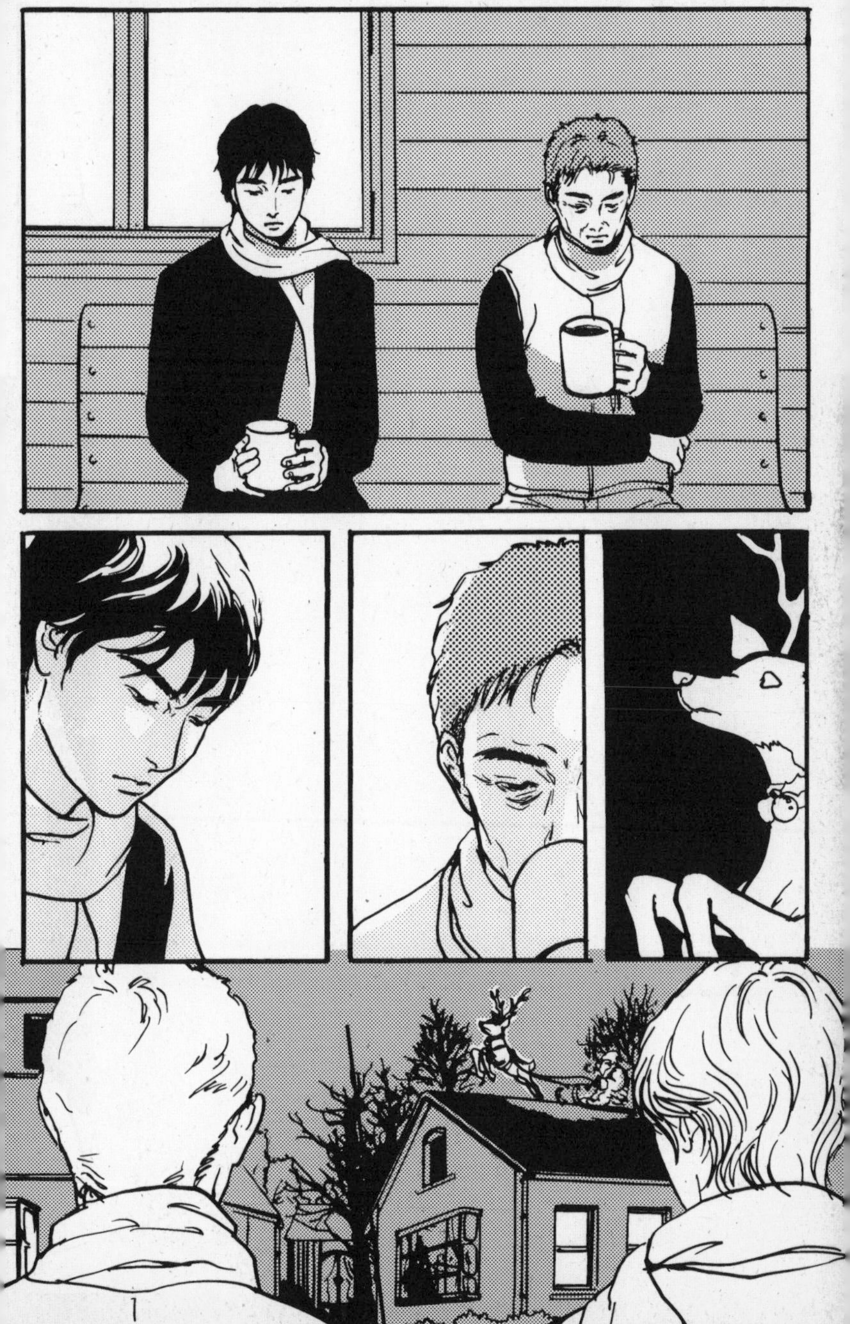

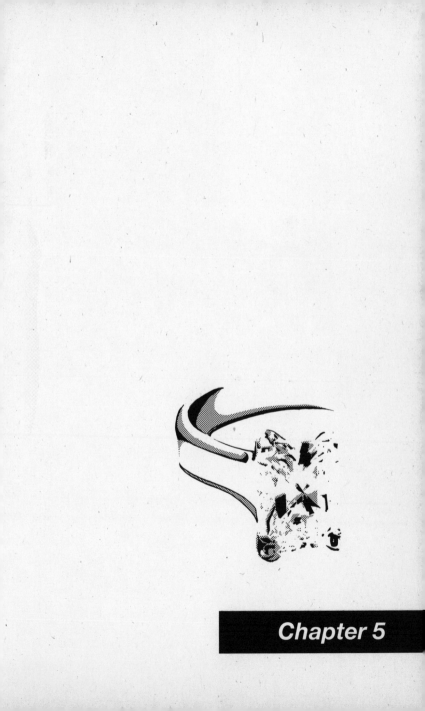

Chapter 5

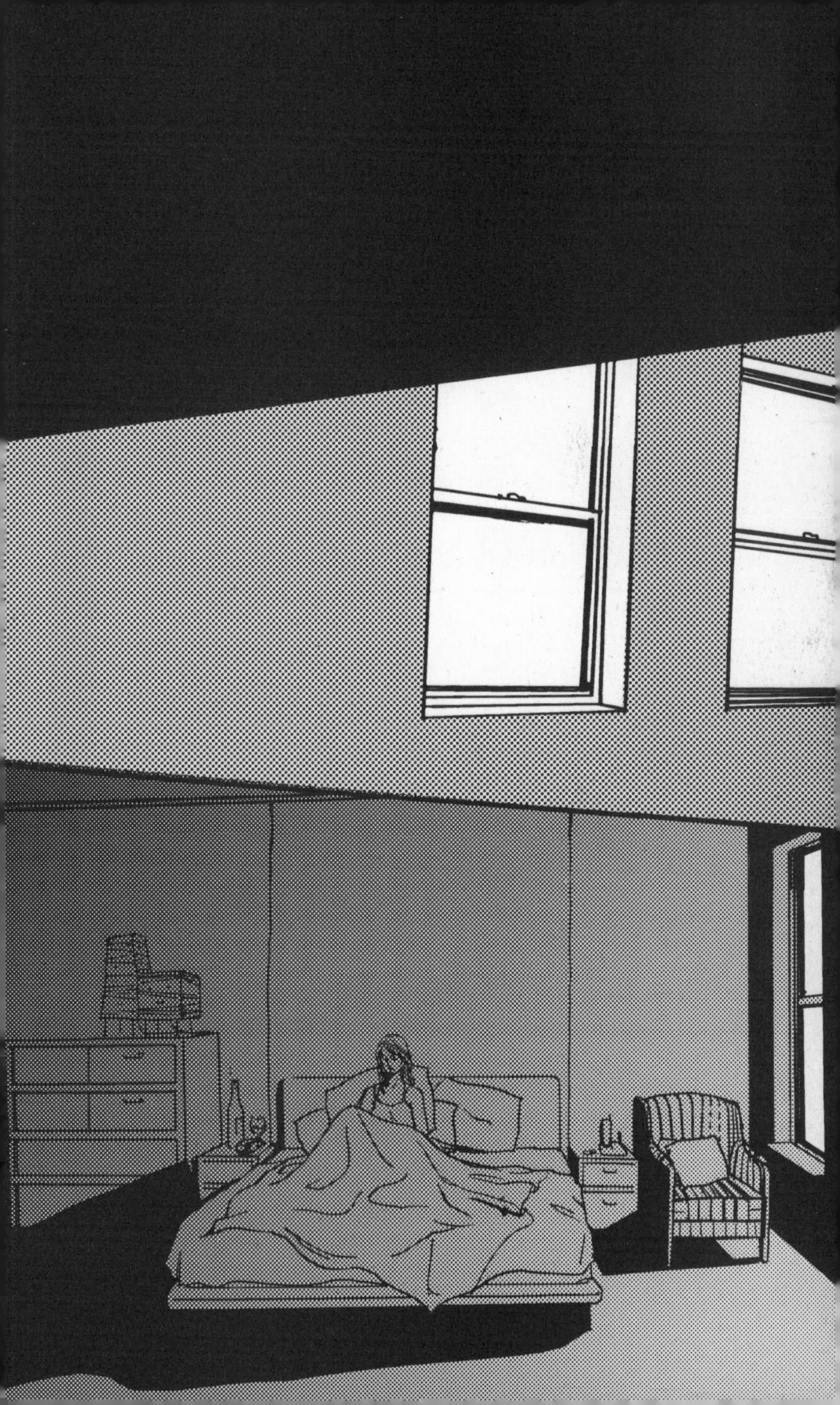

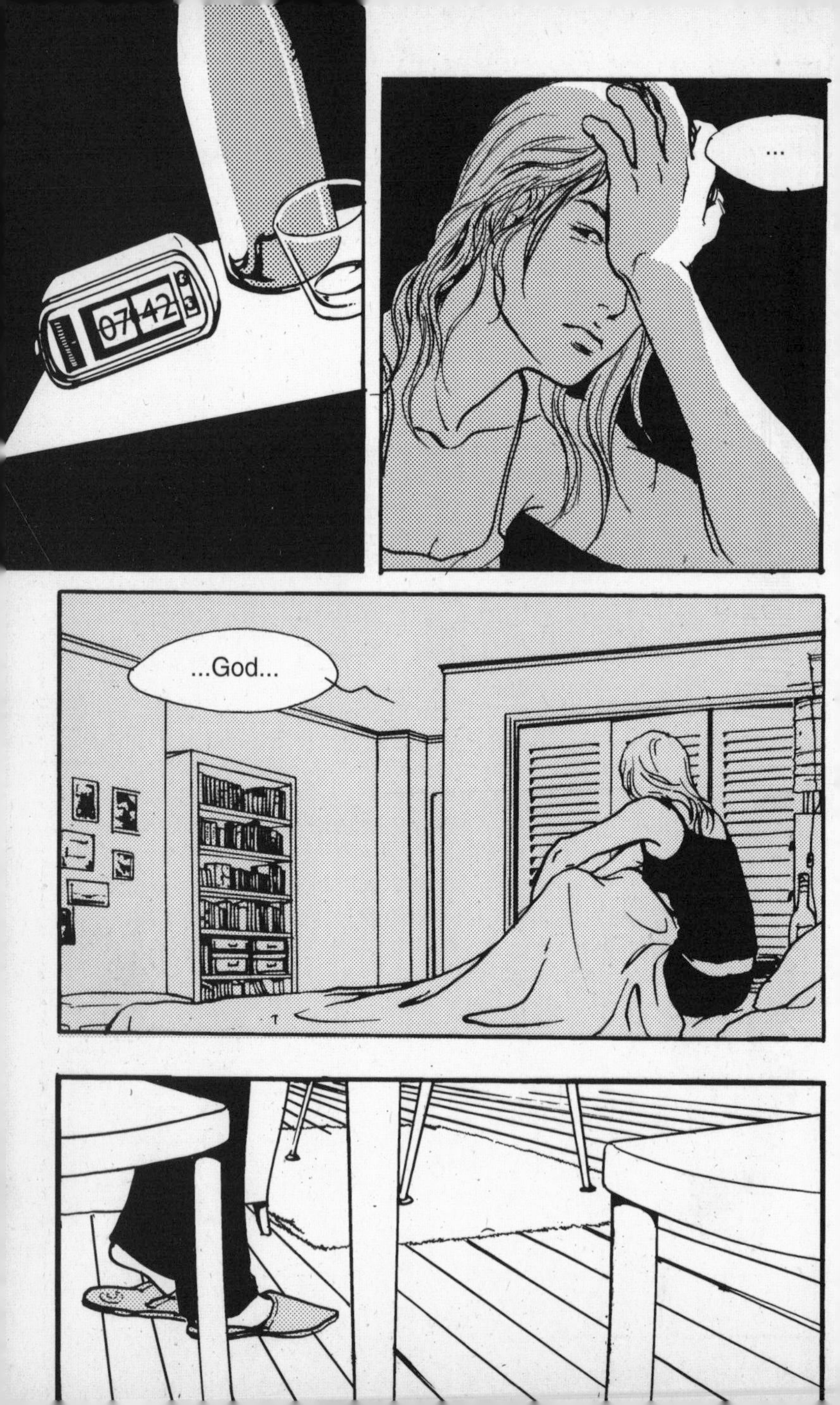
07 42
...
...God...

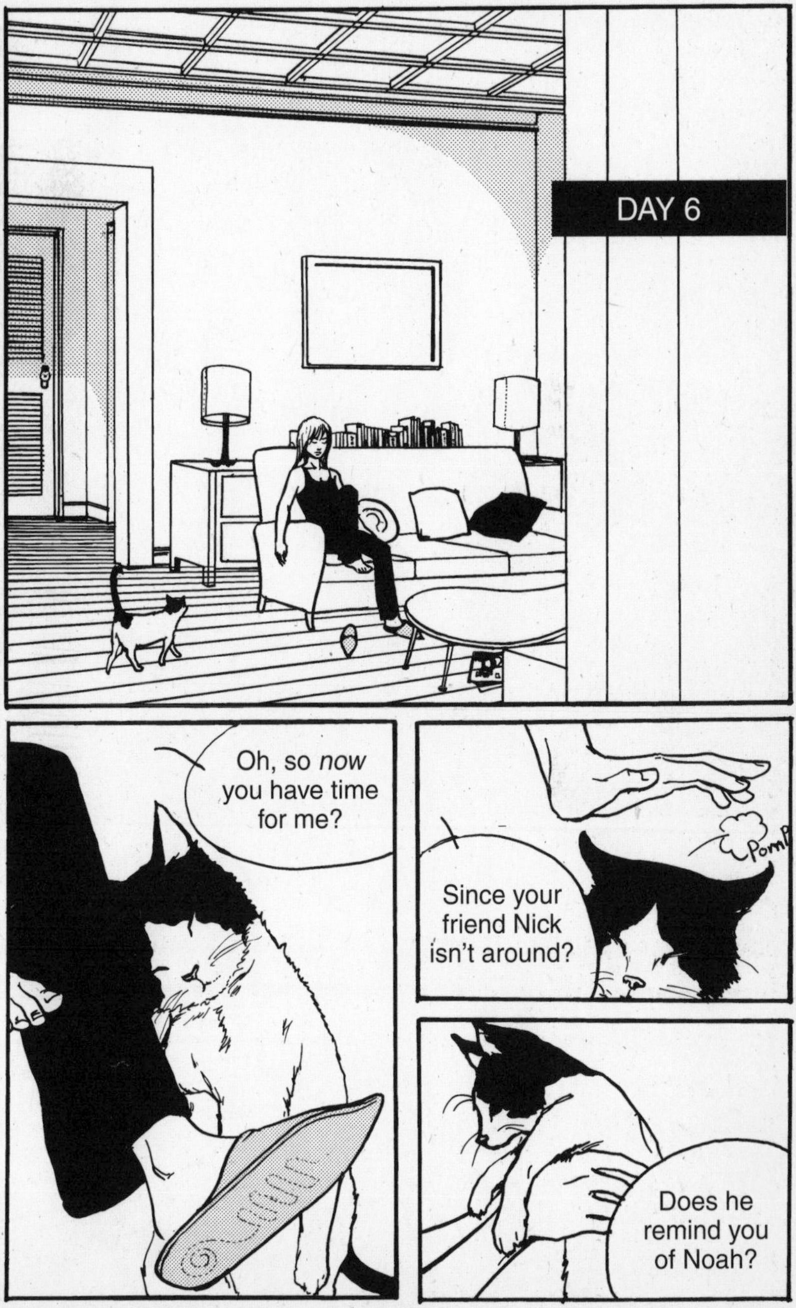
DAY 6
Oh, so *now* you have time for me?
Since your friend Nick isn't around?
Does he remind you of Noah?

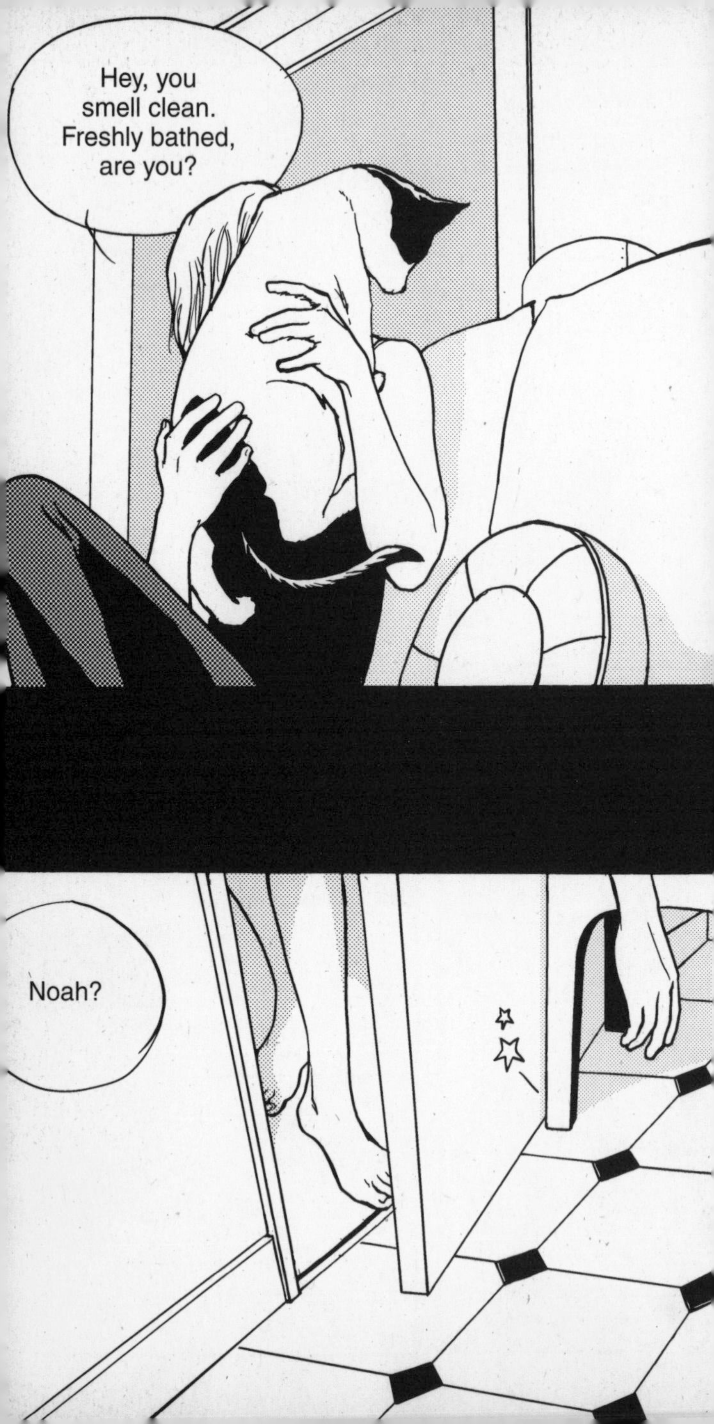
Hey, you smell clean. Freshly bathed, are you?
Noah?

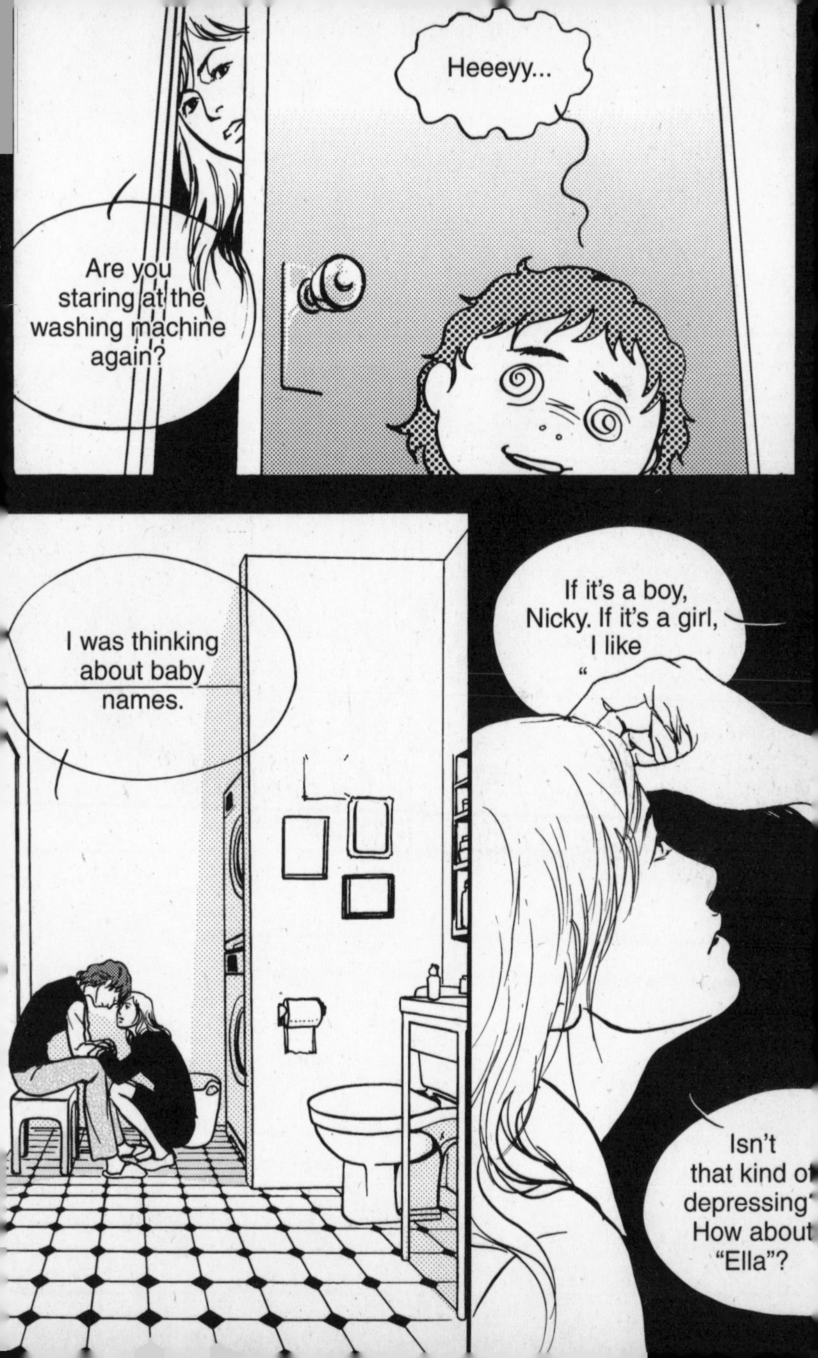
Are you staring at the washing machine again?
Heeeyy...
I was thinking about baby names.
If it's a boy, Nicky. If it's a girl, I like "
Isn't that kind of depressing? How about "Ella"?

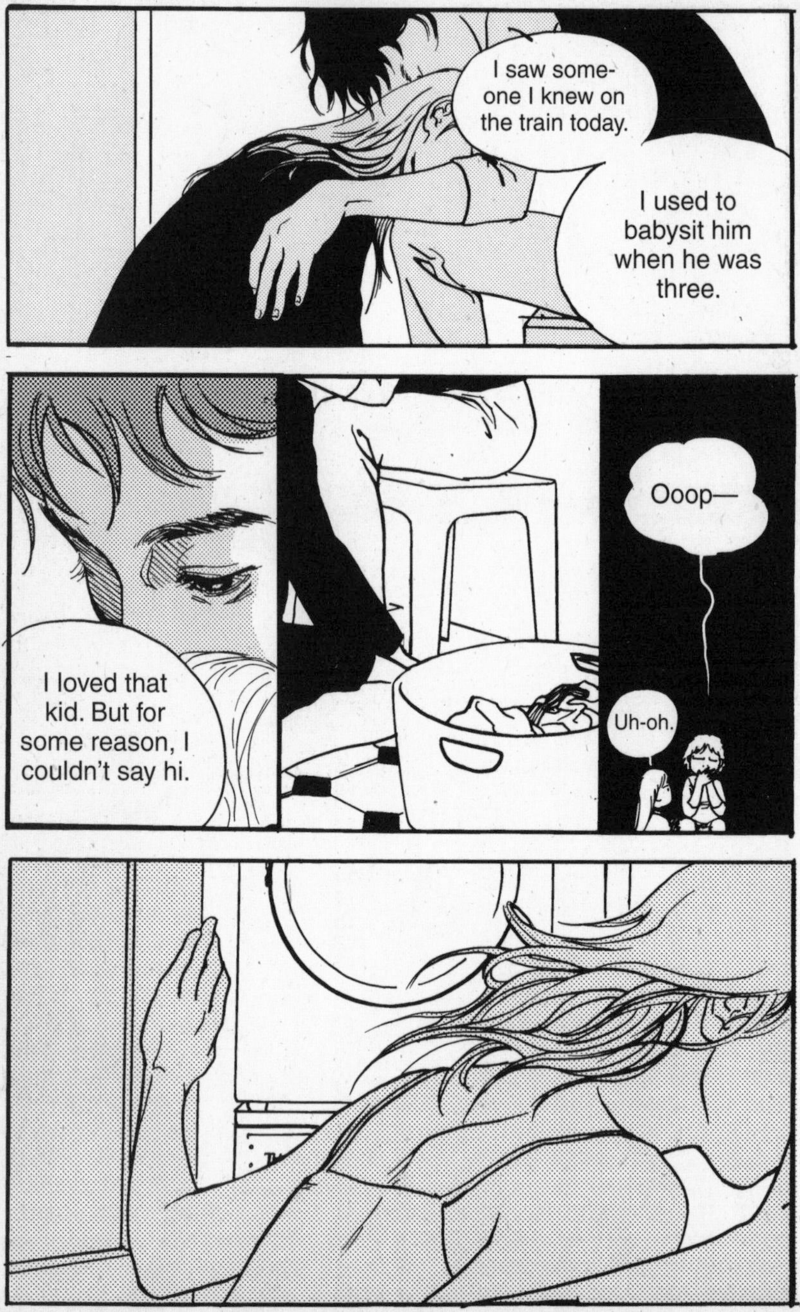
I saw some-one I knew on the train today.
I used to babysit him when he was three.
I loved that kid. But for some reason, I couldn't say hi.
Ooop—
Uh-oh.

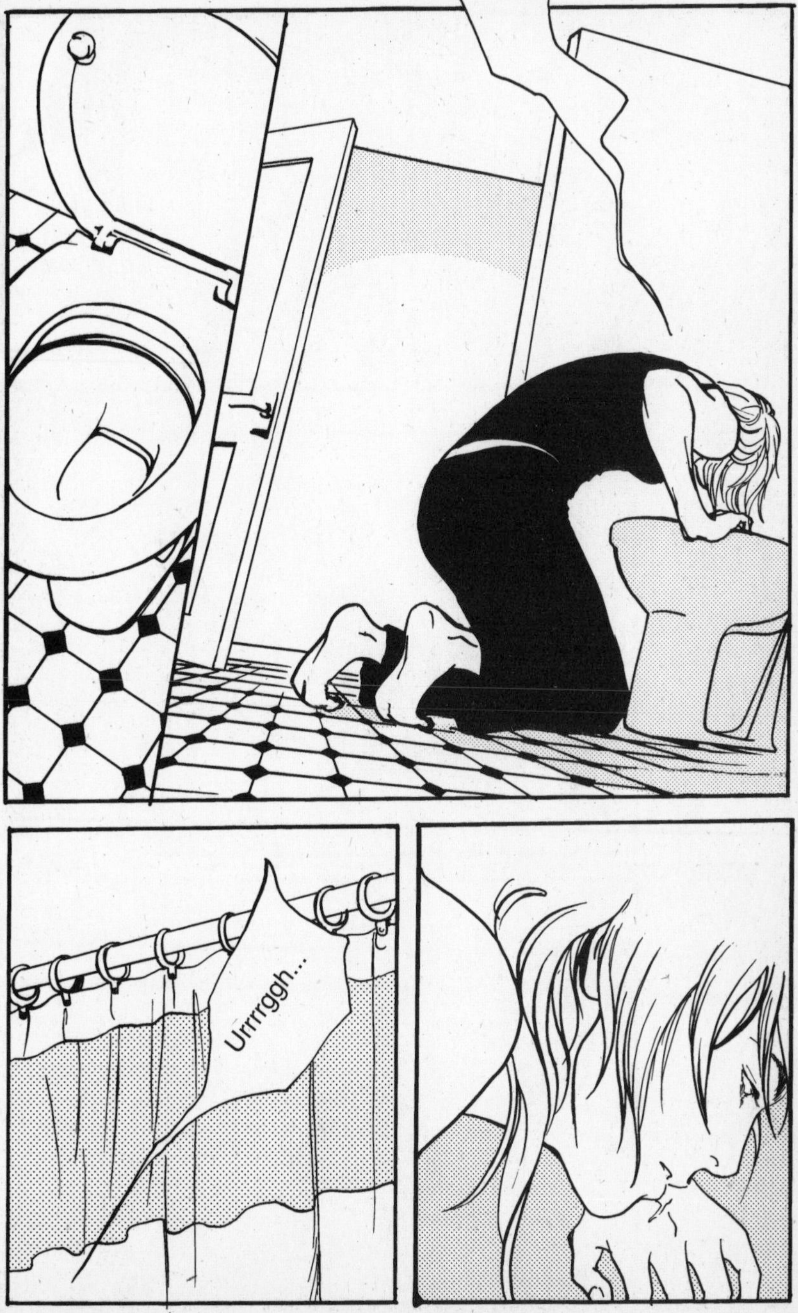
Urrrrggh...

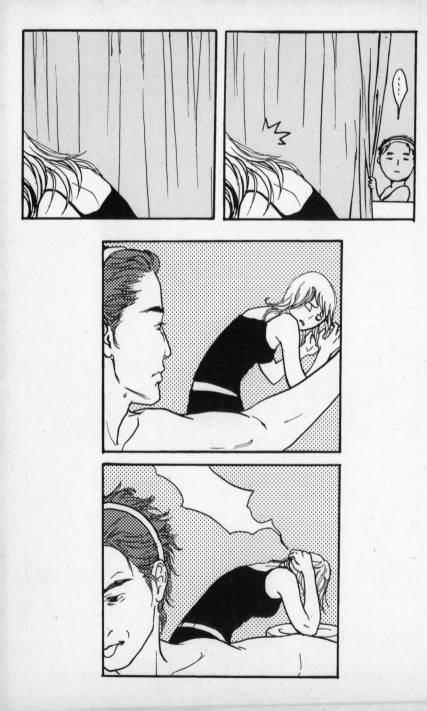

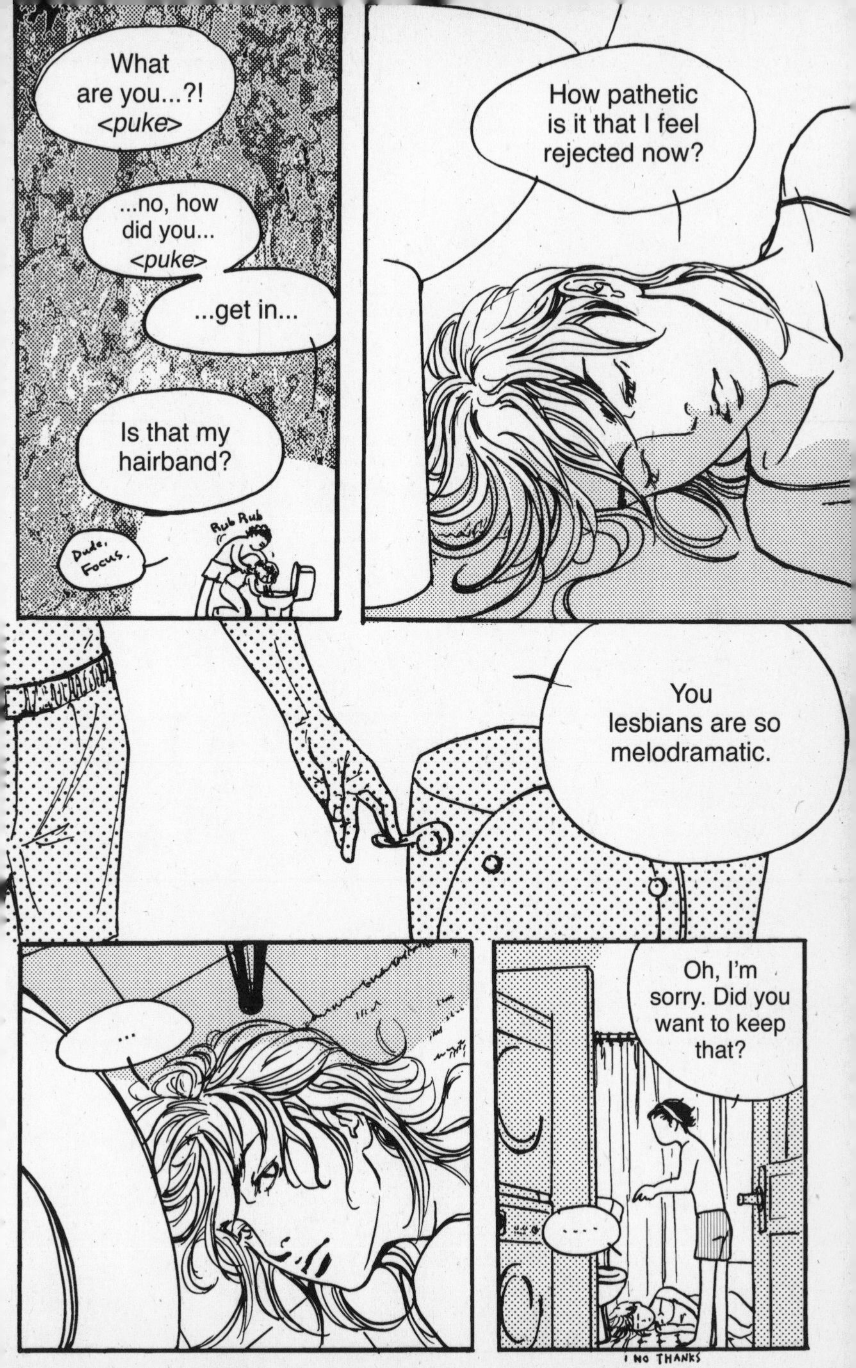
What are you...?! <puke>
...no, how did you... <puke>
...get in...
Is that my hairband?
Rub Rub
Dude, Focus.
How pathetic is it that I feel rejected now?
You lesbians are so melodramatic.
...
Oh, I'm sorry. Did you want to keep that?
....
NO THANKS

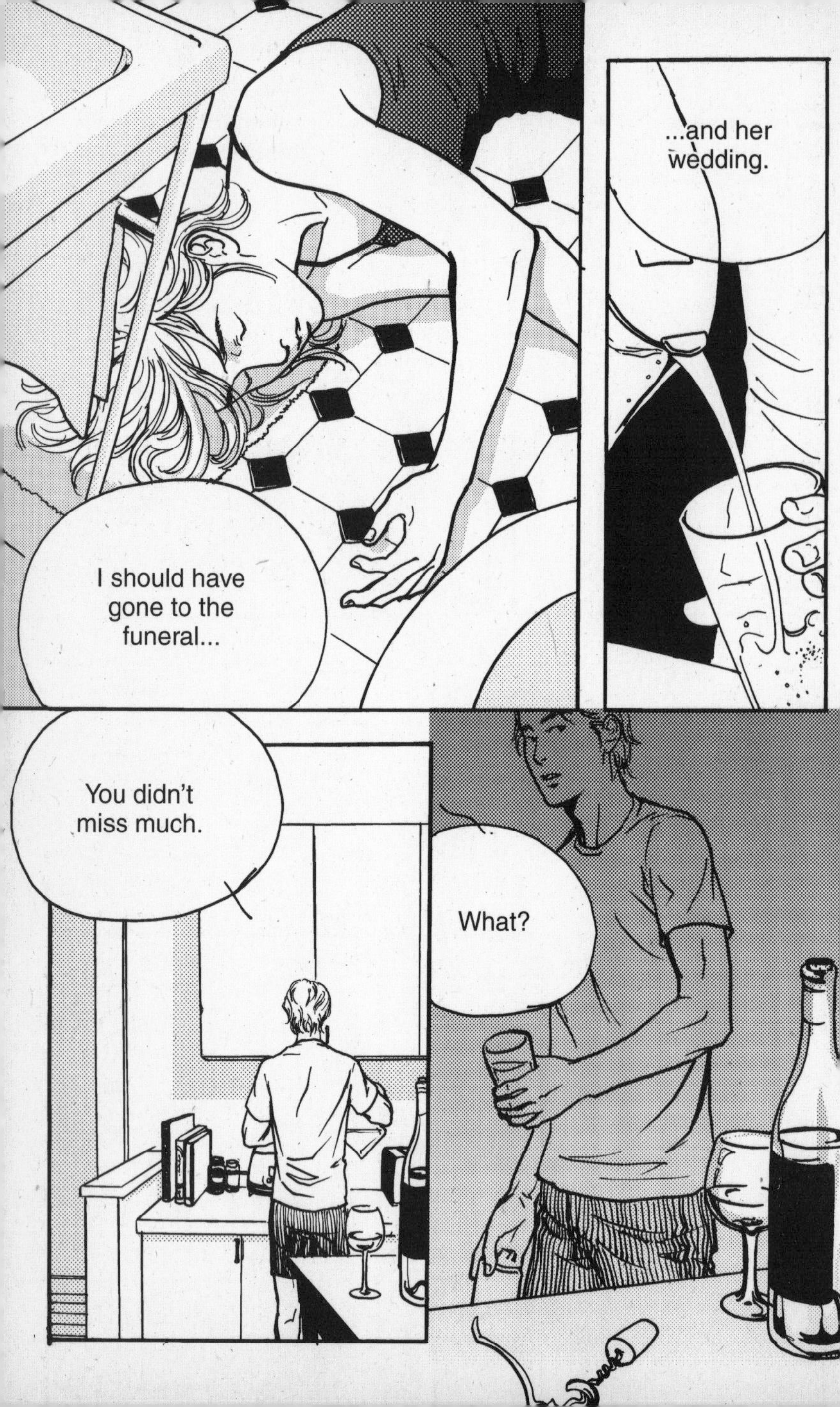
I should have gone to the funeral...
...and her wedding.
You didn't miss much.
What?

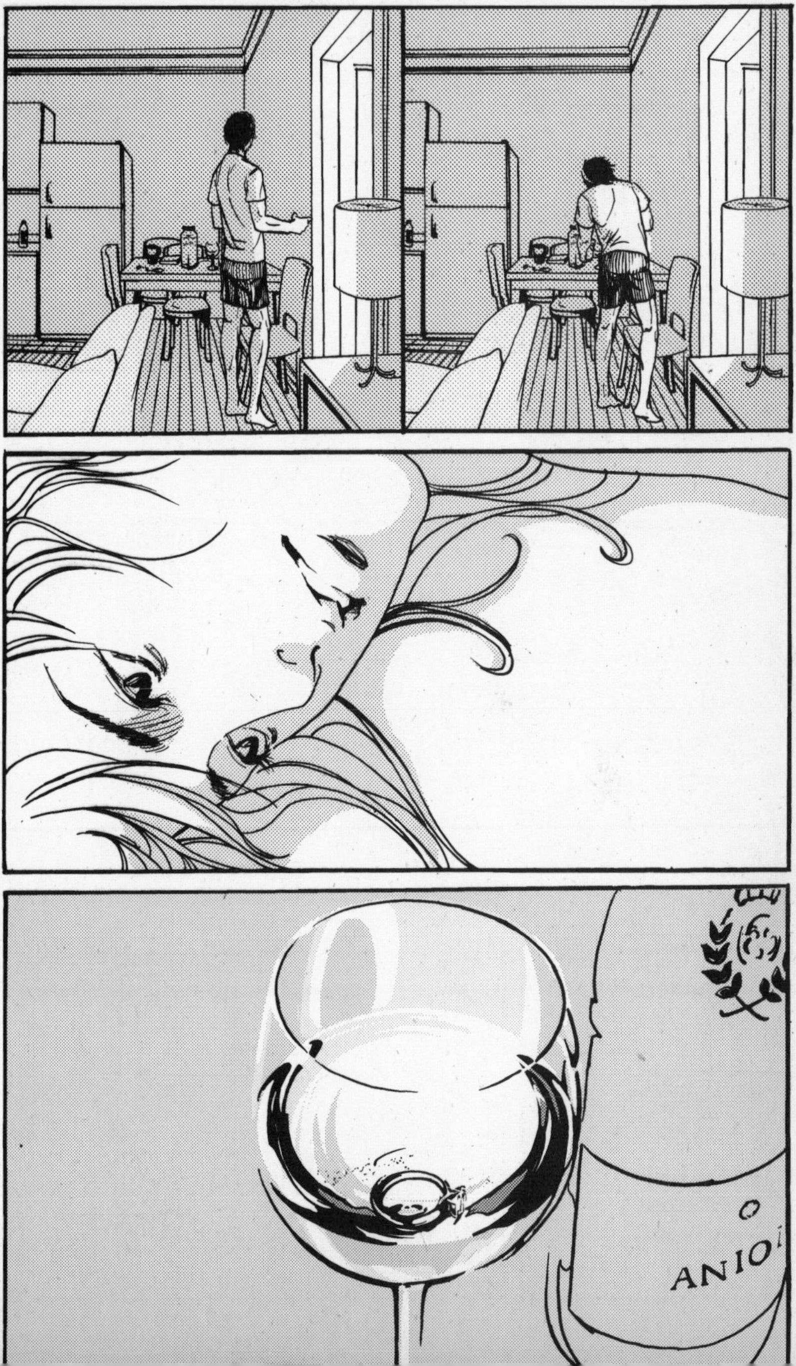
ANIO

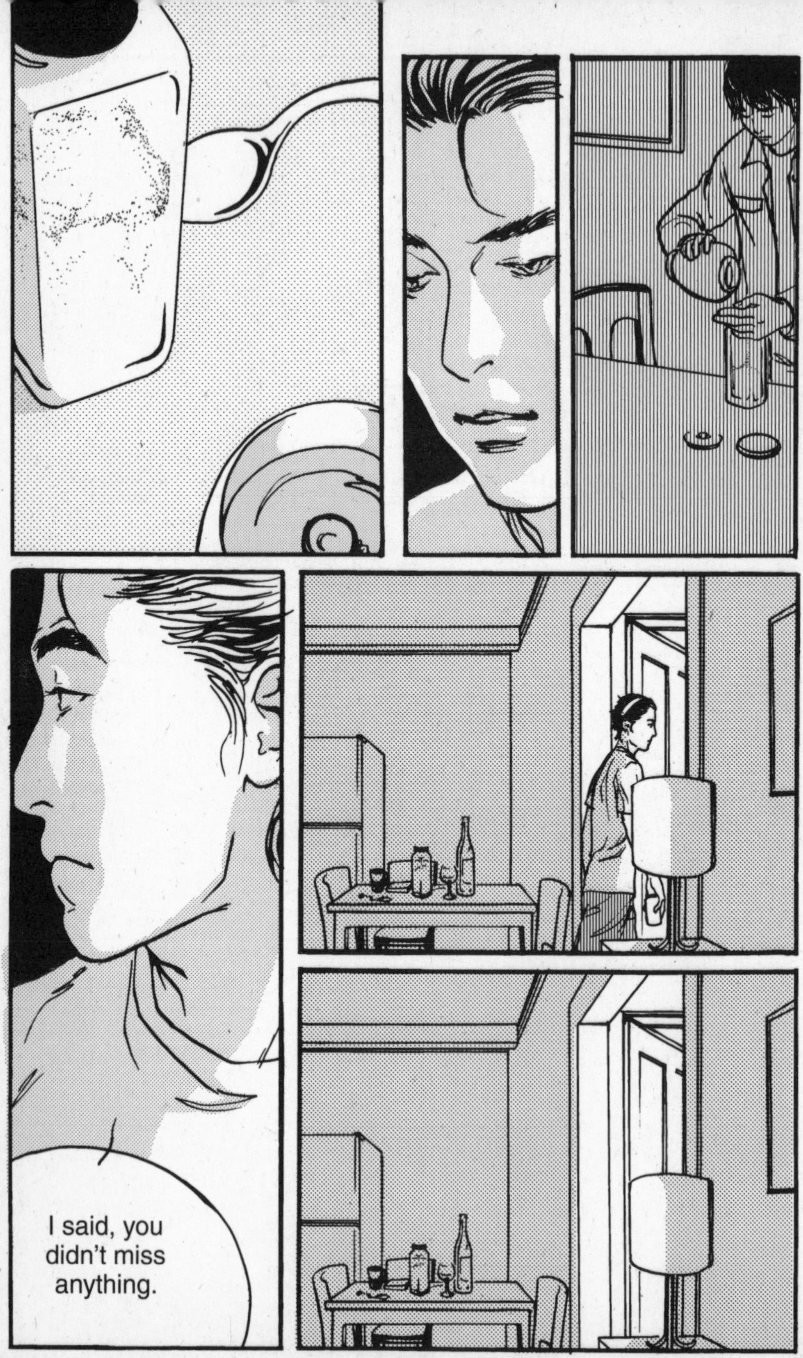
I said, you didn't miss anything.

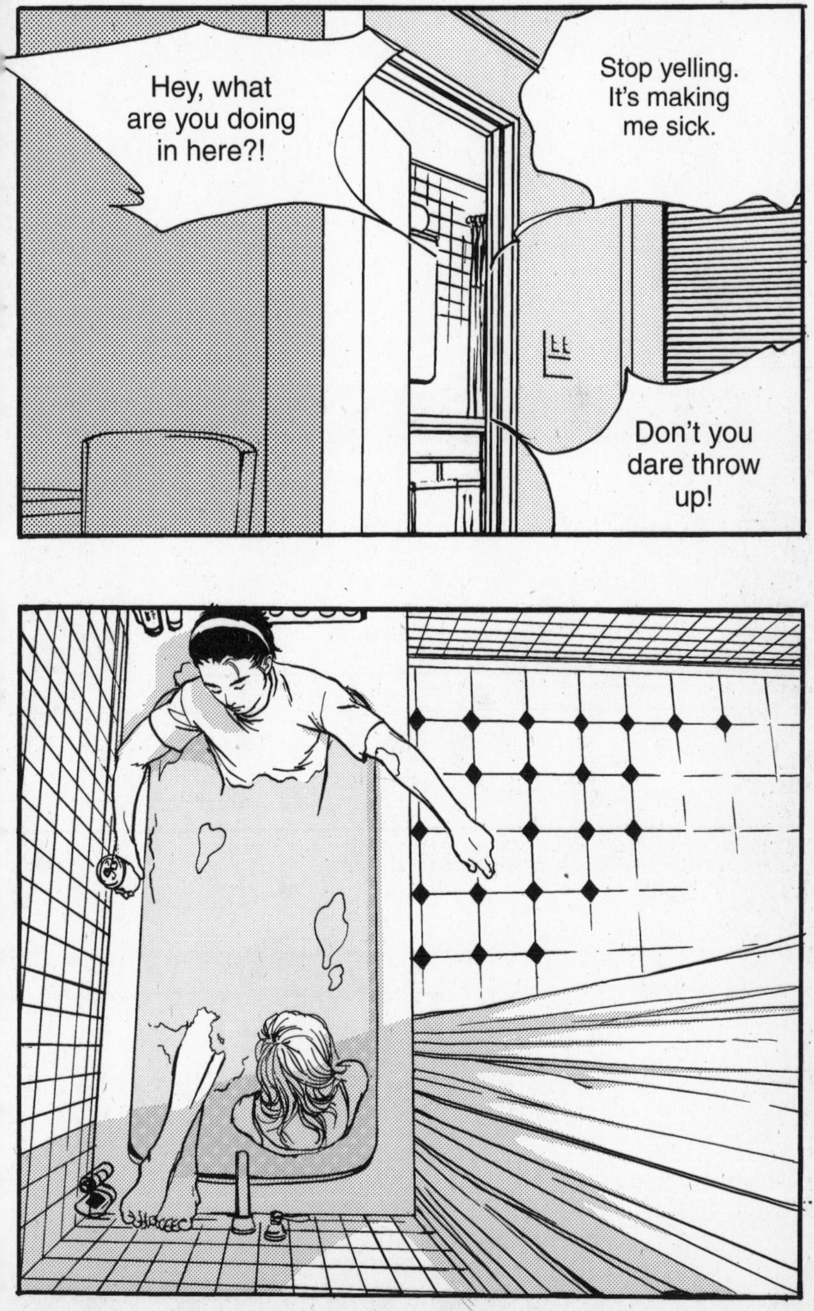
Hey, what are you doing in here?!
Stop yelling. It's making me sick.
Don't you dare throw up!

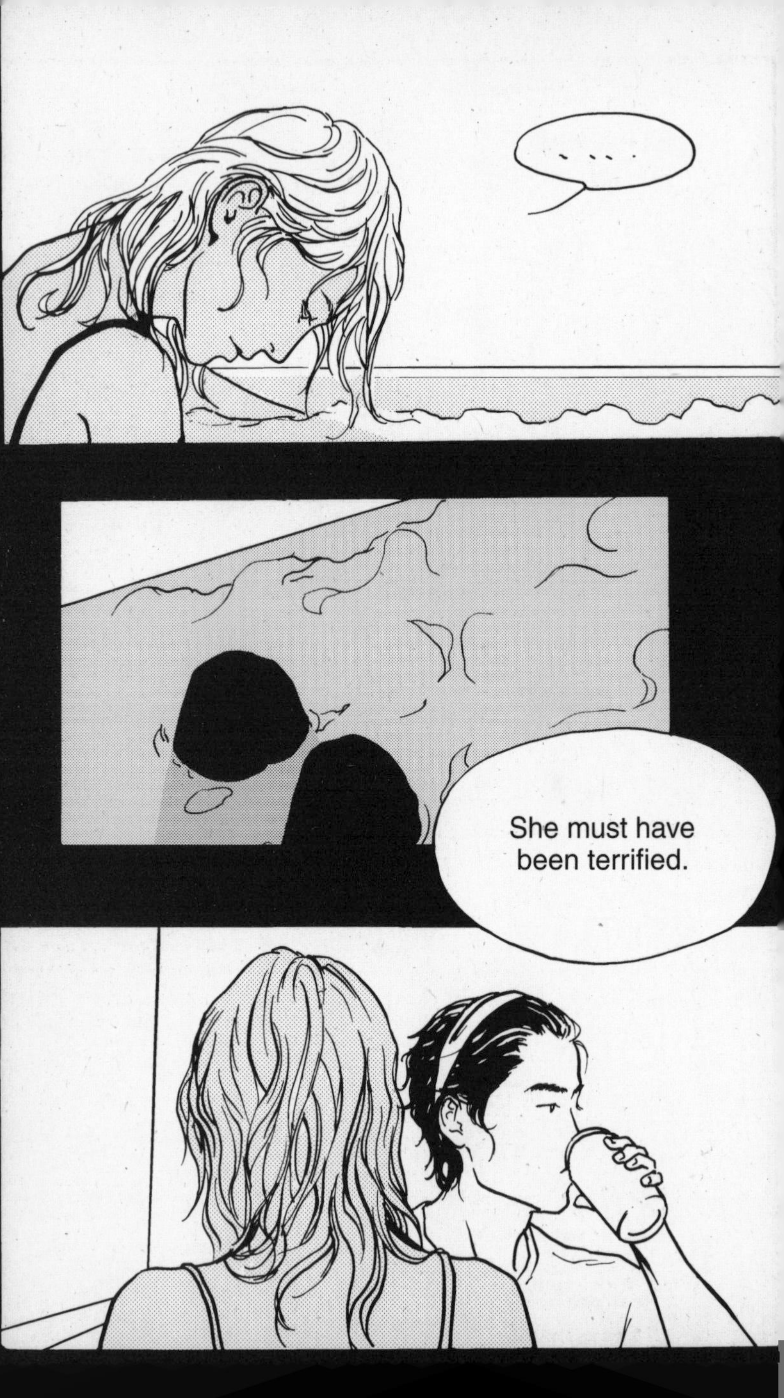
. . . .
She must have been terrified.

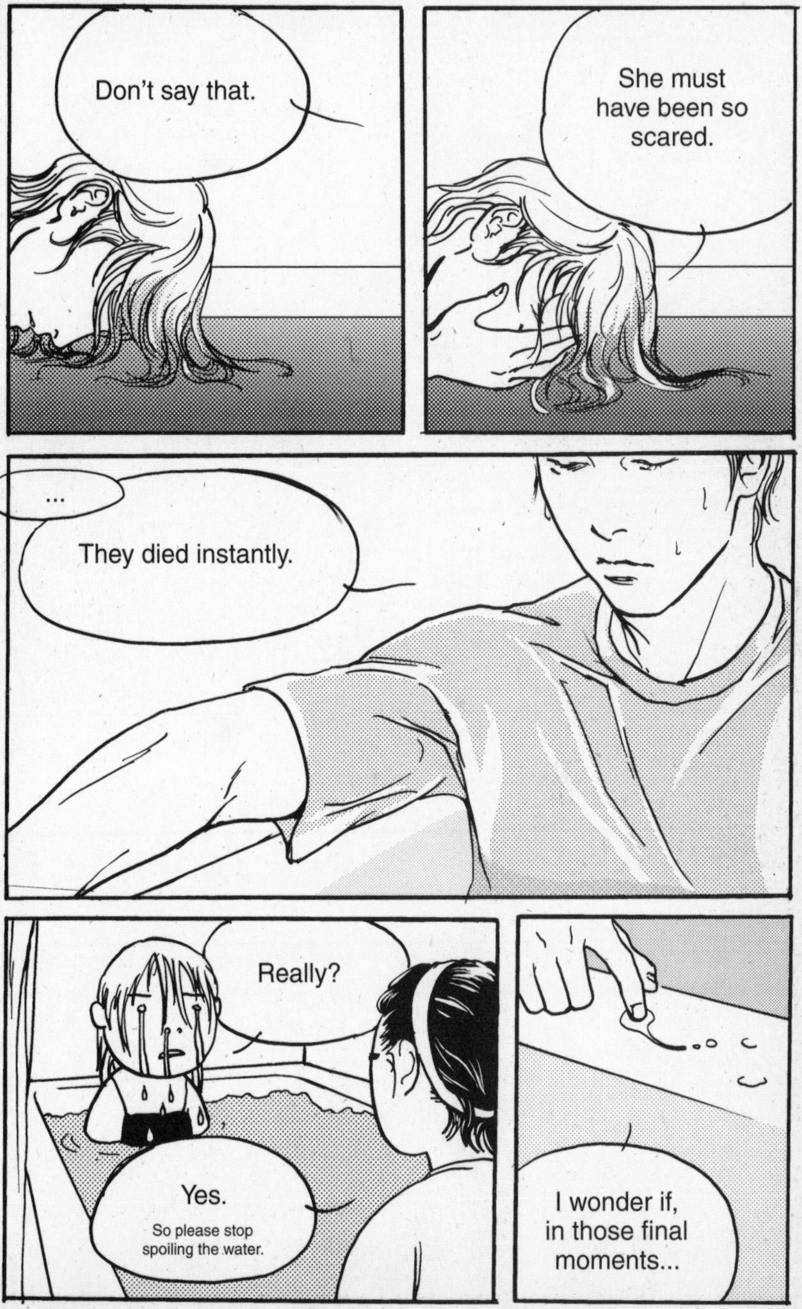
Don't say that.
She must have been so scared.
...
They died instantly.
Really?
Yes.
So please stop spoiling the water.
I wonder if, in those final moments...

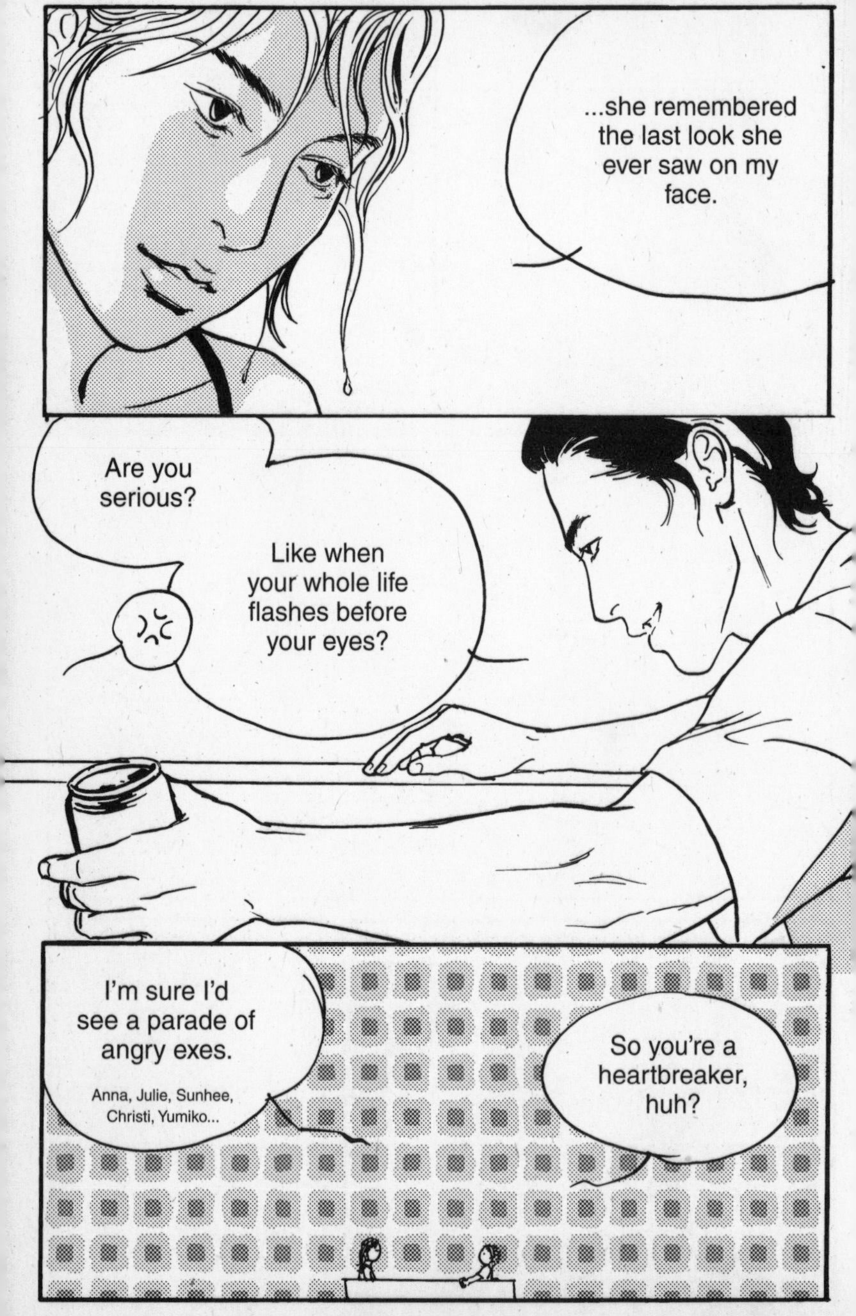
...she remembered the last look she ever saw on my face.
Are you serious?
Like when your whole life flashes before your eyes?
I'm sure I'd see a parade of angry exes.
Anna, Julie, Sunhee, Christi, Yumiko...
So you're a heartbreaker, huh?

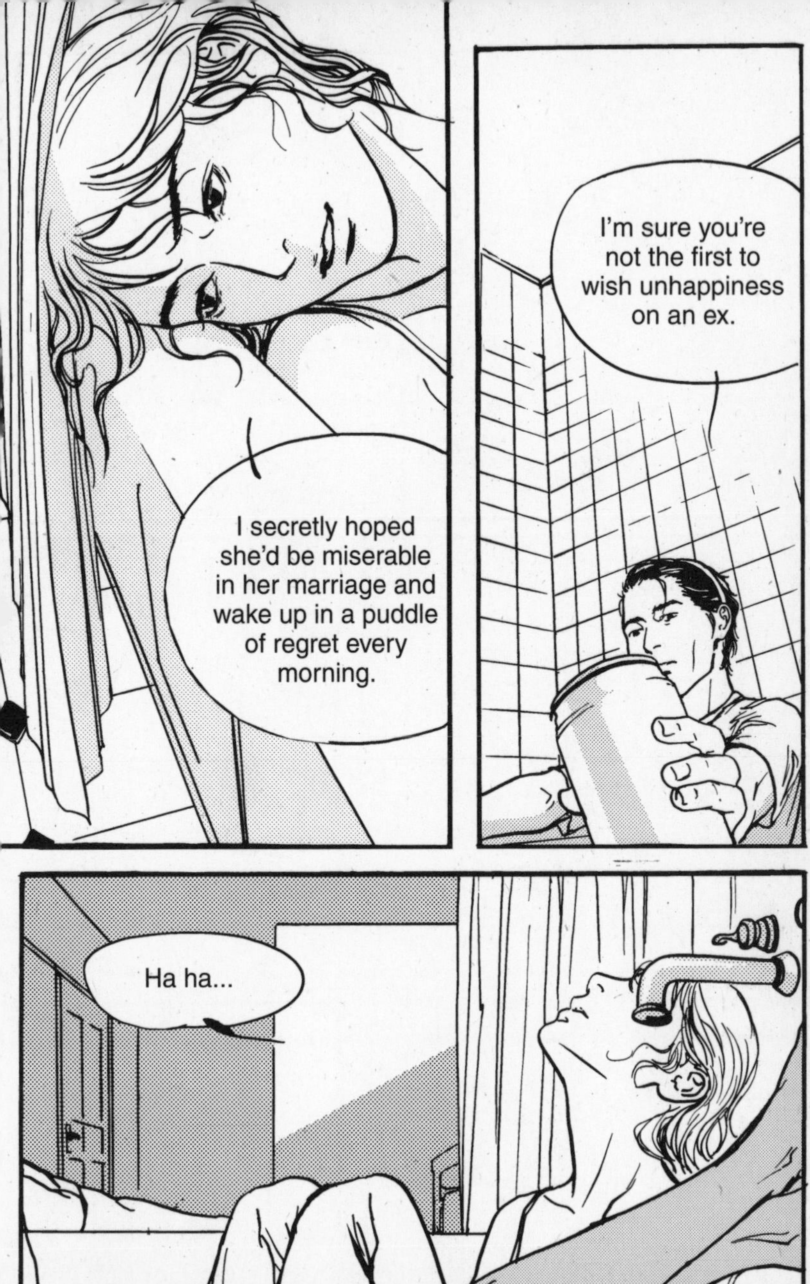
I secretly hoped she'd be miserable in her marriage and wake up in a puddle of regret every morning.
I'm sure you're not the first to wish unhappiness on an ex.
Ha ha...

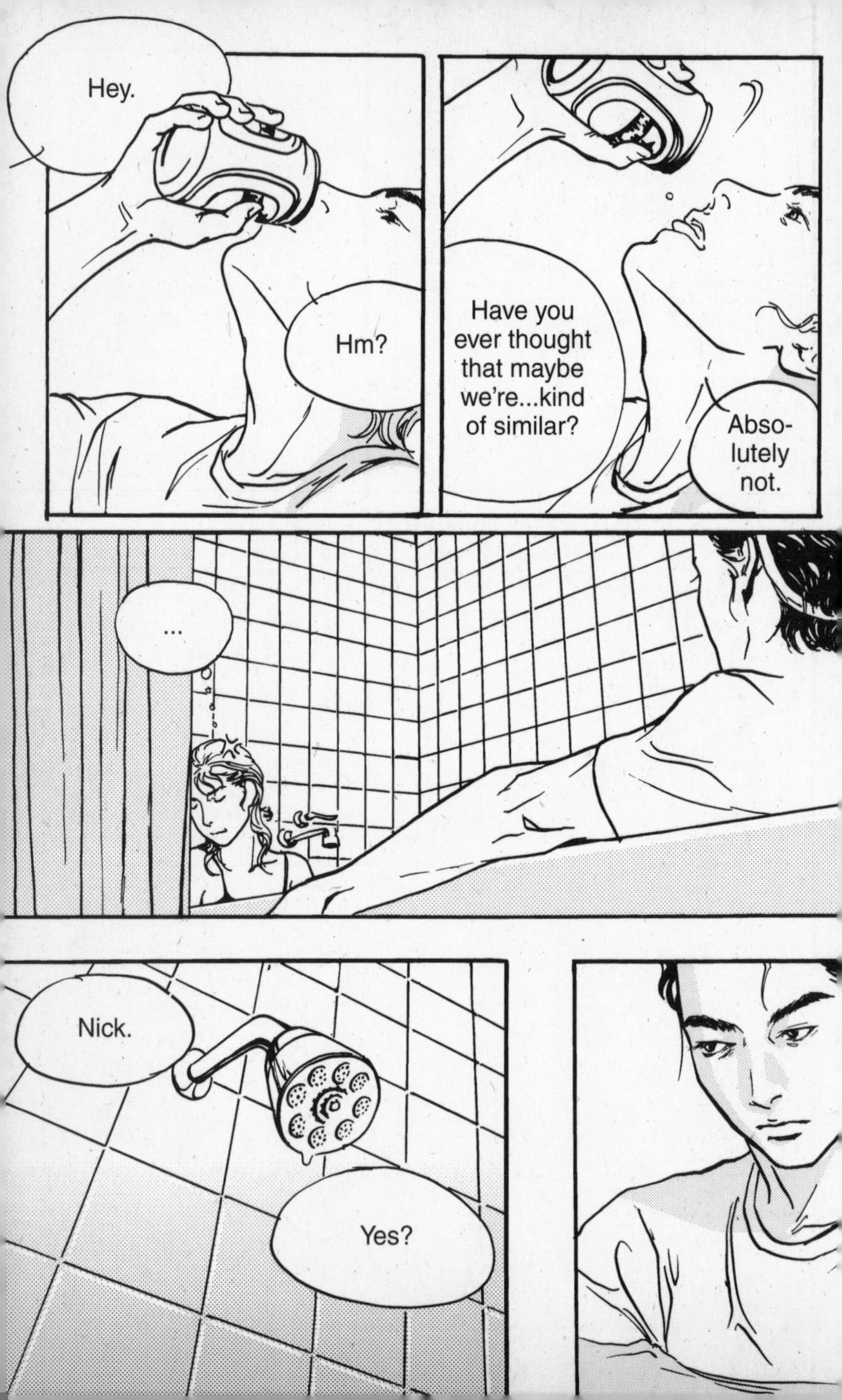
Hey.
Hm?
Have you ever thought that maybe we're...kind of similar?
Abso-lutely not.
...
Nick.
Yes?

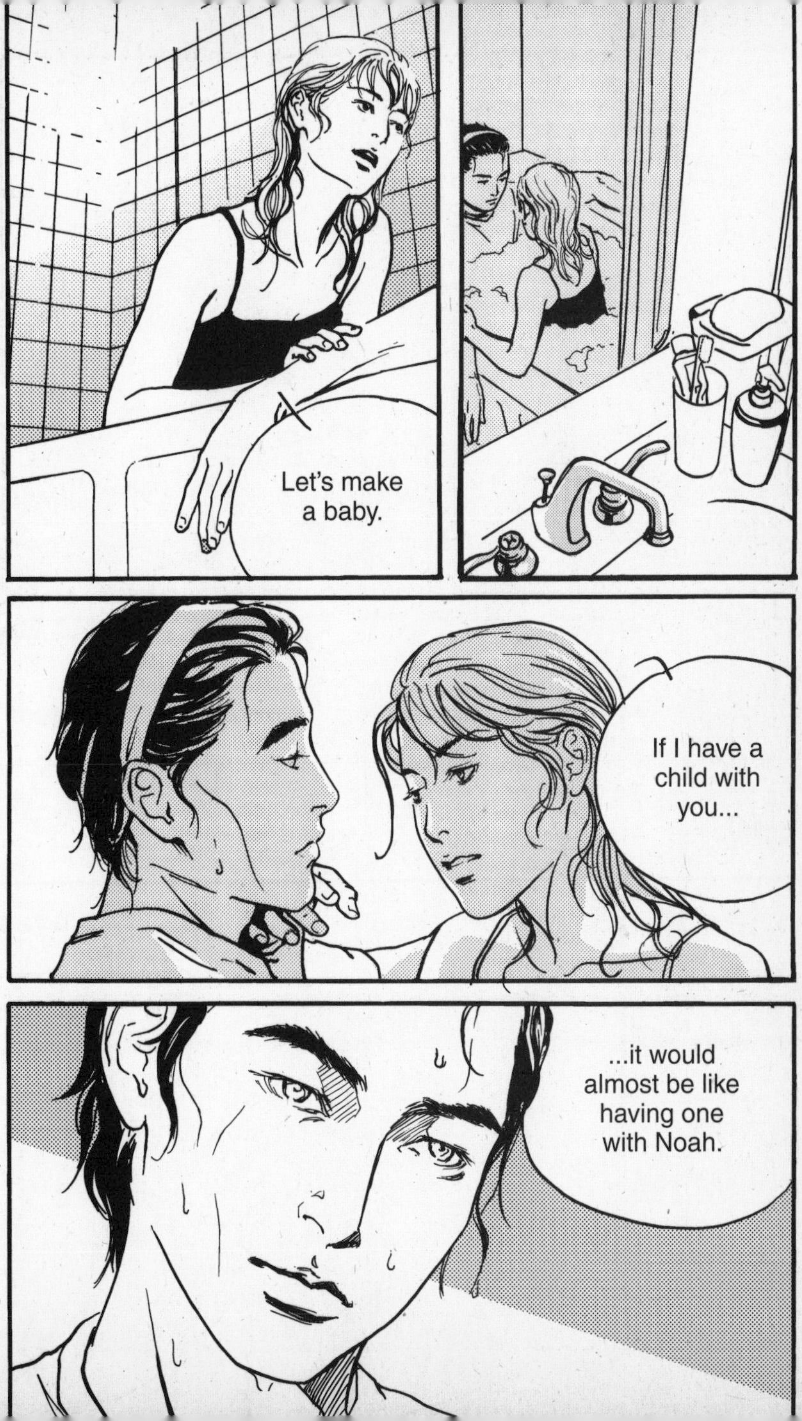
Let's make a baby.
If I have a child with you...
...it would almost be like having one with Noah.

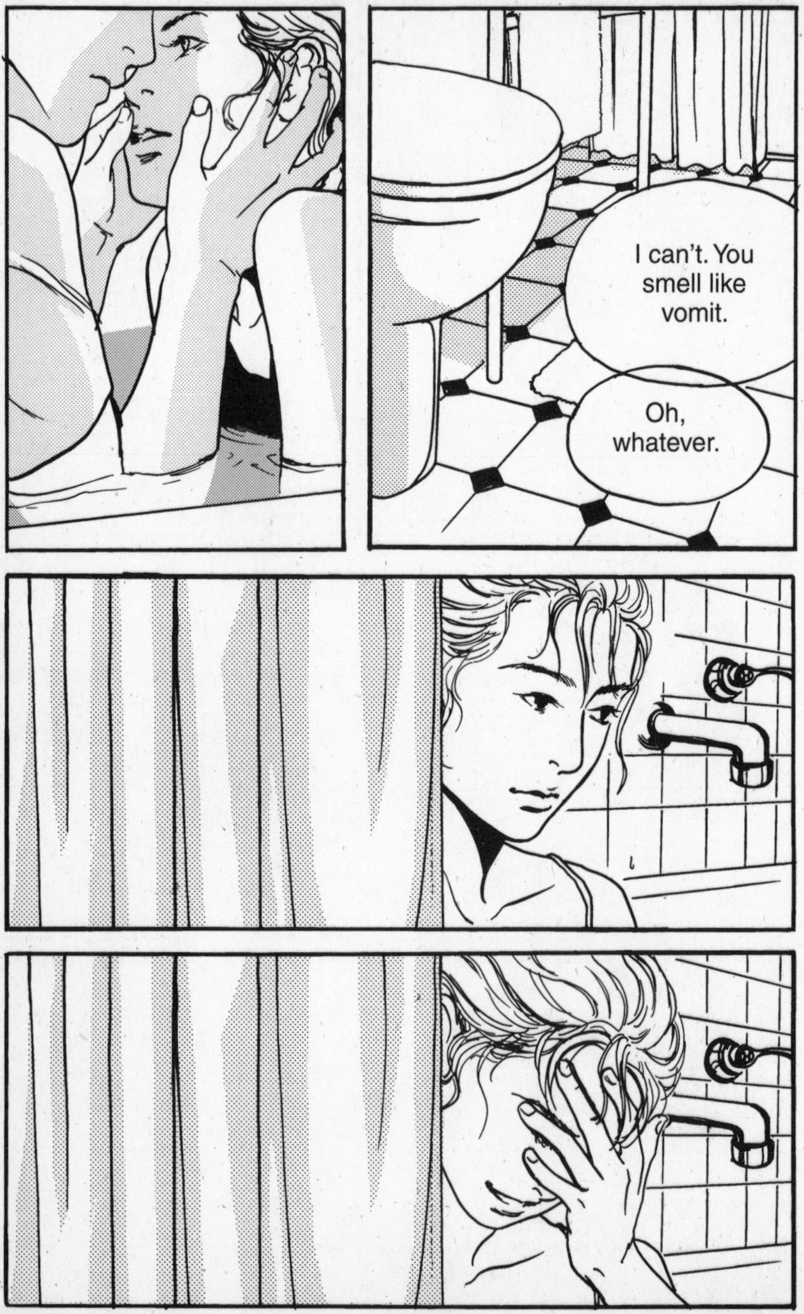
I can't. You smell like vomit.
Oh, whatever.

Chapter 6

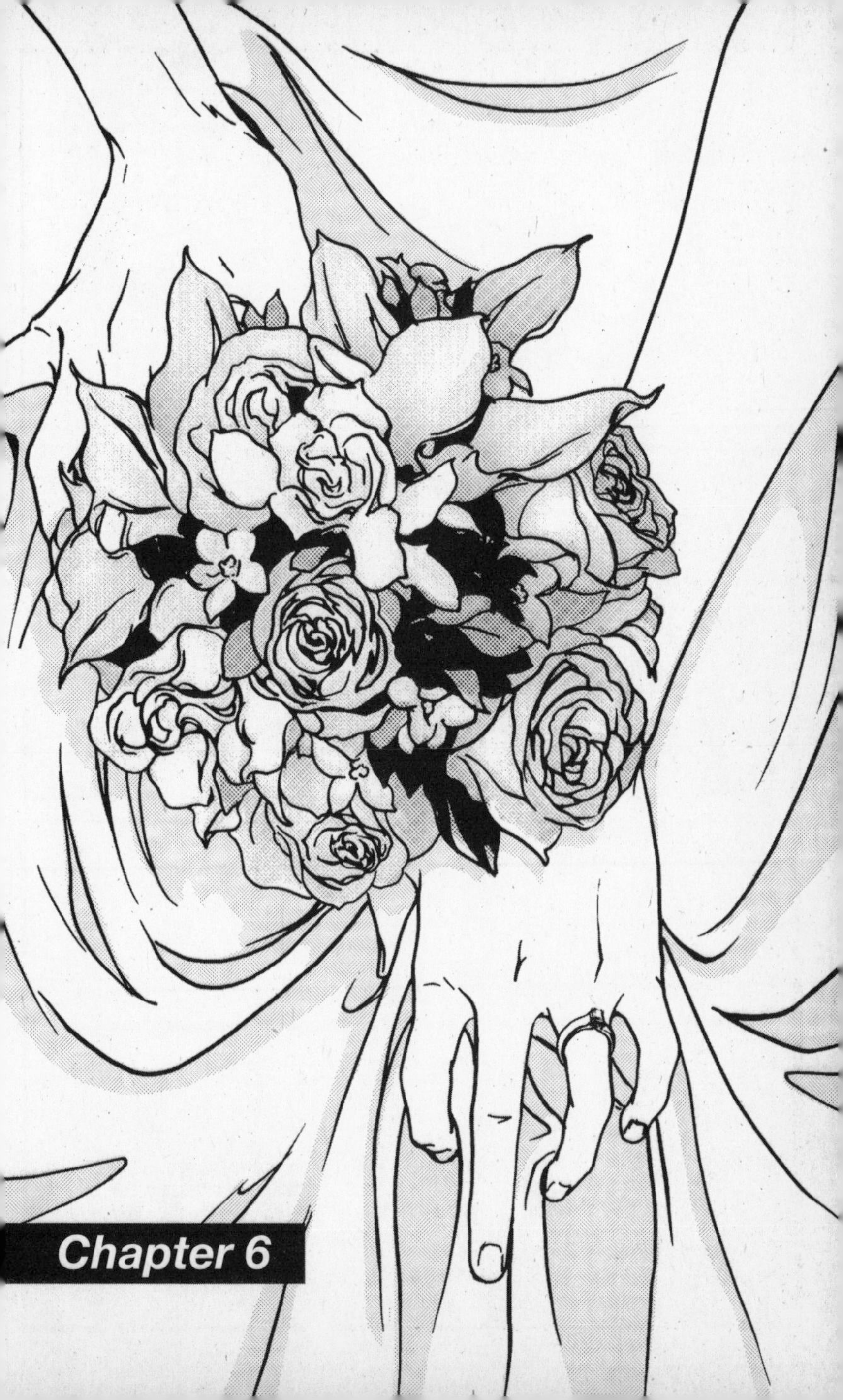

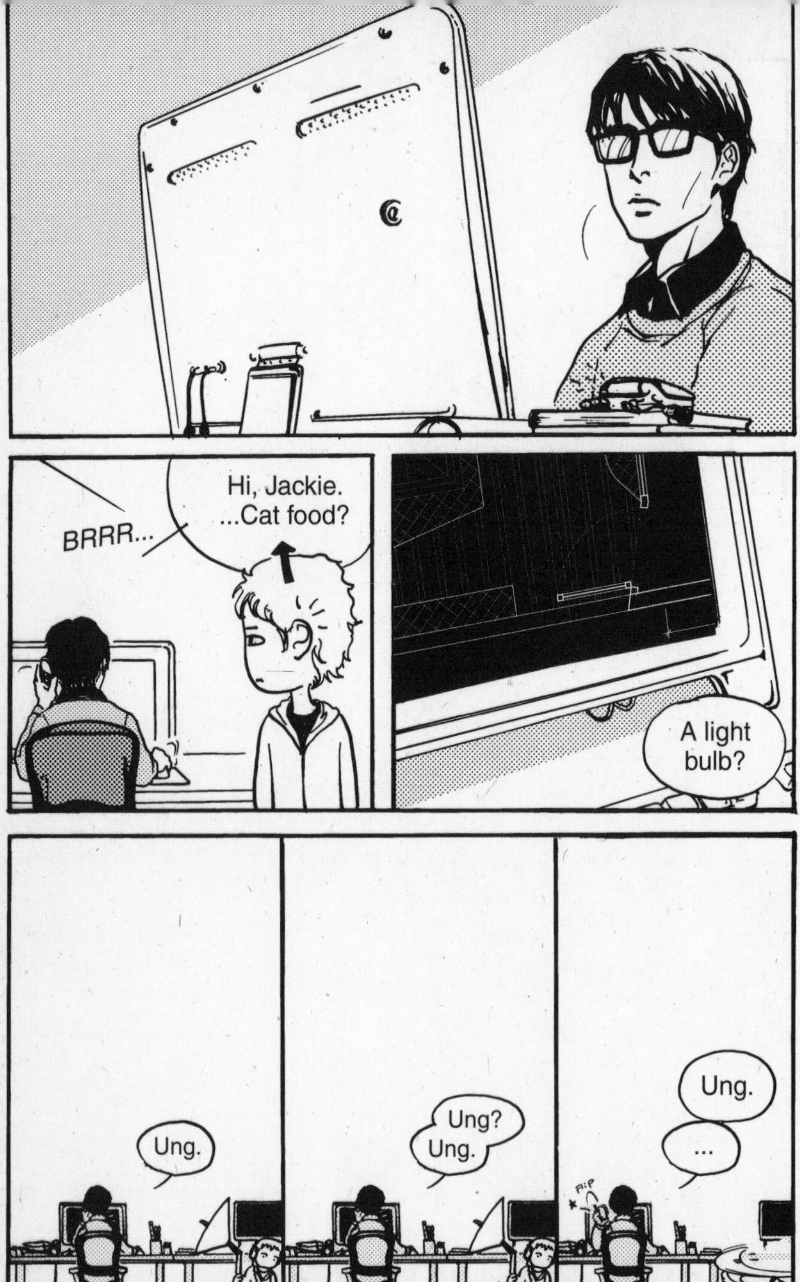
BRRR...
Hi, Jackie.
...Cat food?
A light bulb?
Ung.
Ung?
Ung.
Ung.
...
ung: uh-huh

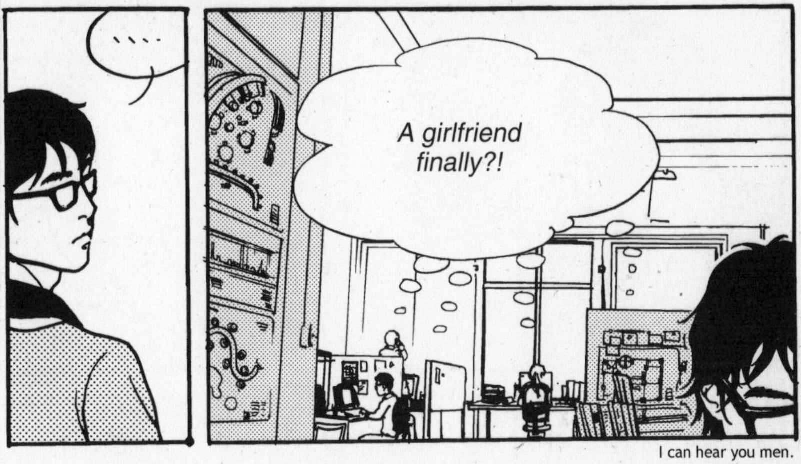
....
A girlfriend finally?!

I can hear you men.

DAY 8

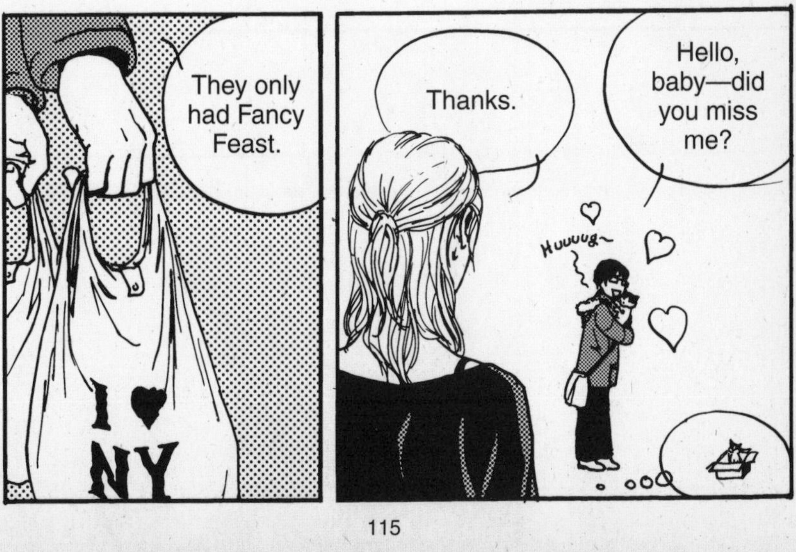
They only had Fancy Feast.
Thanks.
Hello, baby—did you miss me?
Huuuug~

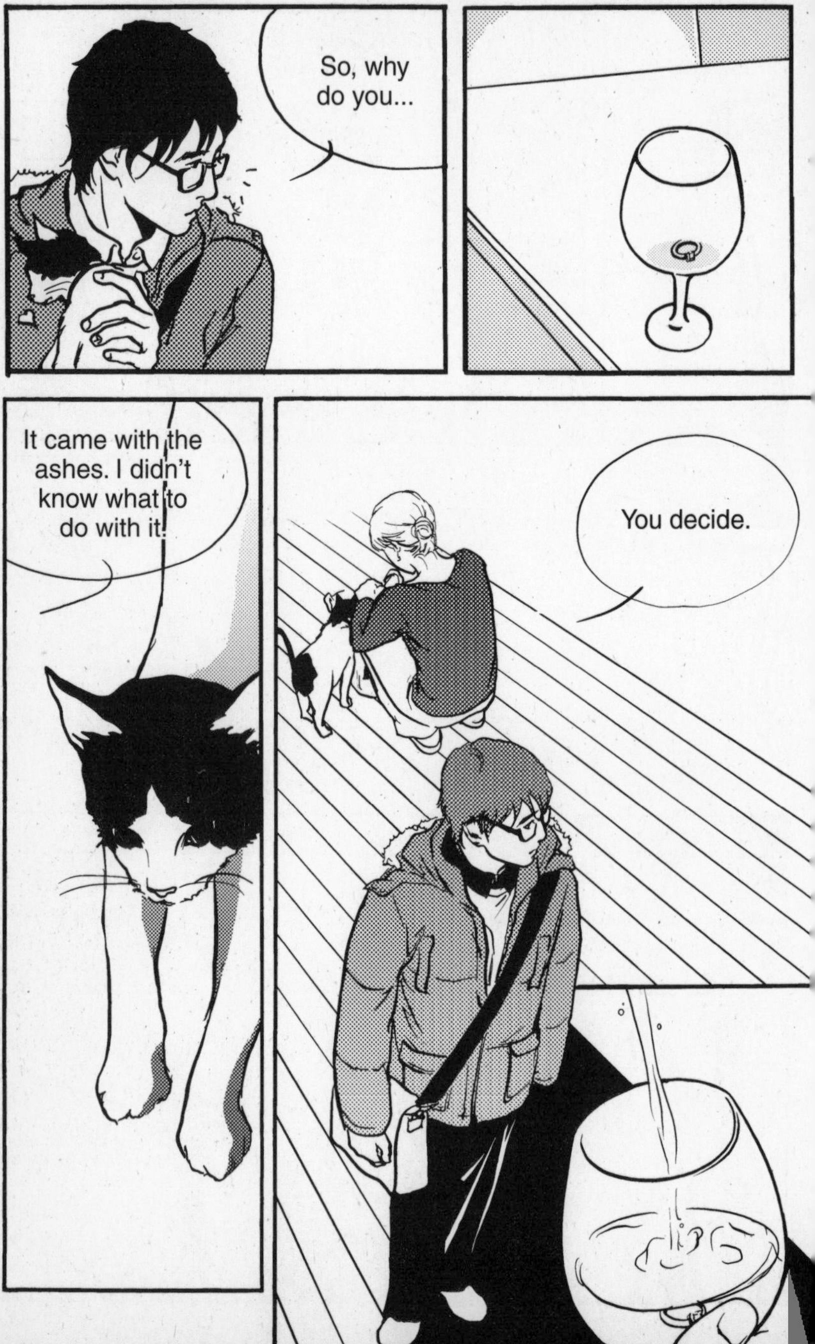
So, why do you...
It came with the ashes. I didn't know what to do with it.
You decide.

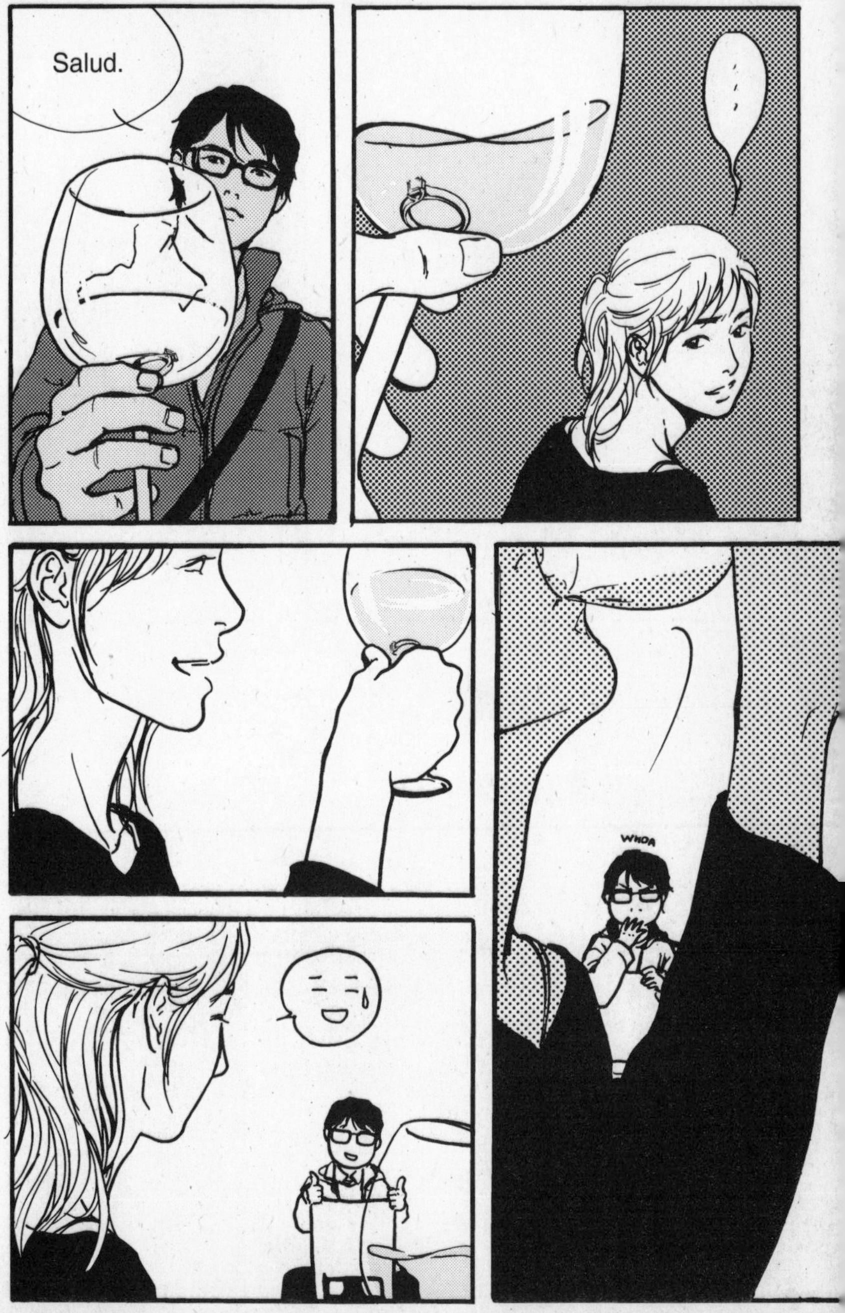
Salud.
. . .
WHOA

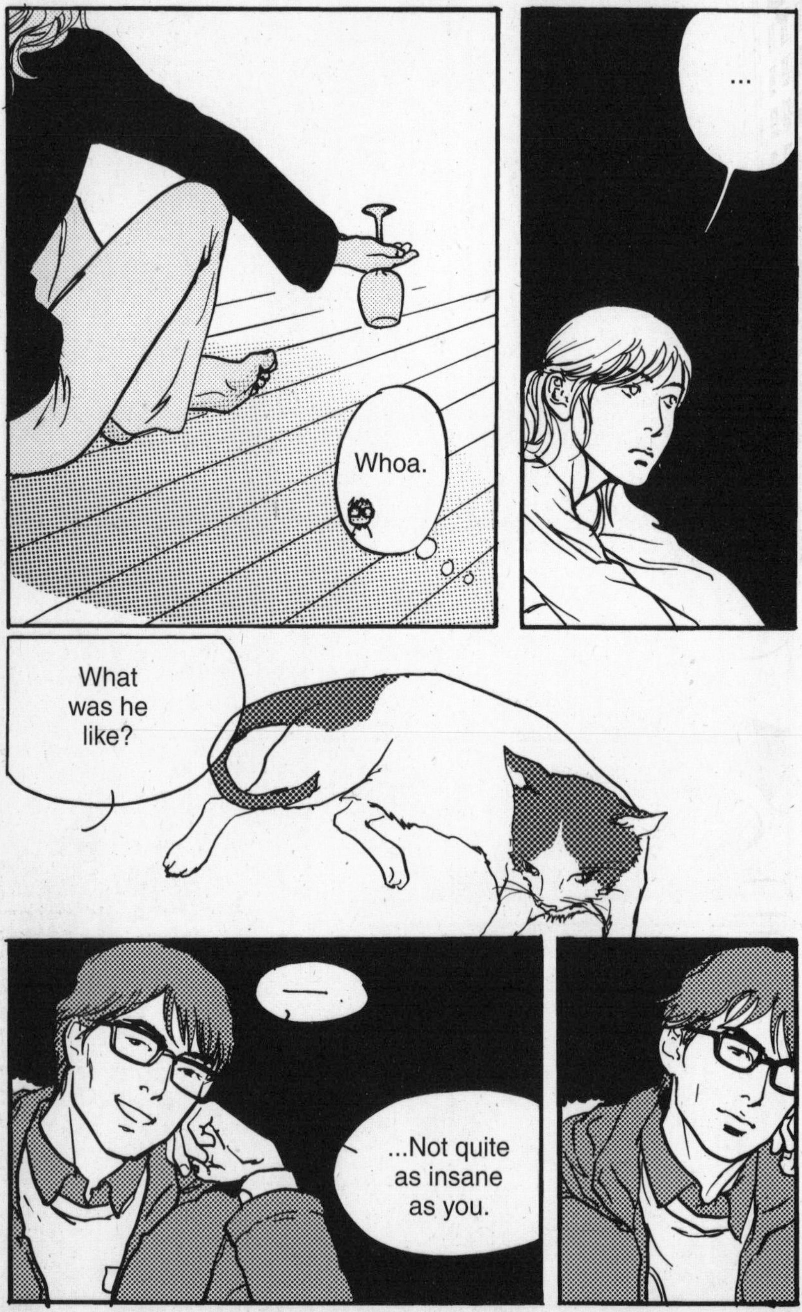
Whoa.
...
What was he like?
—.
...Not quite as insane as you.

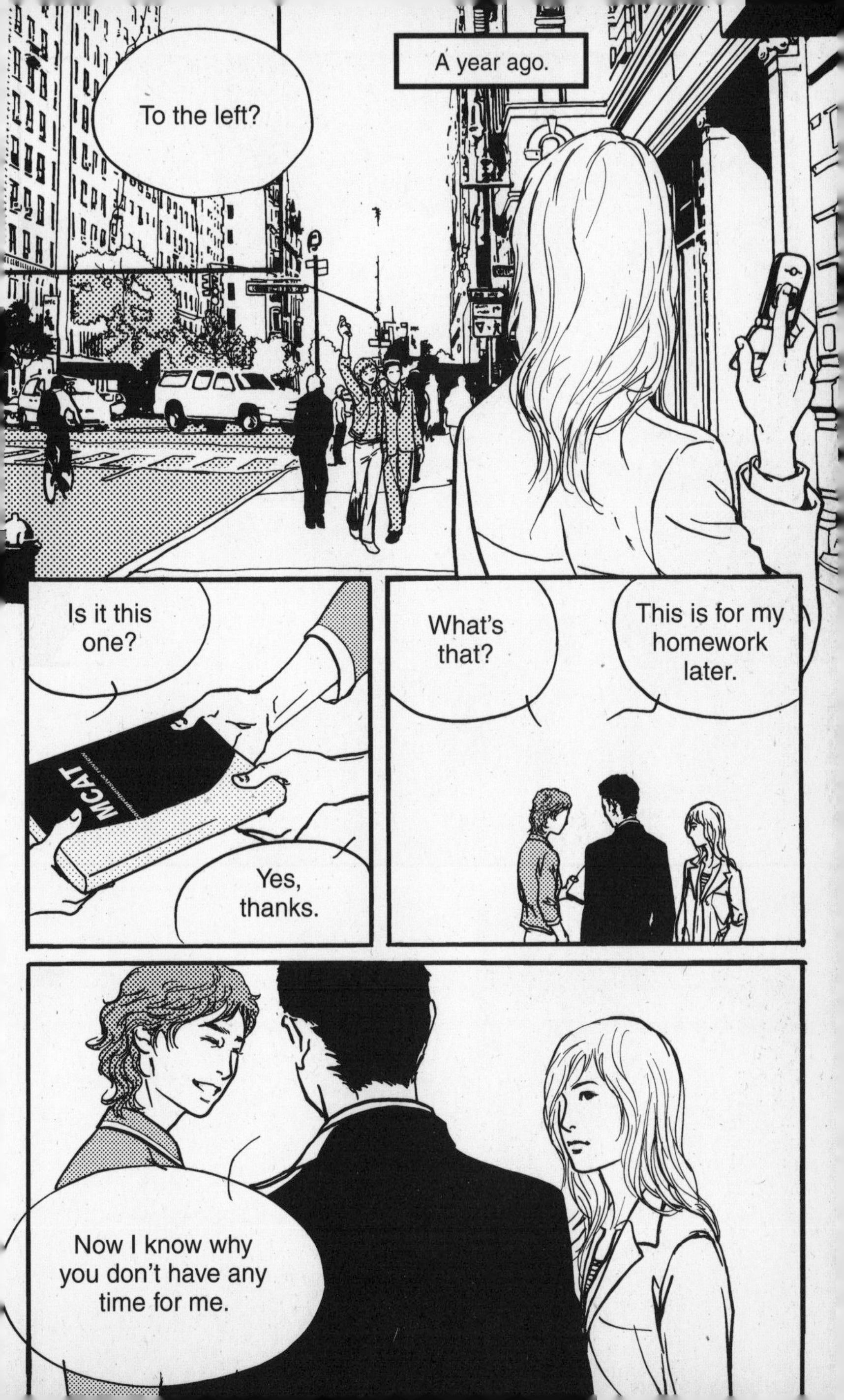
A year ago.
To the left?
Is it this one?
MCAT
Yes, thanks.
What's that?
This is for my homework later.
Now I know why you don't have any time for me.

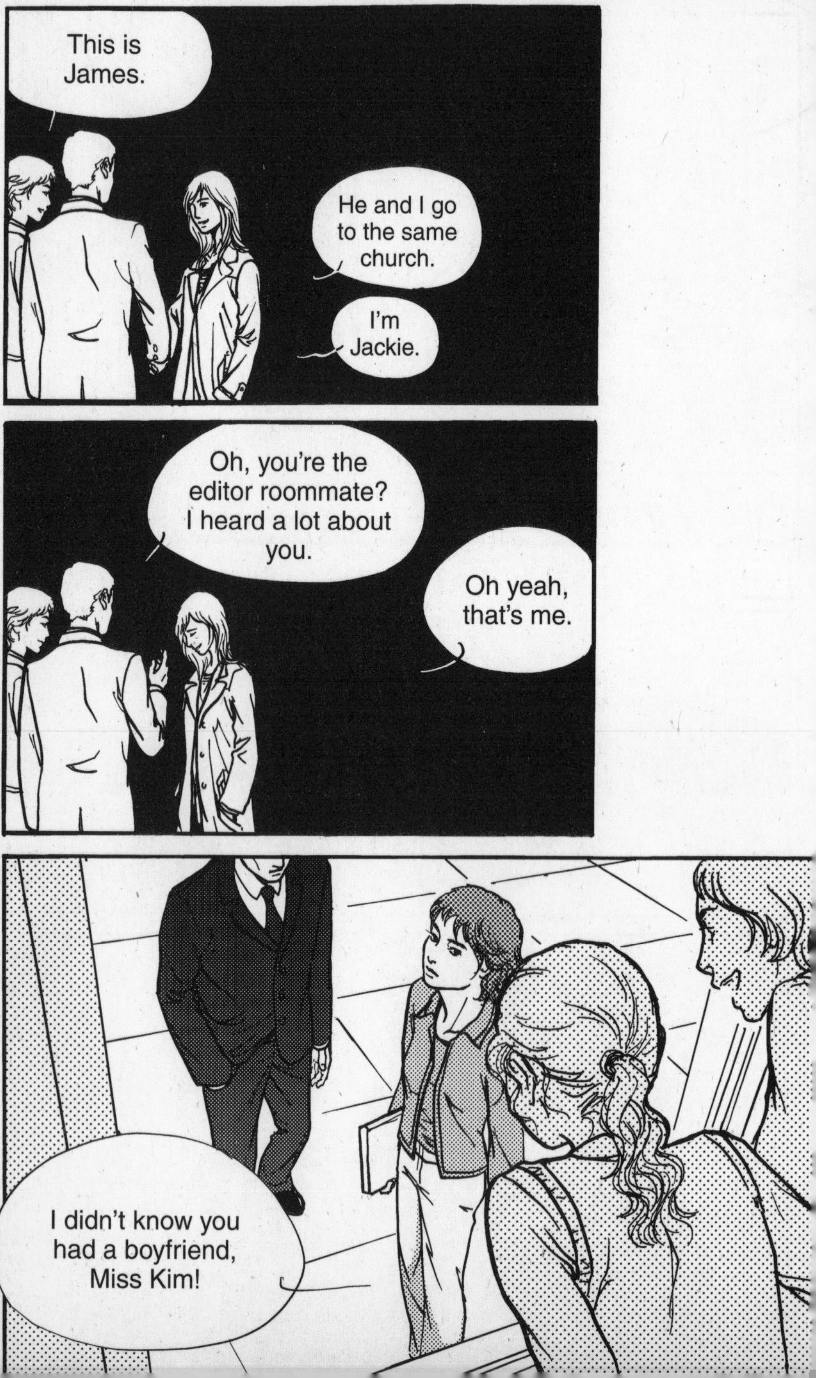
This is James.
He and I go to the same church.
I'm Jackie.
Oh, you're the editor roommate? I heard a lot about you.
Oh yeah, that's me.
I didn't know you had a boyfriend, Miss Kim!

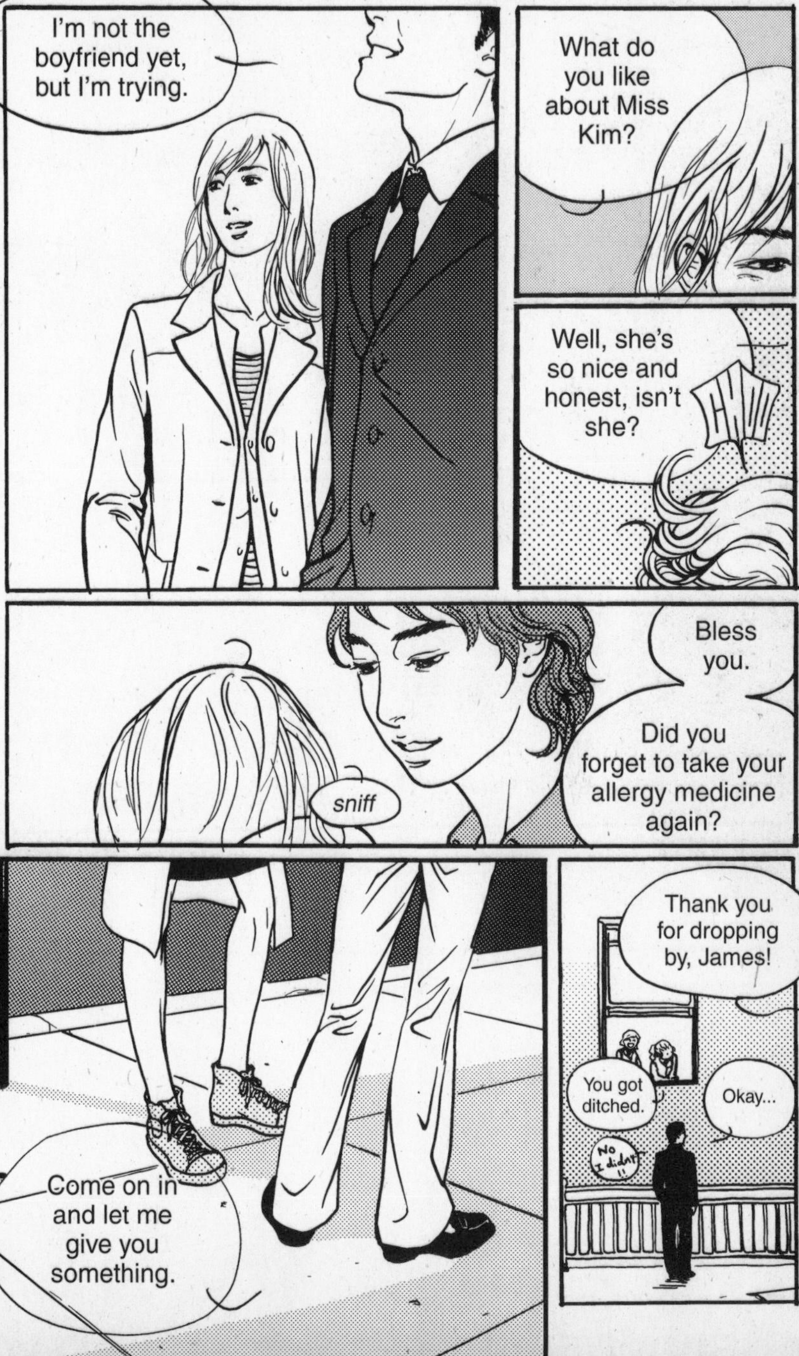

I'm not the boyfriend yet, but I'm trying.
What do you like about Miss Kim?
Well, she's so nice and honest, isn't she?
Bless you.
sniff
Did you forget to take your allergy medicine again?
Come on in and let me give you something.
Thank you for dropping by, James!
You got ditched.
Okay...
No I didn't!!

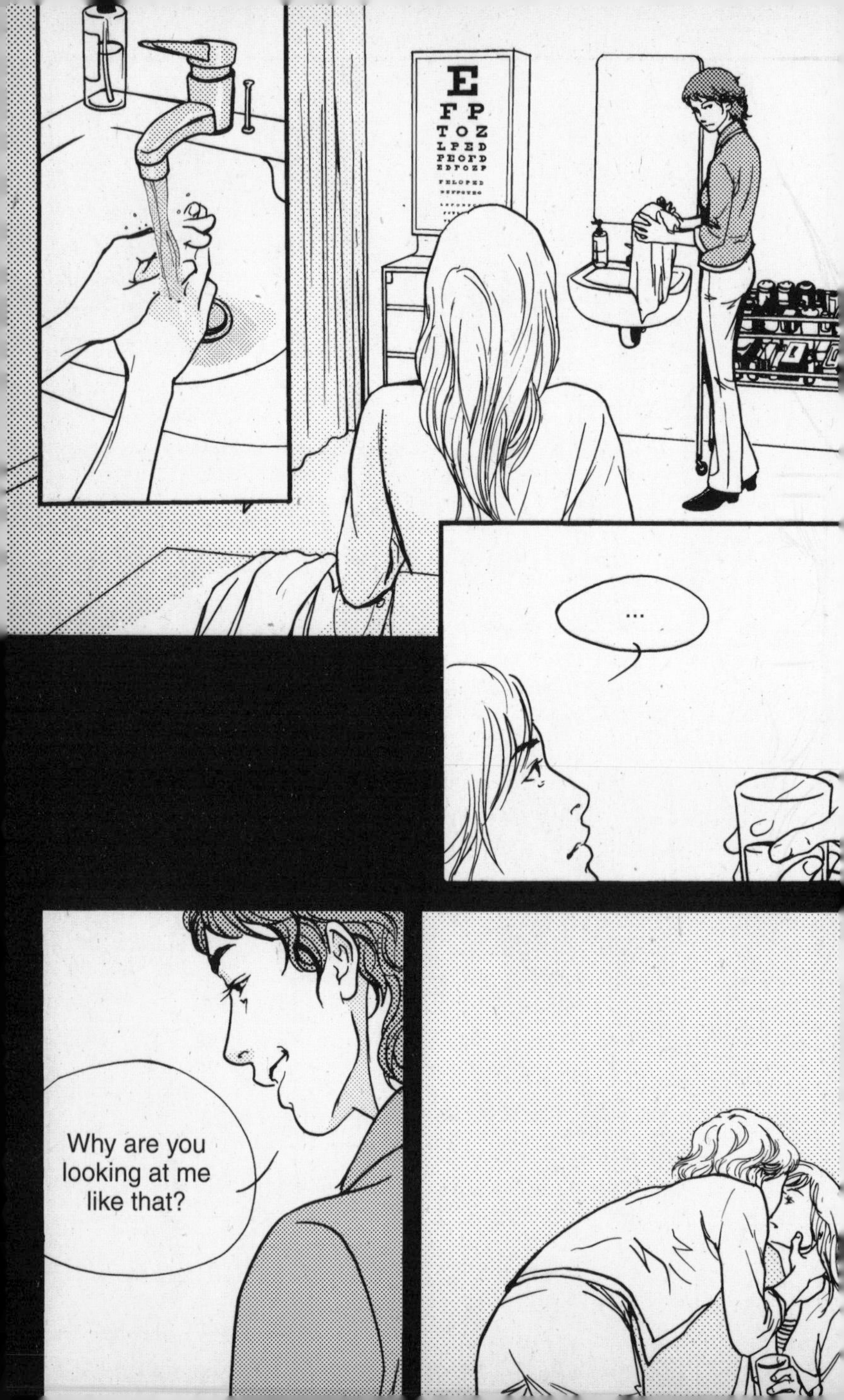
E
F P
T O Z
L P E D
...
Why are you looking at me like that?

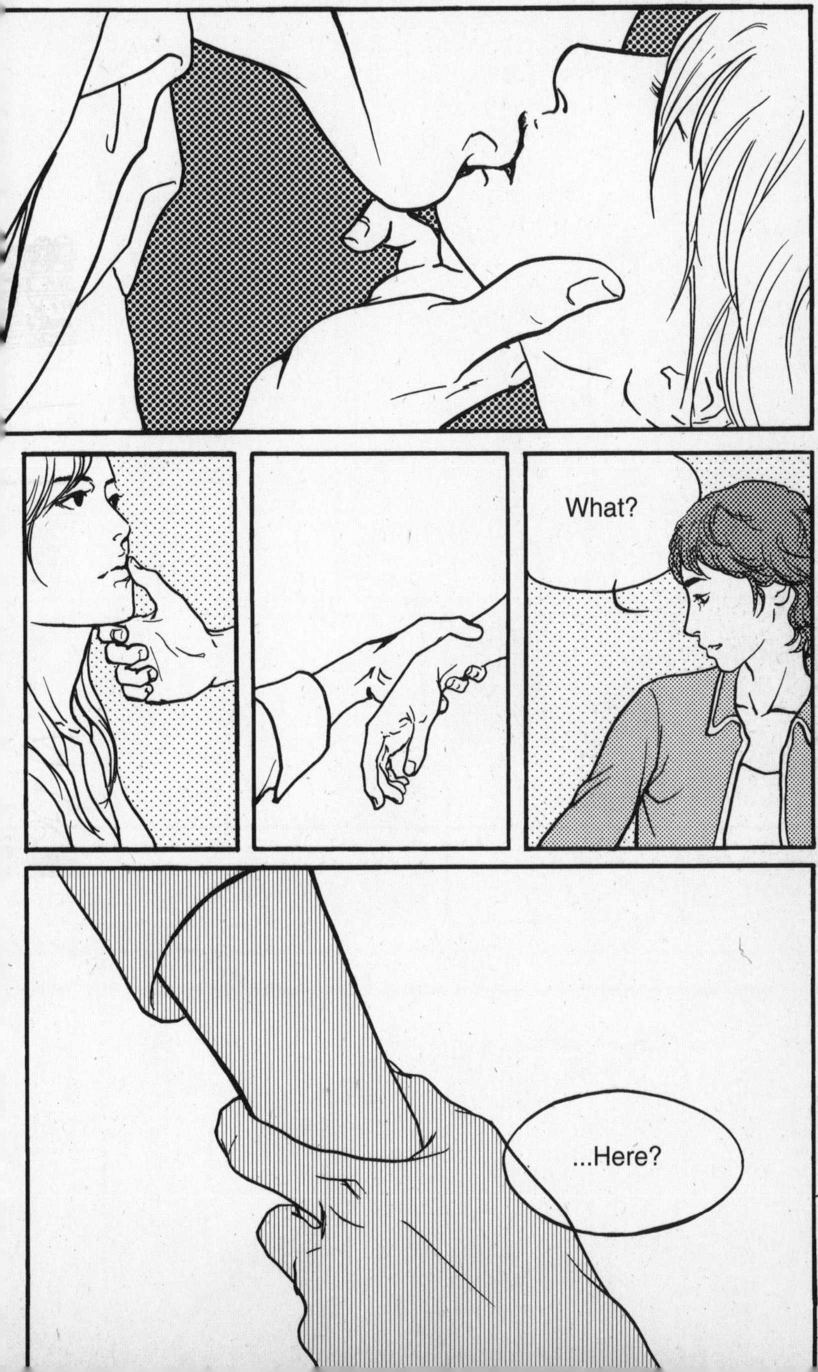
What?
...Here?

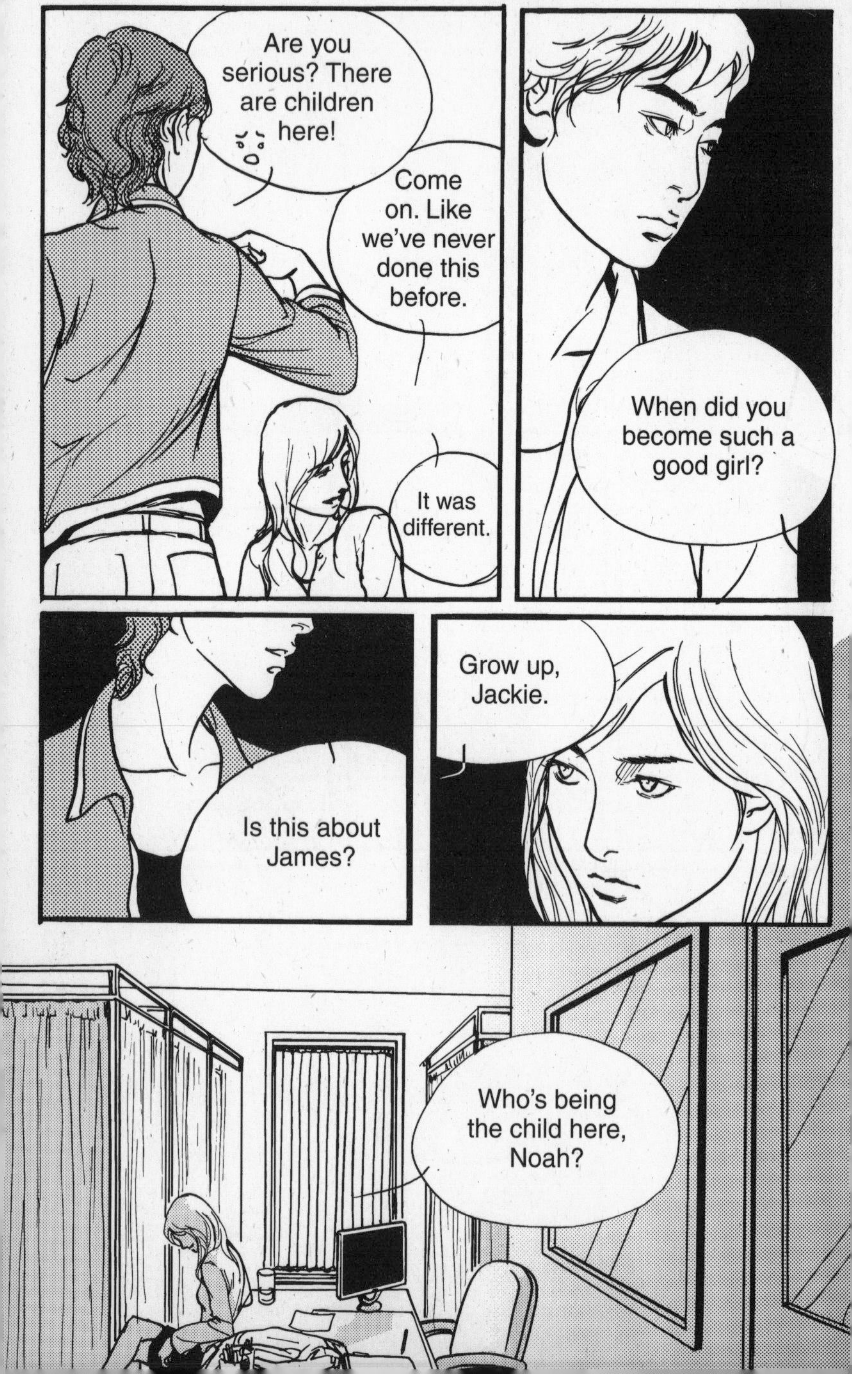
Are you serious? There are children here!
Come on. Like we've never done this before.
It was different.
When did you become such a good girl?
Is this about James?
Grow up, Jackie.
Who's being the child here, Noah?

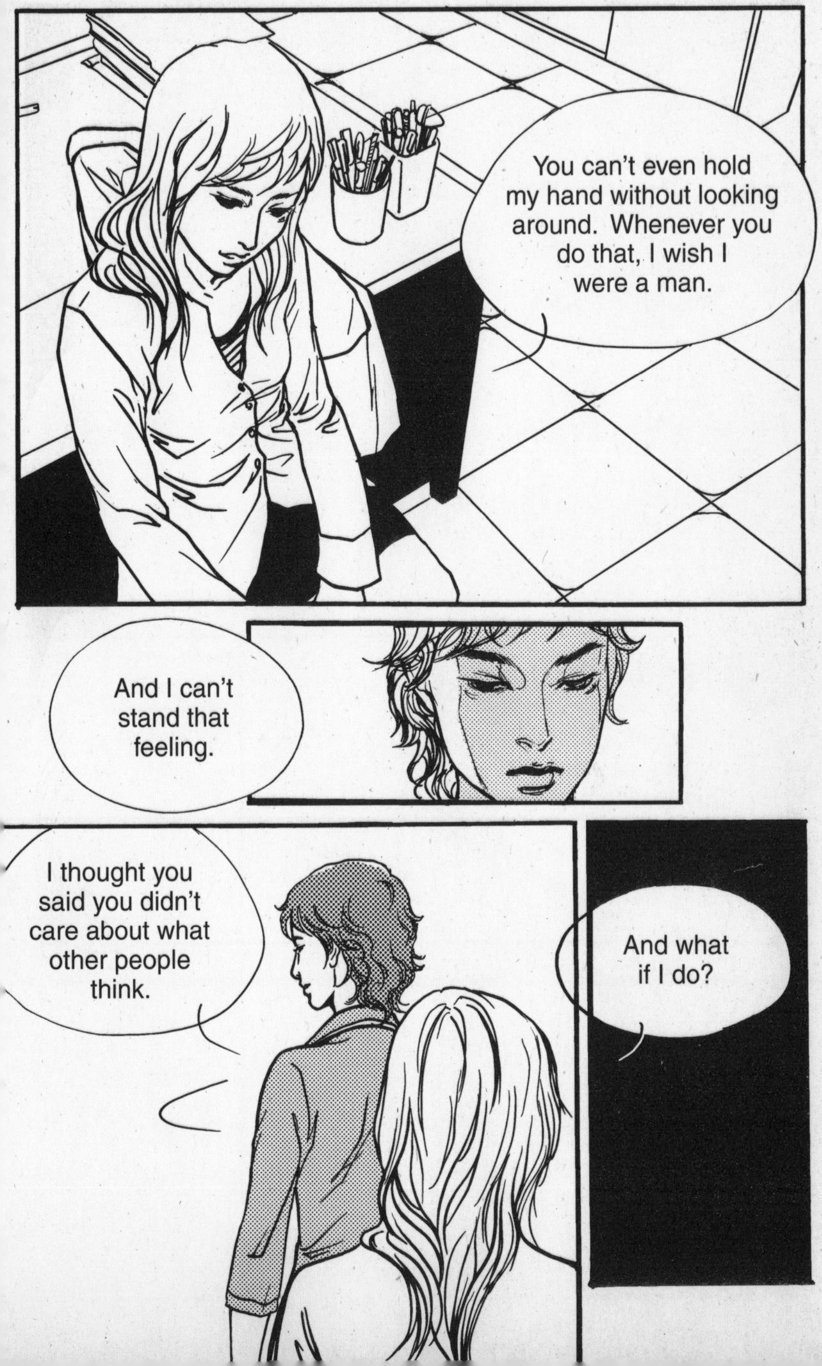
You can't even hold my hand without looking around. Whenever you do that, I wish I were a man.
And I can't stand that feeling.
I thought you said you didn't care about what other people think.
And what if I do?

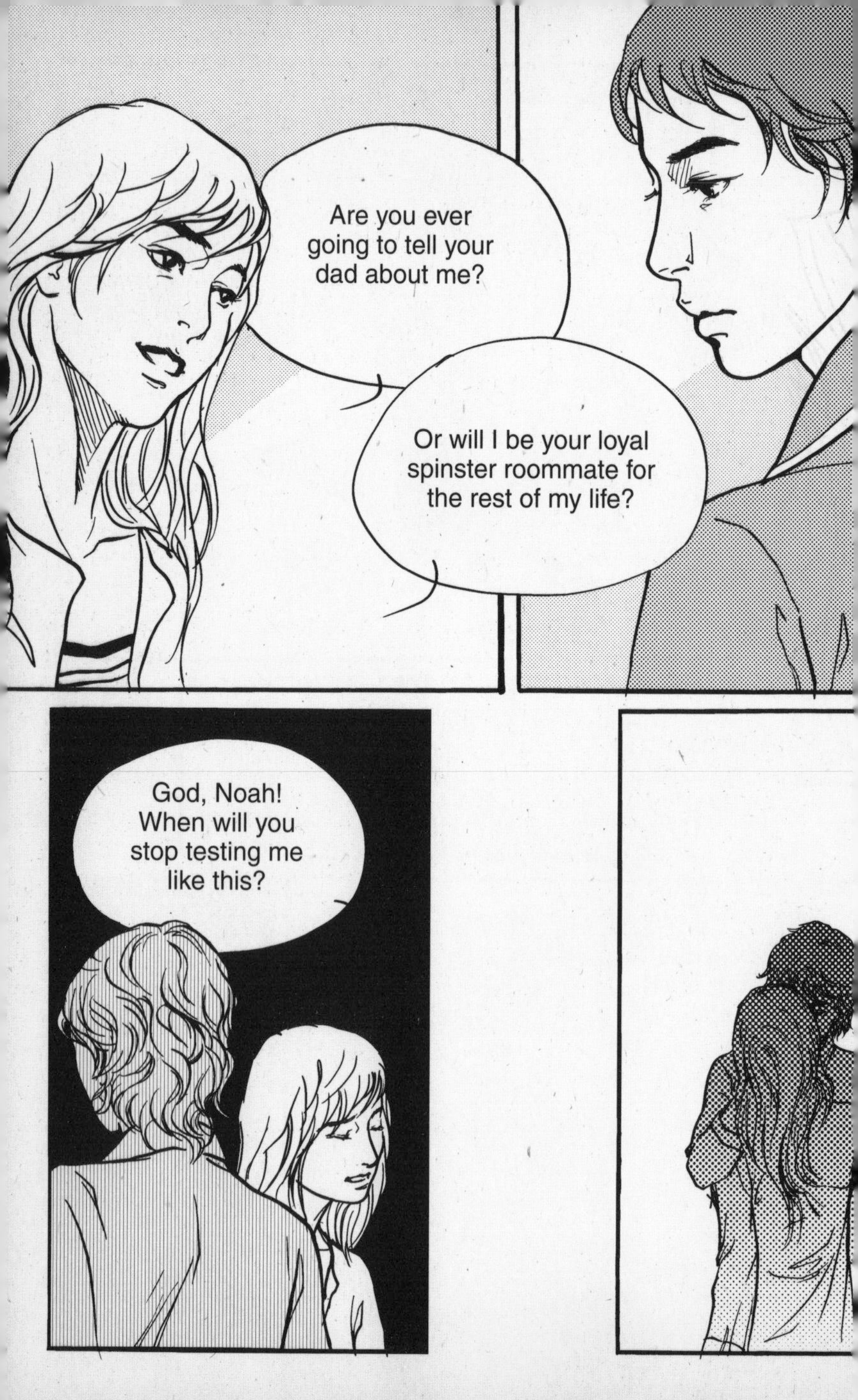
Are you ever going to tell your dad about me?
Or will I be your loyal spinster roommate for the rest of my life?
God, Noah! When will you stop testing me like this?

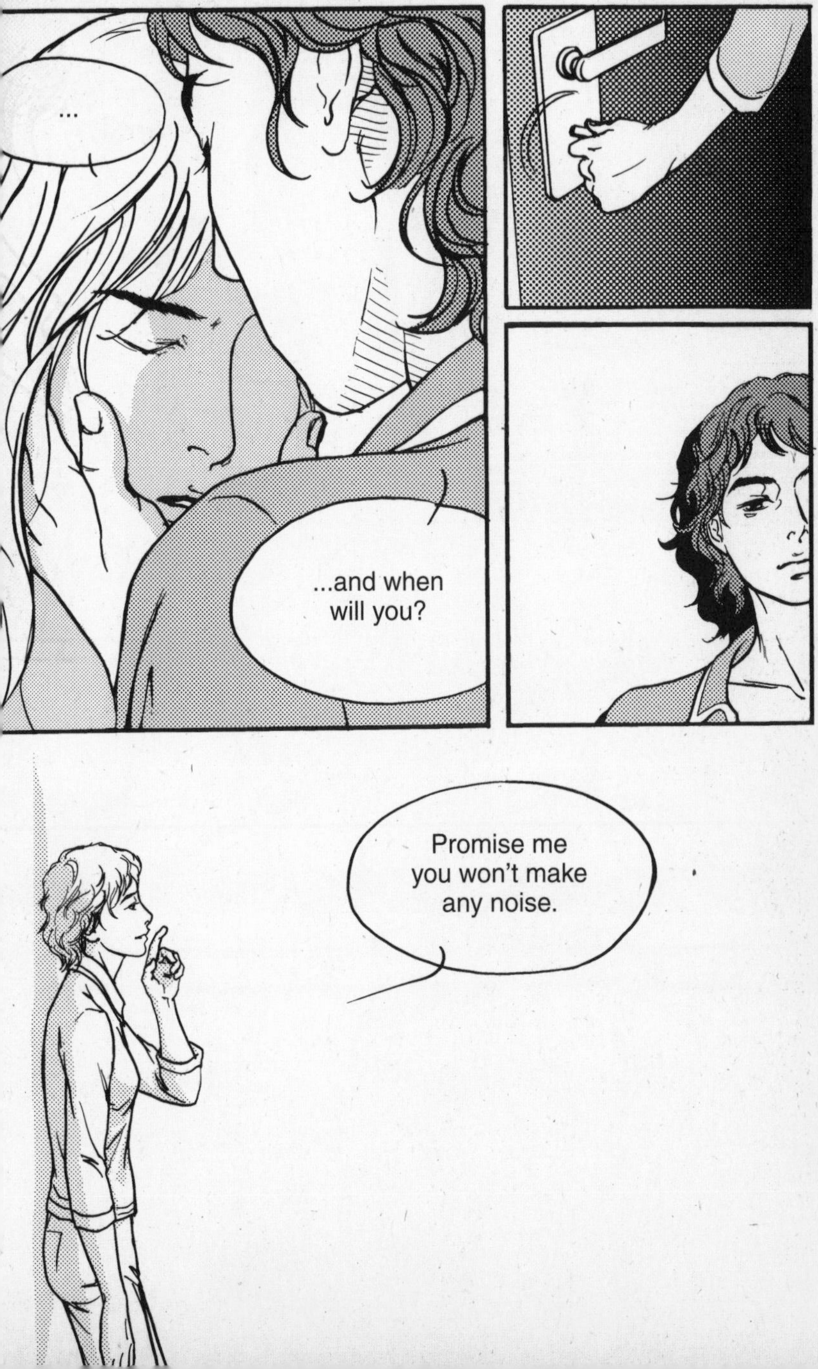
...
...and when will you?
Promise me you won't make any noise.

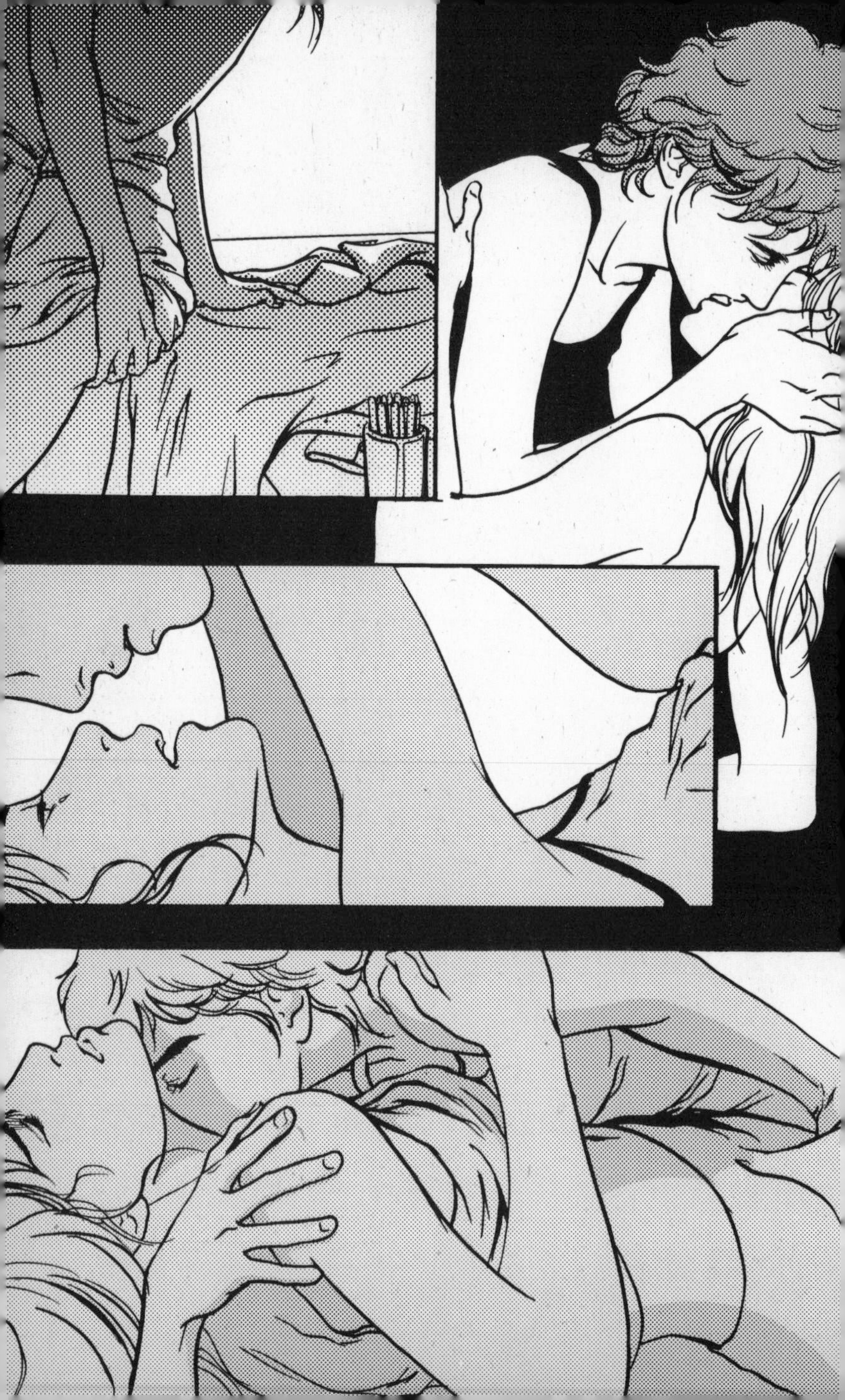

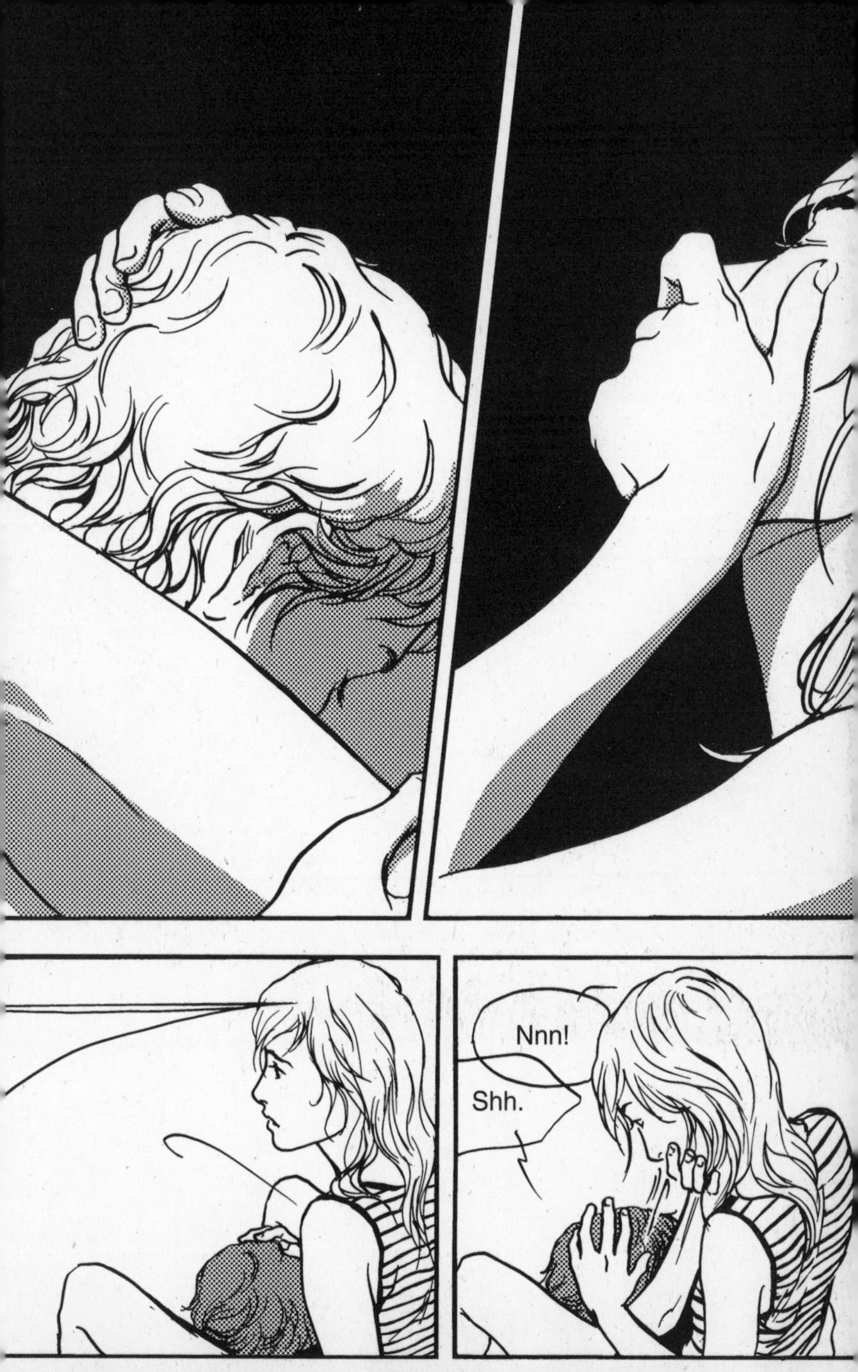
Nnn!
Shh.

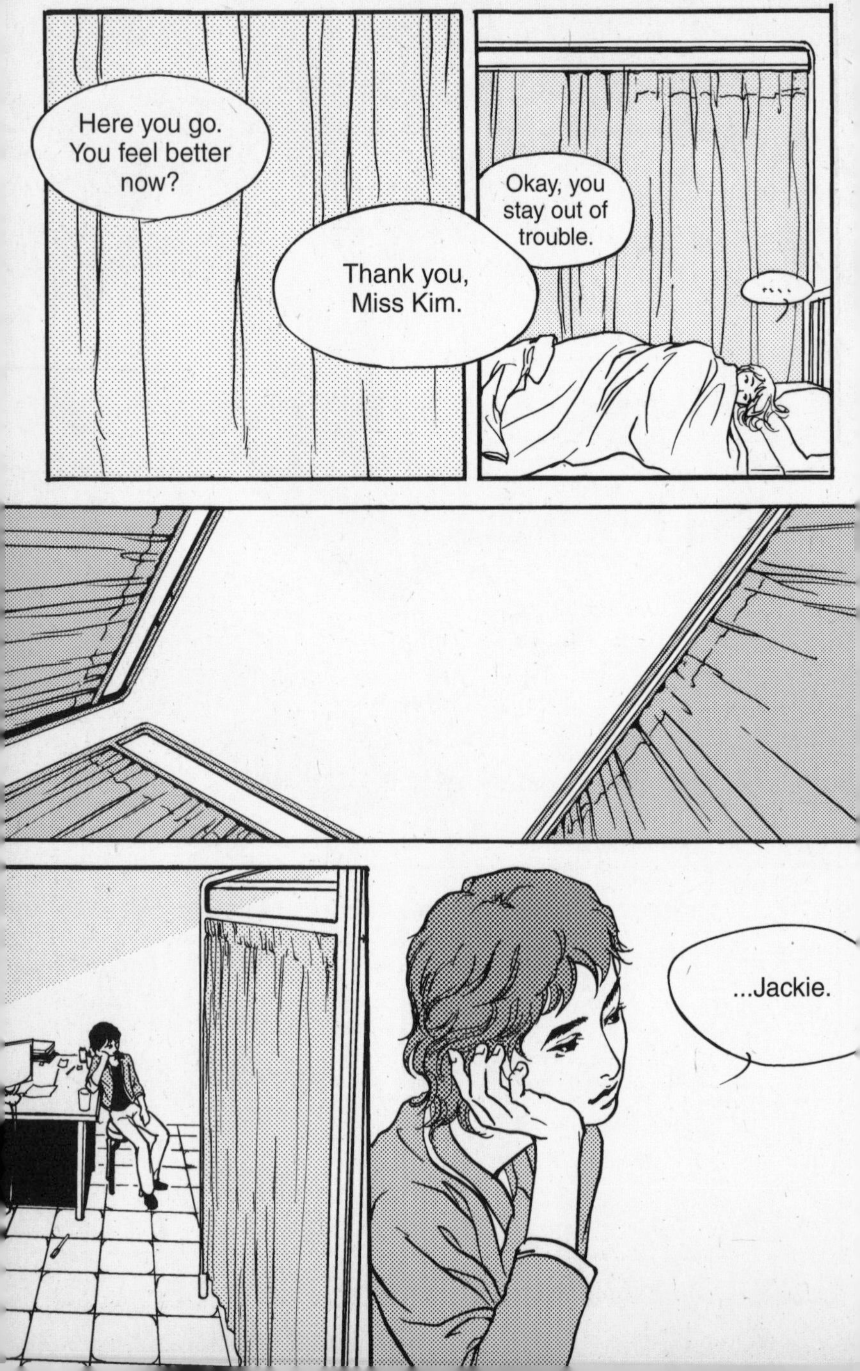
Here you go. You feel better now?
Thank you, Miss Kim.
Okay, you stay out of trouble.
...
...Jackie.

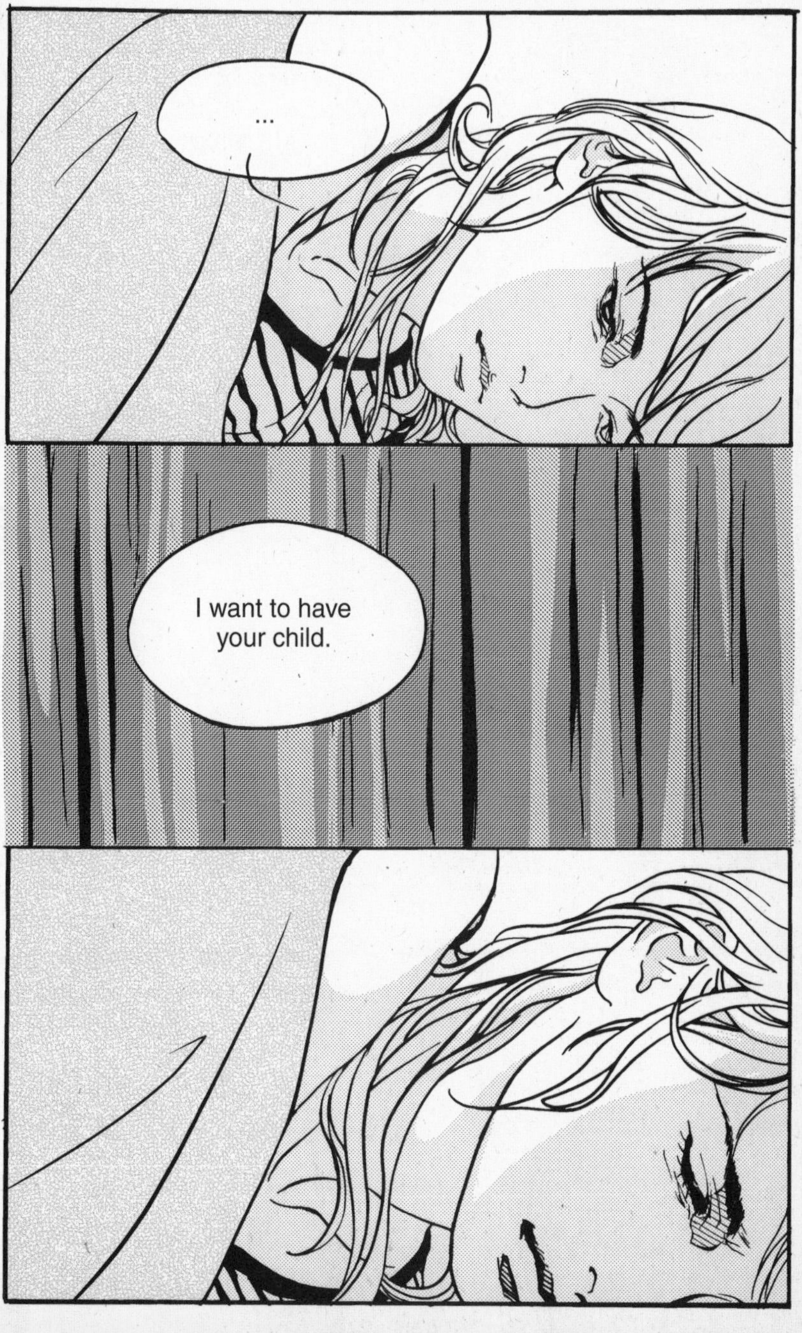
...
I want to have your child.

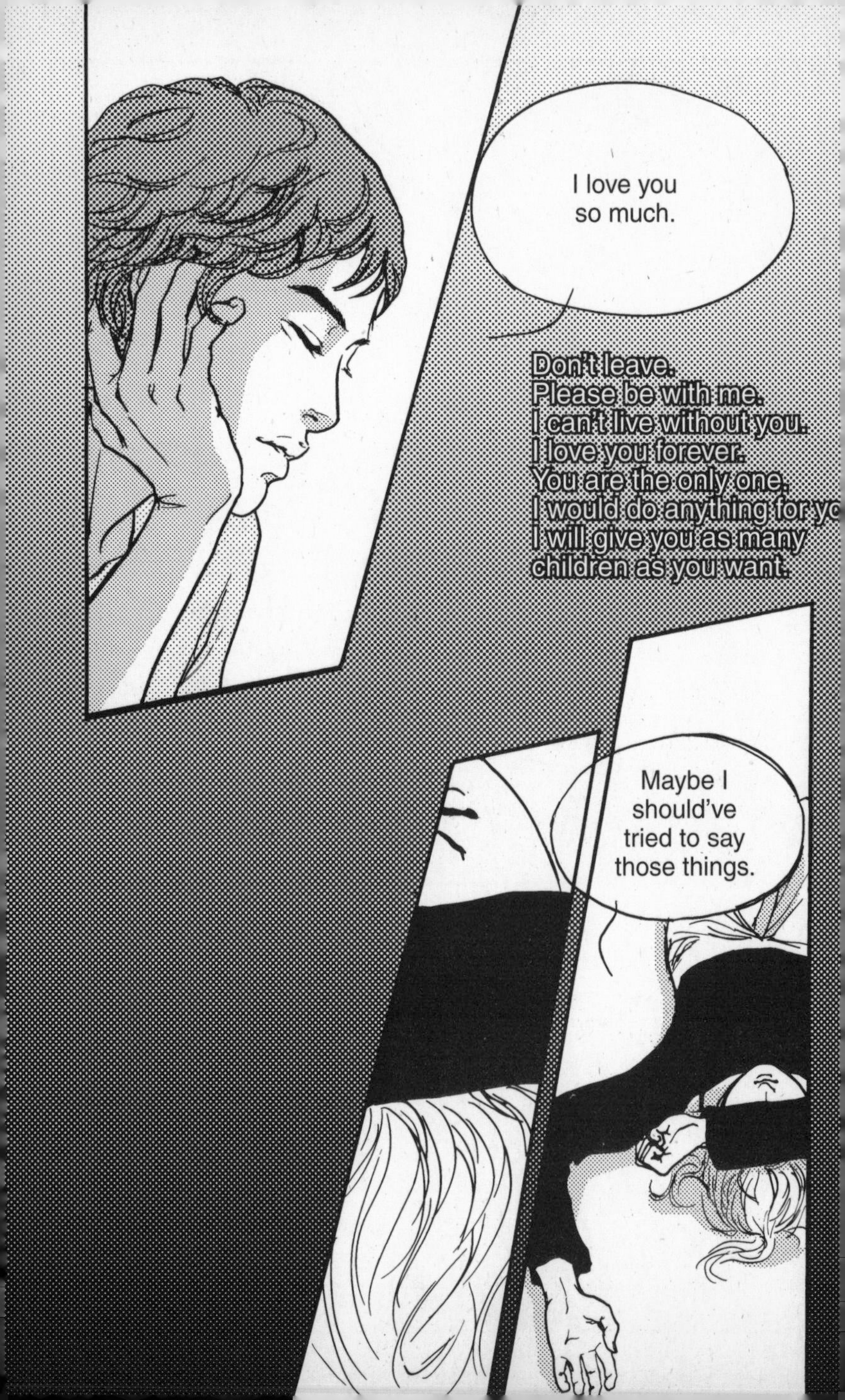
I love you so much.
Don't leave.
Please be with me.
I can't live without you.
I love you forever.
You are the only one.
I would do anything for yo
I will give you as many children as you want.
Maybe I should've tried to say those things.

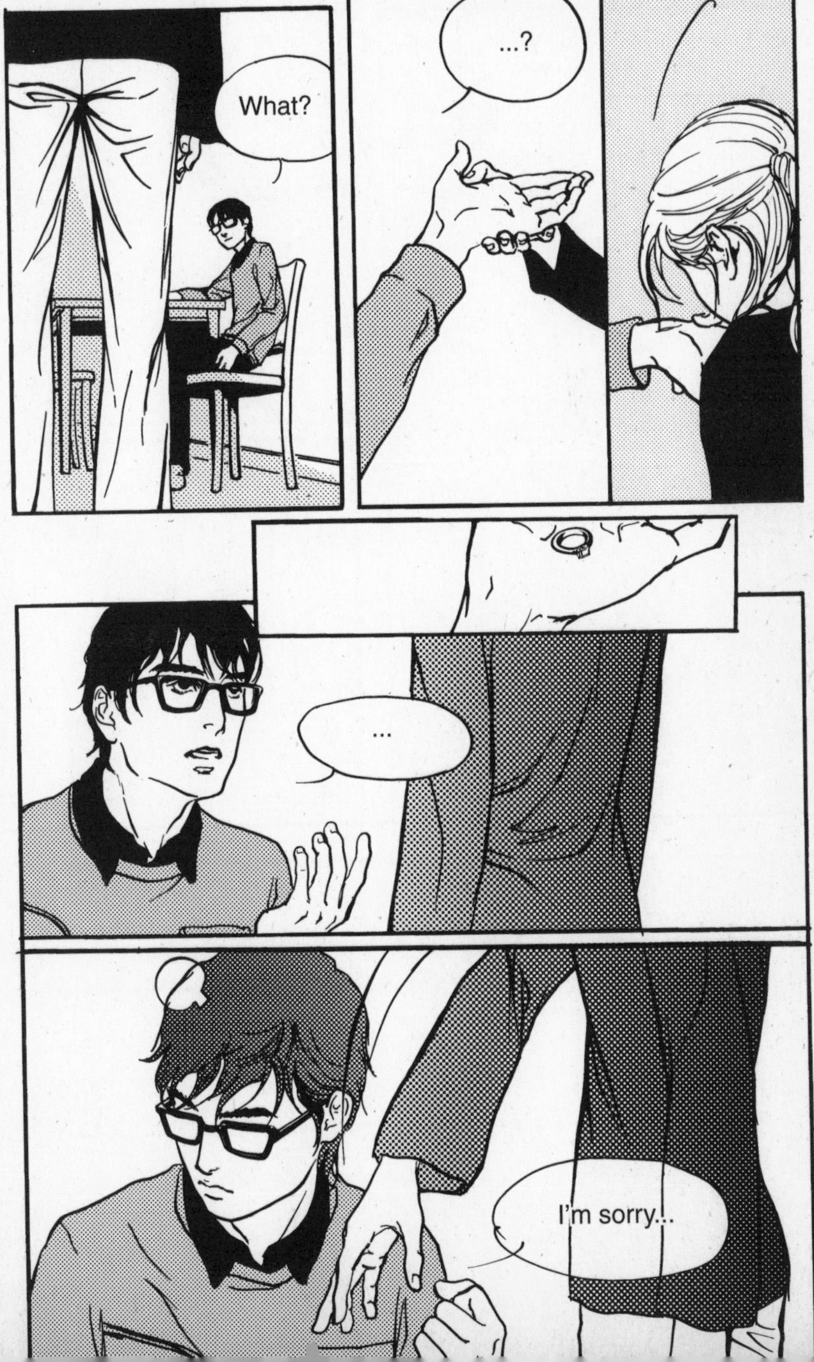
What?
...?
...
I'm sorry...

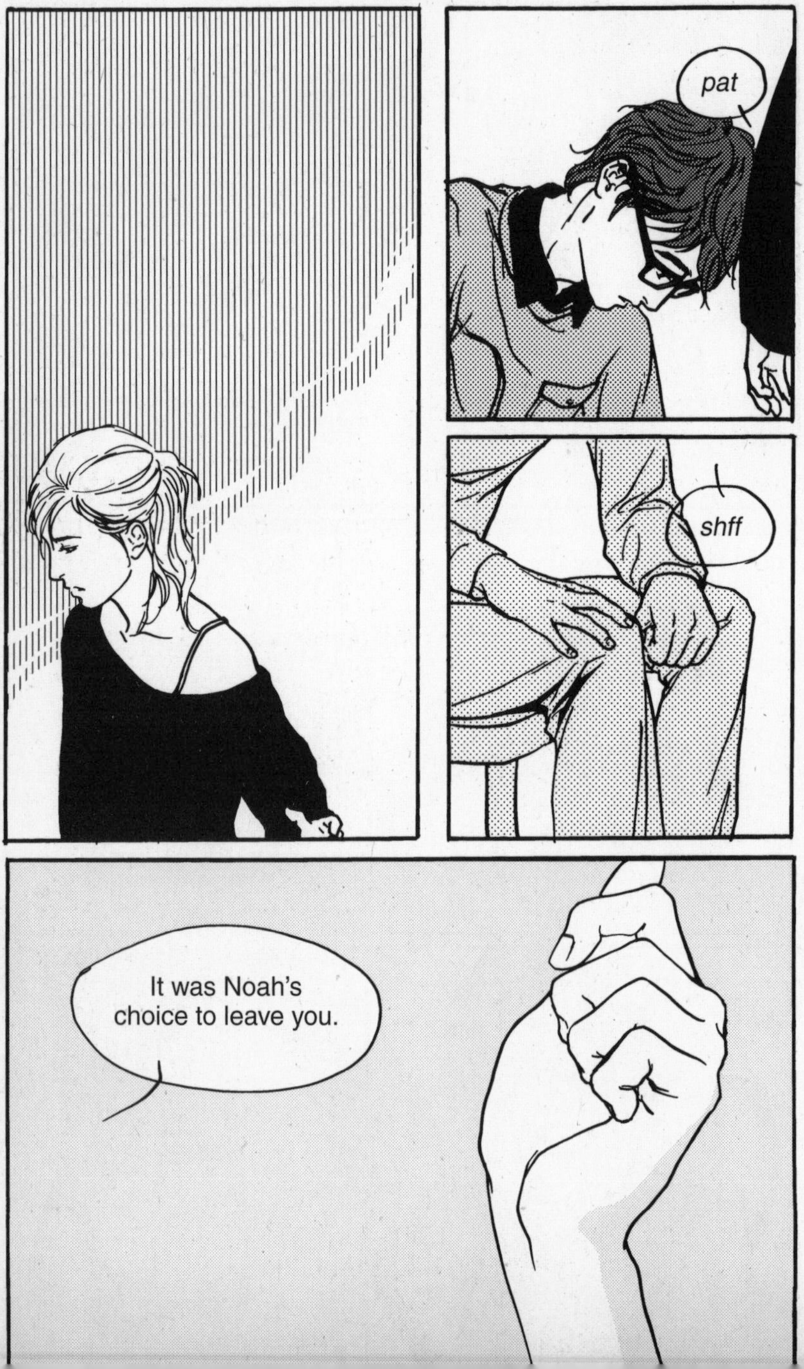
pat
shff
It was Noah's choice to leave you.

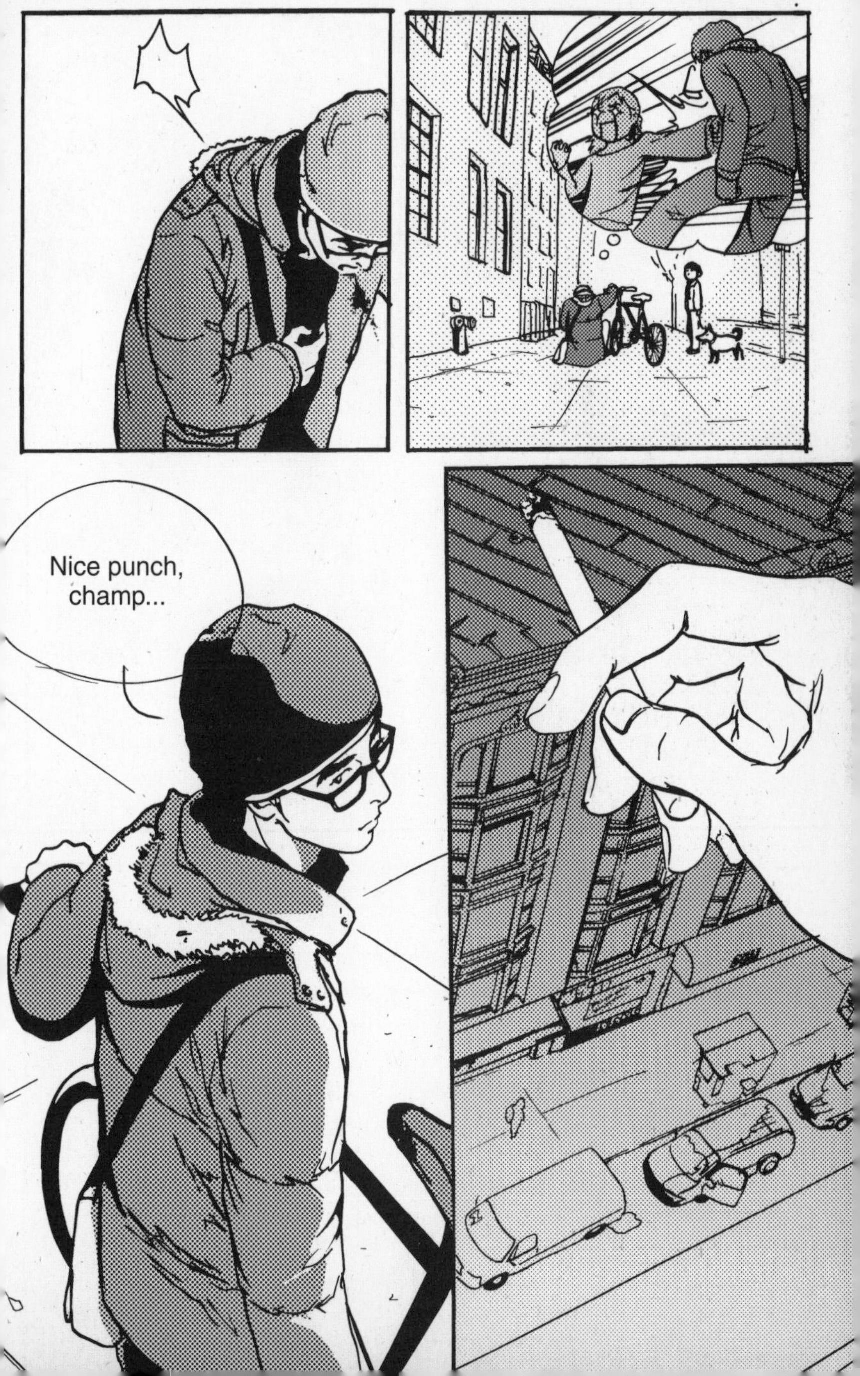
Nice punch, champ...

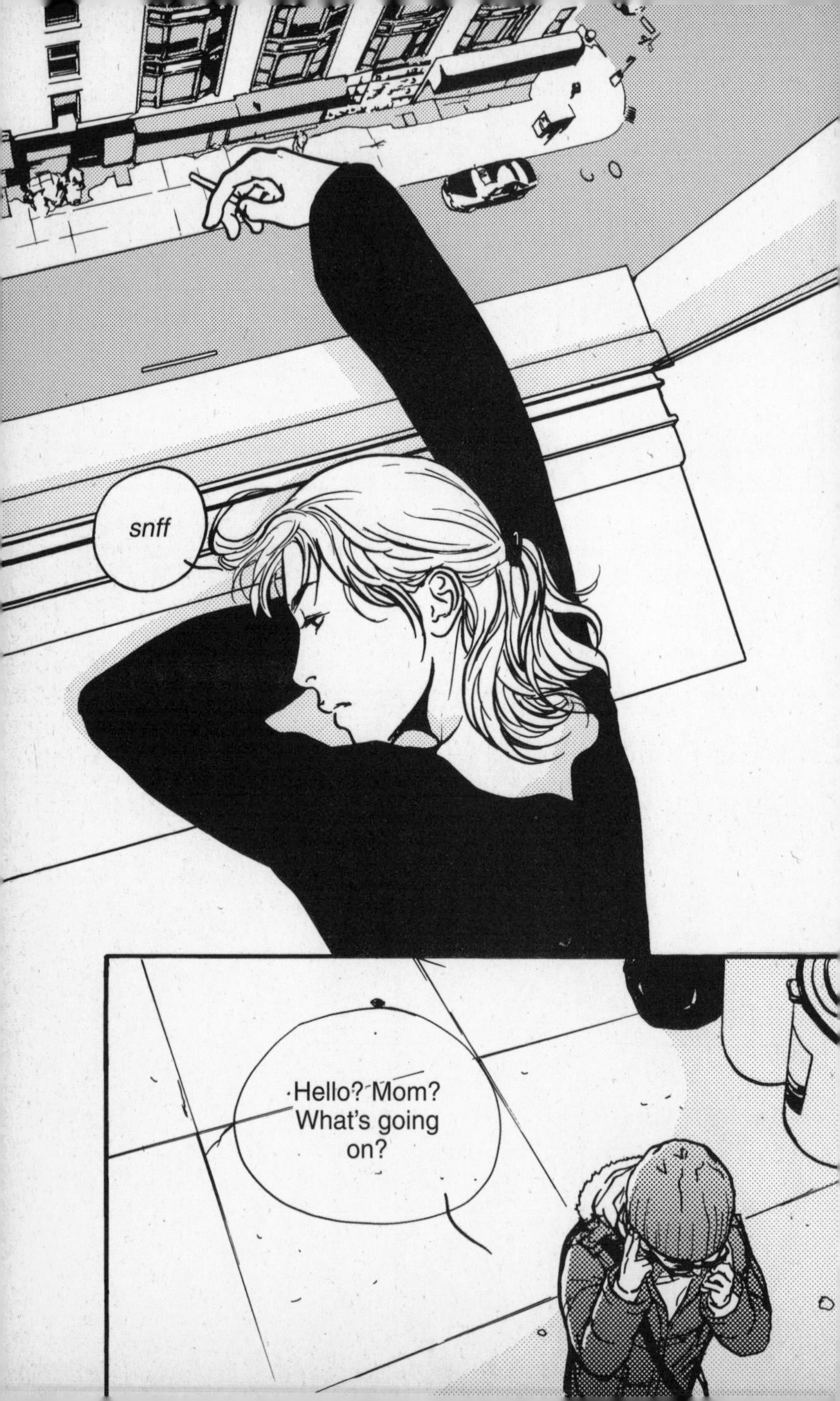
snff
Hello? Mom? What's going on?

Nick, please...

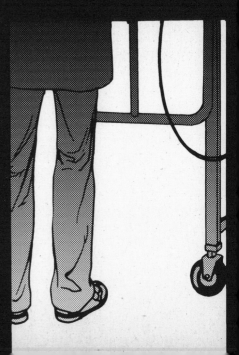

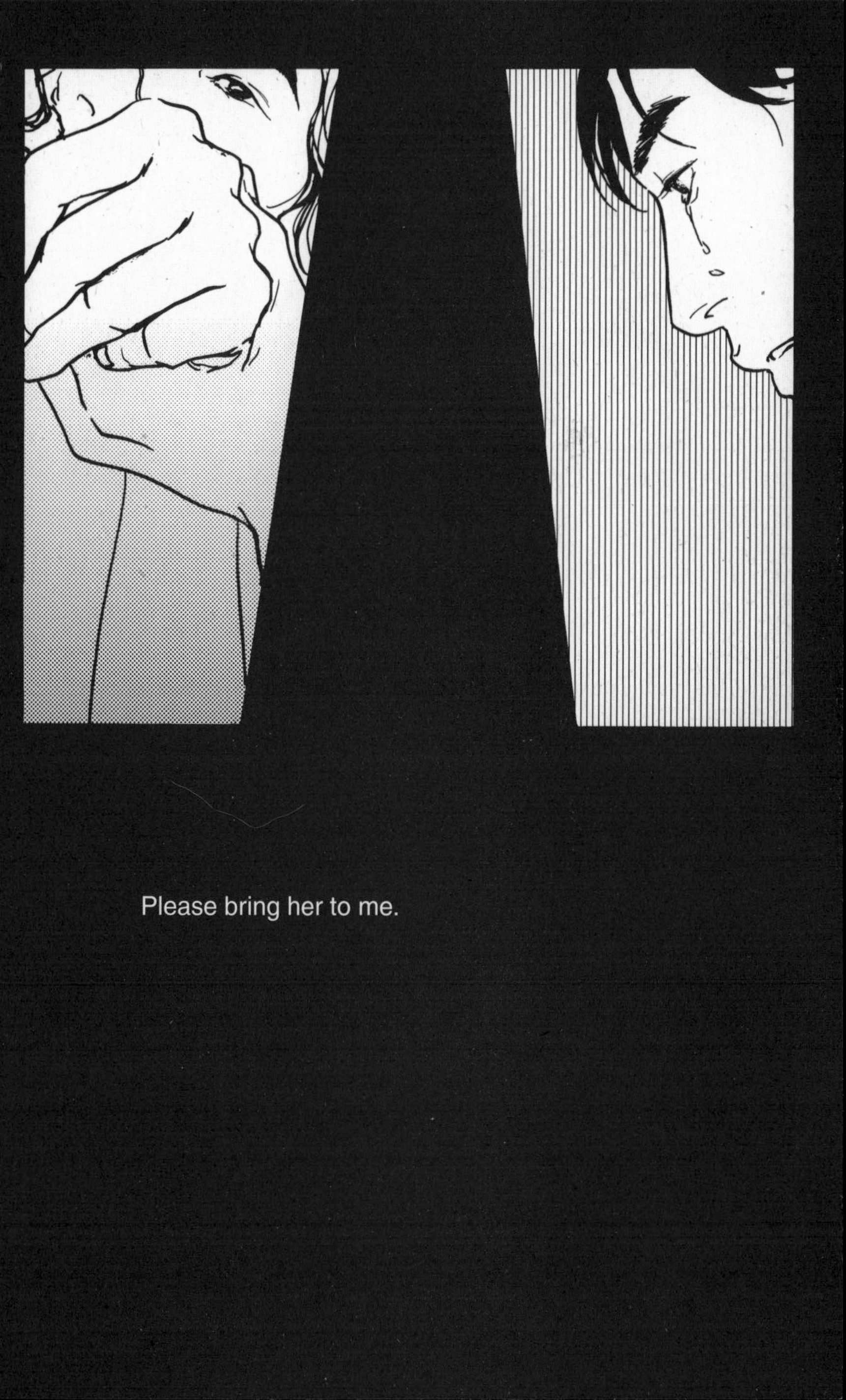
Please bring her to me.

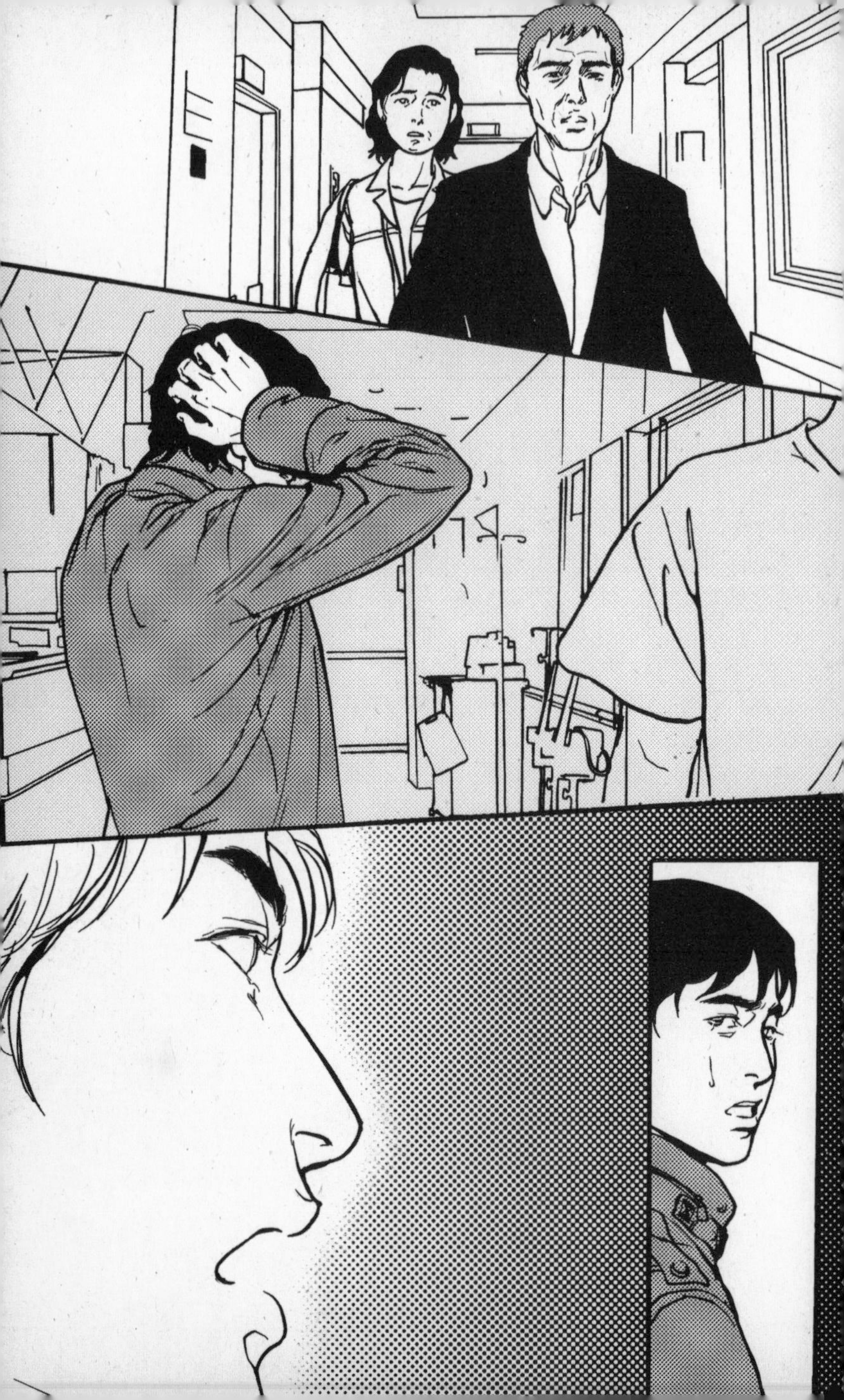

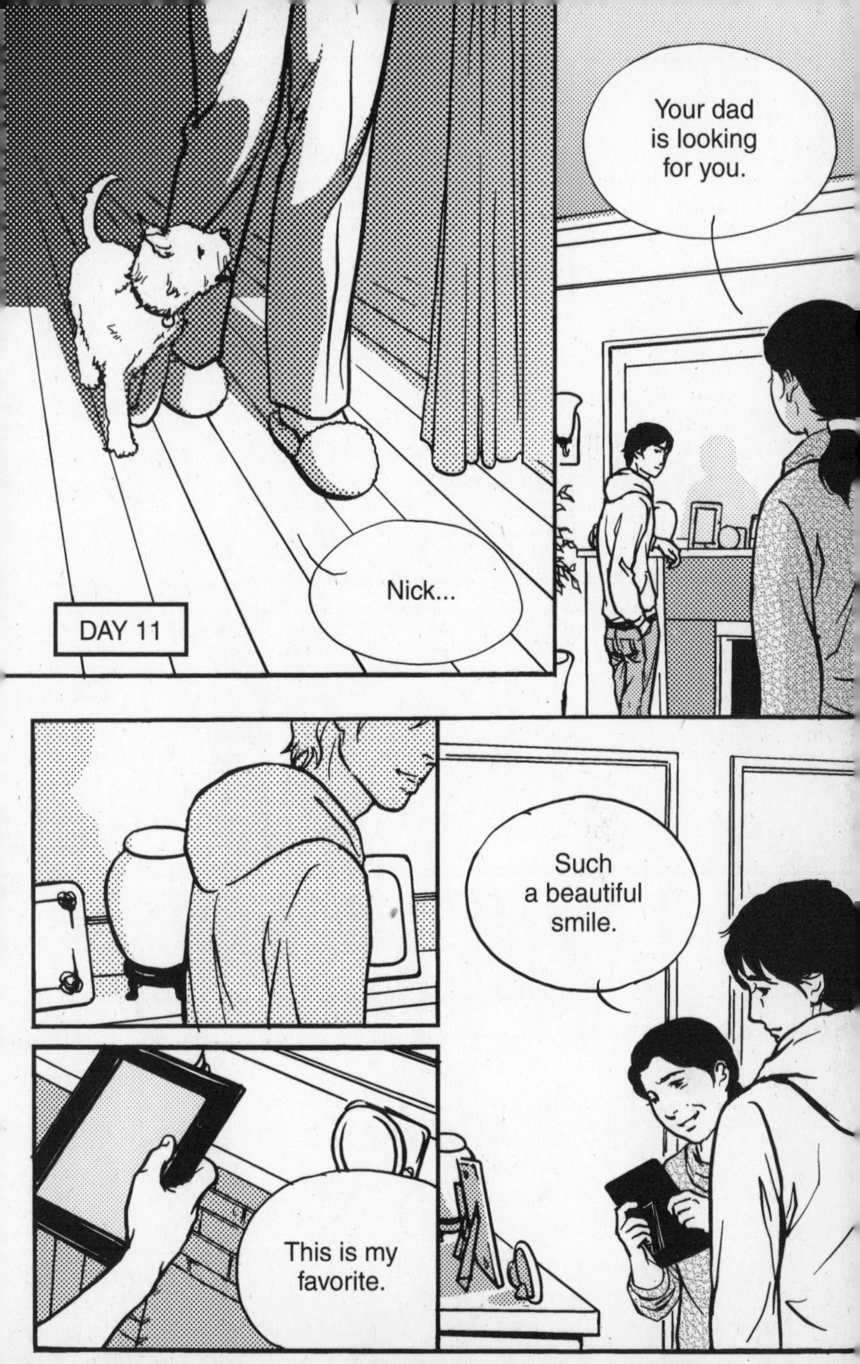
DAY 11
Nick...
Your dad is looking for you.
Such a beautiful smile.
This is my favorite.

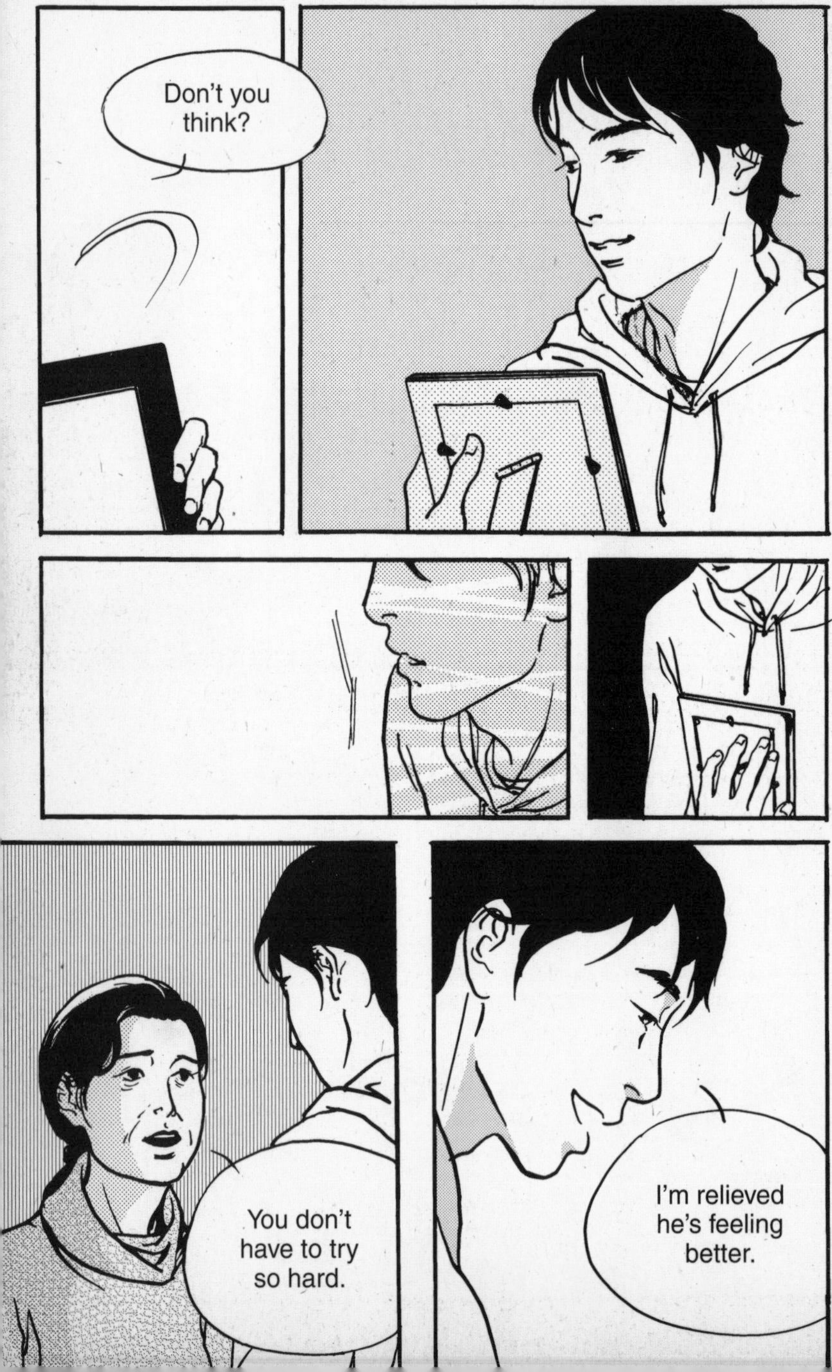
Don't you think?
You don't have to try so hard.
I'm relieved he's feeling better.

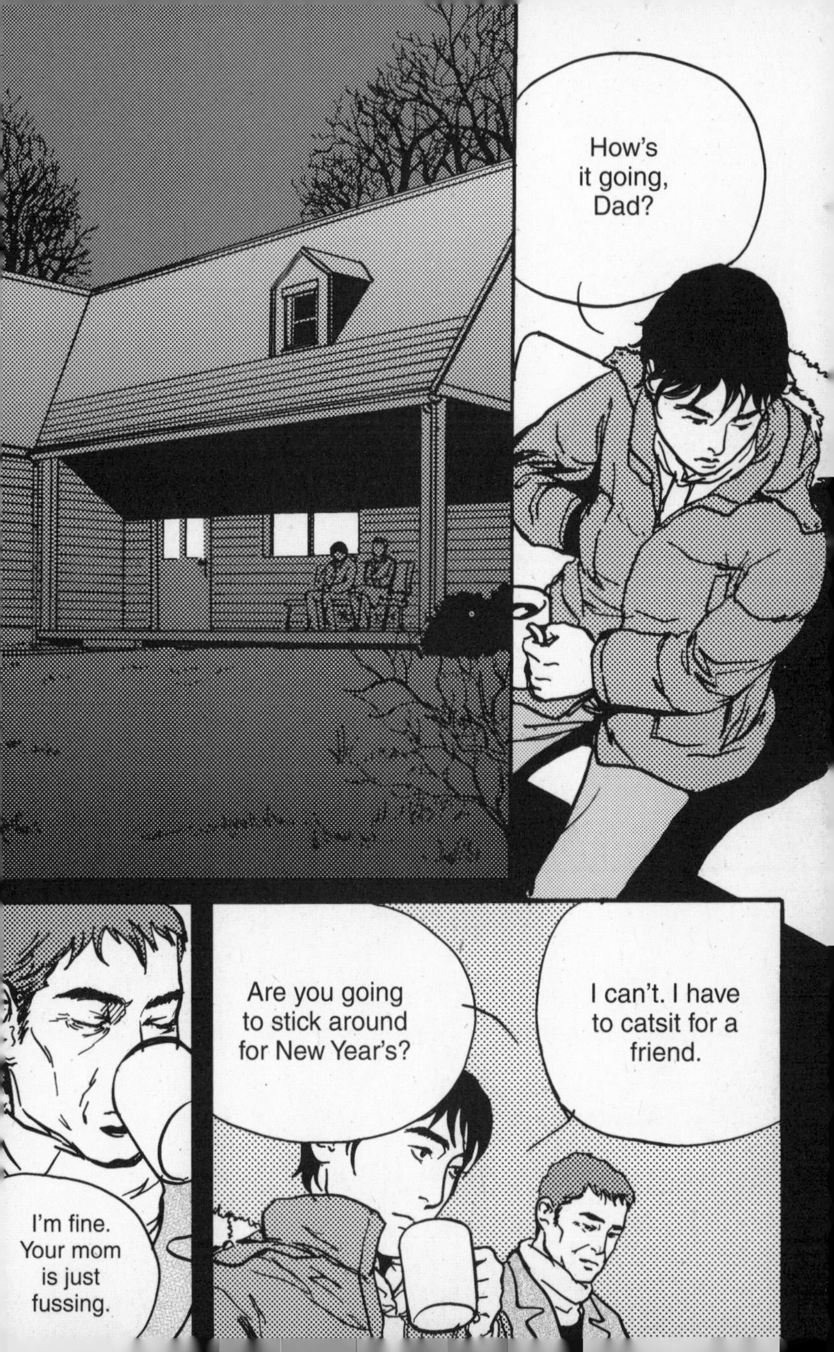
How's it going, Dad?
I'm fine. Your mom is just fussing.
Are you going to stick around for New Year's?
I can't. I have to catsit for a friend.

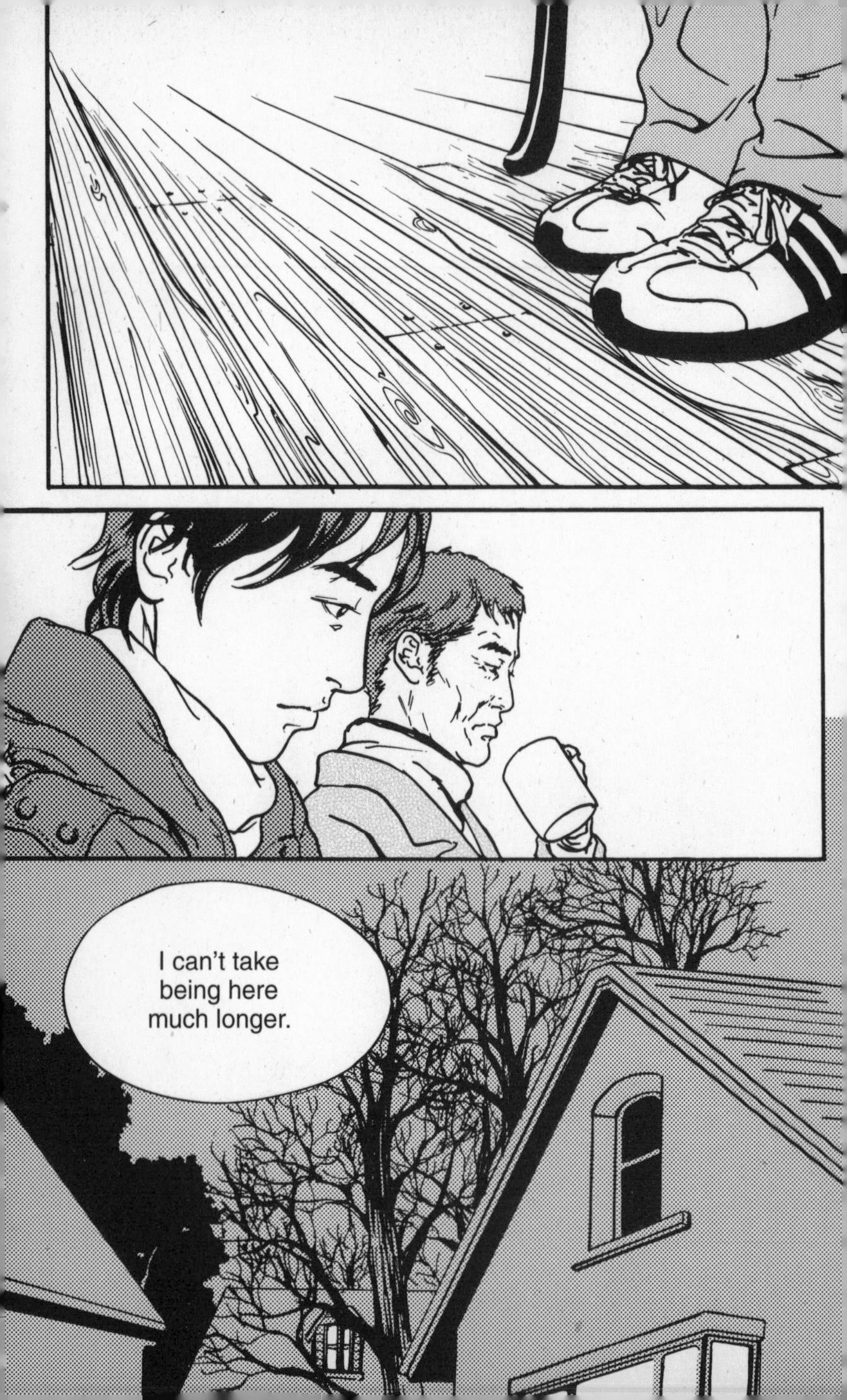
I can't take being here much longer.

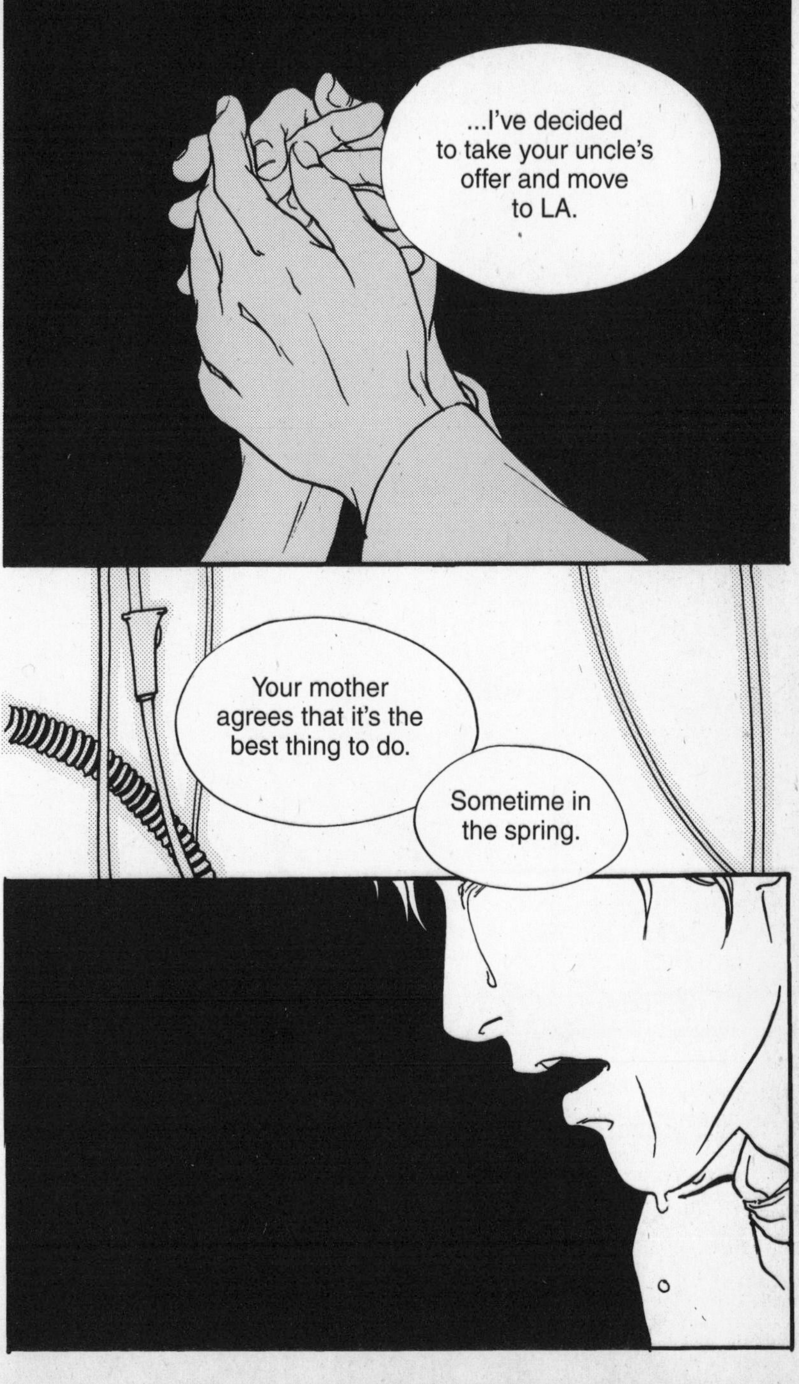
...I've decided to take your uncle's offer and move to LA.
Your mother agrees that it's the best thing to do.
Sometime in the spring.

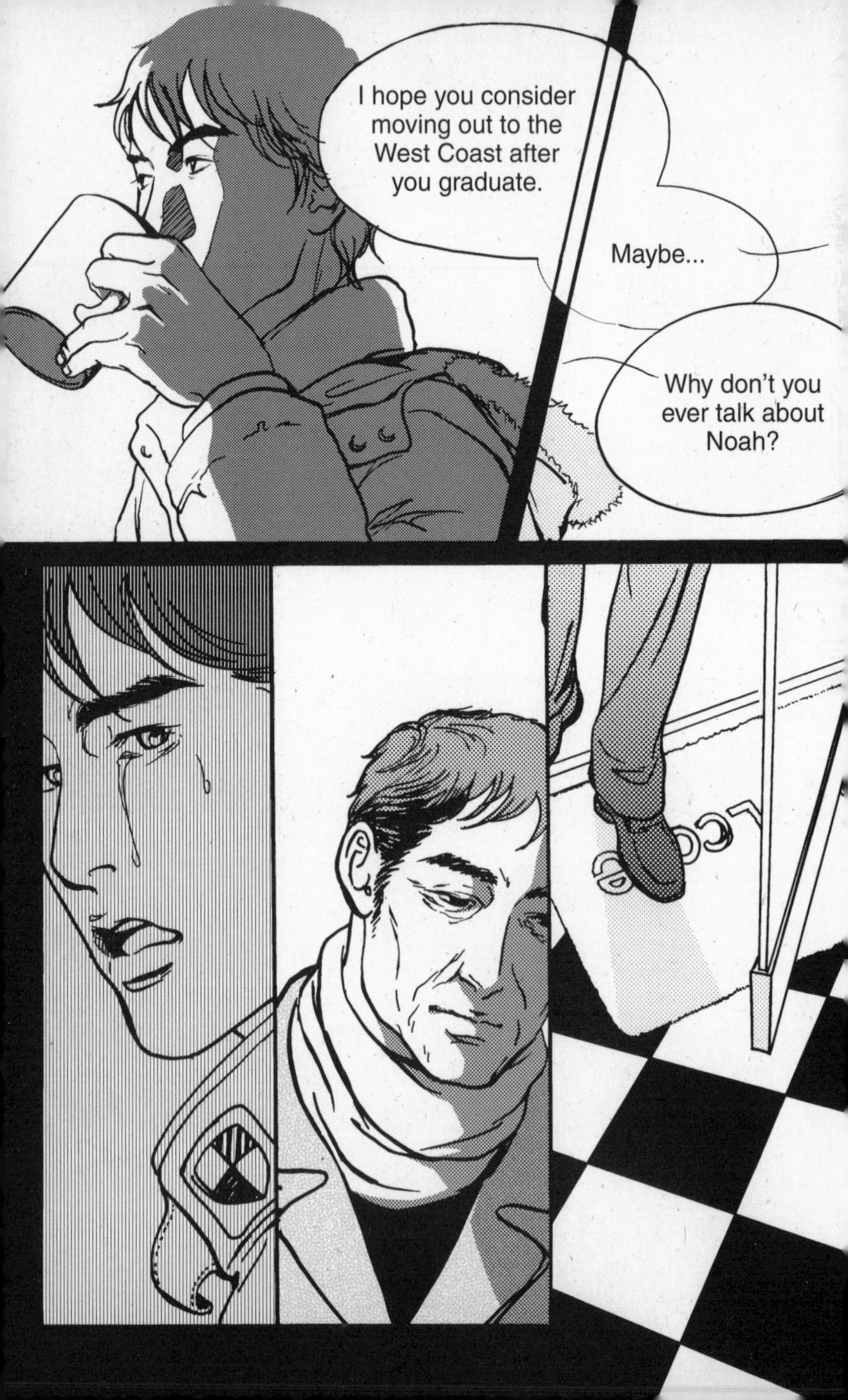
I hope you consider moving out to the West Coast after you graduate.
Maybe...
Why don't you ever talk about Noah?

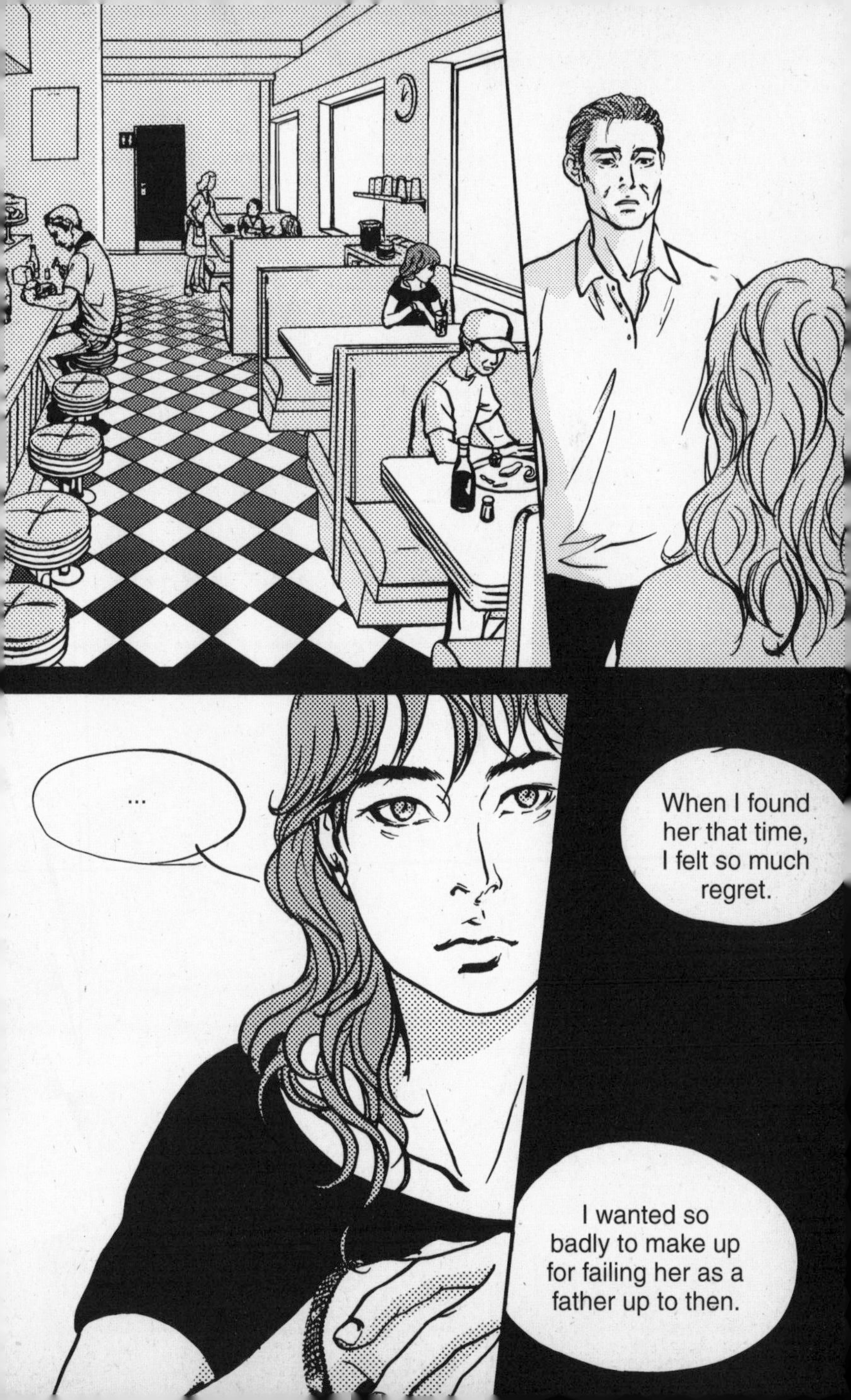
...
When I found her that time, I felt so much regret.
I wanted so badly to make up for failing her as a father up to then.

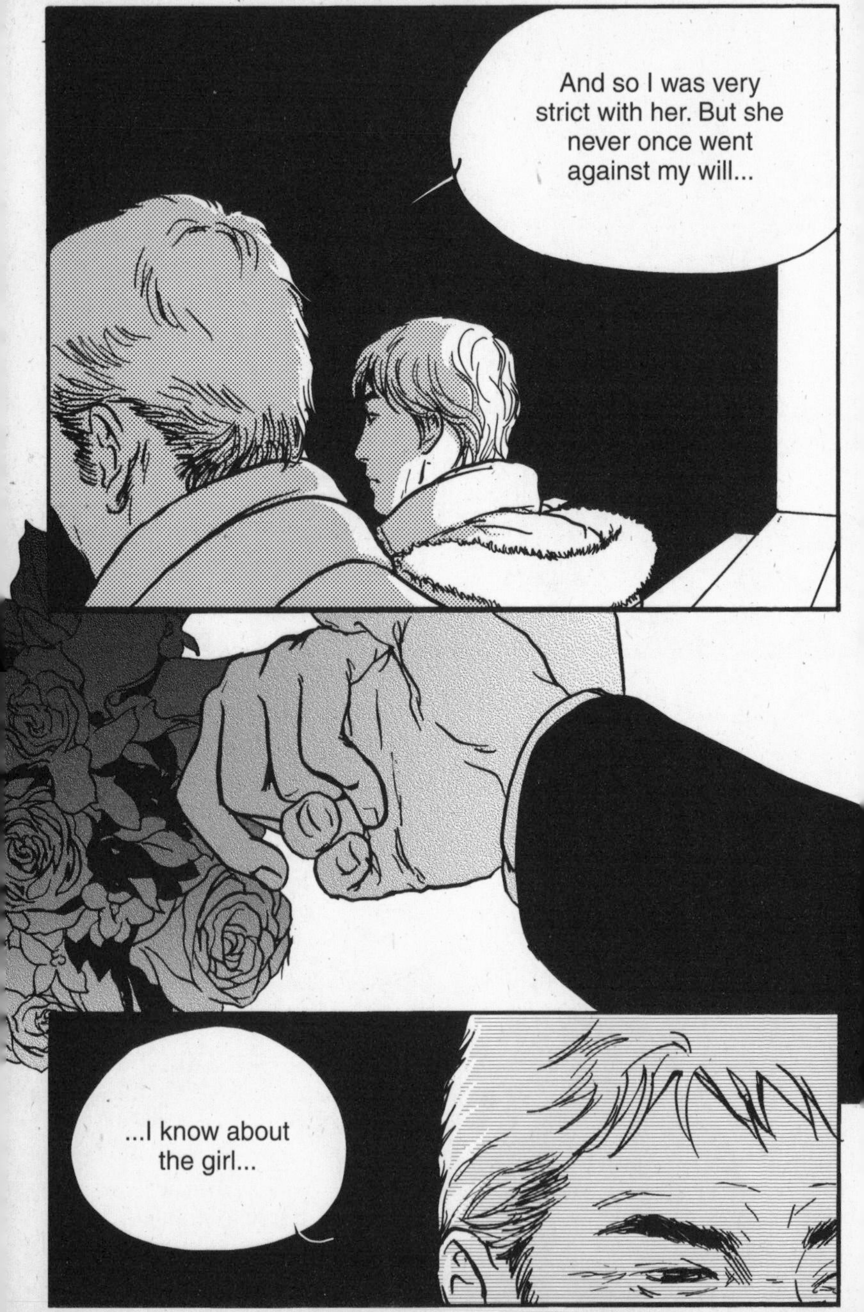
And so I was very strict with her. But she never once went against my will...
...I know about the girl...

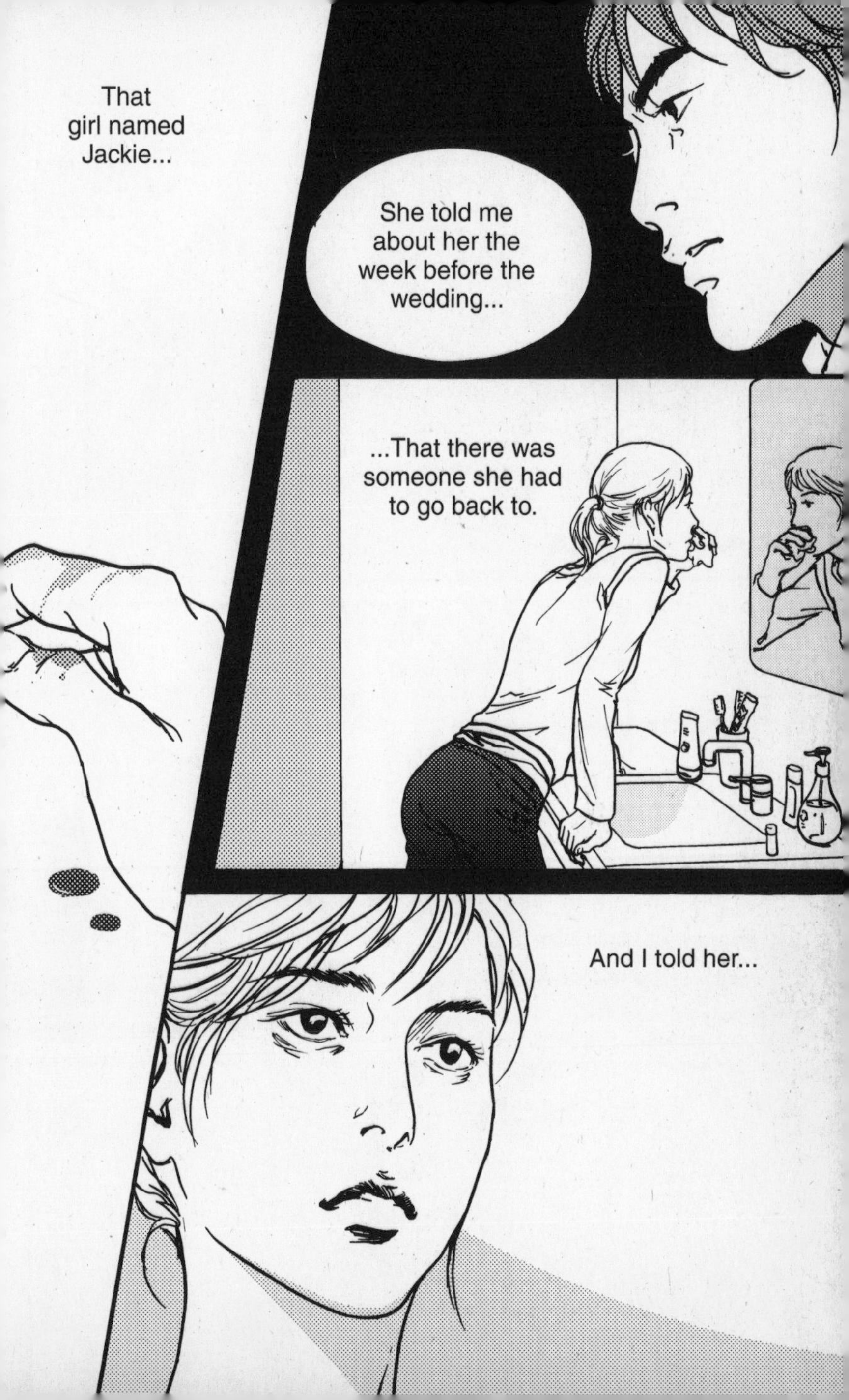

That girl named Jackie...
She told me about her the week before the wedding...
...That there was someone she had to go back to.
And I told her...

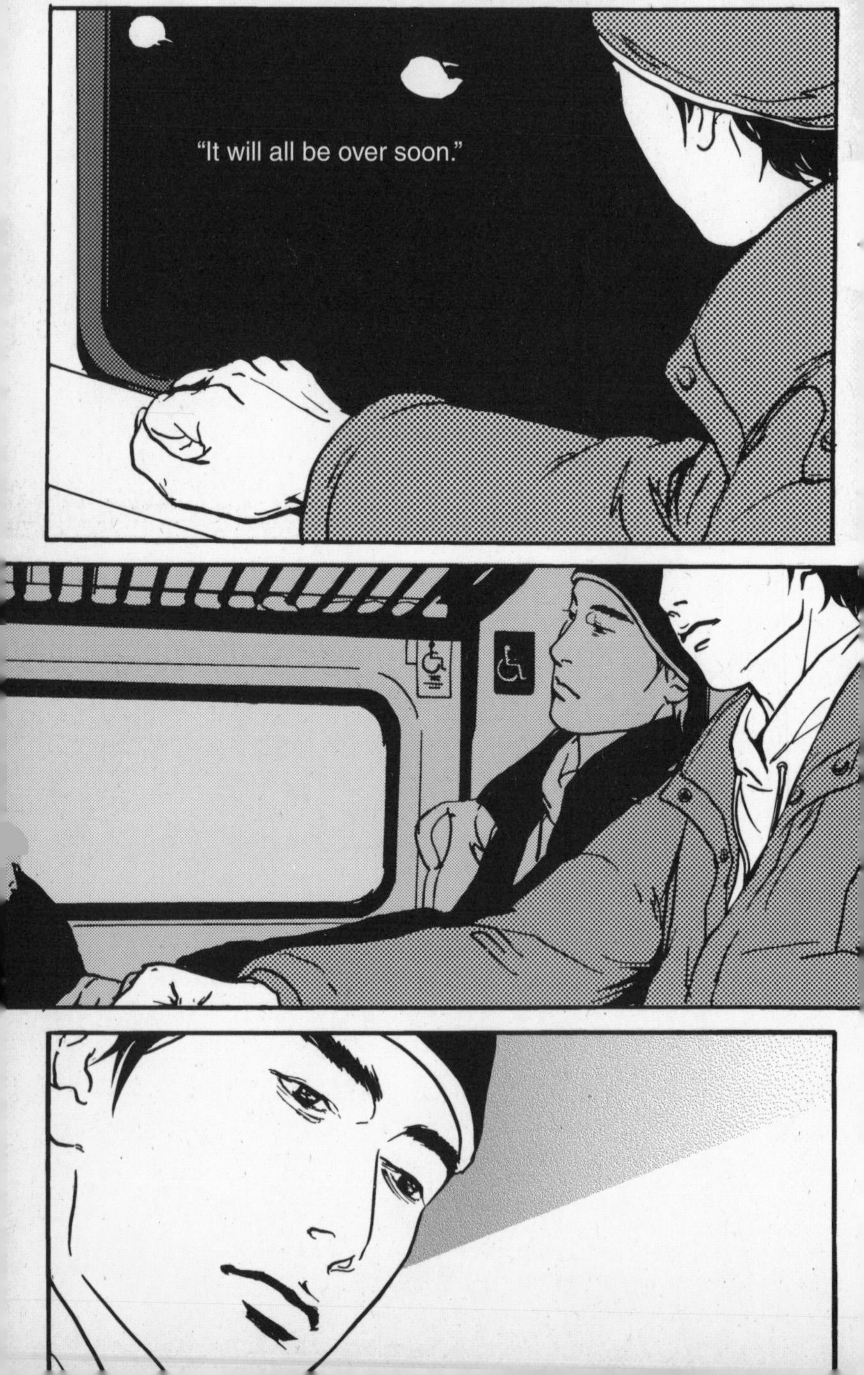
"It will all be over soon."

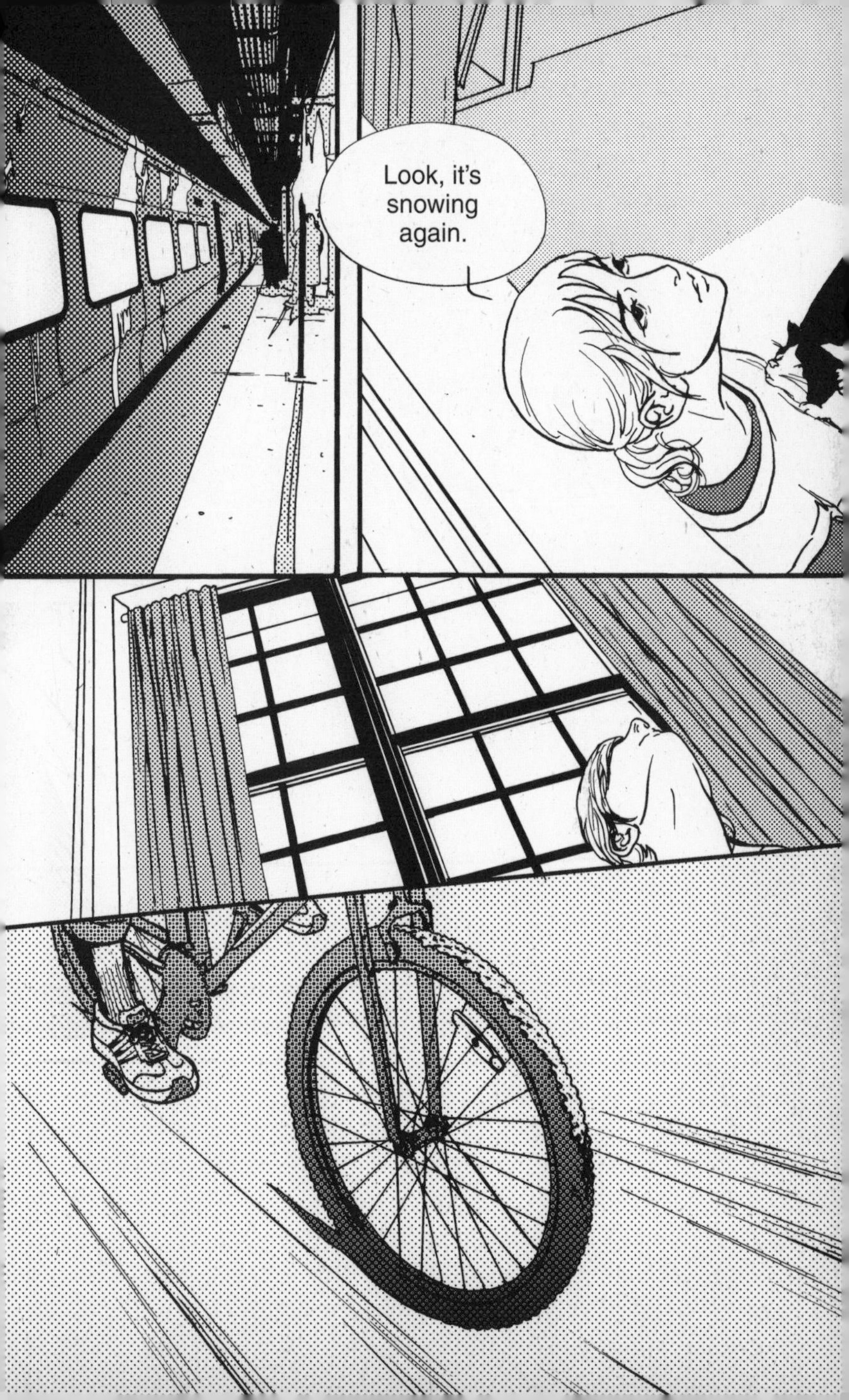
Look, it's snowing again.

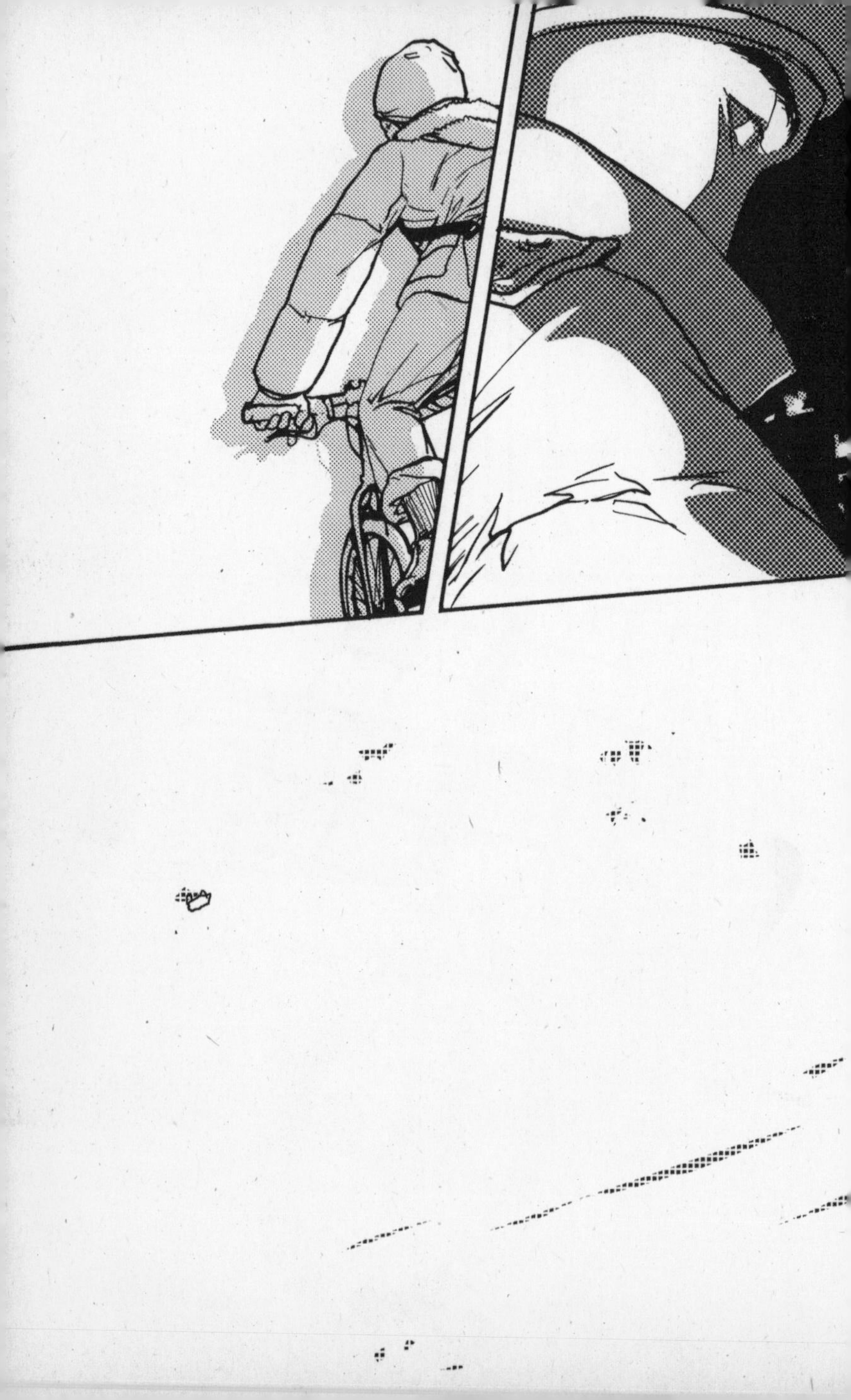

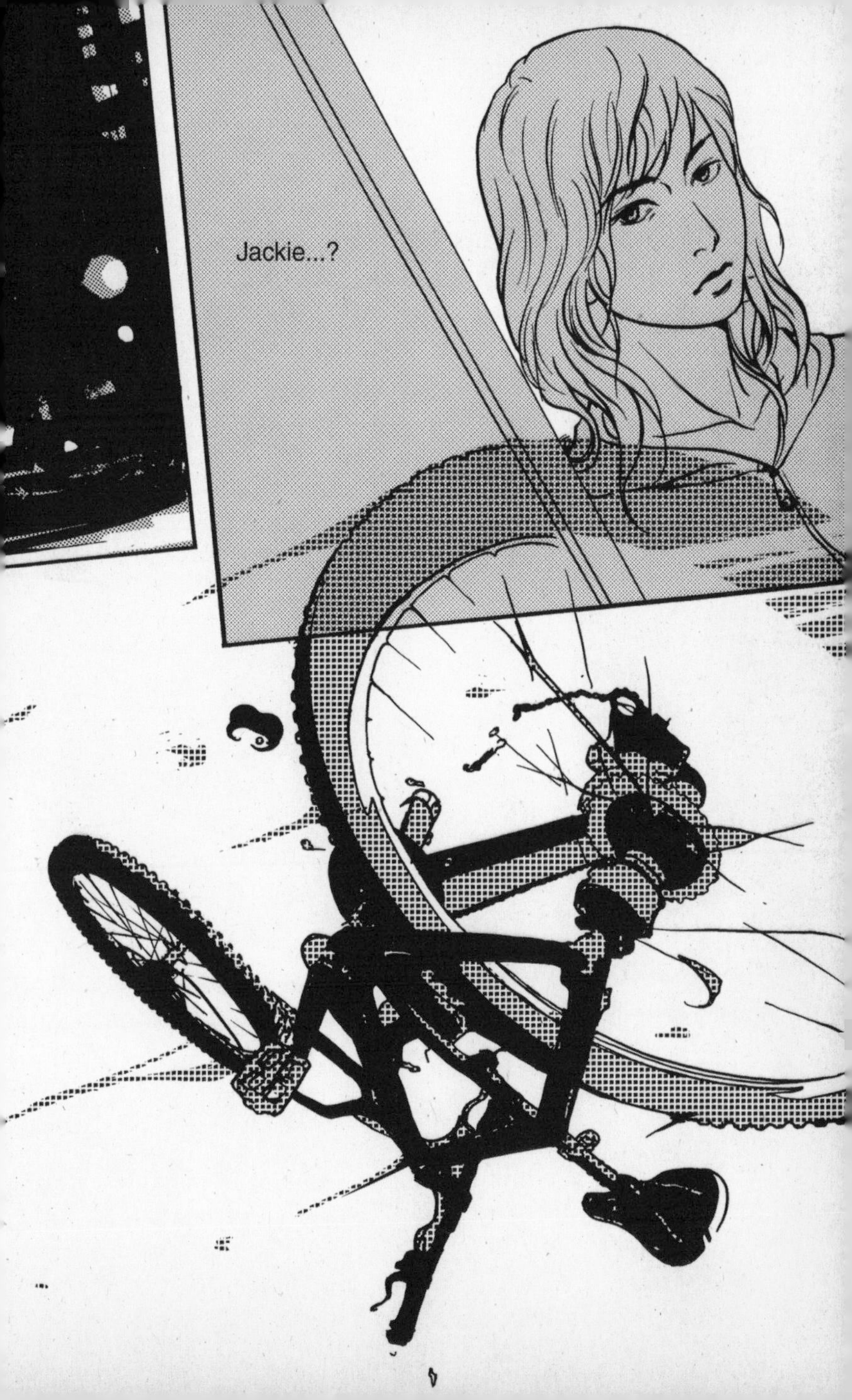
Jackie...?

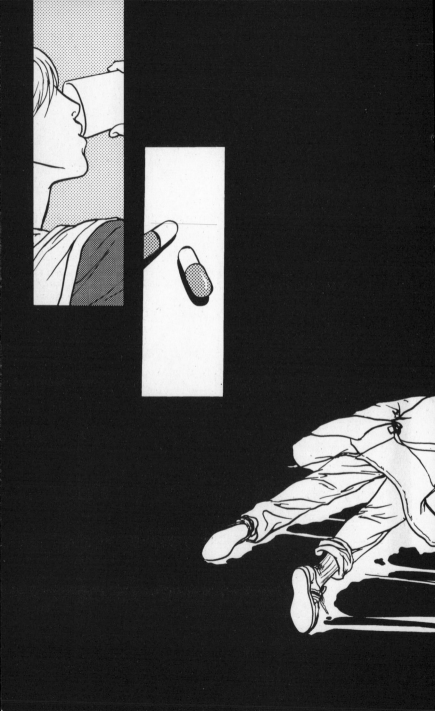

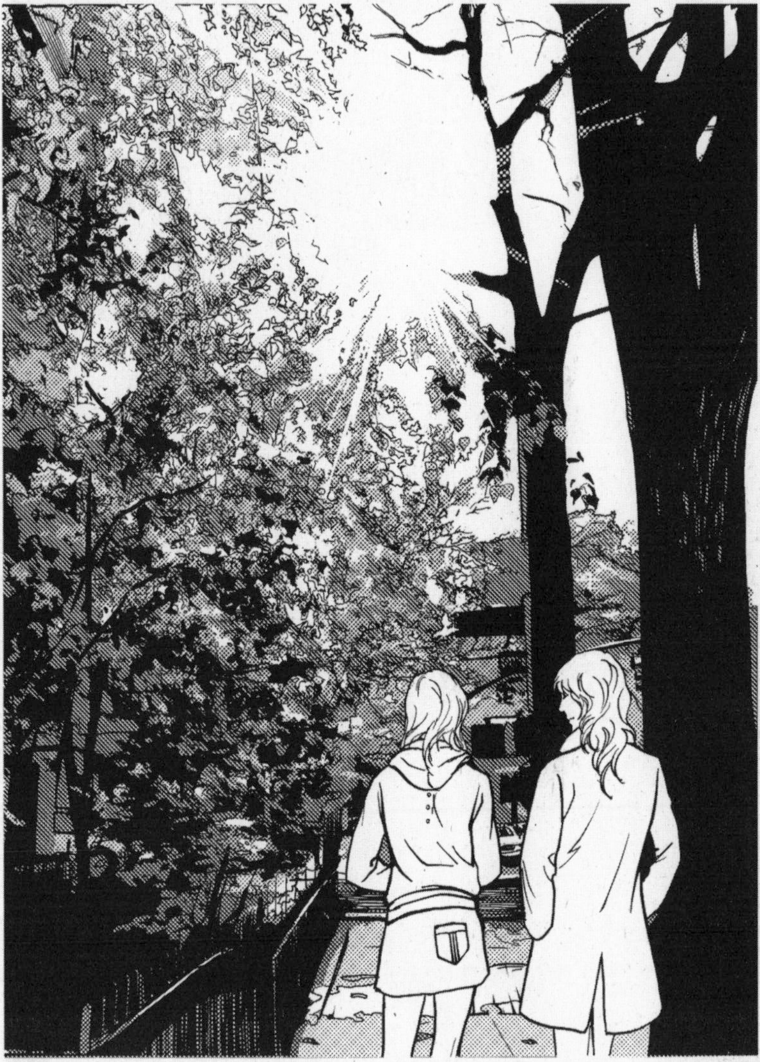

Chapter 7

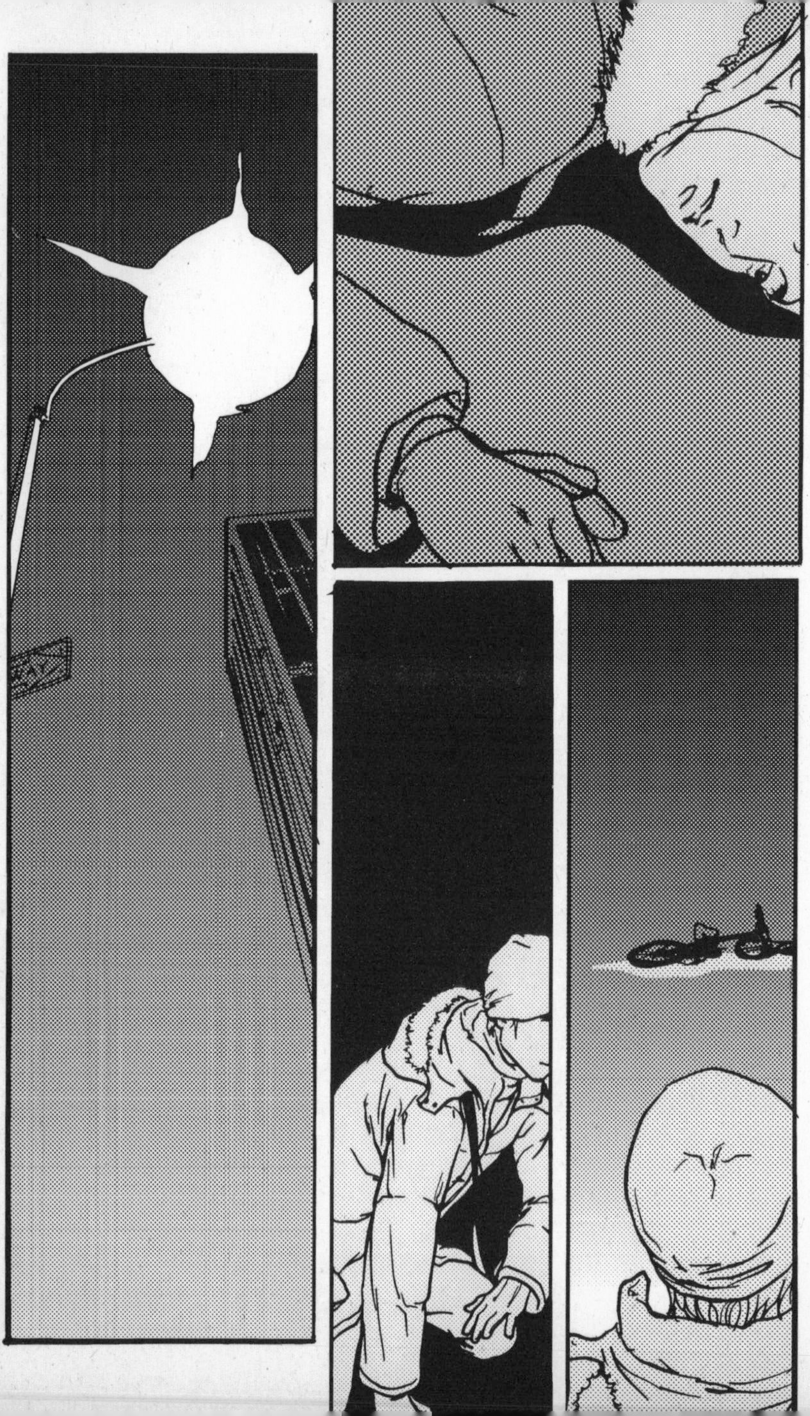

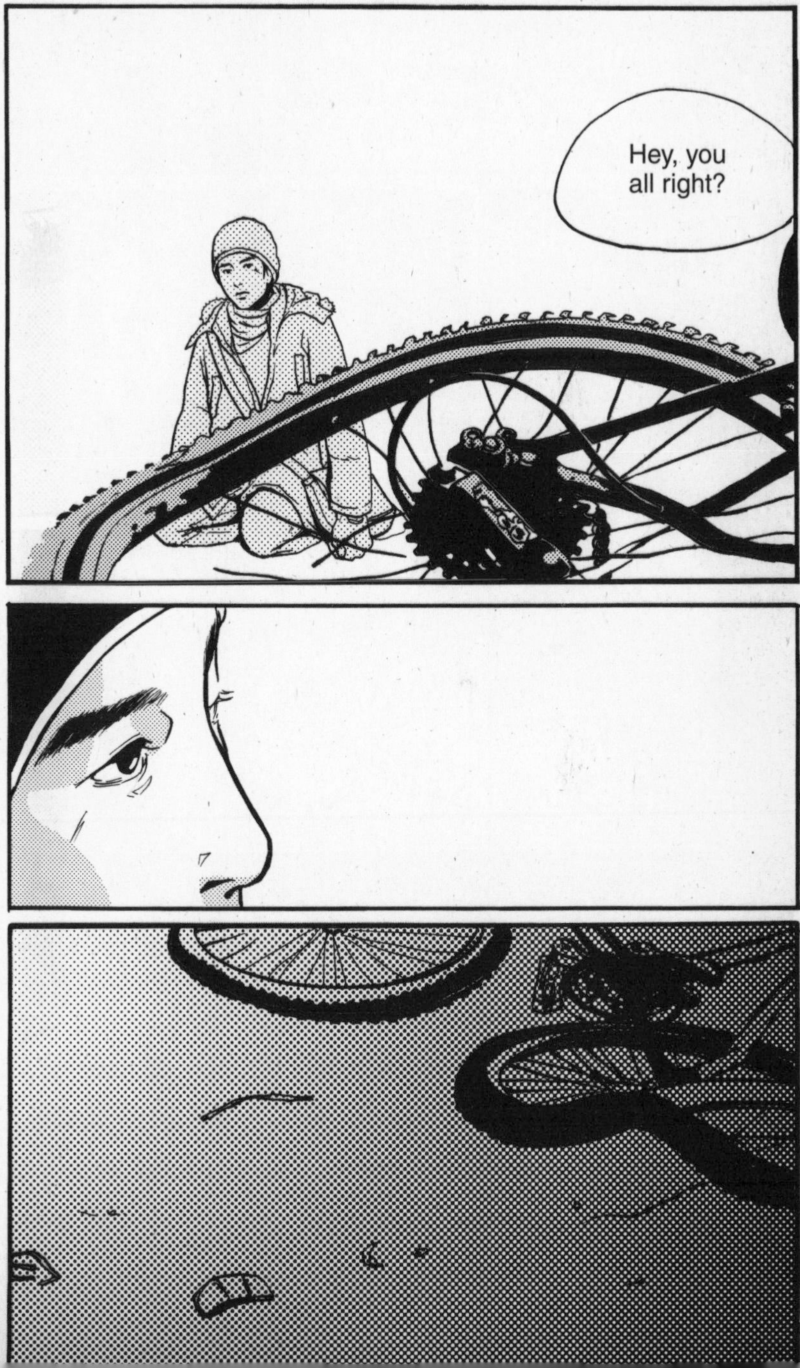
Hey, you all right?

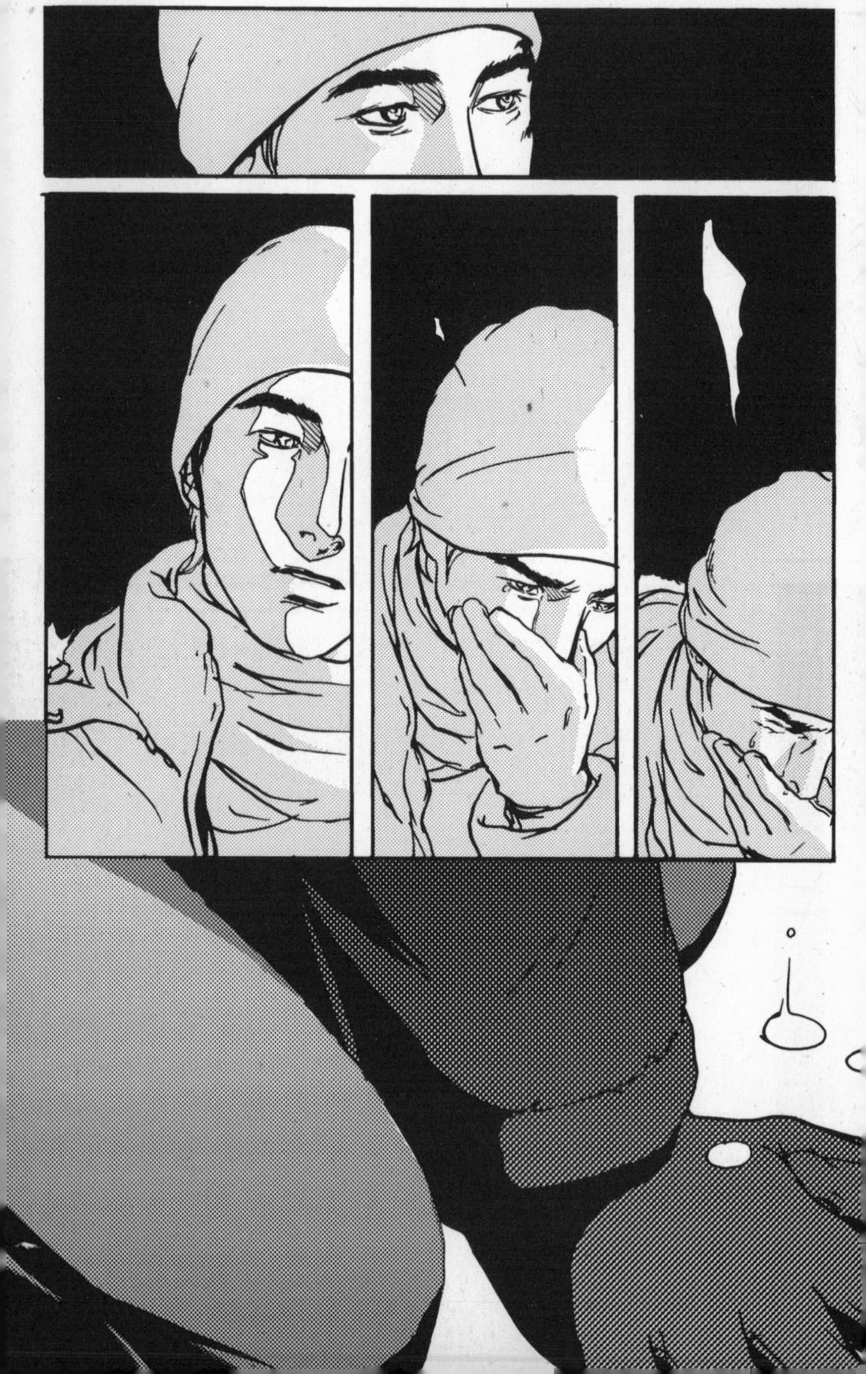

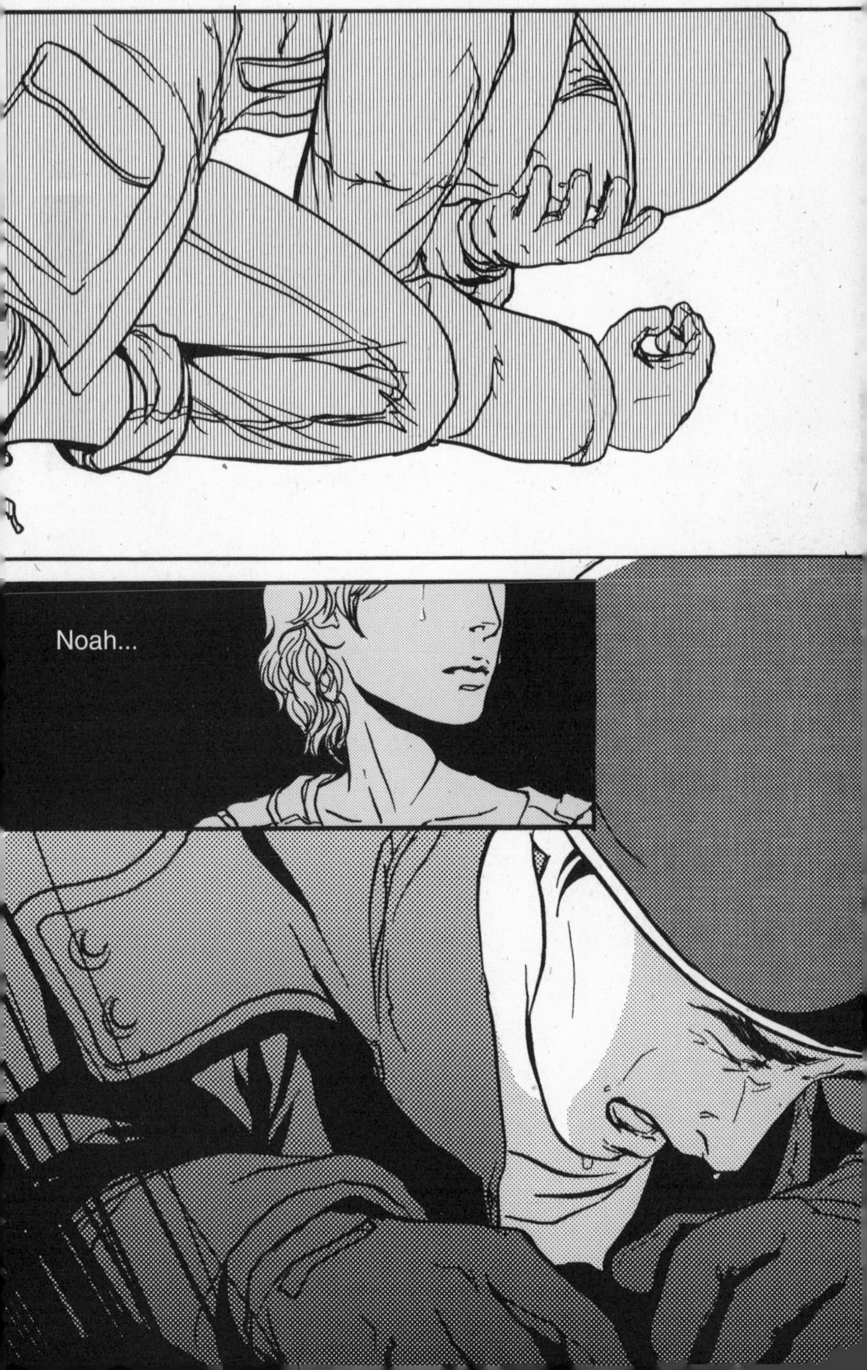
Noah...

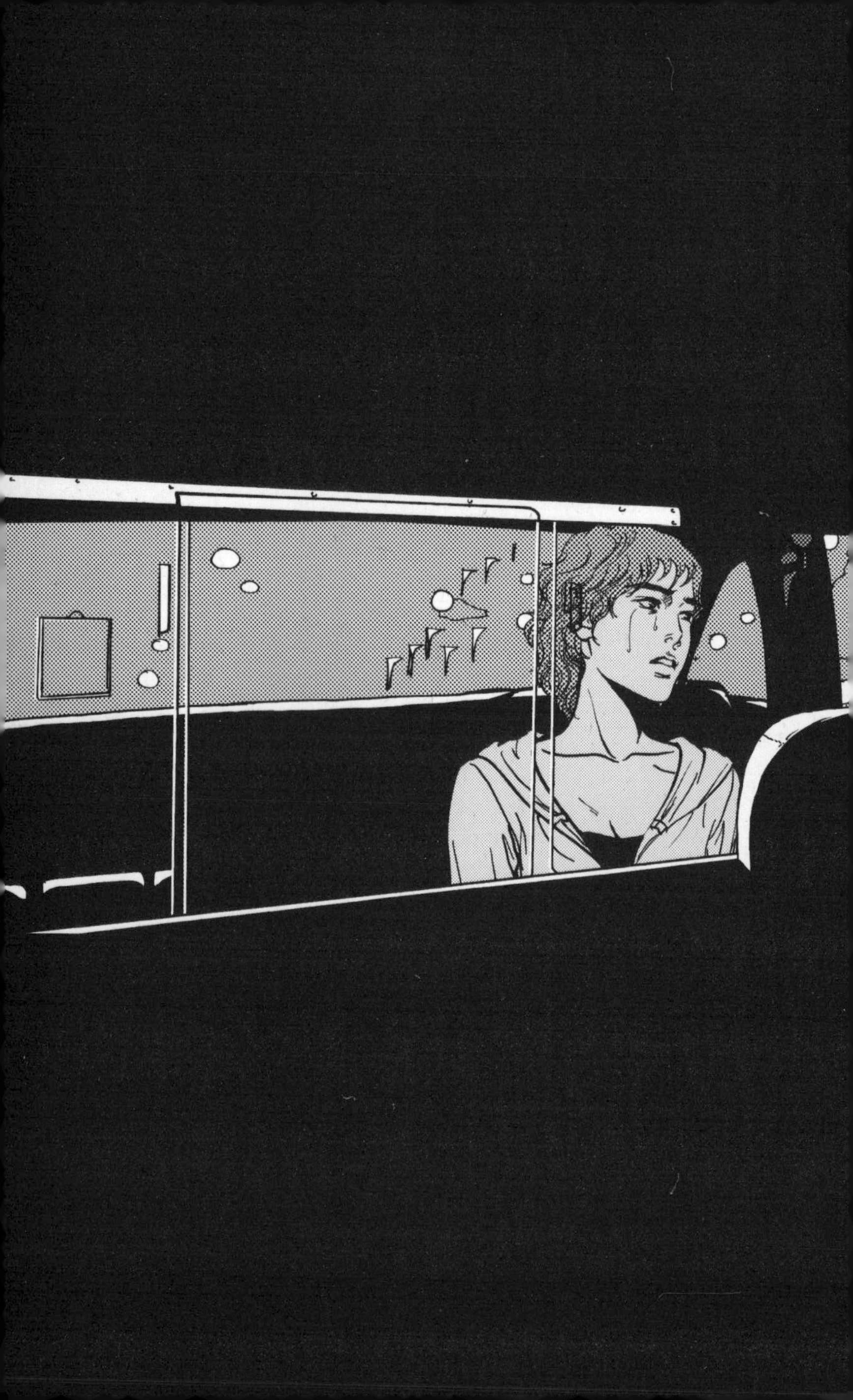

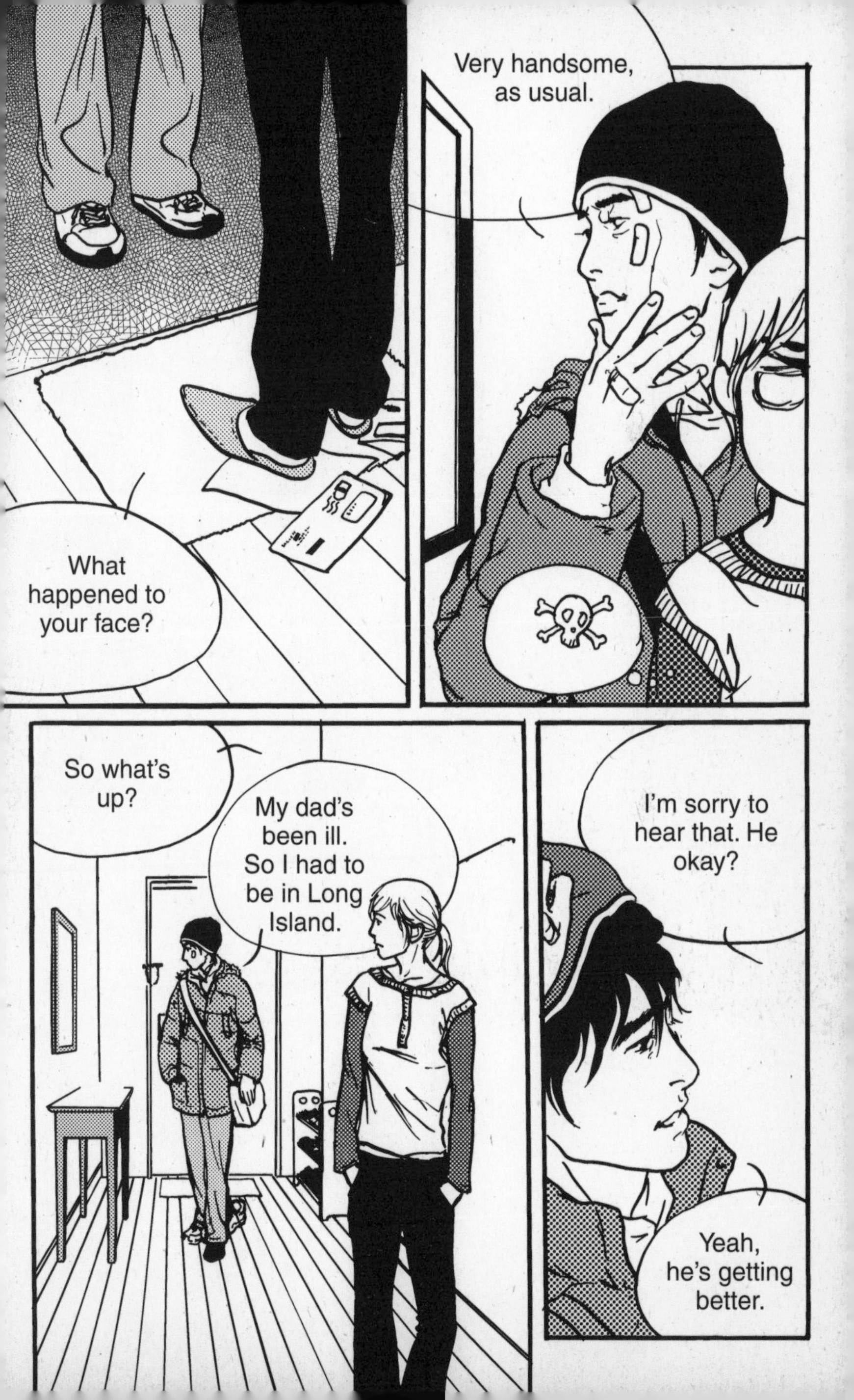
What happened to your face?
Very handsome, as usual.
So what's up?
My dad's been ill. So I had to be in Long Island.
I'm sorry to hear that. He okay?
Yeah, he's getting better.

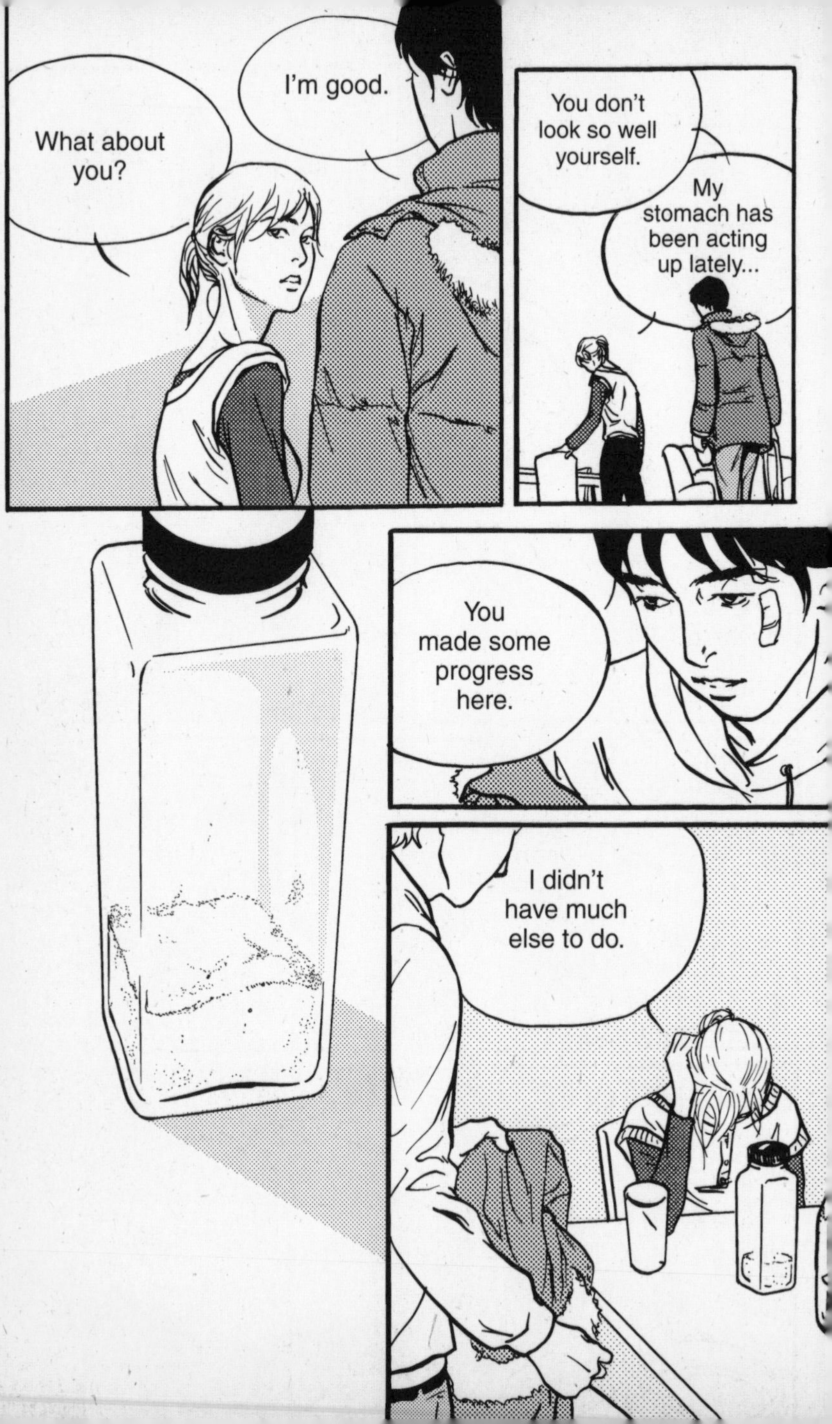
What about you?
I'm good.
You don't look so well yourself.
My stomach has been acting up lately...
You made some progress here.
I didn't have much else to do.

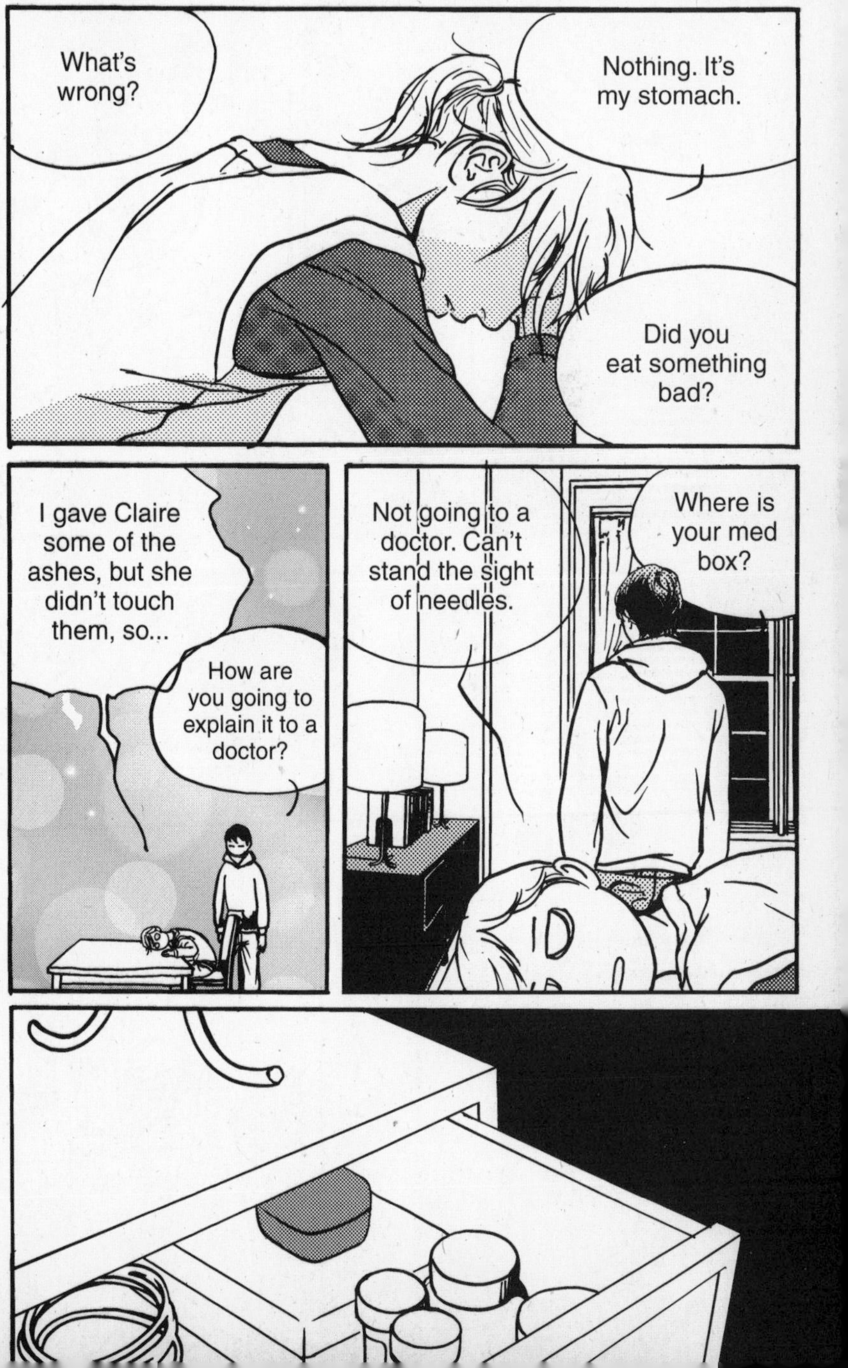
What's wrong?
Nothing. It's my stomach.
Did you eat something bad?
I gave Claire some of the ashes, but she didn't touch them, so...
How are you going to explain it to a doctor?
Not going to a doctor. Can't stand the sight of needles.
Where is your med box?

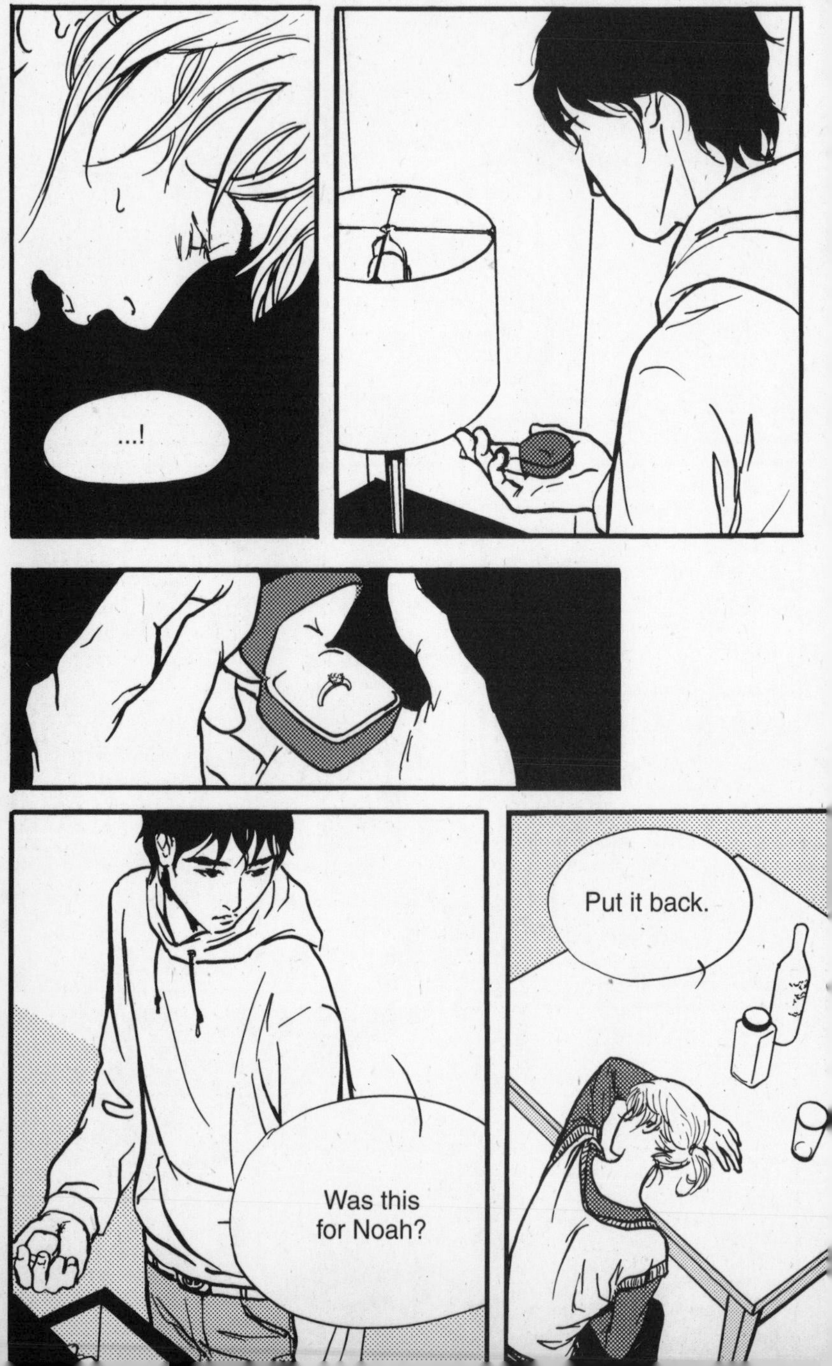
...!
Was this for Noah?
Put it back.

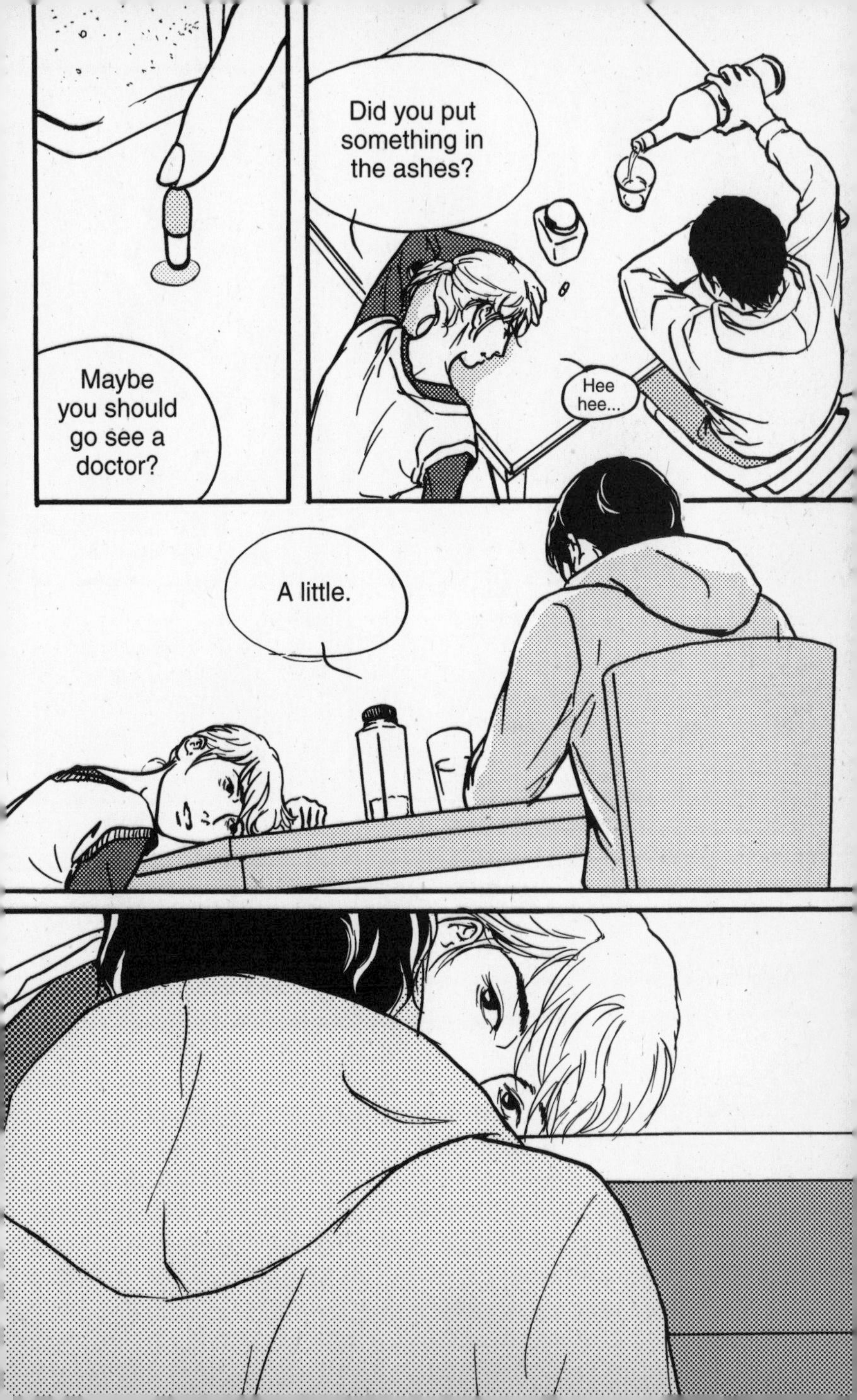
Maybe you should go see a doctor?
Did you put something in the ashes?
Hee hee...
A little.

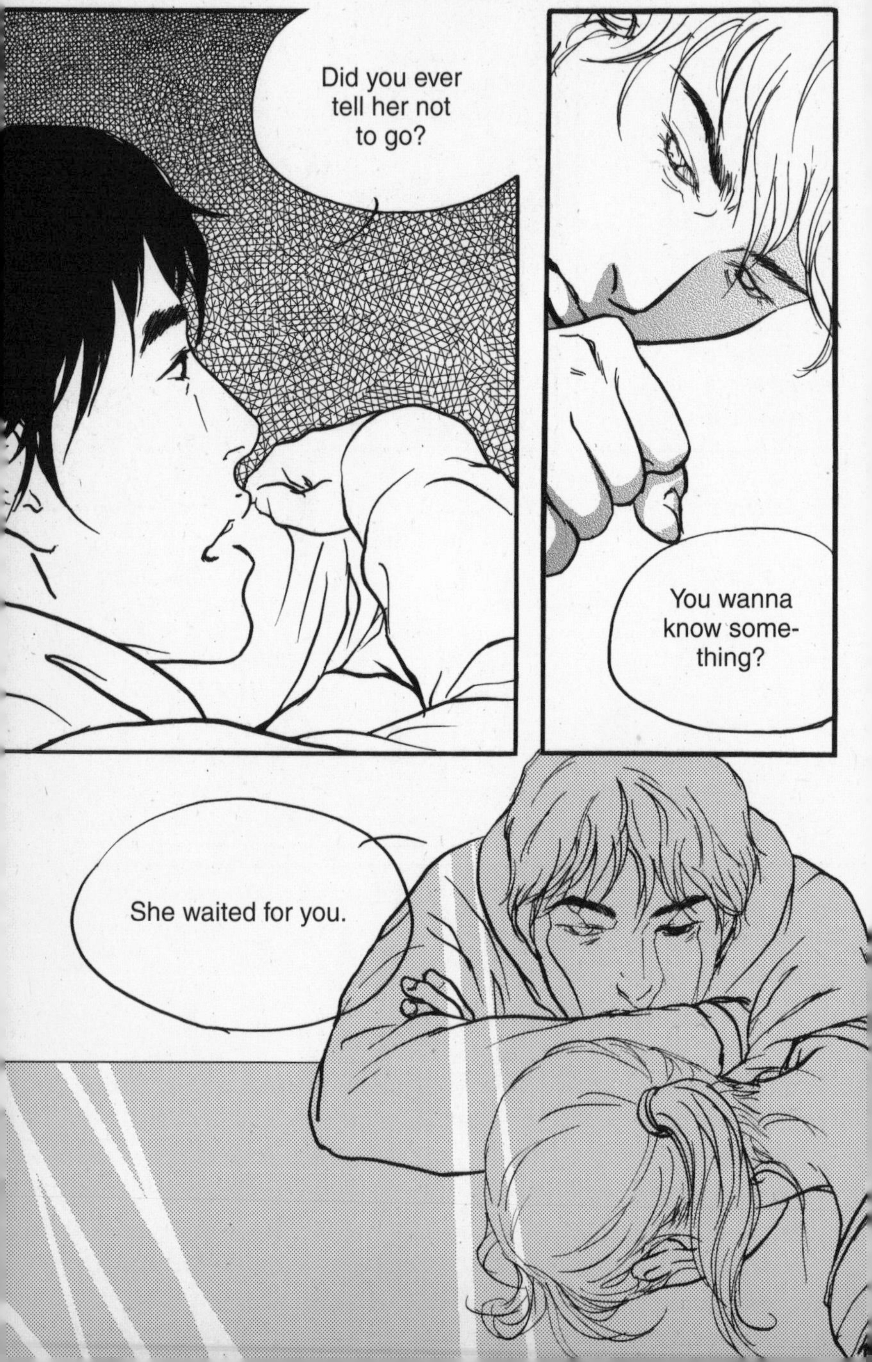
Did you ever tell her not to go?
You wanna know some-thing?
She waited for you.

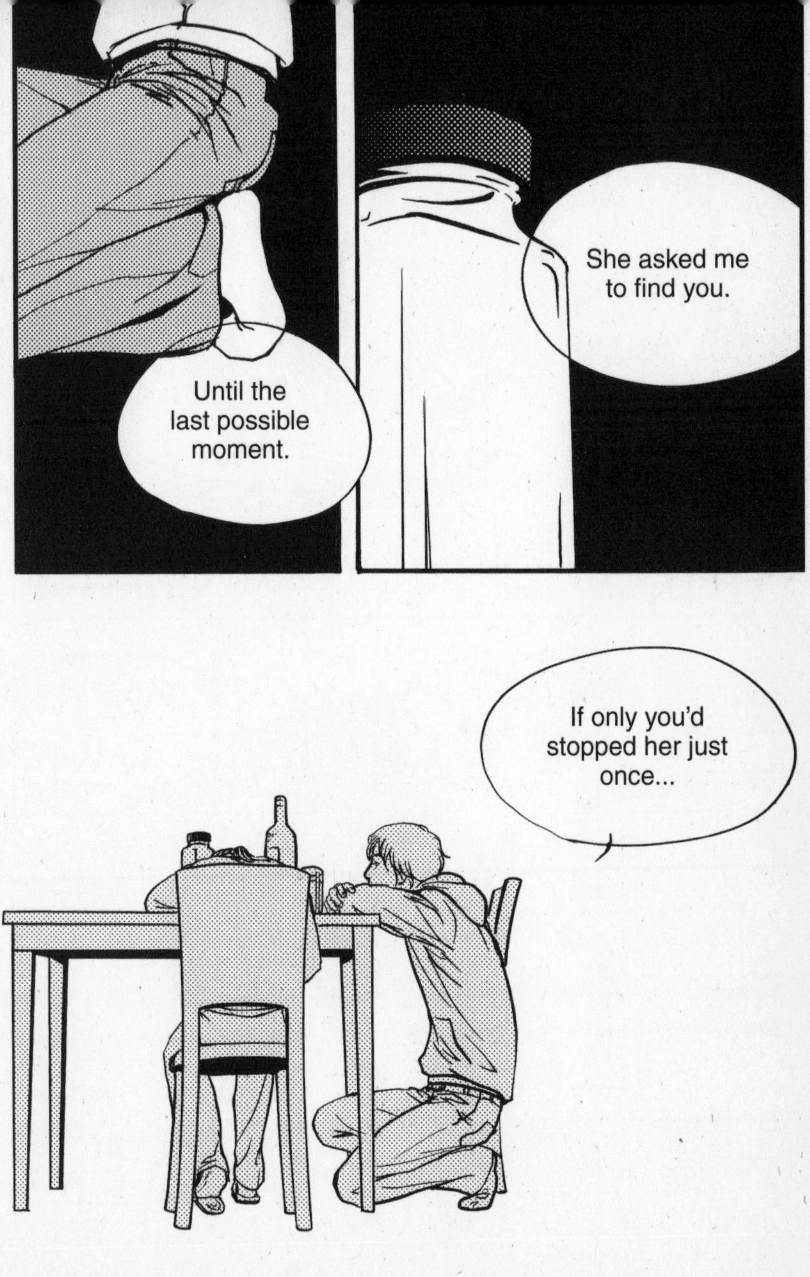
Until the last possible moment.
She asked me to find you.
If only you'd stopped her just once...

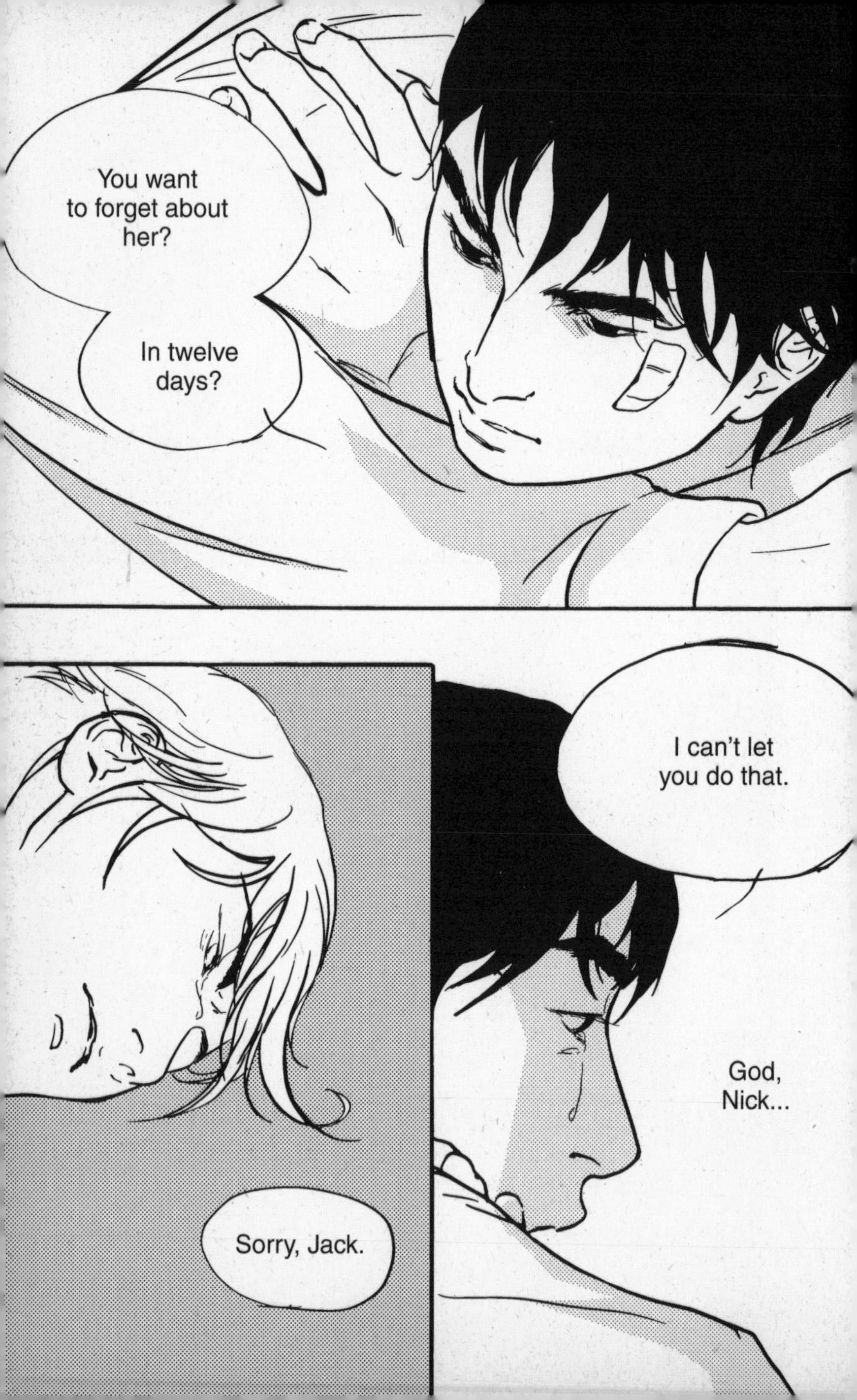
You want to forget about her?
In twelve days?
Sorry, Jack.
I can't let you do that.
God, Nick...

Please stop crying...

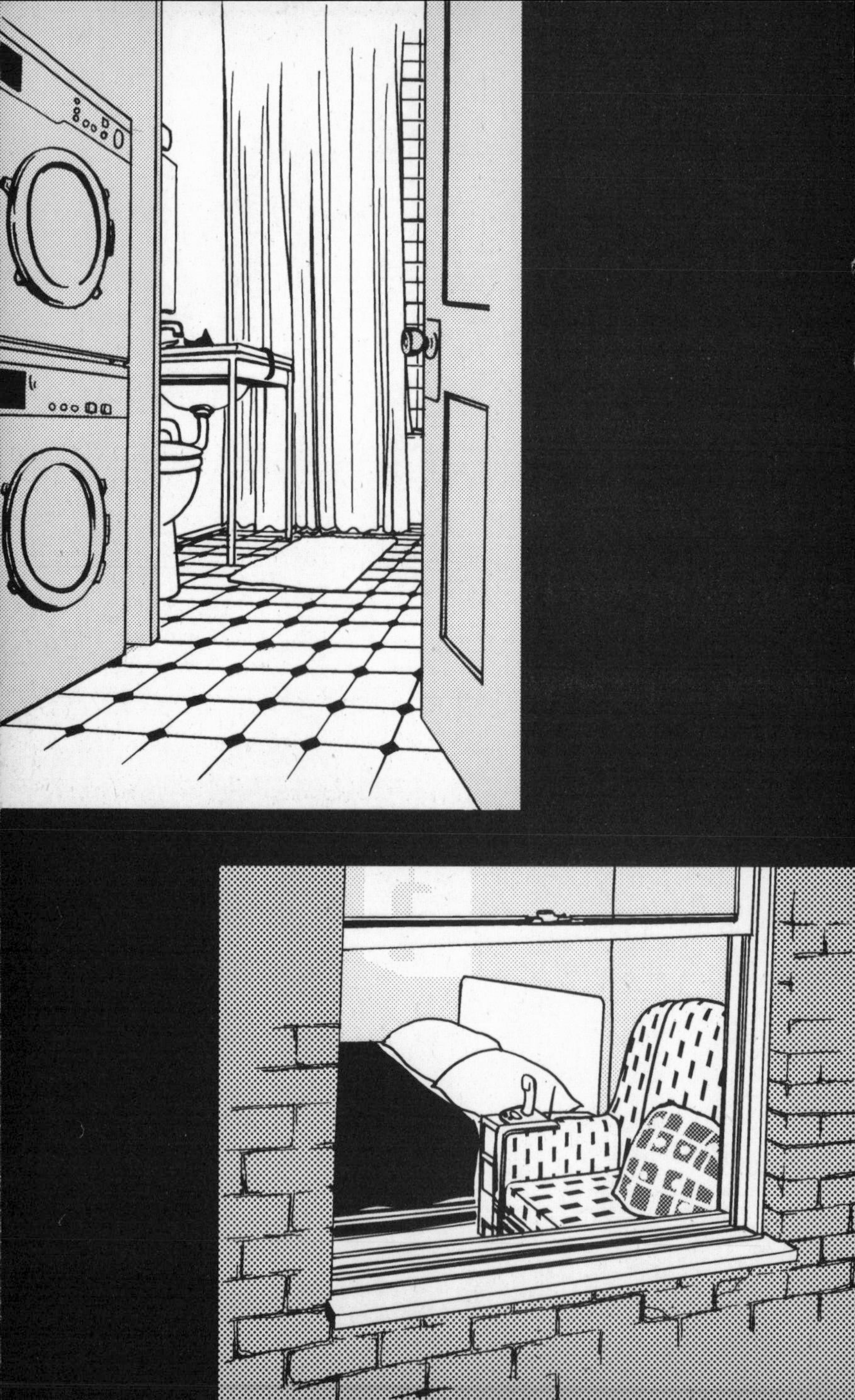

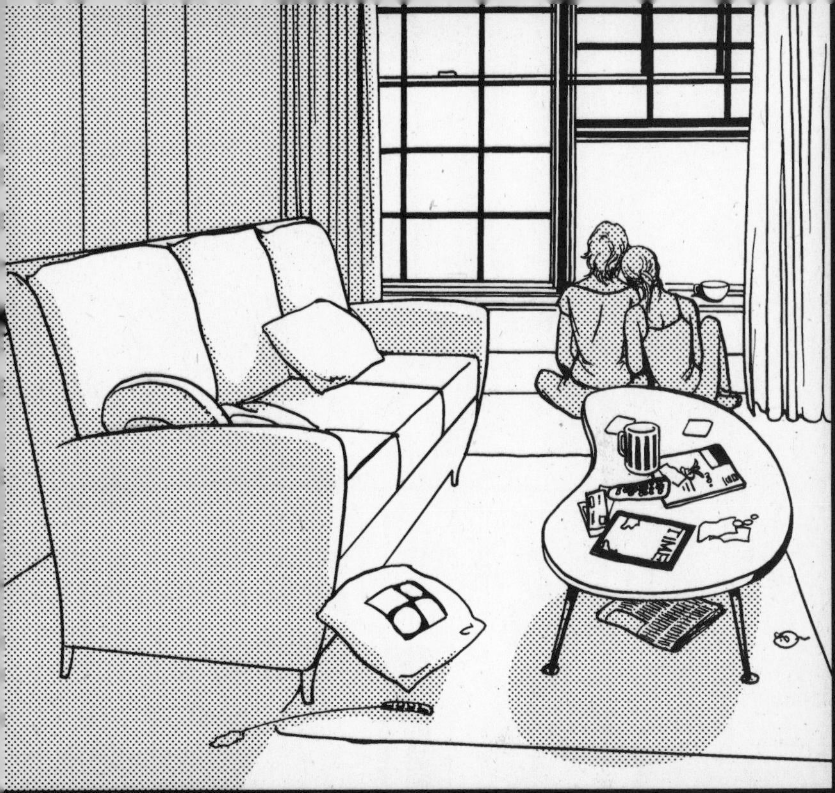
TIME

Chapter 8

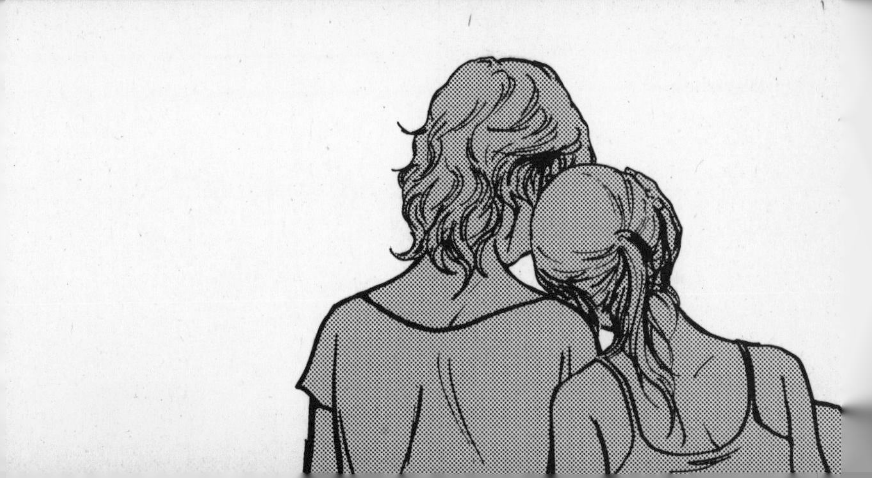

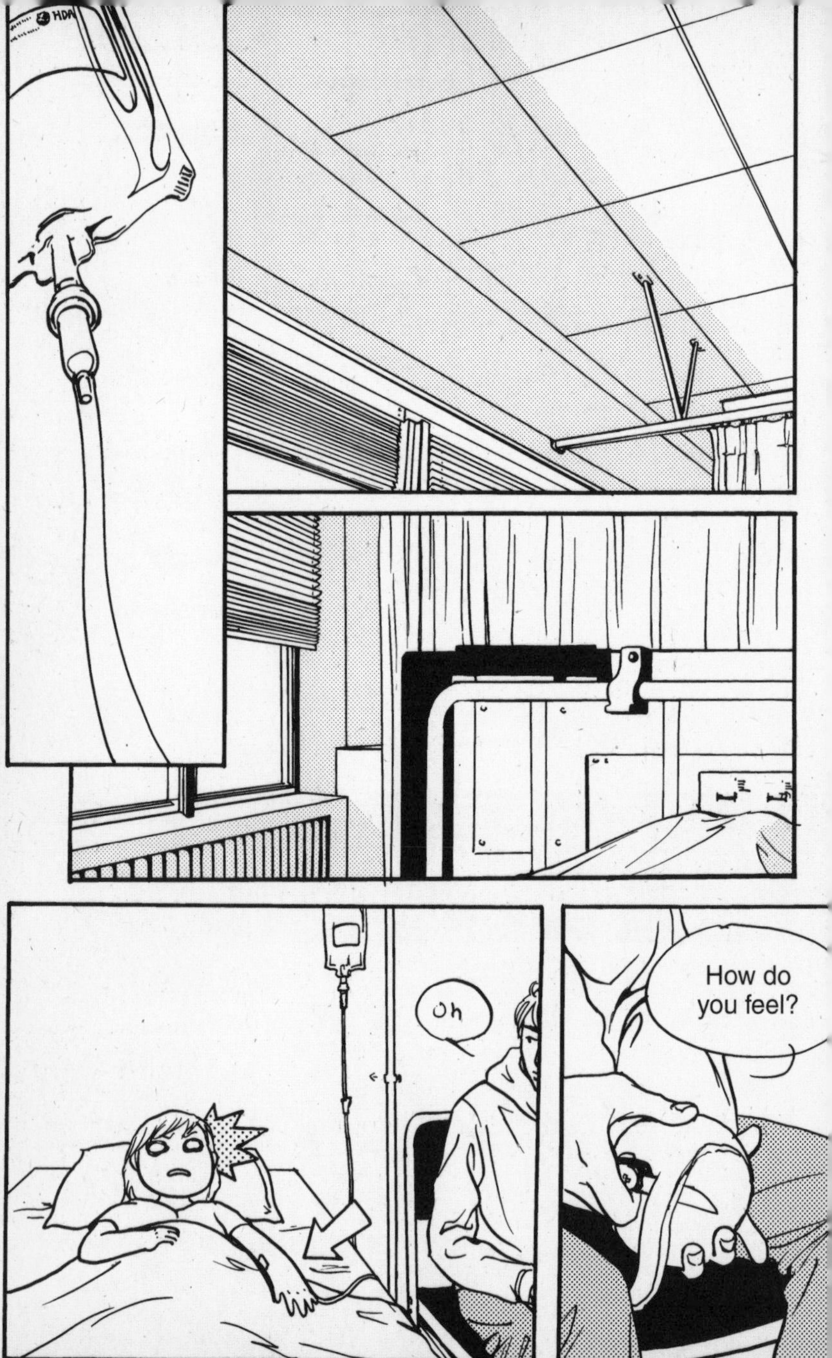
Oh
How do you feel?

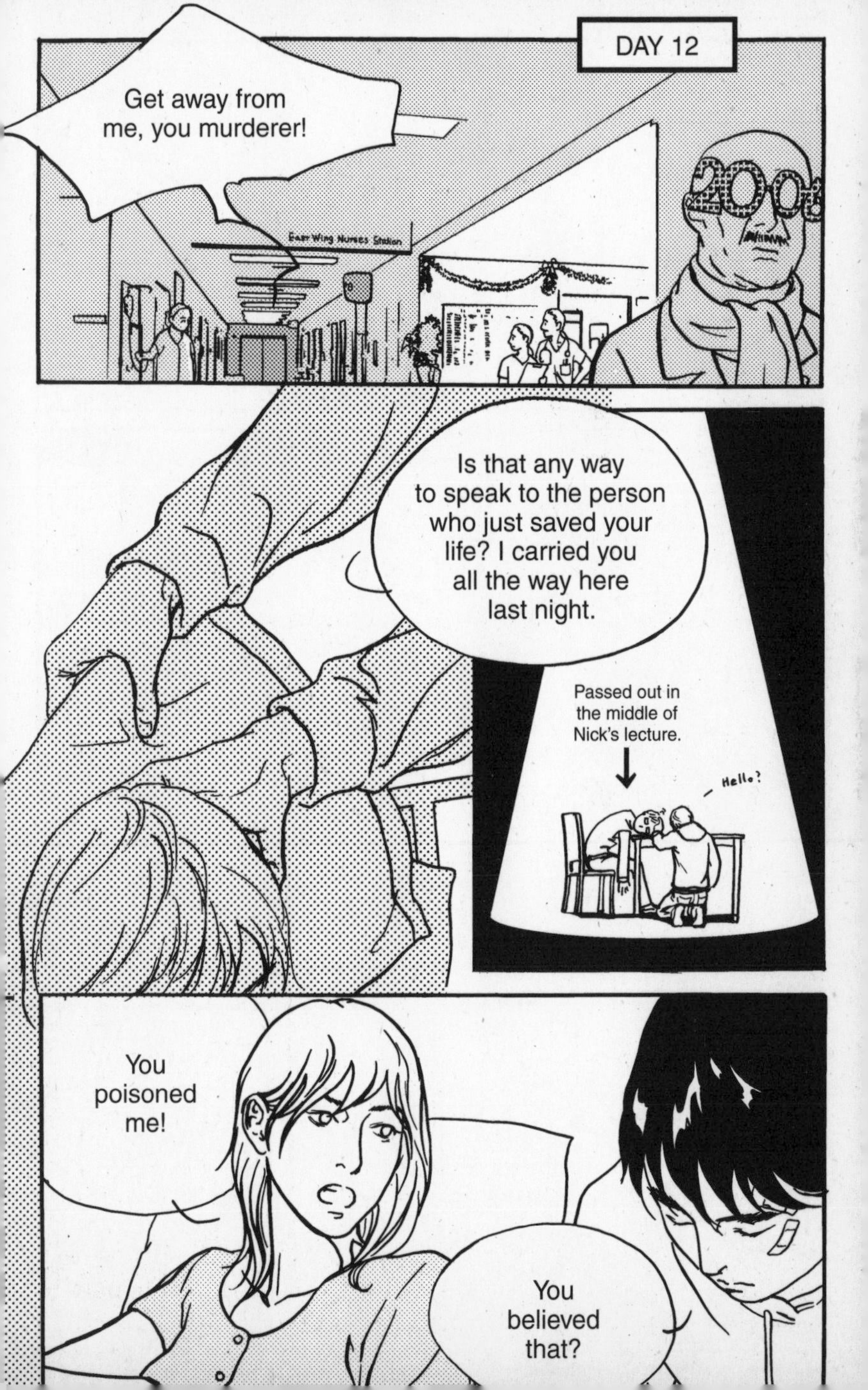
DAY 12
Get away from me, you murderer!
East Wing Nurses Station
Is that any way to speak to the person who just saved your life? I carried you all the way here last night.
Passed out in the middle of Nick's lecture.
Hello?
You poisoned me!
You believed that?

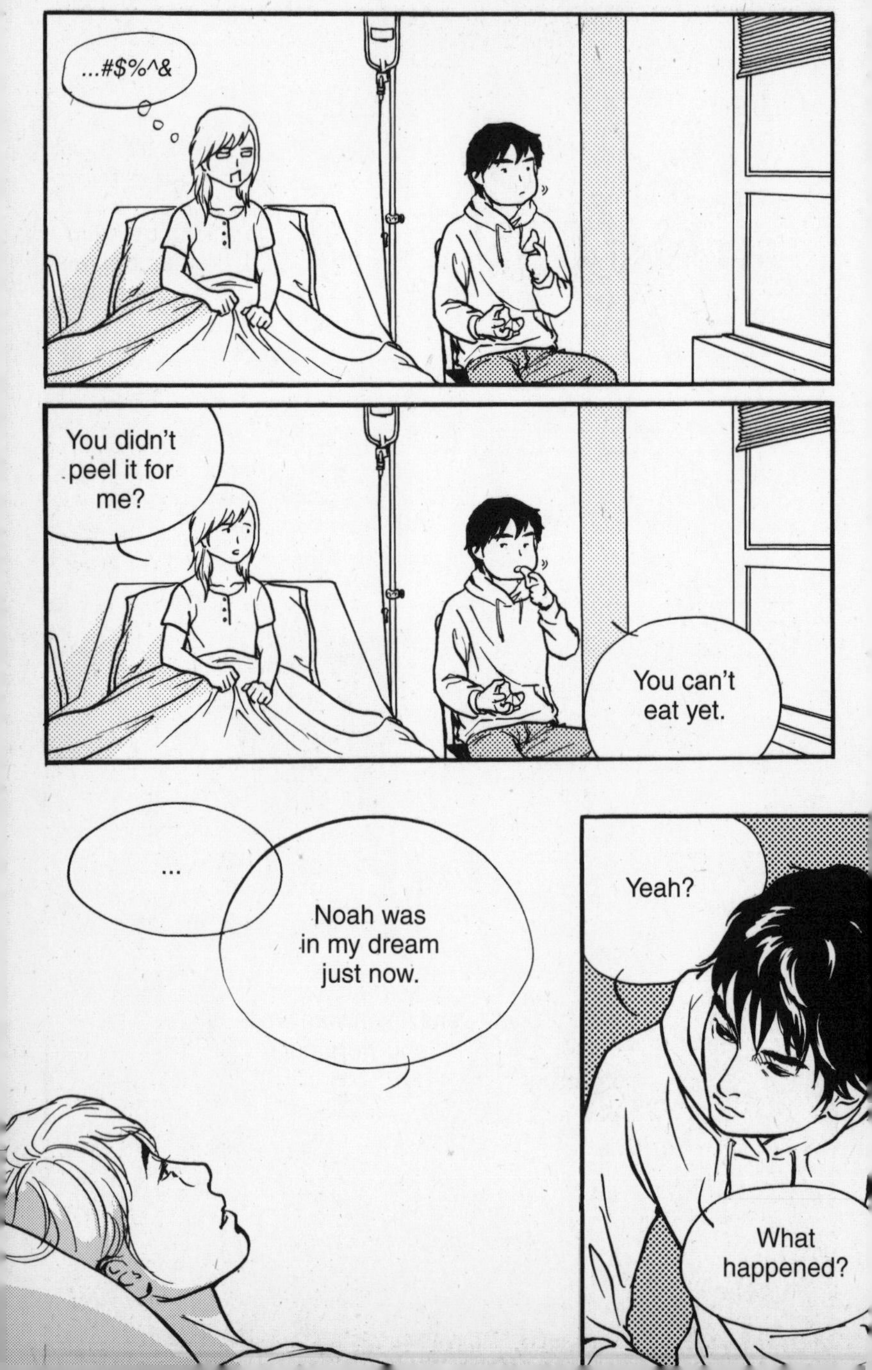
...#$%^&
You didn't peel it for me?
You can't eat yet.
...
Noah was in my dream just now.
Yeah?
What happened?

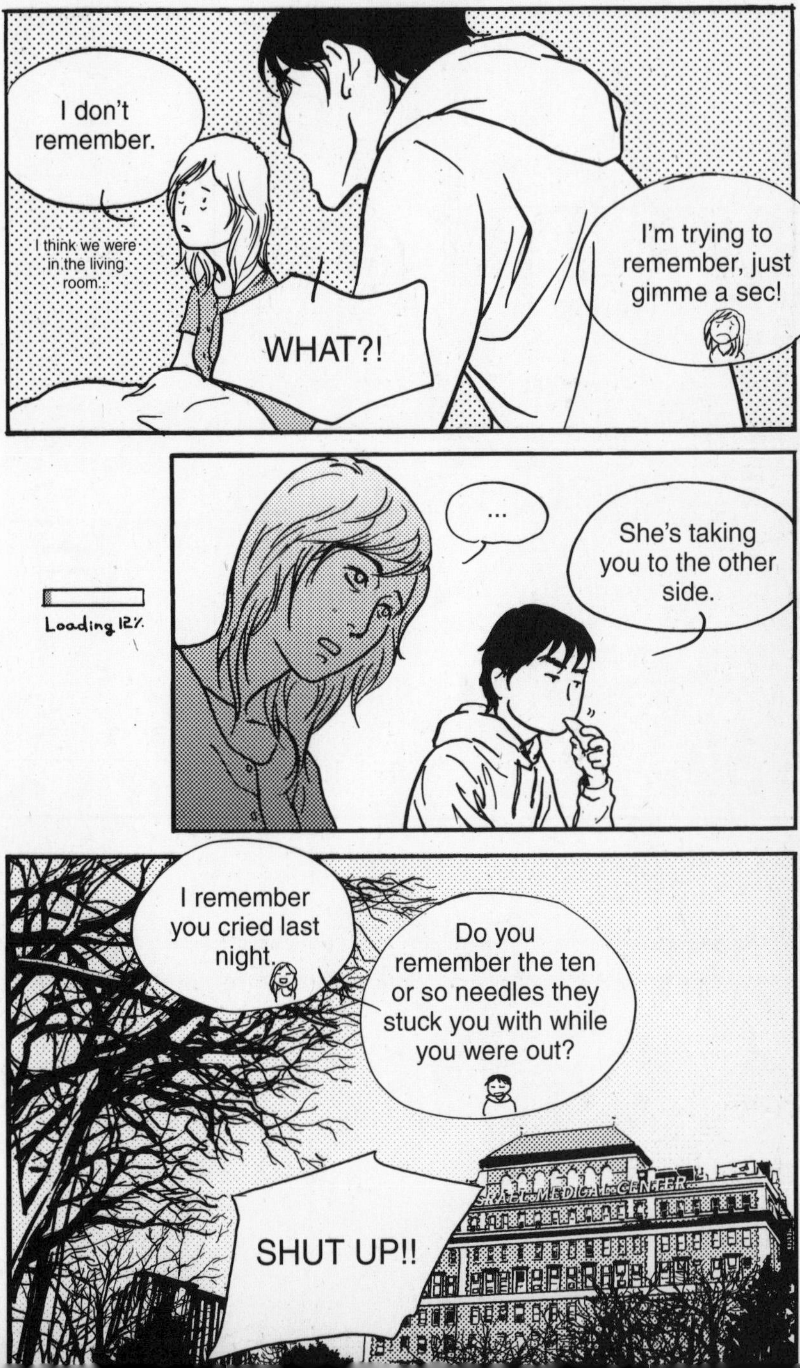
I don't remember.
I think we were in the living room.
WHAT?!
I'm trying to remember, just gimme a sec!
Loading 12%
...
She's taking you to the other side.
I remember you cried last night.
Do you remember the ten or so needles they stuck you with while you were out?
SHUT UP!!

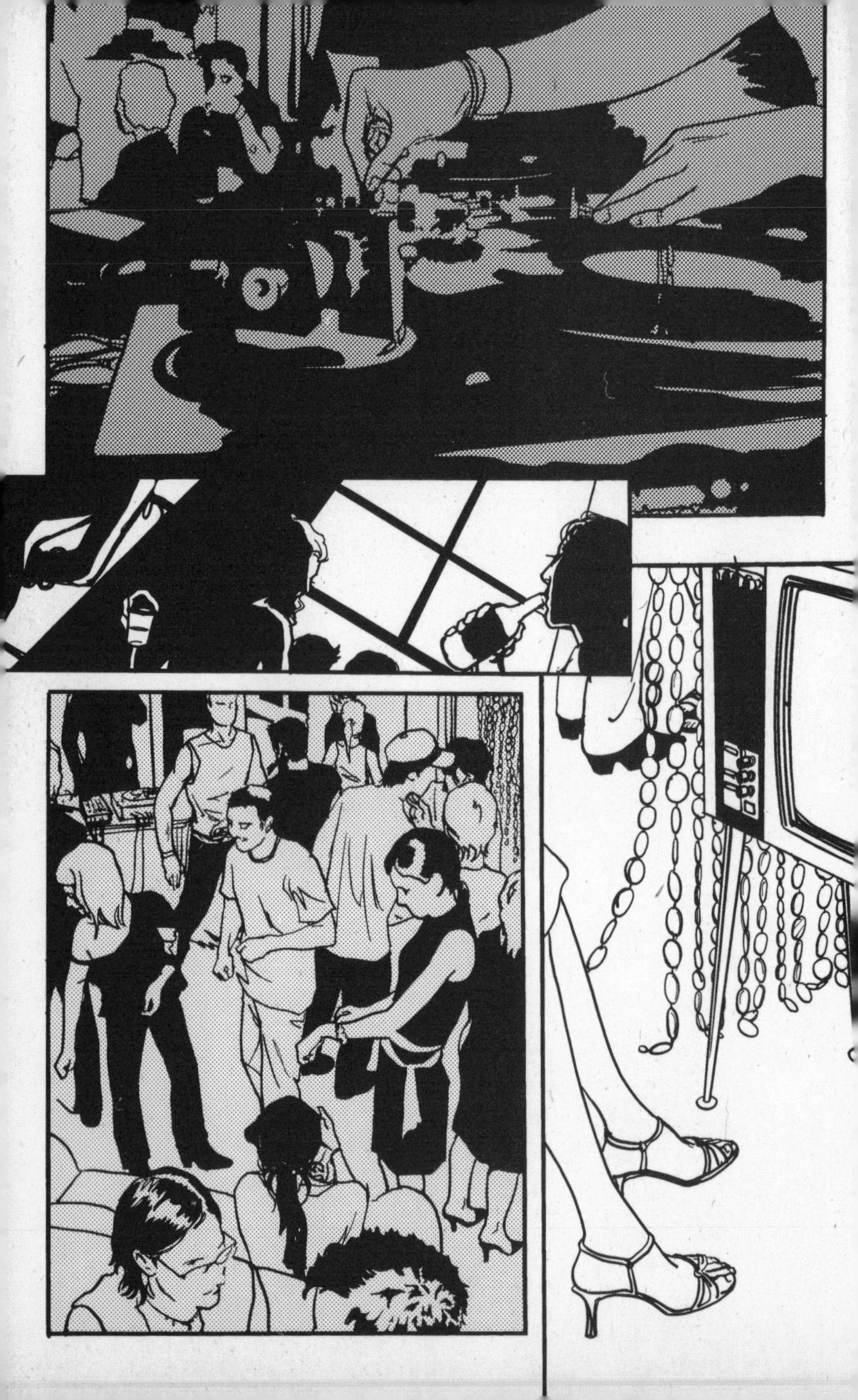

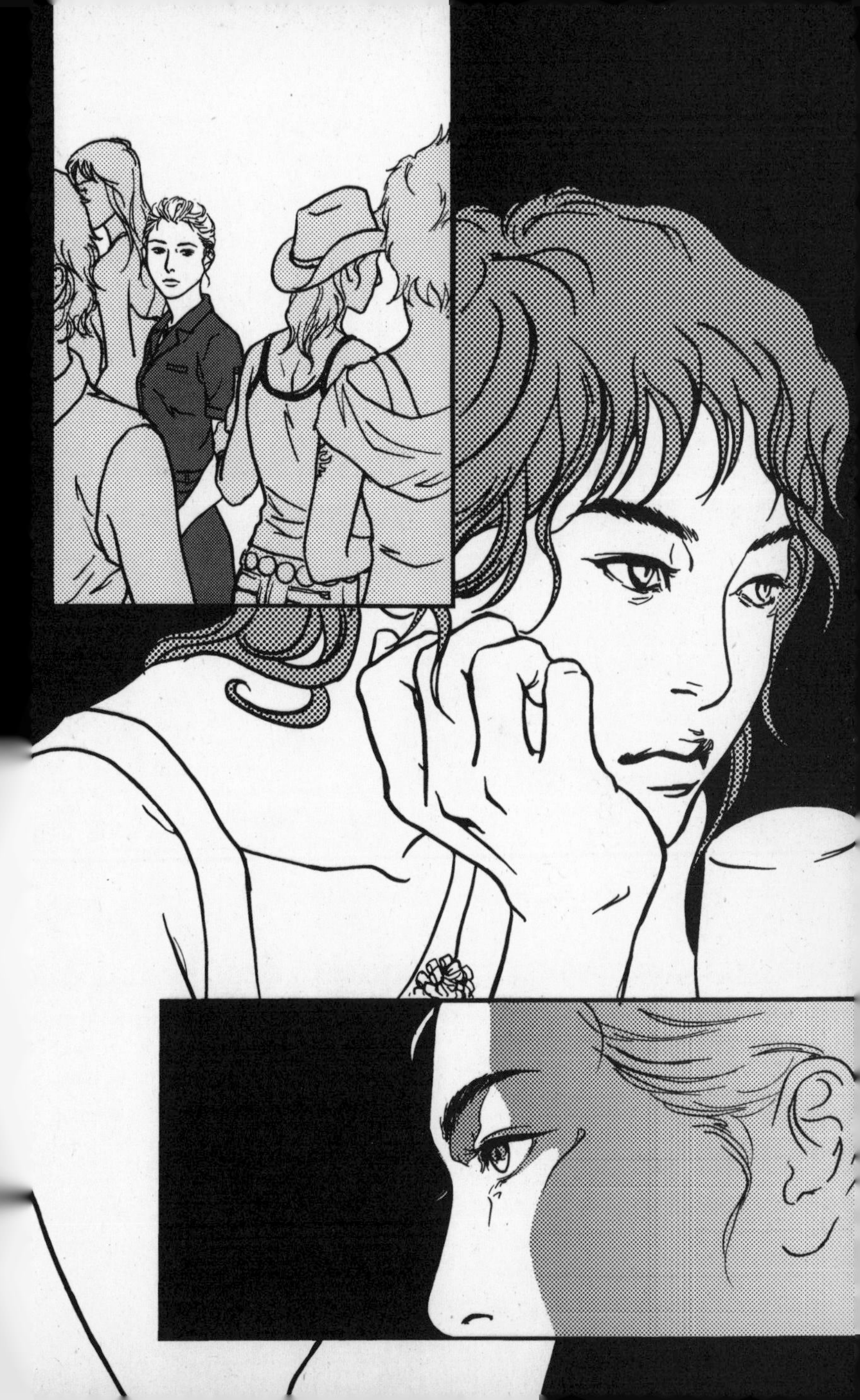

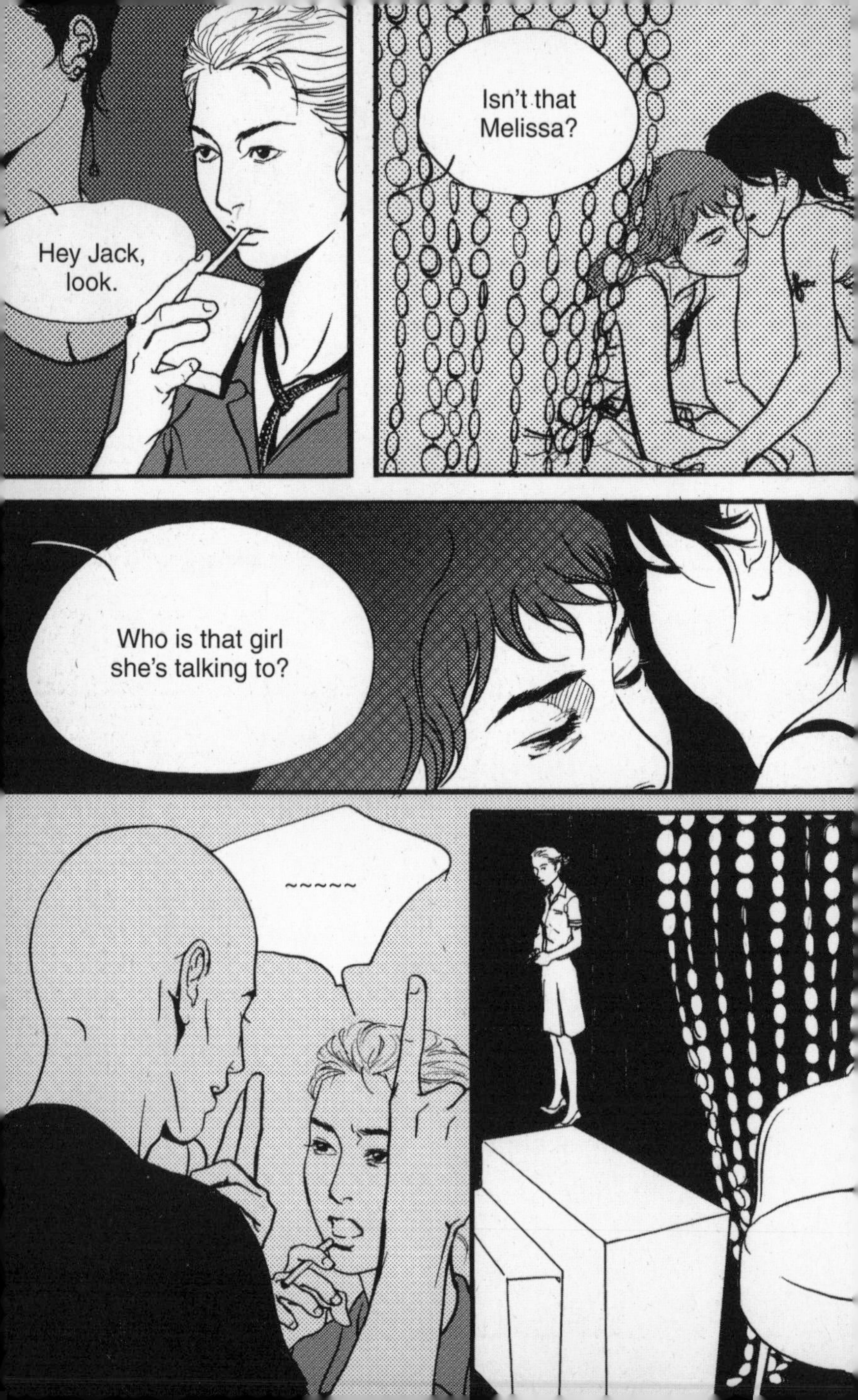
Hey Jack, look.
Isn't that Melissa?
Who is that girl she's talking to?
~~~~~
~~~~~

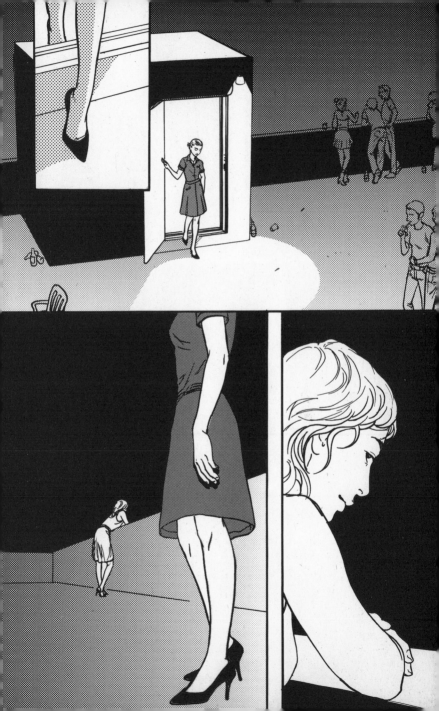

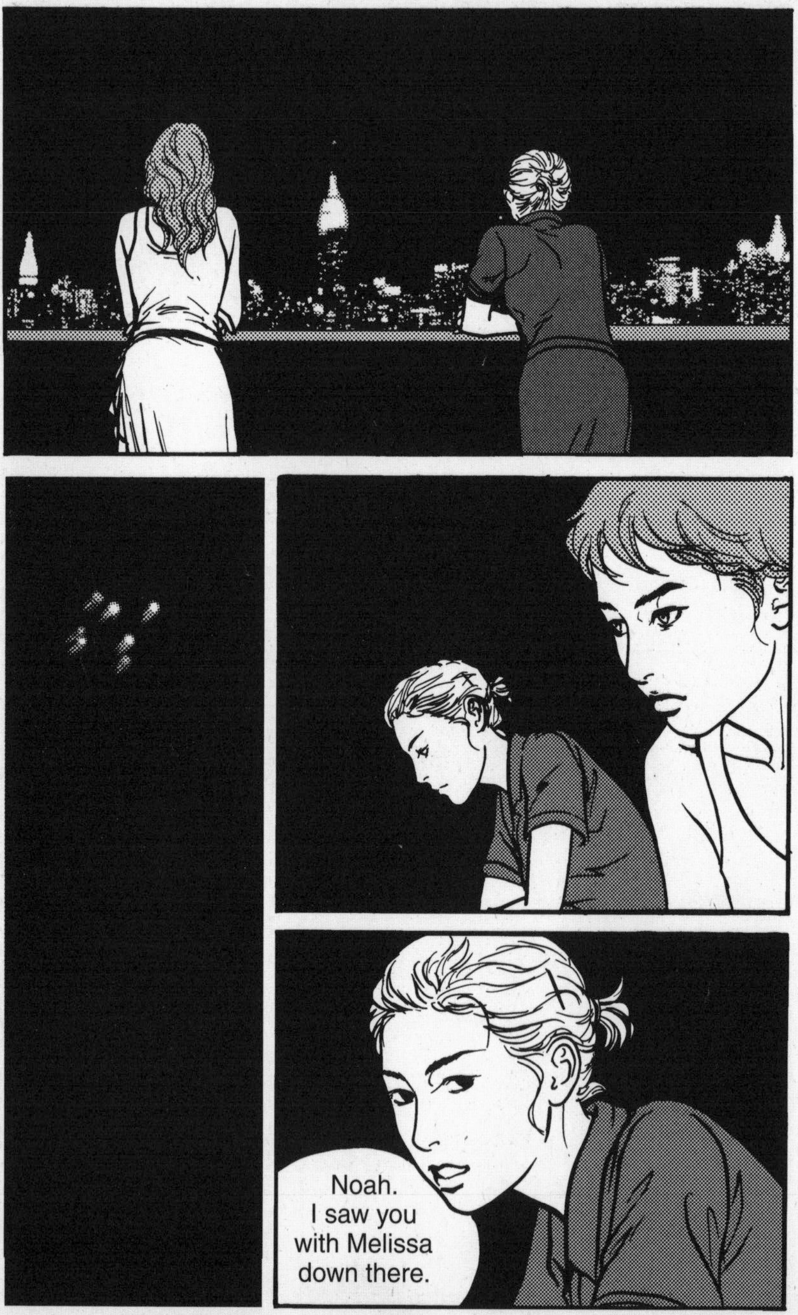
Noah. I saw you with Melissa down there.

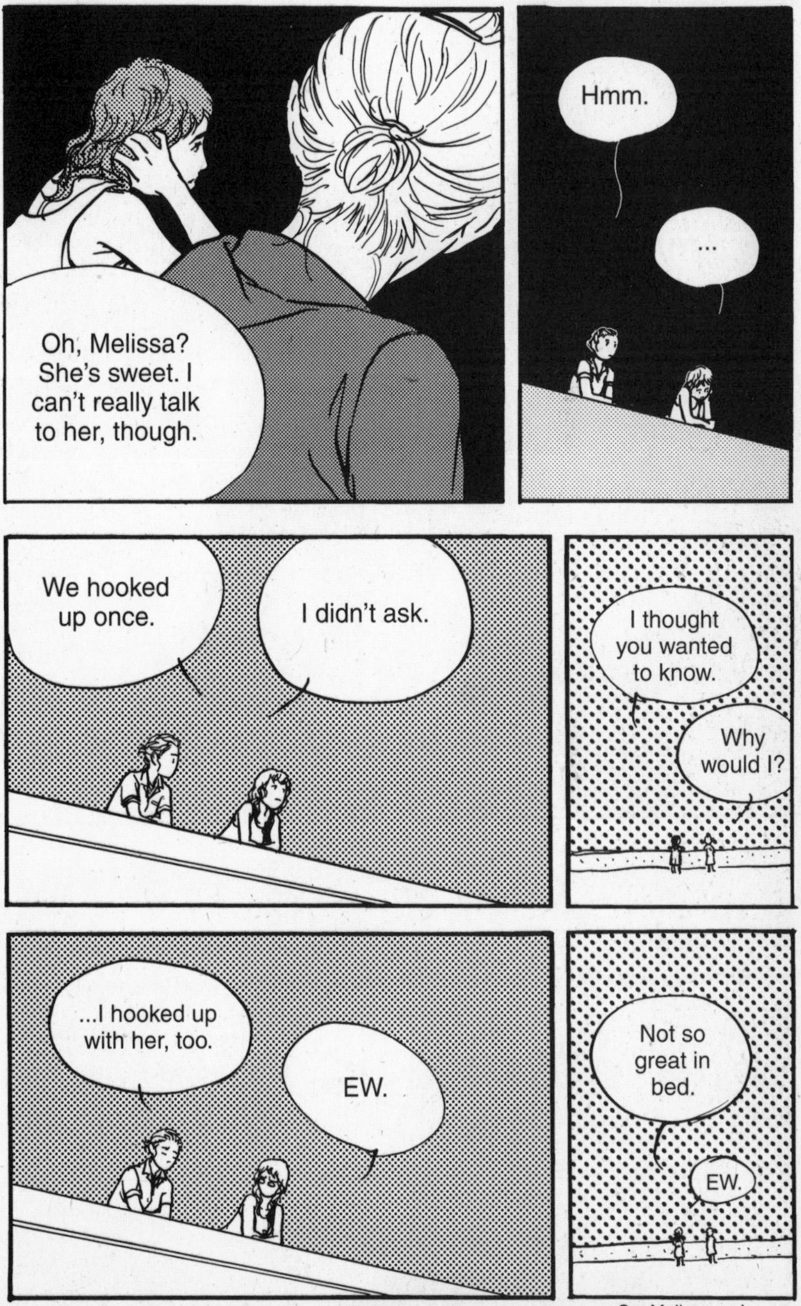
Oh, Melissa? She's sweet. I can't really talk to her, though.
Hmm.
...
We hooked up once.
I didn't ask.
I thought you wanted to know.
Why would I?
...I hooked up with her, too.
EW.
Not so great in bed.
EW.
Go, Melissa, go!

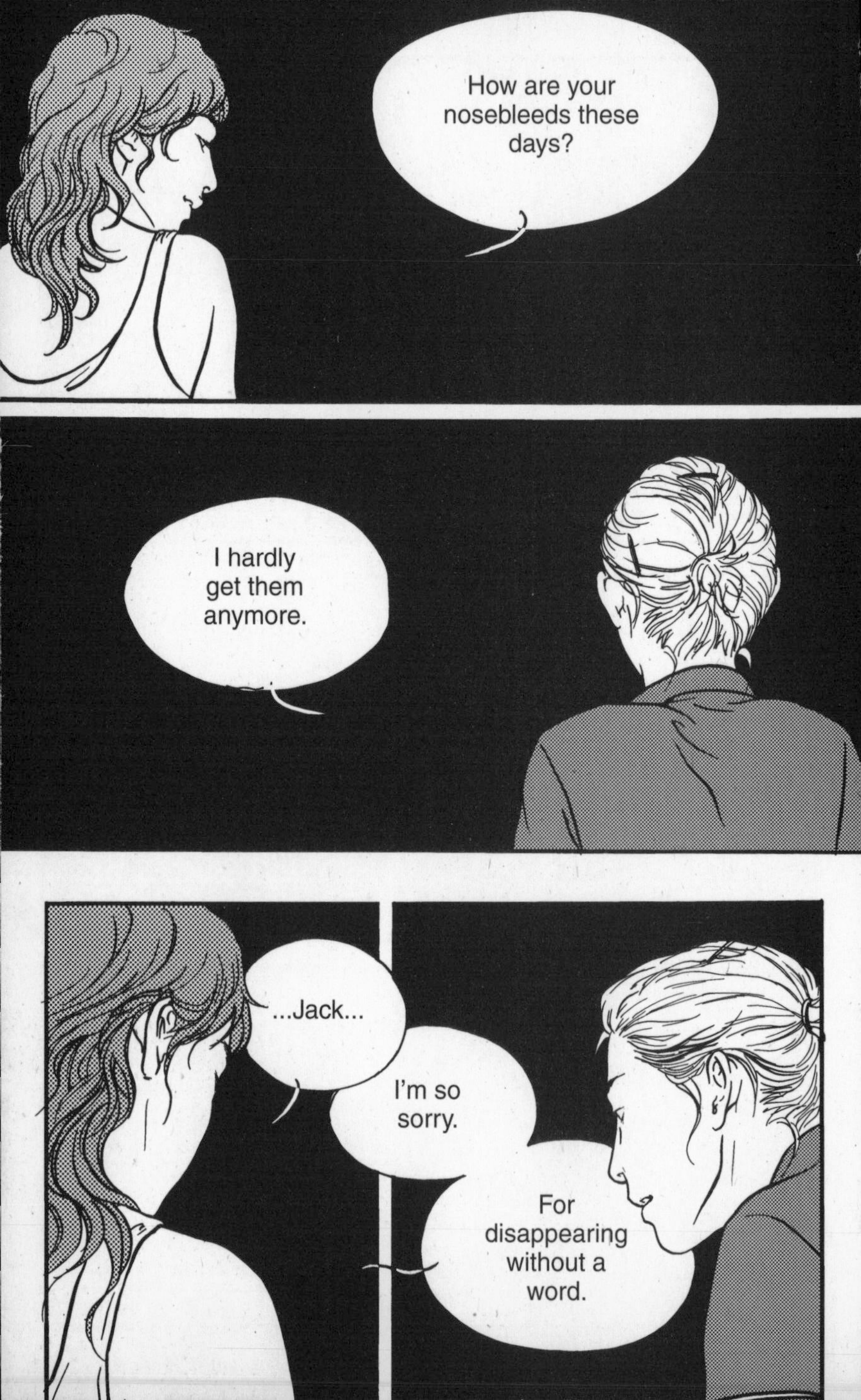
How are your nosebleeds these days?
I hardly get them anymore.
...Jack...
I'm so sorry.
For disappearing without a word.

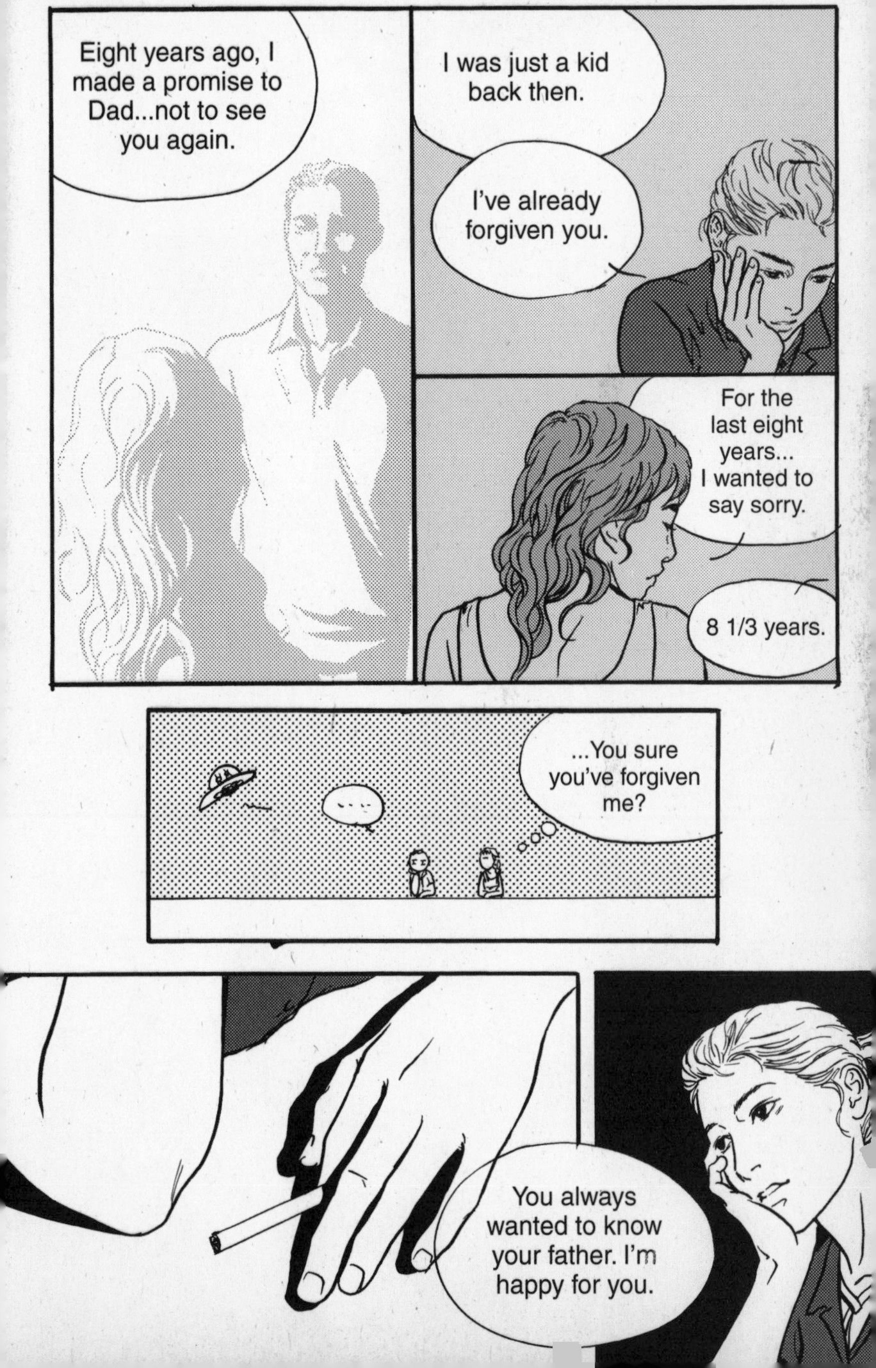
Eight years ago, I made a promise to Dad...not to see you again.
I was just a kid back then.
I've already forgiven you.
For the last eight years... I wanted to say sorry.
8 1/3 years.
...You sure you've forgiven me?
You always wanted to know your father. I'm happy for you.

I remember when we first met, in the nurse's office. Your nose was bleeding all over your hands.
I was so freaked out... I was only a student aide...
It took me a whole bag of chocolate to get it to bleed like that.

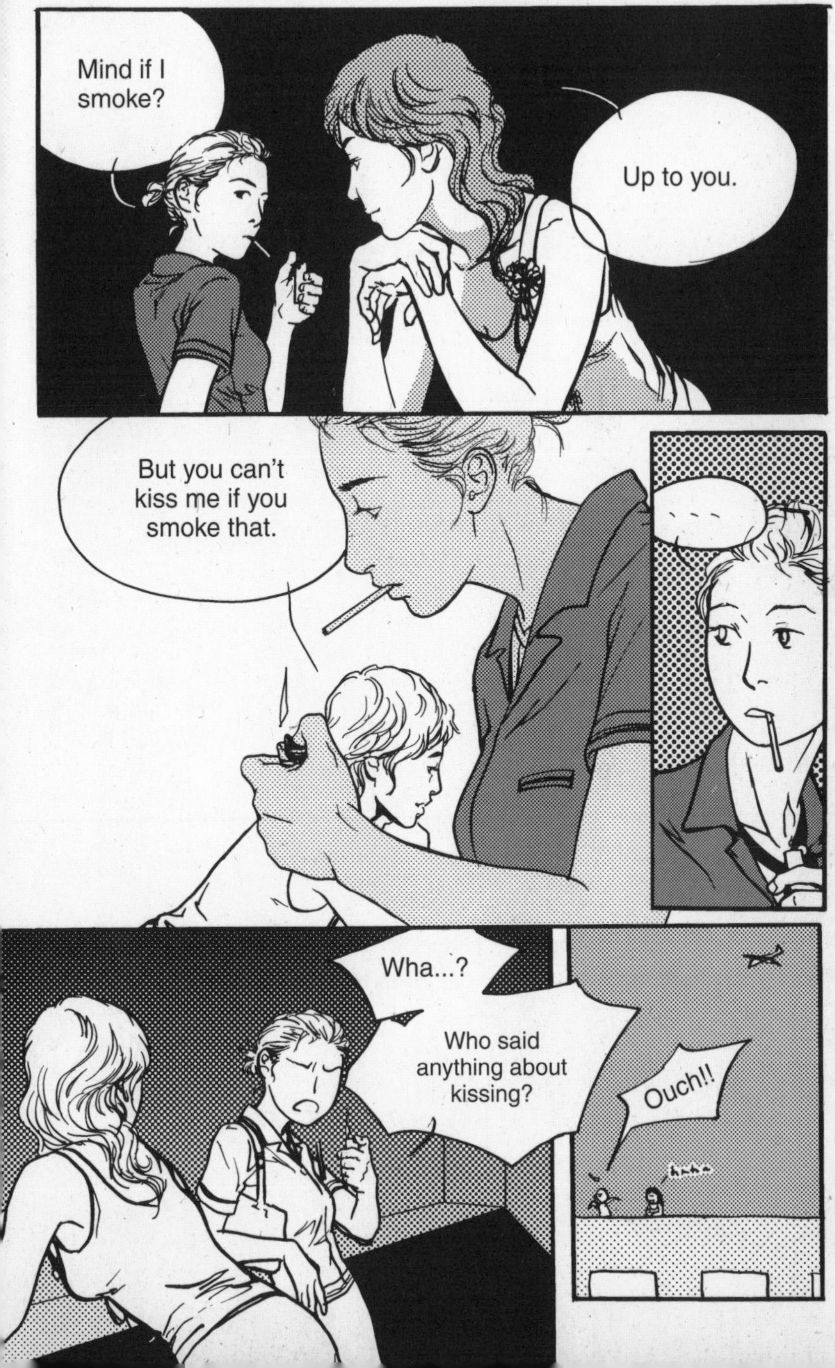
Mind if I smoke?
Up to you.
But you can't kiss me if you smoke that.
...
Wha...?
Who said anything about kissing?
Ouch!!

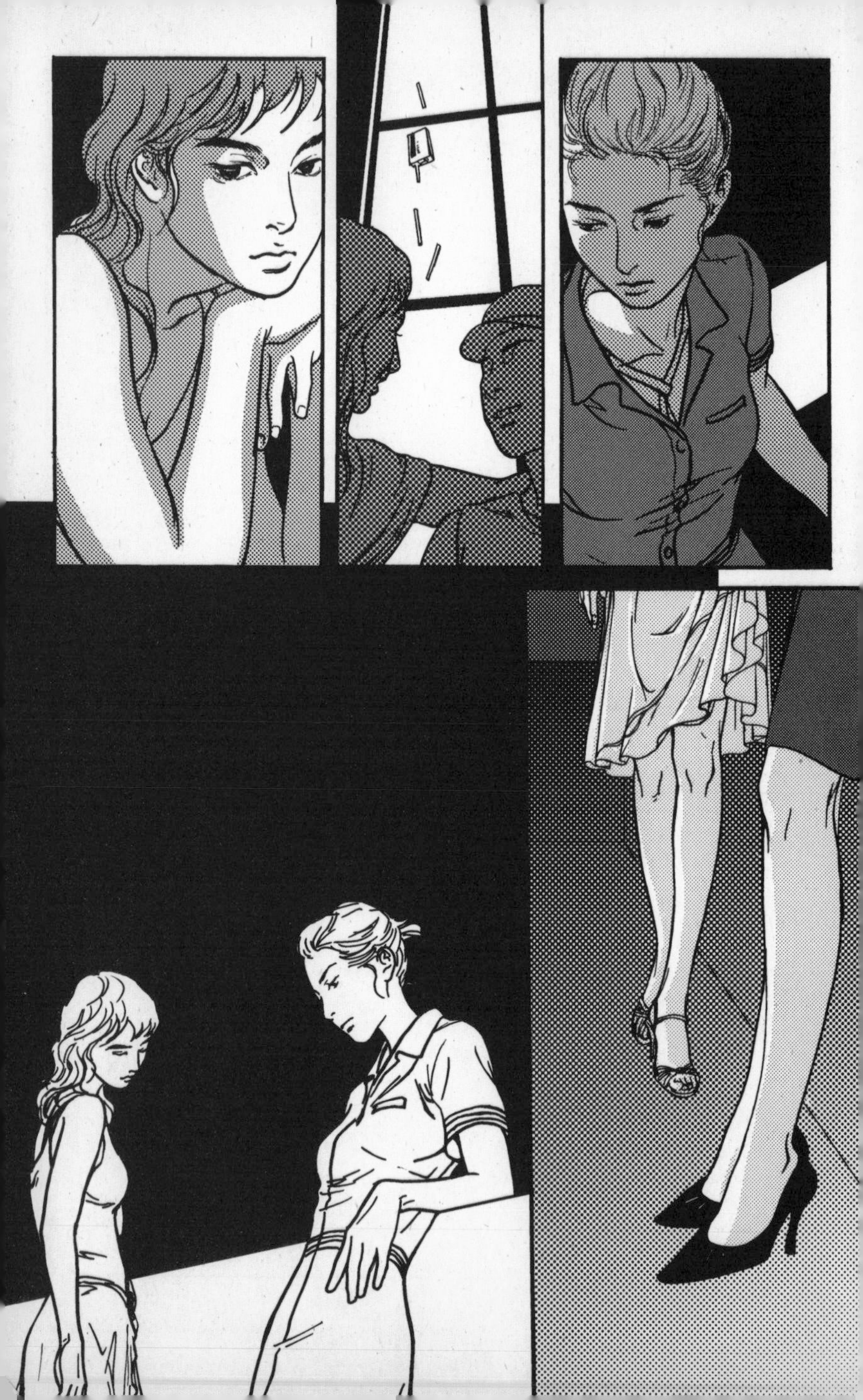

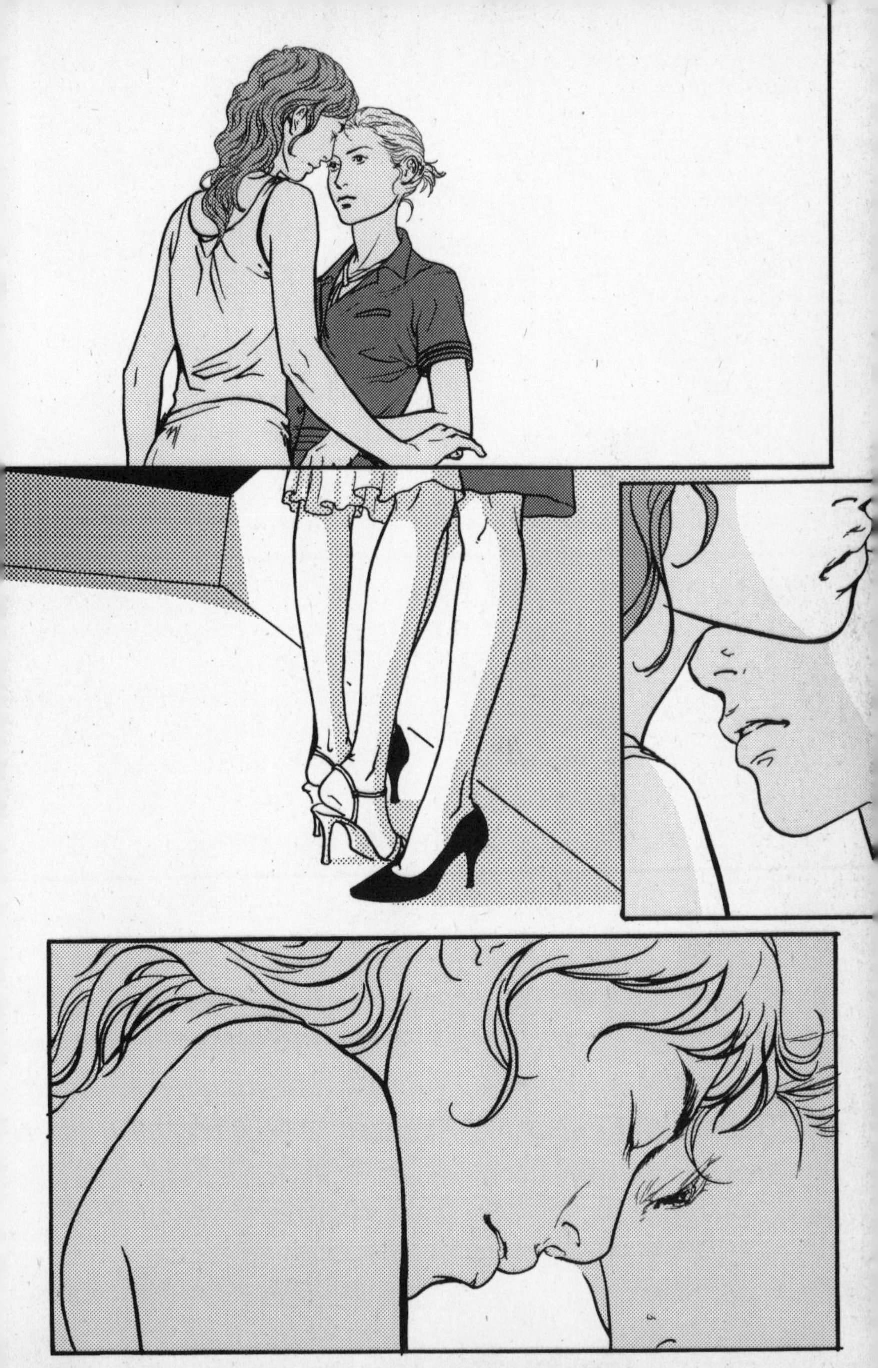

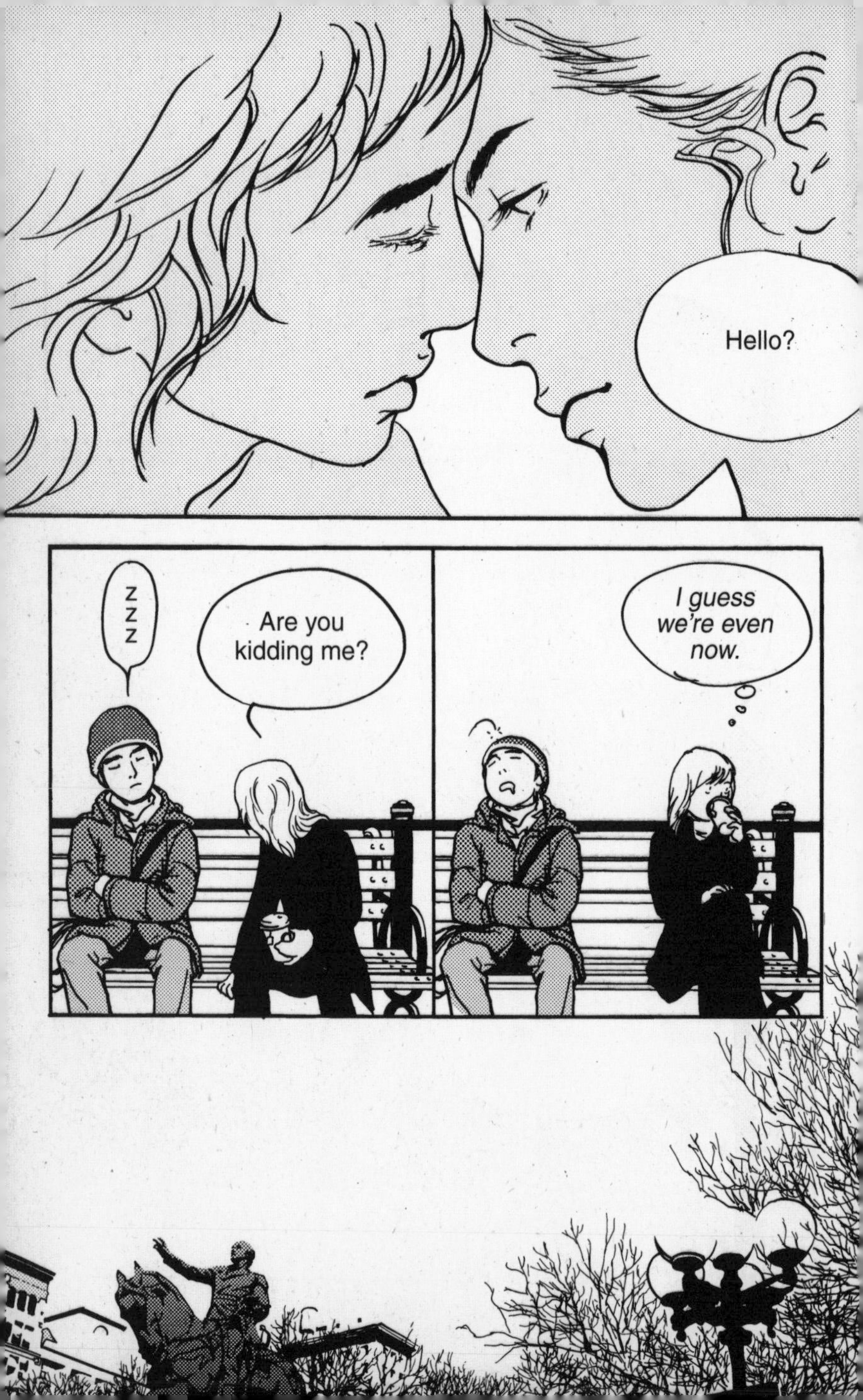
Hello?
ZZZ
Are you kidding me?
I guess we're even now.

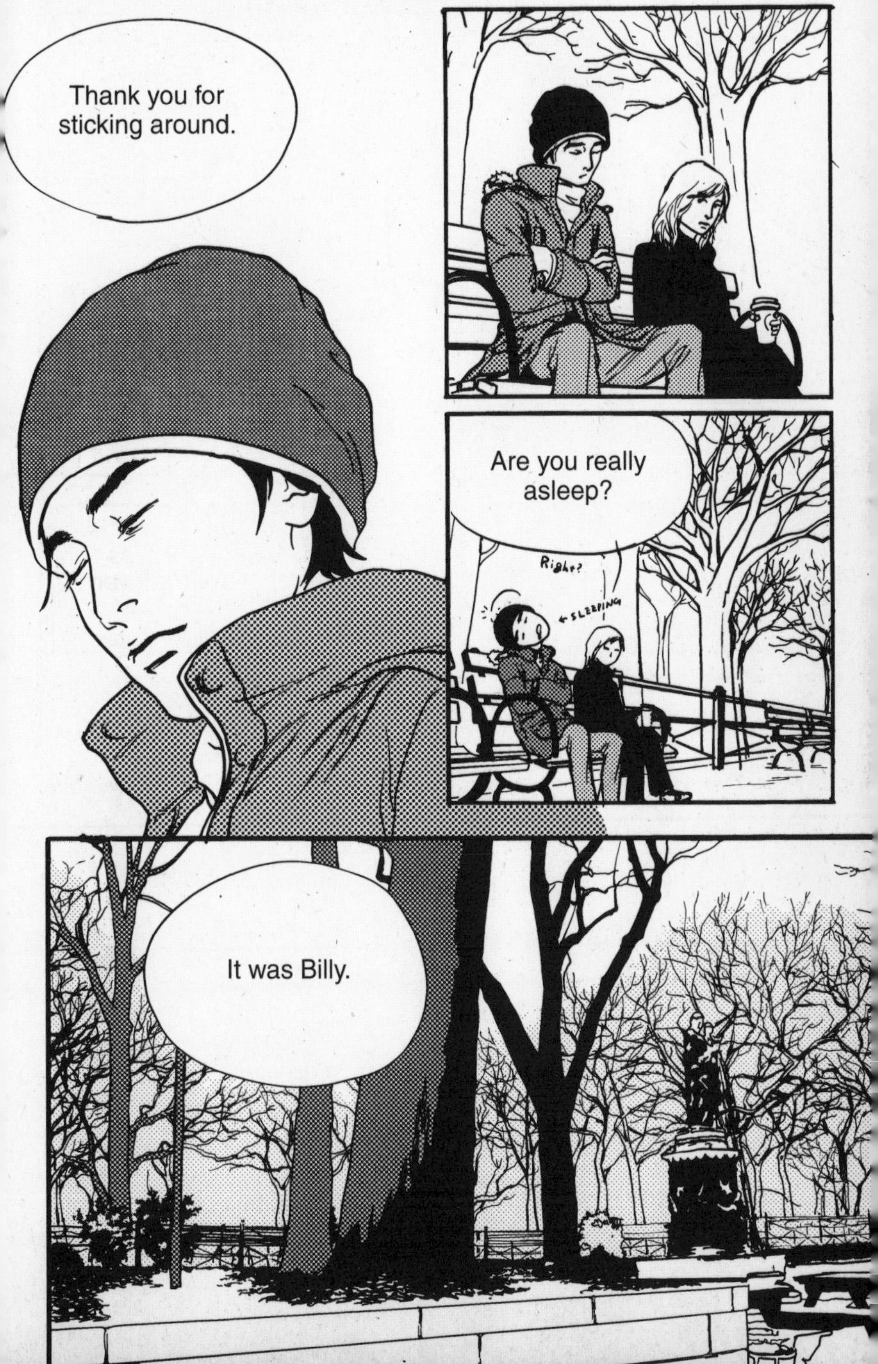
Thank you for sticking around.
Are you really asleep?
Right?
←SLEEPING
It was Billy.

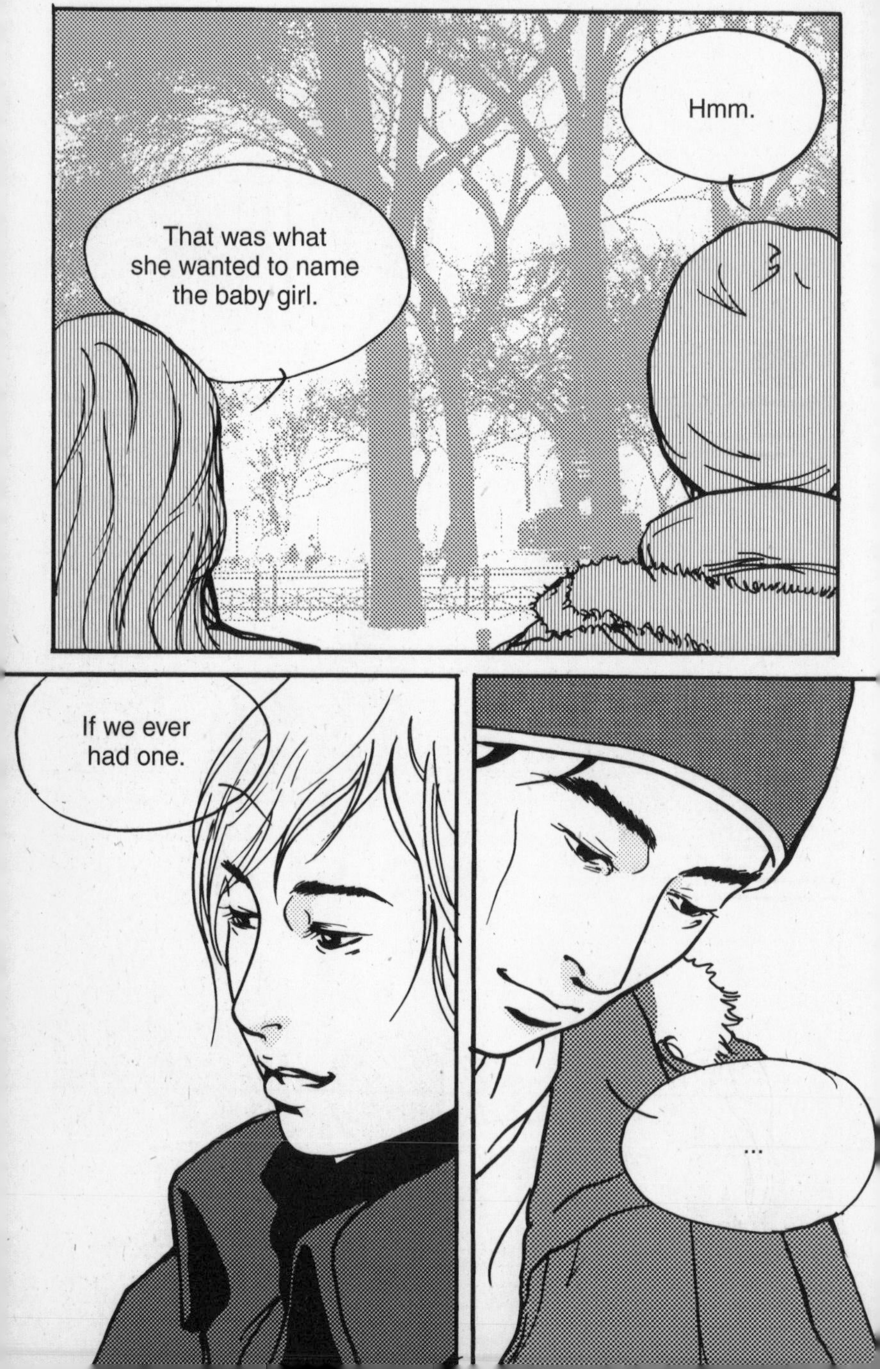
That was what she wanted to name the baby girl.
Hmm.
If we ever had one.
...

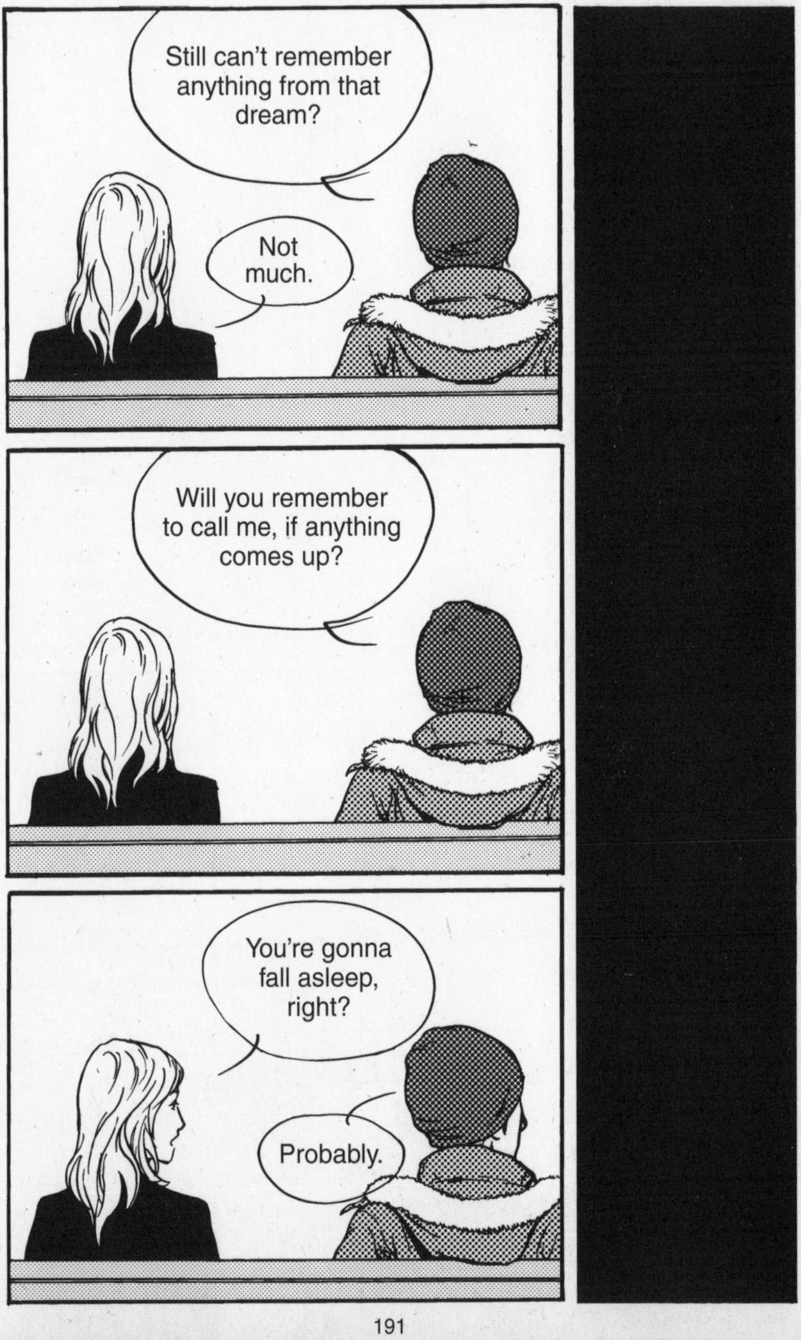
Still can't remember anything from that dream?
Not much.
Will you remember to call me, if anything comes up?
You're gonna fall asleep, right?
Probably.

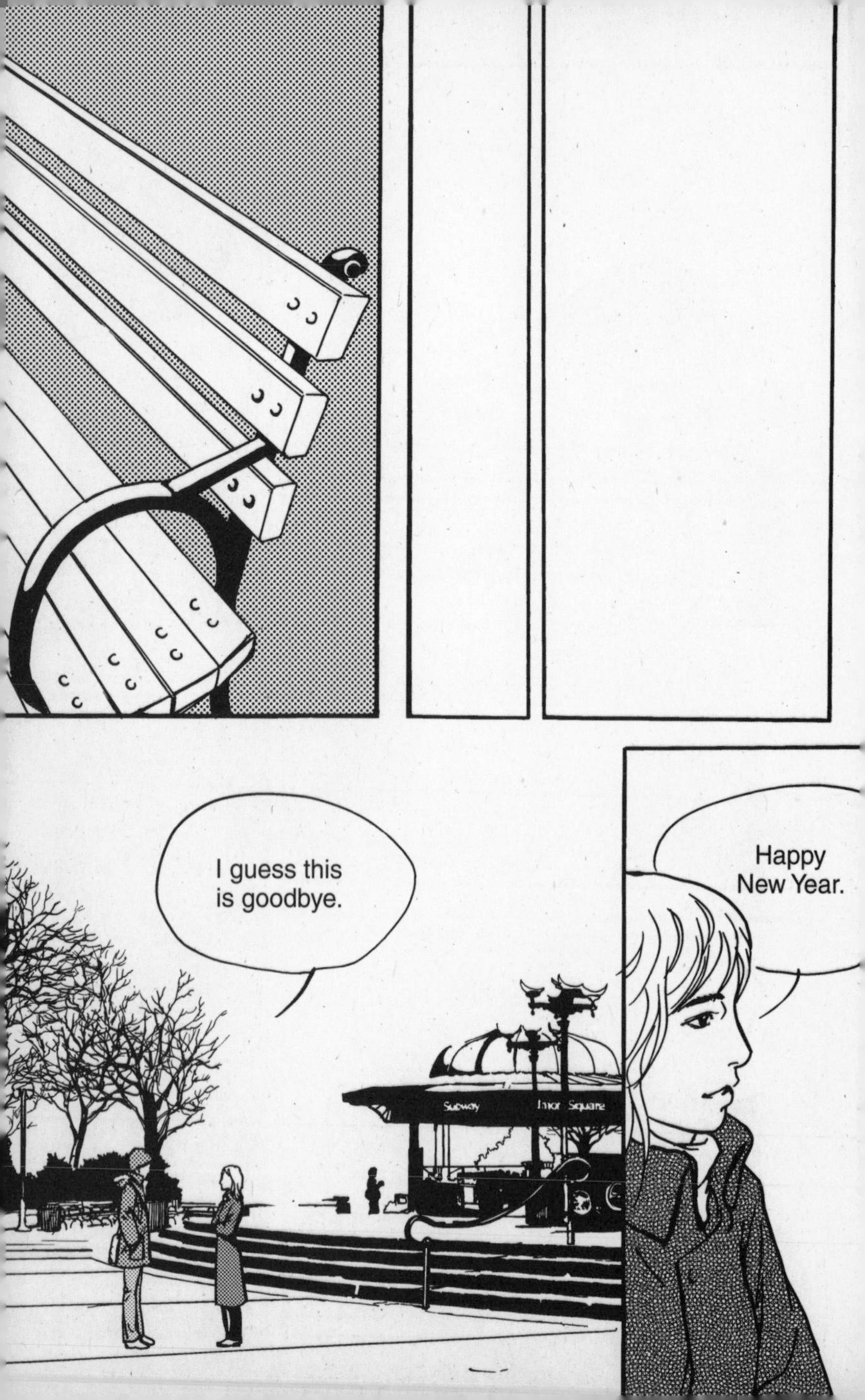
I guess this is goodbye.
Subway
Happy New Year.

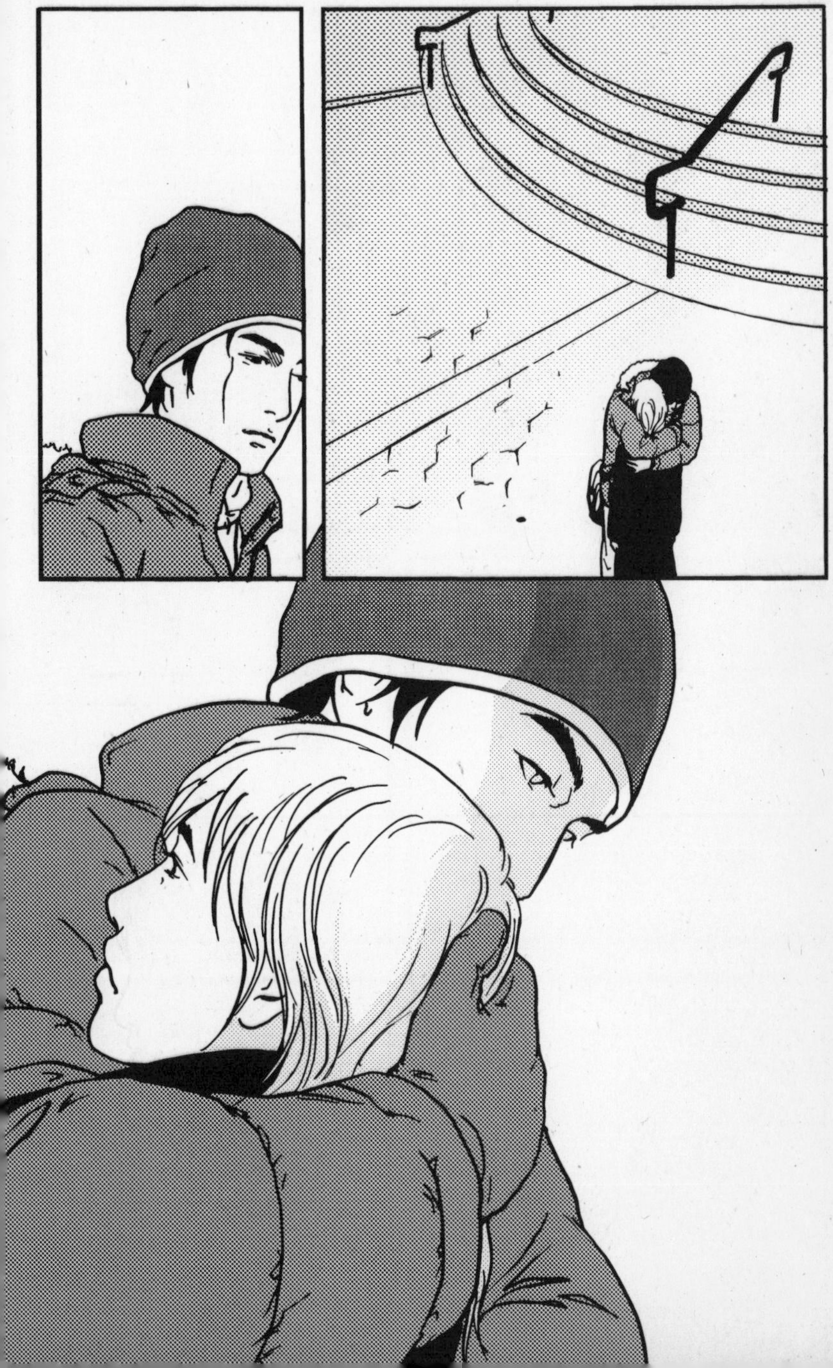

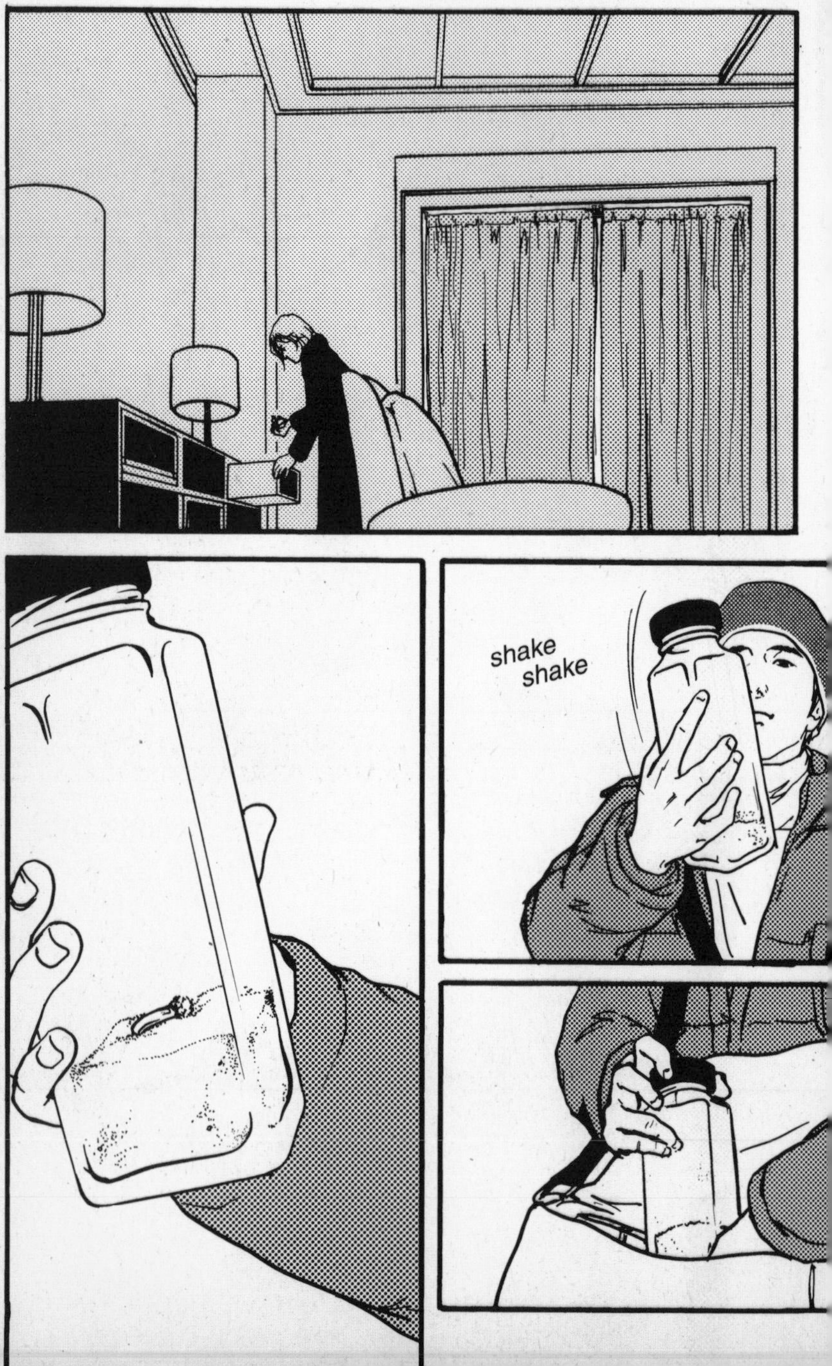
shake
shake

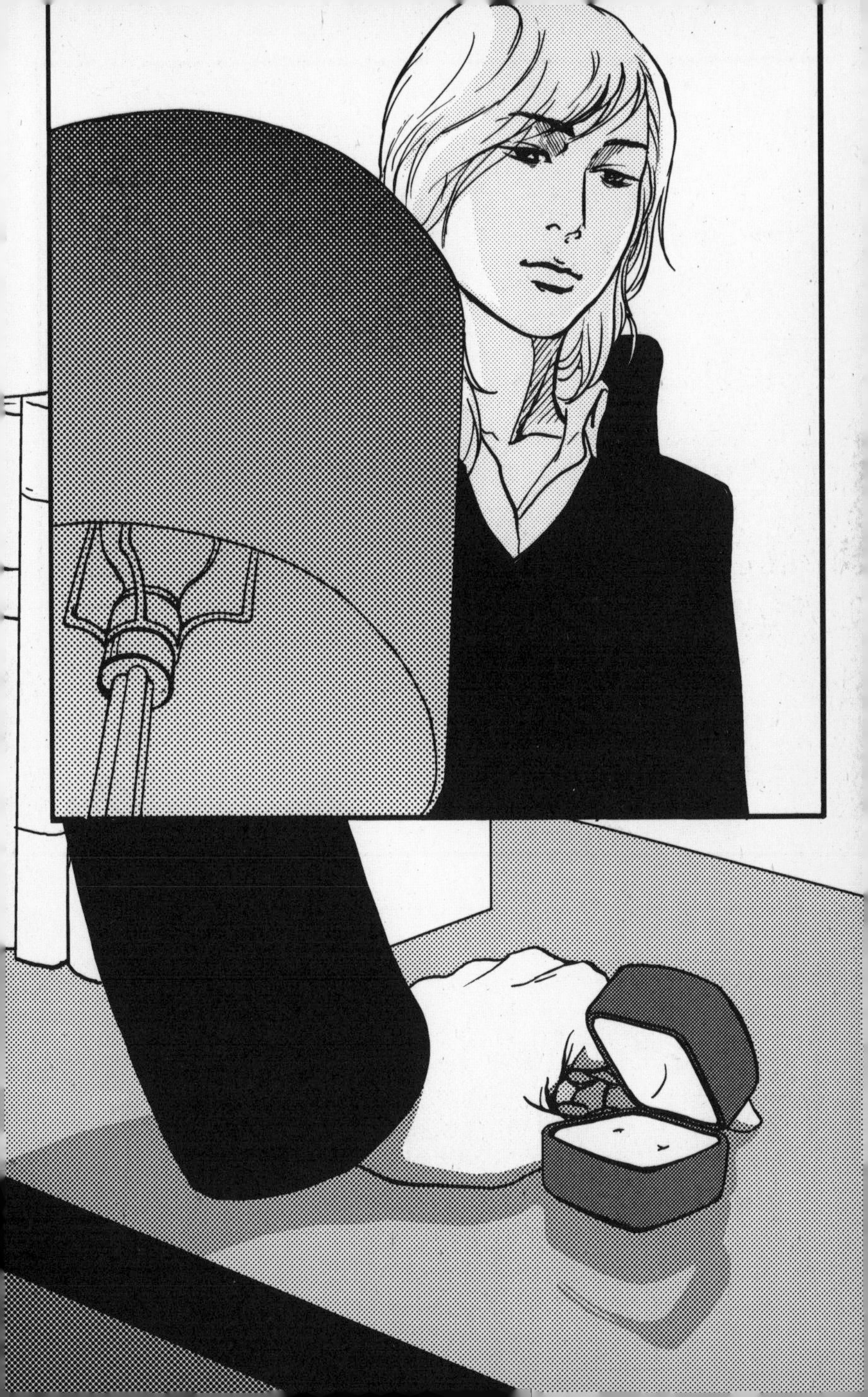

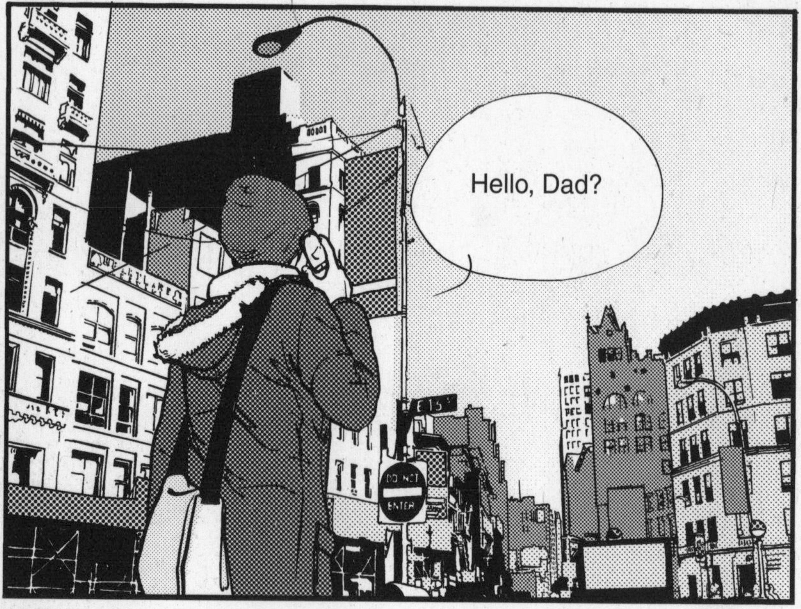
Hello, Dad?
E 13

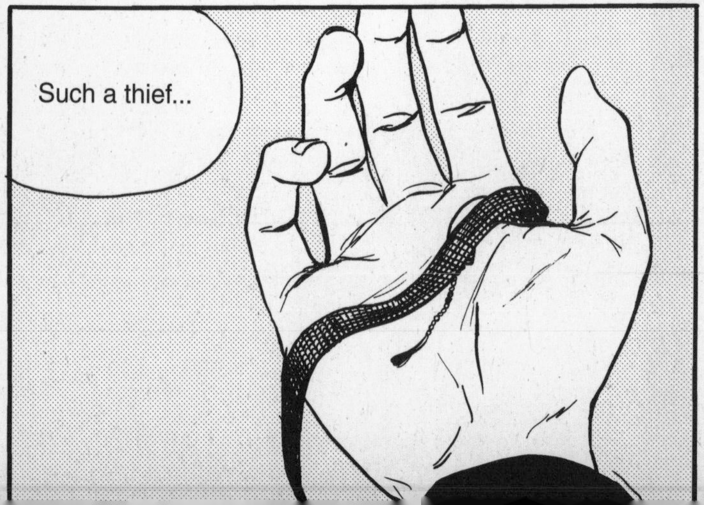
Such a thief...

THANKS

Chapter 0

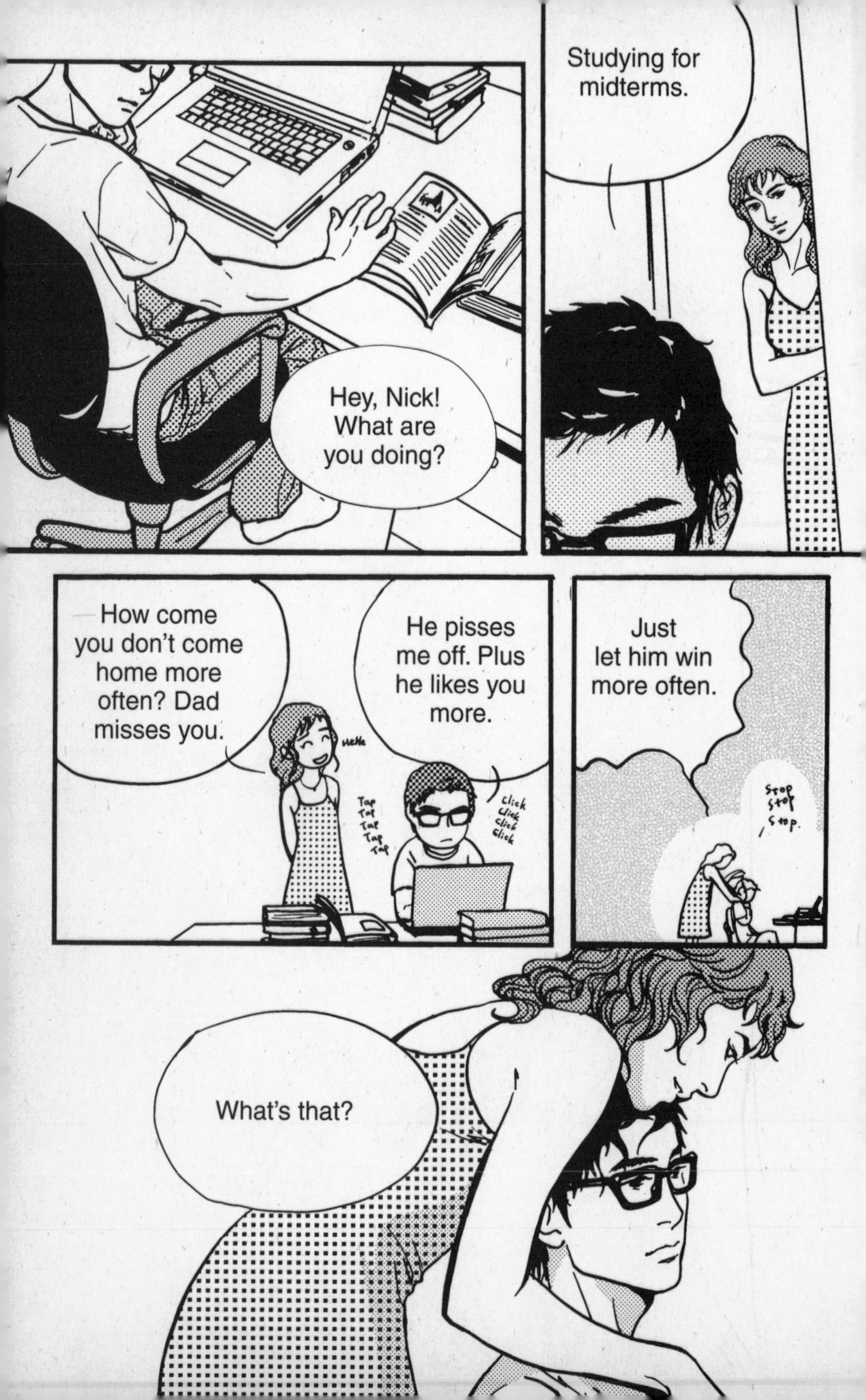
Hey, Nick! What are you doing?
Studying for midterms.
How come you don't come home more often? Dad misses you.
Hello
Tap Tap Tap Tap Tap
He pisses me off. Plus he likes you more.
Click Click Click Click
Just let him win more often.
Stop stop stop.
What's that?

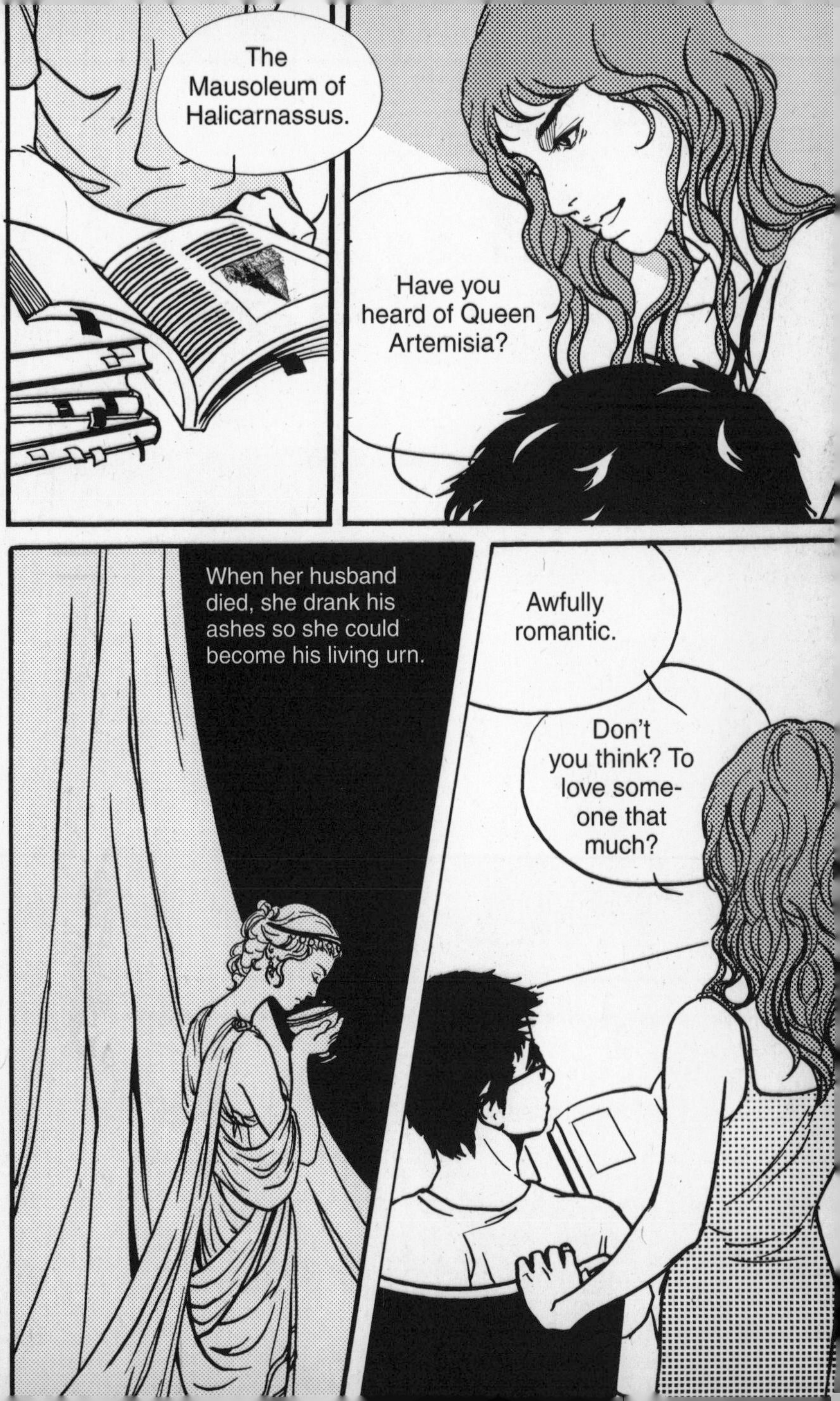
The Mausoleum of Halicarnassus.
Have you heard of Queen Artemisia?
When her husband died, she drank his ashes so she could become his living urn.
Awfully romantic.
Don't you think? To love some-one that much?

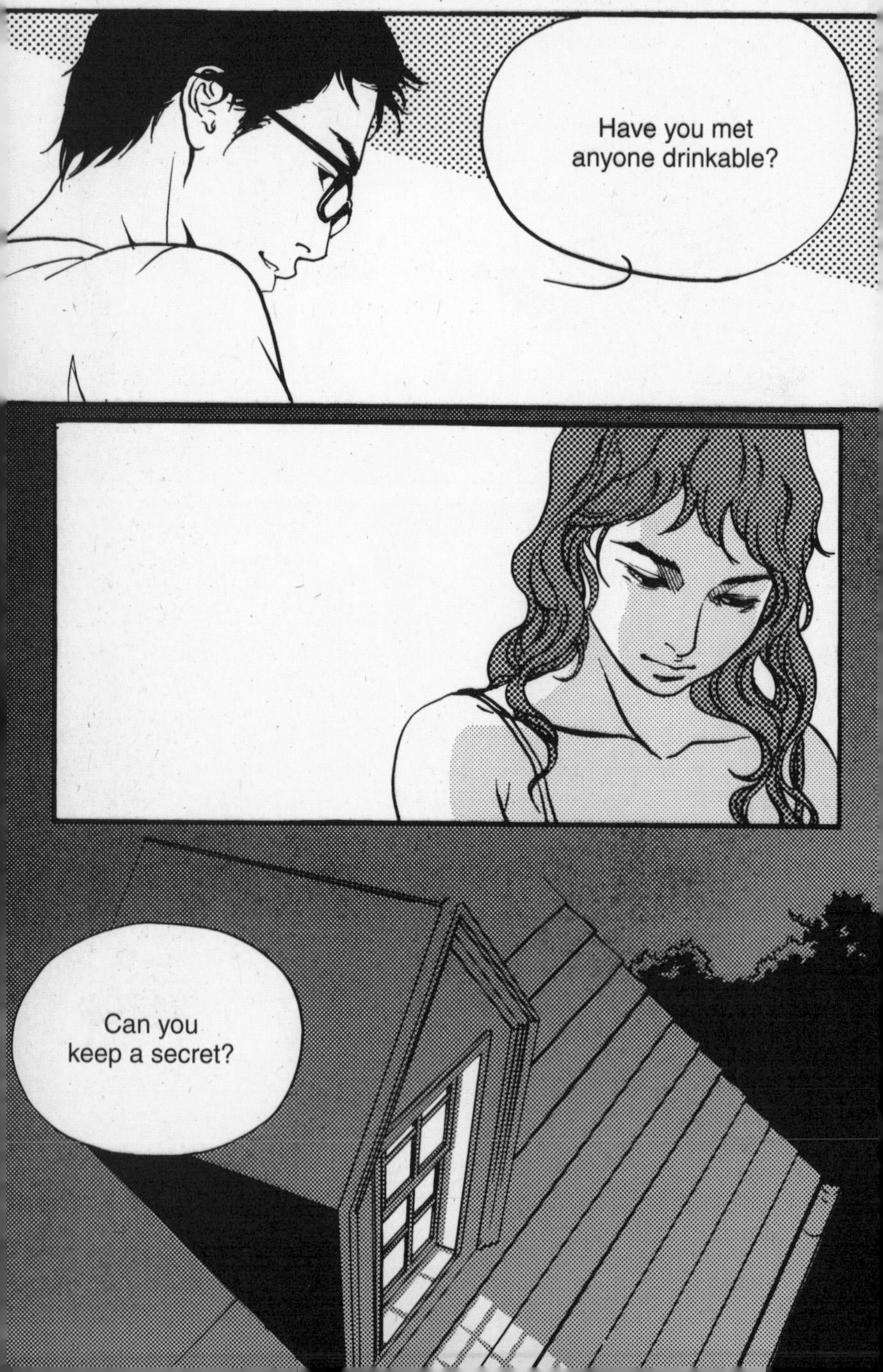
Have you met anyone drinkable?
Can you keep a secret?

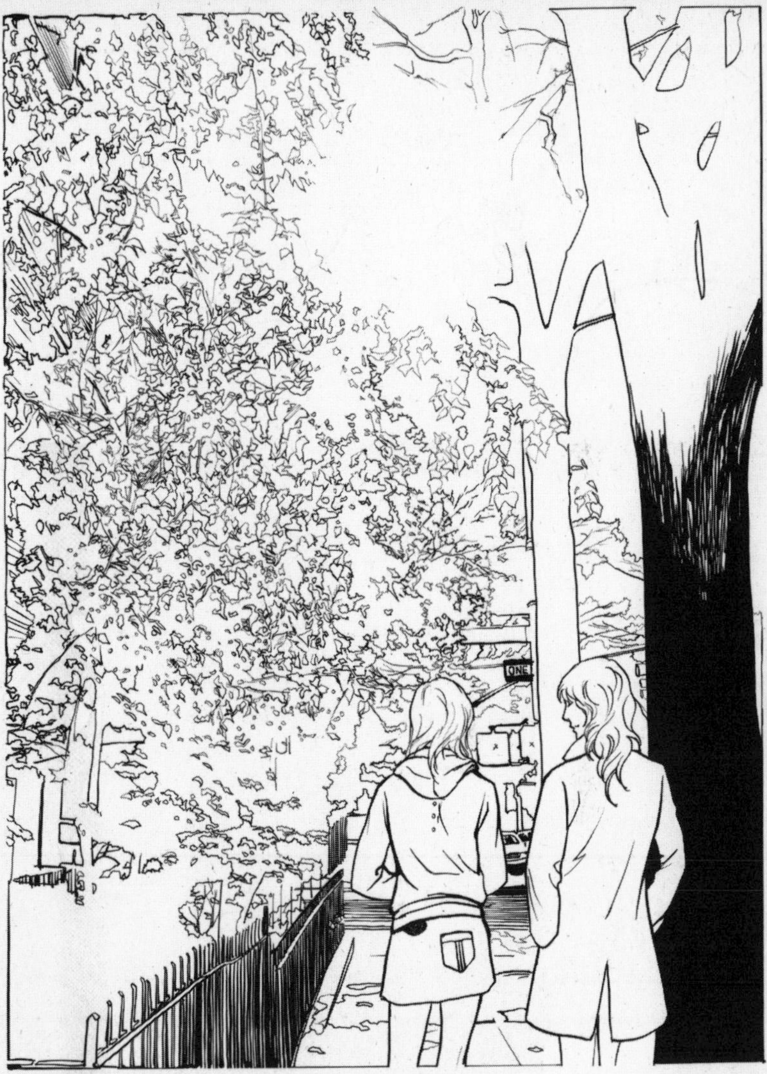
ONE

SPECIAL THANKS TO:
My parents
Betty M. Park
Christi Bertelsen
Hua Msu
the Studio Guild
My editor Lillian

...and the girl who told me a sad story about her ex-girlfriend 10 years ago

12 Days
Created by June Kim

Lettering - Lucas Rivera
Cover Design - Anne Marie Horne
Toning Assistants - Christi Bertelsen, Hyejeong Park, Jane Lim

Editor - Lillian Diaz-Pryzbyl
Digital Imaging Manager - Chris Buford
Pre-Production Supervisor - Erika Terriquez
Art Director - Anne Marie Horne
Production Manager - Elisabeth Brizzi
Managing Editor - Vy Nguyen
VP of Production - Ron Klamert
Publisher - Mike Kiley
Editor-in-Chief - Rob Tokar
President and C.O.O. - John Parker
C.E.O. and Chief Creative Officer - Stuart Levy

A **TOKYOPOP** Manga

TOKYOPOP Inc.
5900 Wilshire Blvd. Suite 2000
Los Angeles, CA 90036

E-mail: info@TOKYOPOP.com
Come visit us online at www.TOKYOPOP.com

ISBN: 1-59816-691-3

First TOKYOPOP printing: November 2006
10 9 8 7 6 5 4 3 2 1
Printed in the USA

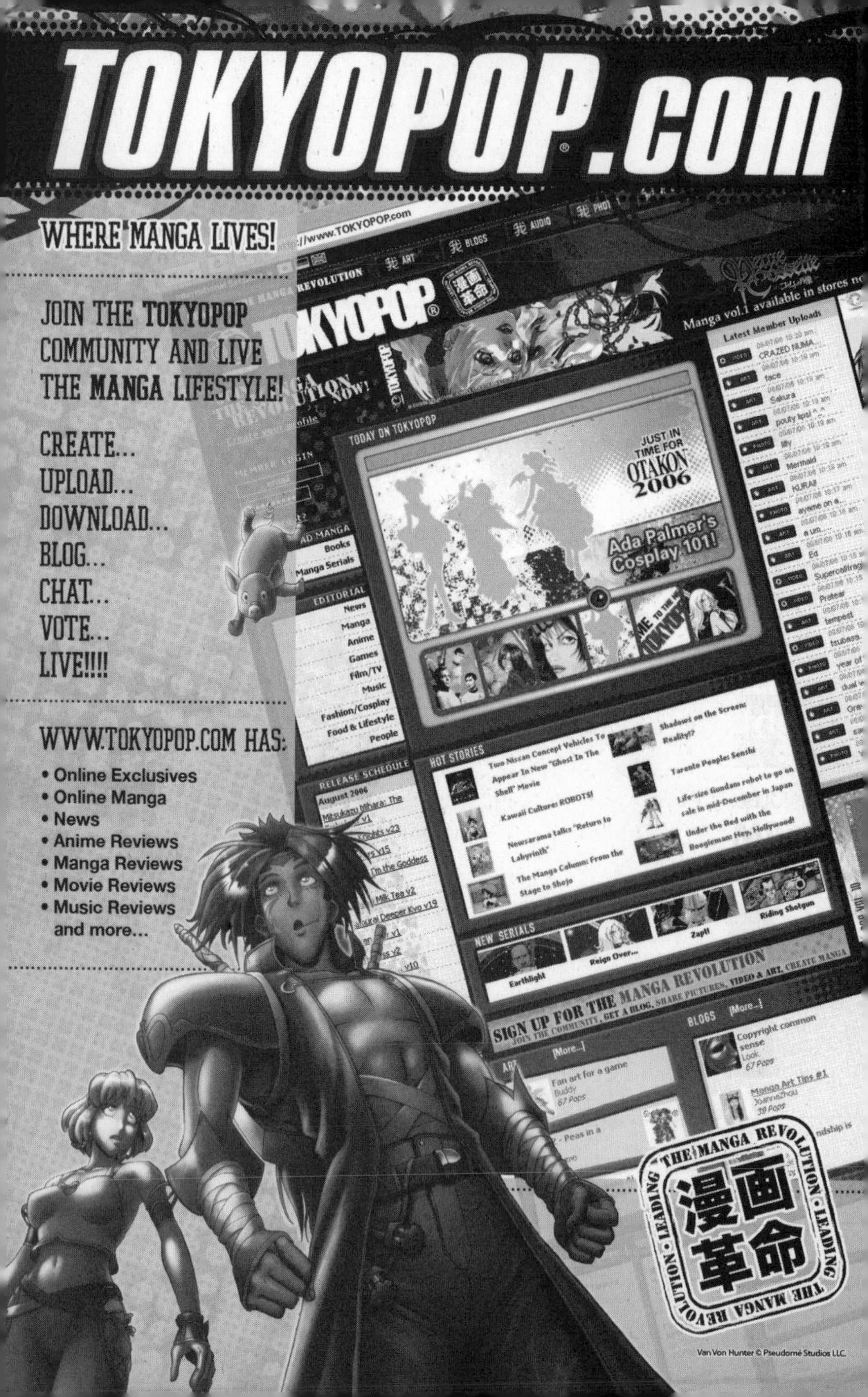
TOKYOPOP®.com
WHERE MANGA LIVES!
JOIN THE TOKYOPOP COMMUNITY AND LIVE THE MANGA LIFESTYLE!
CREATE...
UPLOAD...
DOWNLOAD...
BLOG...
CHAT...
VOTE...
LIVE!!!!
WWW.TOKYOPOP.COM HAS:
• Online Exclusives
• Online Manga
• News
• Anime Reviews
• Manga Reviews
• Movie Reviews
• Music Reviews
and more...
THE MANGA REVOLUTION • LEADING
漫画革命
Van Von Hunter © Pseudomé Studios LLC.

TOKYOPOP MANGA SUPPLEMENT

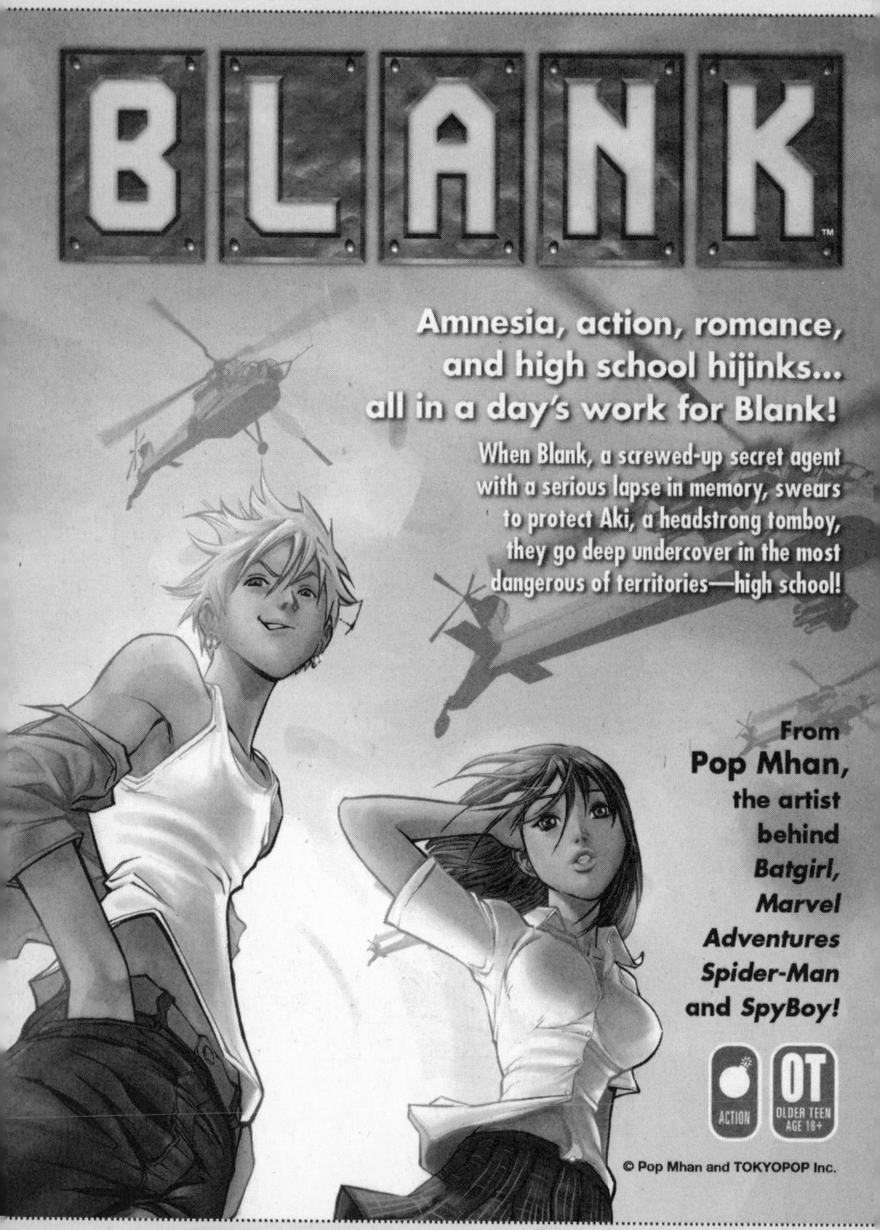
BLANK™
Amnesia, action, romance, and high school hijinks... all in a day's work for Blank!
When Blank, a screwed-up secret agent with a serious lapse in memory, swears to protect Aki, a headstrong tomboy, they go deep undercover in the most dangerous of territories—high school!
From Pop Mhan, the artist behind Batgirl, Marvel Adventures Spider-Man and SpyBoy!
ACTION
OT
OLDER TEEN AGE 16+
© Pop Mhan and TOKYOPOP Inc.

FOR MORE INFORMATION VISIT: WWW.TOKYOPOP.COM